1996

INEQUALITY

INEQUALITY

Radical Institutionalist Views
on Race, Gender, Class, and Nation

EDITED BY

WILLIAM M. DUGGER

Contributions in Economics and Economic History,
Number 178

GREENWOOD PRESS
Westport, Connecticut • London

Library of Congress Cataloging-in-Publication Data

Inequality : radical institutionalist views on race, gender, class,
   and nation / edited by William M. Dugger.
      p.   cm. — (Contributions in economics and economic history,
   ISSN 0084–9235 ; no. 178)
   Includes bibliographical references and index.
   ISBN 0–313–30014–3 (alk. paper)
      1. Radical economics. 2. Institutional economics. 3. Minorities—
Economic conditions. 4. Equality. I. Dugger, William M.
II. Series.
HB97.7.I53   1996
330—dc20   96–3643

British Library Cataloguing in Publication Data is available.

Library of Congress Catalog Card Number: 96–3643
ISBN: 0–313–30014–3
ISSN: 0084–9235

First published in 1996

Greenwood Press, 88 Post Road West, Westport, CT 06881
An imprint of Greenwood Publishing Group, Inc.

Printed in the United States of America

The paper used in this book complies with the
Permanent Paper Standard issued by the National
Information Standards Organization (Z39.48–1984).

10 9 8 7 6 5 4 3 2 1

Contents

Illustrations

Introduction

William M. Dugger

Three volumes have preceded this one in a loosely related series of anthologies produced by an informal group of radical institutional economists. The first three volumes were: *Radical Institutionalism*, edited by William M. Dugger; *The Stratified State*, edited by William M. Dugger and William T. Waller, Jr.; and *The Economic Status of Women Under Capitalism*, edited by Janice Peterson and Doug Brown.

This new anthology focuses radical institutionalism on inequality. Radical institutionalism is a "processual paradigm focused on changing the direction of cultural evolution and the function of social provisioning in order to promote the full participation of all" (Dugger 1989, 133). Mainstream economics is not broad enough to capture the complexities of inequality, but radical institutionalism, with its blend of institutionalism, Marxism, and feminism, is. Radical institutionalists understand that at its root, inequality is social rather than individual in nature. It is a product of social processes more than of individual choices. Furthermore, inequality is not determined by alleged genetic differences between races and ethnic groups or differences between sexes or by cultural differences between classes. Most important, inequality is a social pathology, not an inevitable cost of economic progress.

This volume is in four parts. Basic ways of understanding inequality are discussed in Part 1. The welfare state crisis is discussed in Part 2. Part 3 explores international contexts. Part 4 contains case studies.

Thorstein Veblen is the founder of institutional economics, so this anthology starts with "The Egalitarian Significance of Veblen's Business–Industry Dichotomy," by Rick Tilman. Tilman explains that Veblen's appreciation for equality as an essential element in the fullness of life provides the key to understanding the "Veblenian dichotomy."

The next chapter is "Four Modes of Inequality," by William M. Dugger. Dugger formulates a common framework and vocabulary for understanding inequality as process. Four such interrelated processes or modes are explained in terms of the practices of inequality, the myths that justify it, and the antidotes. The four modes of inequality discussed are gender, race, class, and nation.

Howard J. Sherman produces "A Holistic-Evolutionary View of Racism, Sexism, and Class Inequality." Most important in his chapter is his explanation that racist, sexist, and classist myths are far more than mere individual preferences. Such enabling myths are highly functional. They justify inequality and make it possible for the top class in society to secure its advantages and use them to reap economic rewards at the expense of the lower class.

John E. Elliott's chapter focuses even more closely on class and economic inequality. His "Exploitation and Inequality" clearly sets out the class nature of exploitation. He also relates exploitation to other modes of inequality—gender and race in particular.

James Devine digs deeply into critical Marxist theory in his "Taxation without Representation: A Reconstruction of Marx's Theory of Capitalist Exploitation." He reconstructs a modern Marxist theory of exploitation, relates it to other attempts at reconstruction, and approaches exploitation as ethically objectionable in the same way that taxation without representation is objectionable.

Part 1 concludes with Edythe S. Miller's "Seen through a Glass Darkly: Competing Views of Equality and Inequality in Economic Thought," which contrasts the problem-solving nature of institutional economics with the Pollyanna nature of neoclassical economics.

Most industrial democracies have responded to inequality with the welfare state. However, the welfare state has come under strong attack and entered a period of crisis. This is the context for Part 2 of the anthology. Marc R. Tool's opening chapter for Part 2 is particularly significant. His "Choose Equality" uses the American instrumentalist philosophy to show why equality is an economic necessity and a social imperative. He explores meritocracy, efficiency, and equality of opportunity in terms of instrumental social value theory, laying the philosophical foundation for the welfare state as an egalitarian institution instead of a mere sop to the poor.

The second chapter in Part 2 is "Reconstructing the Welfare State in the Aftermath of the Great Capitalist Restoration," by James Ronald Stanfield and Jacqueline Bloom Stanfield. The Stanfields use institutionalist theory to identify and analyze a nurturance gap in the U.S. social economy. Closing the gap will require the financial empowerment of women and children, regardless of whether a man has conferred on them a "legitimate" relation to his patriarchy.

Janice Peterson's chapter, "Social Provisioning and Inequality: Women and the Dual Welfare State," explains how invidious distinctions have led to the evolution of a dual welfare state in the United States, which fails to meet the social provisioning requirements of the most needy. On one—the higher—level, social insurance is provided for those who meet white, middle-class, male standards of legitimacy. The supports provided are almost adequate for a full life for many of the beneficiaries of social insurance. On the other—the lower—level, "welfare" is provided for those who are not white or middle class and do not meet male standards of legitimacy. The supports provided here are not adequate. Reform must address this fundamental inequity.

Part 2 concludes with Zahid Shariff's "Inequality and Government," a timely examination of the egalitarian potential of different levels of government in the United States. He finds that equality is best served by policies of the federal government and that decentralizing will increase economic inequality and reduce participatory democracy.

Part 3 addresses the international contexts of inequality. It opens with a philosophical statement provided by Doug Brown's "East Meets West: Dewey, Gandhi, and Instrumental Equality for the Twenty-First Century." Brown explores the crisis of sustainability created by the insatiable dynamic of global capitalism. Drawing on the thought of Mohandas Gandhi to provide a culture of sustainability and on that of John Dewey to provide a method of sustainability, Brown argues that we must achieve an "instrumental equality" for the global economy of the next century.

The next chapter is Brent McClintock's "International Inequality and the Economic Process." McClintock compares neoclassical and institutional theories of growth and development in the context of growing global inequality and shows that international policies based on the neoclassical faith in the market and its assumed ability to naturally generate convergence, instead of divergence, will not work. Instead, supranational governance structures must be instituted that will actually channel more resources to the poorest nations.

Part 3 concludes with "Inequality in the 1980s: An Institutionalist View," by Charles M. A. Clark. Clark's chapter focuses on the recent experience of developed market economies and shows that the level of inequality and the recent changes in inequality in the countries studied are due to institutional factors and state policies. There is nothing "natural" or inevitable about the distribution of income, even in market economies.

Institutional economists love case studies so much that no anthology like this would be complete without them. Consequently, three strikingly different case studies are provided in Part 4. The section begins with Jim Horner's "The War on Drugs: A Legitimate Battle or Another Mode of Inequality?" in which Horner shows that the U.S. war on drugs is as much a war on women, minorities, foreigners, and the lower class as it is an honest attempt to reduce the social harm caused by drug abuse. Waged so intensely against the underdogs by the top dogs, it now vies with the predatory effects of racism, sexism, classism, and jingoism. "Drugism," anyone?

The next case study is by James Peach and entitled "Regional Income Inequality Revisited: Lessons from the 100 Lowest-Income Counties in the United States." Those lessons include the significance of high unemployment, low education, race and ethnicity, rural isolation (not always), and the extraordinary persistence of regional inequality. There is no natural tendency built into market forces that provides for regional income convergence.

The last chapter is Steven Shulman's "Racial Inequality and Radical Institutionalism: A Research Agenda," in which he argues that institutional economists have not lived up to the potential of their paradigm. Except for Gunnar Myrdal, they have paid little research attention to racism in America. However, institutionalism is well suited to the analysis of racism, as its facility with cultural norms, cumulative causation, evolutionary holism, and normative evaluations makes it ideal for such research.

That is how such anthologies should end—with a call for further research.

REFERENCE

Dugger, William M. 1989. *Radical Institutionalism*. Westport, Conn.: Greenwood Press.

Part I

BASIC APPROACHES

1

The Egalitarian Significance of Veblen's Business–Industry Dichotomy

Rick Tilman

Except for his theory of status emulation, no Veblen concept receives more attention than his distinction between business and industry. However, no consensus exists as to its meaning or its contemporary relevance for social and economic analysis. Indeed, conservatives Frank Knight and Ludwig von Mises expressed grave misgivings regarding its moral and political import as a rationale for the social control of industry and "interference" with consumer sovereignty; liberals have castigated it for exaggerating the social disserviceability of the profit system, while radicals, particularly Marxists, view it as a poor, or at least inadequate, substitute for Marxian theories of exploitation.[1] Even institutional economists have criticized it for being too simplistic because it indicates neither the degree to which business promotes industry indirectly nor the extent that working principles of industry and business are intermeshed in the production or technological system.[2] Nevertheless, I contend that if fully developed, it could be one of Veblen's most powerful analytical and normative devices; however, its full import can still only be understood in relationship to his "generic ends of life," of which equality is an organic part. Consequently, his argument must be deconstructed so as to link the business-industry dichotomy with his larger vision of social reconstruction, which encapsulates "fullness of life."[3]

Specifically, I will (1) further clarify the meaning of the dichotomy by providing a list of business and industrial pursuits drawn from examples actually used by Veblen, (2) explain why business and industrial pursuits are not, strictly speaking, always dichotomous in his analysis, (3) link the dichotomy with his ideas regarding community serviceability and its opposites—exploit, waste and predation—and most important, (4) demonstrate that the dichotomy has little significance if divorced from Veblen's "generic ends of life," an essential part of which is equality.[4]

THE BUSINESS-INDUSTRY DICHOTOMY

In Veblen's analysis of the dichotomy between business and industrial pursuits, no sharp dividing line is established between what is business and what is industrial. He studied, at length and in detail, the actual practices of U.S. financiers and industrialists. Veblen was a keen observer and drew on his observations in formulating his dichotomy. He was well aware of the complexity of many occupational pursuits and the difficulty of ascertaining whether a particular kind of work provided serviceability to the community or simply consisted of exploit, predation, and waste. This was particularly true of those occupations conventionally regarded as businesslike in nature. In Veblen's words: "The traffic of these business men shades off insensibly from that of the bona fide speculator who has no ulterior end of industrial efficiency to serve, to that of the captain of industry or entrepreneur as conventionally set forth in the economic manuals."[5] Veblen is careful, then, to give some examples that display the shades and nuances of business pursuits, although it should be remembered that on the whole, these remain on the business side of the spectrum (see Table 1.1).

Table 1.1
Business Pursuits

Speculators in Securities	Attorneys
Realtors	Brokers
Business Promoters	Bankers

Clearly, the intent of this classification, if not always its conceptual result, is to show that business pursuits as ideal types are largely self-regarding and pecuniary; if they produce any social benefits, it is coincidentally a by-product of the main thrust of both motive and activity. However, Veblen does not believe that all businesslike activities are solely of this nature; rather there are degrees of this, so that some economic activities provide socially serviceable commodities with only a modicum of predation and waste, whereas with other business pursuits, the opposite is true. As illustrated in Table 1.1, speculators in securities and realtors engage in mostly predatory activities, while business promoters, attorneys, brokers and bankers, although exploitive, provide some service to the community.

On the other hand, industrial pursuits appear to be largely serviceable to the community, although the likelihood of some industrial goods serving the purposes of emulatory consumption must be considered. Nonetheless, it is Veblen's claim that pursuits having the following traits are wholly, or at least largely, of a serviceable nature: pursuits "directing the processes of industry and contriving aims and ideals of industry"[6] and those "material situations reducible to objective mechanical, chemical and physiological impact."[7] Veblen then gives these examples (Table 1.2).

Table 1.2
Industrial Pursuits

Farming(ers)	Steel Workers
Assembly Line Workers	Engineers
Technicians	Mechanics
Artists	Inventors
Designers	Engineers
Foremen	Scientists

Finally, there is that category of employments that apparently has the characteristics of both business and industrial pursuits; it is where lines of employment blend and cross. Perhaps tongue-in-cheek, Veblen lists these marginal cases, which have the traits of both kinds of occupations (Table 1.3).

Table 1.3
Business and Industrial Pursuits

Retail Shopkeeping
Newspaper Work
Popular Art
Preaching
Sleight-of-hand, etc.

Not only are all these employments (except preaching) stated in the vaguest possible ways, they are not definitions of occupations at all. Instead, they each could encompass several kinds of work. "Retail shopkeeping," for example, could include tending the cash register, keeping accounts, stocking the shelves, cutting meat, culling vegetables and fruit, and sweeping floors. "Newspaper work" (Veblen may once have worked as a printer), could involve journalism, reporting, accounting, advertising, public relations, selling and delivering newspapers, and setting type. The impossibility of classifying such employments as either "business" or "industry" is evident.[8]

Veblen can thus be criticized by both heterodox and orthodox economists for his lack of conceptual and epistemological clarity. He is accused of, not only failing to adequately define *business* and *industry*, but of not showing how the two are related to each other, that is, how they overlap. Most specifically, it is argued that he failed to show how and when the price system is serviceable and when it is not. Some of these complaints are merely the reflexive ideological carping of market-oriented, politically conservative, neoclassical economists fixated on moral agnosticism or radical cultural relativism. Others emanate from the positivist epistemology, with its rigid distinctions between the *is* and the *ought*. More perceptive comments, come however, from those who are genuinely puzzled by the vagueness of the Veblen dichotomy. Although this area lies outside the realm of the present analysis, it may even suggest a need for a redefinition of the terms *business* and *industry*, if they are to continue to be used by political economists working in the Veblenian tradition.

MARGINAL PRODUCTIVITY THEORY: VEBLEN'S SEVERANCE OF PRODUCTIVITY FROM REMUNERATION

Traditionally, economists have divided the factors of production into land, labor, and capital. However, as Veblen put it:

The theoretical aim of the economists in discussing these factors and the activities for which they stand has not remained the same throughout the course of economic discussion, and the three-fold division has not always lent itself with facility to new points of view and new purposes of theory, but the writers who have shaped later theory have, on the whole, not laid violent hands on the sacred formula. ... It is accordingly not the aim of this paper to set aside the time-honored classification of factors, or even to formulate an iconoclastic amendment, but rather to indicate how and why this classification has proved inadequate for certain purposes of theory which were not contemplated by the men who elaborated it.[9]

However, although a substantial part of the essay is devoted to a satirical discussion of the taxonomy, production, and distribution theory of neoclassical economics, his claims that this theory and its variants are either tautological, irrelevant, or trivial are familiar to most Veblen scholars. In any case, it is the meaning of his distinction for political economists between pecuniary and industrial pursuits that is at issue here, and his tongue-in-cheek comments should not divert attention from the main thrust of his analysis.

The ambiguity of the business-industry dichotomy for operational purposes is evident, but the limitation of the neoclassical taxonomy of the factors of production in explaining the distribution of income is even more stark. If, as Veblen suggests, many elements in the business community do not contribute, directly or indirectly, to the production of goods and services, how are they able to obtain an income? His explanation, which appears tentative at first, is as follows:

There is in modern society a considerable range of activities, which are not only normally present, but which constitute the vital core of our economic system; which are not directly concerned with production, but which are nevertheless lucrative. Indeed, the group comprises most of the highly remunerative employments in modern economic life. The gains from these employments must plainly be accounted for on other grounds than their productivity, since they need have no productivity.[10]

The reader should note, however, that Veblen does not assert that the highly rewarded employments never have a connection (direct or indirect) with the production of goods and services; he simply claims that the bulk of them must have their income explained on grounds other than productivity. He further explains:

A result of the acceptance of the theoretical distinction here between industrial and pecuniary employments and an effective recognition of the pecuniary basis of the modern economic organization would be to dissociate the two ideas of productivity and remuneration. In mathematical language, remuneration could no longer be conceived and handled as a "function" of productivity—unless productivity be taken to mean pecuniary serviceability to the person who pays the remuneration. In modern life remuneration is, in the last analysis, uniformly obtained by virtue of an agreement between individuals who commonly proceed on their own interest in point of pecuniary gain. The remuneration may, therefore, be said to be a "function" of the pecuniary service rendered the person who grants the remuneration; but what is pecuniarily serviceable to the individual who exercises the discretion in the matter need not be productive of material gain to the community as a whole. Nor does the algebraic sum of individual pecuniary gains measure the aggregate serviceability of the activities for which the gains are got.[11]

The industry-pecuniary dichotomy thus breaks the link between production and distribution and lies at the heart of Veblen's critique of neoclassical marginal productivity theory. The egalitarian thrust of his argument remains central for, as he explains:

It is not only as regards the pecuniary employments that productivity and remuneration are constitutionally out of touch. It seems plain, from what has already been said, that the like is true for the remuneration gained in the industrial employments. Most wages, particularly those paid in the industrial employments proper, as contrasted with those paid for domestic or personal service, are paid on account of pecuniary serviceability to the employer, not on grounds of material serviceability to mankind at large. The product is valued, sought and paid for on account of and in some proportion to its vendibility, not for more recondite reasons of ulterior human welfare at large. It results that there is no warrant, in general theory, for claiming that the work of highly paid persons (more particularly that of highly paid business men) is of greater substantial use to the community than that of the less highly paid.[12]

Finally, in regard to the relationship between his dichotomy and the distribution of income, Veblen advances his favorite thesis, which concerns the absurdity of claiming that it is possible to accurately or objectively measure or ascertain the value of individual input.

In a community organized, as modern communities are, on a pecuniary basis, the discretion in economic matters rests with the individuals, in severalty; and the aggregate of discrete individual interests nowise expresses the collective interest. Expressions constantly recur in economic discussions which imply that the transactions discussed are carried out for the sake of the collective good or at the initiative of the social organism, or that "society" rewards so and so for their services. Such expressions are commonly of the nature of figures of speech and are serviceable for homiletical rather than for scientific use.[13]

In Veblen's view, some ways and means of distributing the income stream of the community may be more serviceable than others in terms of enhancing the community's adaptive powers to a continuously changing environment; but the claim that the input of individuals can be measured objectively is simply nonsense. He concludes:

The fact has come to be gradually more and more patent that there are constantly, normally present in modern economic life an important range of activities and classes of persons who work for an income but of whom it cannot be said that they, either proximately or remotely, apply themselves to the production of goods.[14]

Veblen portrays the evolution of industrial capitalism as a historical process requiring continuous modification in regard to both economic theory and policy analysis. The changing role of the entrepreneur, or "undertaker," thus comes under his scrutiny:

In the later development, the specialization of work in the economic field has at this point progressed so far, and the undertaker now in many cases comes so near being occupied with business affairs alone, to the exclusion of technological direction and supervision, that, with this object lesson before us, we no longer have the same difficulty in drawing a distinction between business and industrial employments. ... [T]he characteristic fact about [the undertaker's] work is that he is a businessman, occupied with pecuniary affairs.[15]

Veblen's point is that the pecuniary, or business, side of entrepreneurship has advanced a considerable distance toward marked differentiation from the industrial side. He then advances an interesting hypothesis about what this means in terms of enhanced serviceability to the community:

Its [the pecuniary, entrepreneurial side's] objective point is an alternative of the distribution of wealth. His business is, essentially, to sell and buy—sell in order to buy cheaper, buy in order to sell dearer. It may or may not, indirectly, and in a sense incidentally, result in enhanced production. The business man may be equally successful in his enterprise, and he may be equally well remunerated, whether his activity does or does not enrich the community. Immediately and directly, so long as it is confined to the pecuniary or business sphere, his activity is incapable of enriching or impoverishing the community as a whole except, after the fashion conceived by the mercantilists, through his dealings with men of other communities. The circulation and distribution of goods incidental to the business man's traffic is commonly, though not always or in the nature of the case, serviceable to the community; but the distribution of goods is a mechanical, not a pecuniary transaction, and it is not the objective point of business nor its invariable outcome.[16]

Purely business (that is, pecuniary), pursuits, by their very nature, differ from purely industrial pursuits, which is partly explained by Veblen on the basis of the applicability of different criteria of valuation. As he put it:

On the other hand, industrial capital, being a matter of mechanical contrivances and adaptation, cannot similarly vary through a revision of valuations. If it is taken as an aggregate, it is a physical magnitude, and as such it does not alter its complexion or its mechanical efficiency in response to the greater or less degree of appreciation with which it is viewed. Capital pecuniarily considered rests on a basis of subjective value; capital industrially considered rests on material circumstances reducible to objective terms of mechanical, chemical and physiological effect.[17]

Even in Veblen's time, conventional economists confused (or, more often, simply conflated), the two kinds of valuation and the different processes that give rise to them. Indeed, it was commonplace then, as now, to use the terms *pecuniary capital* and *physical capital* interchangeably or as synonymous simply with *capital*. Veblen was determined to press upon his readers the seriousness of this intellectual confusion, in part because he knew that the business community and its ideological satellites in the economics profession would simply seize upon it to claim legitimacy or even privileged status for rent, interest, and profit for originating in the production of serviceable goods and services. Moreover, his use of the dichotomy aimed at exposing and delegitimizing the control of industry by businessmen for purely business ends.

The businessman, through his pecuniary dispositions, enforces his choice of what industrial processes shall be in use. He can, of course, not create or initiate methods or aims for industry; if he does so he steps out of the business sphere into the material domain of industry. But he can decide whether and which of the known processes and industrial arts shall be practised, and to what extent.[18]

Veblen also develops his thesis that many business leaders are technologically incompetent to efficiently pursue industrial aims (a claim that will be discussed later).

Veblen makes two other important comments on how pecuniary and industrial values are related to each other in terms of their linked fluctuations. In a sense, this may be his closest approximation to distinguishing between values that are "subjective" and those that are "objective":

Any industrial venture which falls short in meeting the pecuniary exigencies of the market declines and yields ground to others that meet them with better effect. Hence shrewd business management is a requisite to success in any industry that is carried on within the scope of the market. Pecuniary failure carries with it industrial failure, whatever may be the cause to which the pecuniary failure is due—whether it be inferiority of the goods produced, lack of salesmanlike tact, popular prejudice, scanty or ill-devised advertising, excessive truthfulness, or what not. In this way industrial results are closely dependent upon the presence of business ability; but the cause of this dependence of industry upon business in a given case is to be sought in the fact that other rival ventures have the backing of shrewd business management, rather than in any help which business management in the aggregate affords to the aggregate industry of the community.[19]

It is interesting to note that the "subjective" values expressed in the market by price thus determined whether more "objective" values could flourish in the technological-industrial sector.   Veblen offered the following discerning comments to this effect, yet without an adequate explanation as yet as to how the process of valuation in the latter realm is superior to that in the former.

The point has frequently been noted that it is impossible to get at the aggregate social (industrial) capital by adding up the several items of individual (pecuniary) capital. A reason for this, apart from variations in the market values of given material means of production, is that pecuniary capital comprises not only material things but also conventional facts, psychological phenomena not related in any rigid way to material means of production,—as, e.g., good will, fashions, customs, prestige, effrontery, personal credit.   Whatever ownership touches, and whatever affords ground for pecuniary discretion, may be turned to account for pecuniary gain and may therefore be comprised in the aggregate of pecuniary capital.[20]

It should be noted once again, however, that to Veblen, *industry* strongly connotes the production of socially serviceable goods and services and these, in turn, enhance the possibility that the community will succeed in its quest for the "generic ends of life"; all of which signifies that it is "fullness of life," or at least his version thereof, that determines whether an activity or process is business or industry.

THE LINK BETWEEN EQUITY AND EFFICIENCY

As Veblen's analysis of the dichotomy between pecuniary and industrial pursuits progresses, his views on social equity and efficiency become more forcefully articulated and the questions to which he demands answers take on increasingly rhetorical overtones:

Neither the practical questions of our generation, nor the pressing theoretical questions of the science, run on the adequacy or equity of the share that goes to any class in the normal case. The questions are rather such realistic ones as these: Why do we, now and again, have hard times and unemployment in the midst of excellent resources, high efficiency and plenty of unmet wants? Why is one-half our consumable product contrived for consumption that yields no material benefit? Why are large coordinations of industry, which greatly reduce cost of production, a cause of perplexity and alarm? Why is the family disintegrating among the industrial classes, at the same time that the wherewithal to maintain it is easier to compass? Why are large and increasing portions of the community penniless in spite of a scale of remuneration which is very appreciably above the subsistence minimum? Why is there a widespread disaffection among the intelligent workman who ought to know better?[21]

Veblen is not merely repudiating, and then reconceptualizing, economic theory as it was understood in the early years of the twentieth century, although that is what has most commonly attracted the attention of economists. He is also constructing an ethical vision with a consciously intended aesthetic import. Alan Dyer has penetratingly commented:

On the one hand, capital displays qualities like physical cause and effect, cooperation, and social productiveness in industrial employments. His [Veblen's] discussion of these effects also showed that a sign may cause different responses in different actors. On the one hand, capital displays qualities like physical cause and effect, cooperation, and social productiveness in industrial employments. On the other hand, capital displays qualities like competition, customary privilege, and personal gain in pecuniary employments. The direction of theoretical inquiry depends upon whose aesthetic response the theoretician chooses to build upon in constructing his theory of capital.[22]

However, Veblen's distinction between pecuniary and industrial employments has little meaning unless his views on community serviceability are understood as the fulcrum of both his social philosophy and his economic analysis. Beyond the mere fulfillment of biological and functional imperatives lies the achievement of the generic ends of life impersonally or objectively considered, and an adequate supply of serviceable goods and services is obviously necessary to gain these ends. However, the composition, or nature, of the output is at least as important to Veblen as the quantity, and it is in these qualitative considerations that Veblen's views on serviceability become most explicit. Purely pecuniary motives and processes in his view often retard or at least do not lead toward a fulfillment of the criterion of serviceability as measured by progress toward the generic ends of life.[23]   Thus, the distinction between business and industry must invoke instrumental valuation in order to reaffirm the validity and the usefulness of the distinction itself, for Veblen clearly understood the difficulty of making these judgments in problematic situations.

In summation, Veblen's dichotomy between business and industry, while a potentially powerful analytical/normative device, remains inadequately developed and always in danger of obsolescence. This means that the links between the two elements, the things that make for the dichotomy as related "potentials," needs to be fleshed out. Part of what will have to constitute an adequate theory of institutional change is how the two elements of the dichotomy differ over time, are defined in new form, and then change again. The nature of any evolving system, including one that can be understood with the dichotomy, is such that its efficiency and equity are always changing. Its rules for understanding both are evolving, since the elements of the dichotomy are themselves changing. This, in turn, means that the process of determining value is also changing. It is not simply a matter of change occurring—it is also a matter of the rate and direction of change—but which rate and in which direction? Moreover, is the division between the elements of the dichotomy a "clean" one? Indeed, the pecuniary and industrial spheres are sometimes so intertwined as to make it difficult to distinguish between them and thus impossible to assign a position of causal primacy or institutional dominance to either.

THE GENERIC ENDS OF LIFE

The discussion of how a progressive outlook in contemporary society is maintained needs more than the "generic ends of life" as a focus. This is an evasive term and needs a fuller explication than it has yet received. The meaning of Veblen's generic ends of life is rarely discussed in specific terms by those who specialize in moral or ethical discourse; consequently, such analysis has been left in the hands of historians and social scientists like this author, who are ill-equipped to engage in it. Nevertheless, clarity's sake demands that the meaning and significance of the term be examined and its use related to Veblen's business-industry dichotomy.

The generic ends of life are those traits Veblen hoped would be most highly developed and visible in the "industrial republic" of his dreams. Such are the common goals of social existence that are transculturally shared, that is, the conscious, shared goals of what C. Wright Mills was later to call a "properly developing society."[24] They crystallize in "fullness of life," which is best exemplified by the flowering of the "instincts" of workmanship, idle curiosity, and parenthood.

Parsimony requires a short list of ends, but much spin-off is possible from Veblen's concept of instincts. Clearly, they incorporate other ends; "workmanship," for example, clearly implies a striving for excellence; "parenthood" signifies altruism, not only toward one's children but, writ large, on a scope that transcends family, clan, class, ethnicity, race, and nation. "Idle curiosity" may involve only speculation, legend construction, and myth making, but in higher stages of social development, it signifies the growth of critical intelligence, scientific inquiry and so on. Veblen's three instincts, then, are not narrowly focused, particularized values but instead require adaptation to changing social environments; rather than being rigid value constants, they have transcultural significance in an instrumental sense as ends-in-view, rather than as ends-in-themselves in an absolute sense.

Veblen clearly believed, unlike many of the neoclassicals, that interpersonal comparisons of well-being are both possible and imperative.[25] Although he did not show how individual and social ends could be made congruent with each other (this was not one of his aims), he did assume that what more conventional economists referred to as "interpersonal comparisons of utility" were appropriate. He made this assumption because he could not otherwise fathom how communities could exist. After all, if people living in close physical and social proximity to one another did not possess widely shared aims and values, how could they coexist with each other?

Veblen's viewpoint was thus social rather than competitive; hence his unwillingness to invidiously promote the interest of any group or class. At the same time, he saw that the private gain aimed at in business activities was pecuniary rather than a beneficent interest in a maximum of goods, as assumed by the neoclassical theorists. Accordingly, he emphasized the perversion of the instinct of workmanship through short-term gain, shoddy workmanship, and price maintenance. No contemporary American economist had so penetrating a theory to explain the secular trend in terms of the conflict between business interests and the social good, and no other economist of any stature so persistently and effectively explained American culture in terms of conflict between business and the public interests.

A student once asked John R. Commons, Veblen's contemporary, what determined the division of national wealth among the various producers in any economy. Commons replied that neoclassical economics was logical in theory, but that in reality, the pressure brought to bear by various producing classes through institutions in the society on the social product more often determined their share of the national product.[26] From this, Commons concluded that various groups in society do not possess effective institutions to compete for a share of the total national product. If more social equity were to be achieved, reform was needed, which clearly suggests the creation and implementation of institutional mechanisms and policies that divert income away from purely market-governed and -driven objectives. Commons was certainly not a radical like Veblen, but he, too, recognized the existence of a dichotomy between business and industry and the significance this had for the adoption of more egalitarian public policies.

The normative thrust of Veblen's "industrial republic," which he hoped would be an "ungraded commonwealth" of "masterless" men and women, points to a strong sense of community. To Veblen this clearly meant a lessening in the four modes of inequality: race, class, gender, and nation. Indeed, he believed that no genuine or authentic sense of community could exist without equality—but how far would Veblen proceed with the flattening, or leveling, of society? He never specifically said, but he clearly believed, that existing degrees of inequality were unjustifiable on grounds of both equity and efficiency. How to answer the basic questions of (1) what to produce, (2) with which resources, and (3) who gets the output cannot be adequately answered by the factorial taxonomy, according to Veblen. Thus, the issue of productivity, including its measurement and remuneration for it, is indeed a social or cultural issue, and not merely a pecuniary one. Indeed, it was Veblen's debunking of the mythical link between large income and large social contribution that has provided many heterodox economists with the rationale they needed to function as egalitarians in an economics profession dominated by neoclassical, marginal productivity theorists.

If there is, as Veblen contended, little or no relationship between production and remuneration, there can be no justification for the degrees of economic inequality that presently exist in the United States and many other industrial nations. Why is it, then, that so many economists continue to defend the bulk of the inequalities that persist? Is their behavior not simply a form of self-fulfilling prophecy, and are they not engaged in the legitimation of a system that perpetuates self-serving myths? These are not rhetorical questions, for they suggest a need for closer examination of the antiegalitarian biases of neoclassical economists and the social and economic elites (and the journalists and politicians, to boot). The relationship between vested interests and vested ideas is sometimes a complex one, but the inequality that now exists is buttressed by the ideologically hegemonic work of intellectuals who apparently believe that equality is a revolt against human nature.

MARXIAN THEORY AND THE BUSINESS-INDUSTRY DICHOTOMY

Many heterodox economists have viewed the business-industry dichotomy as an alternative to Marxian exploitation theory; although they are correct in doing so, there are points of convergence between institutionalism and Marxism in their theories of (1) accumulation, (2) domination, (3) alienation, (4) inequality, and (5) expropriation.[27] Veblen was too different a thinker to be regarded as a Marxist or even as working in any of the Marxian traditions, yet the business-industry dichotomy has affinities with, or bears a significant relationship to, each of these five theories. In fact, however, it is to the "business" side of the dichotomy that Veblen attributes many of the social pathologies of capitalism, while it is to the "industrial" side that he assigns the production of socially useful goods and services.

In regard to accumulation theory, in the Marxism paradigm, the exploitation of workers explains profits and accumulation under capitalism; this is the source of capitalist expansion. However, in the Veblen dichotomy, "business" activity is perceived as largely wasteful in many industries, for it is in qualitative and quantitative changes in the state of the industrial arts—primarily physical, cultural, and institutional processes—rather than in pecuniary ones that Veblen finds the motor of economic growth; thus, the persistence of inequality is primarily a business phenomenon. In regard to Marxian domination theory, exploitation is due to the domination of workers by capitalists, especially at the point of production, and domination is, moreover, viewed as dehumanizing. Although for Veblen domination occurs at the point of production through hierarchical relationships, he focused more strongly on the cultural and ideological hegemony of the dominant classes and on the inculcation of subjugative habits of mind in the underlying population as the facilitators of inequality.

The problem of alienation, which was so central to Marx, takes a different form in Veblen. As John Diggins has argued, he saw the "worship of money as a form of social alienation deeply rooted in the emulative nature of man, a phenomenon that had its origins in primitive man's respect for power and success."[28] Of course, in Veblen's analysis, emulation and emulatory processes are mostly rooted in, or arise from, the business side of the business-industry dichotomy. To overcome alienation in this sense strongly suggests either reducing the scope and intensity of business as such or else its "humanization," which Veblen probably thought unlikely.

Finally, there is expropriation theory; in the Marxian analysis, exploitation is a measure of expropriation, of one agent owning part of the product that should rightfully belong to another. In Veblen's analysis, the main institutional focus in this regard is absentee ownership, and especially absentee ownership of corporate stock which, not surprisingly, most directly impacts on the business side of the business-industry dichotomy.

All five of these processes and the theories that underlie them enhance and explain inequality in industrial society, and all, in the Veblen dichotomy, are located primarily in the business realm. In his analysis, it is thus clear that inequality originates, not primarily in the genes, but in "business" as Veblen construed it.

An important question not yet dealt with here is that of the relationship between the dichotomy, on the one hand, and consumption, on the other. Consumption is usually broken into two categories by Veblen; emulatory consumption, which aims at status enhancement, and functional consumption, which fulfills utilitarian or biological needs. Obviously, many commodities will serve both needs (often simultaneously). The "business" realm of the dichotomy seems most likely to be linked with emulatory consumption, and "industry," with functional consumption, yet the relationship is much more complex than this. For example, many large, expensive automobiles serve emulatory and functional consumer needs together and seem to be the product of both business and industry, but the suspicion lingers that even though Veblen failed to clarify the relationship, he somehow believed that "business" and emulation are closely linked, as are "industry" and functional consumption. In this vein, Dennis Smith recently wrote

Veblen sought to separate and to polarize elements of American culture which are, in fact, closely related. His writings may be interpreted, in large part, as an attempt to establish the existence of a dialectical contradiction whose tension and dynamic would provide the promise of radical social transformation. For example, Veblen proposed a misleading opposition between a predatory inclination and a readiness to engage in regular, purposeful and productive labor. In fact, both traits are typically found in the same individual or group.[29]

Smith neglected Veblen's point, which is that the polarized traits are not present in the same classes in stable quantities, the mixture is unstable even between individuals, and thus it will simply not do to assume the existence of immutable or constant moral traits. Nevertheless, he may be correct in implicitly suggesting that the pursuit of self-interest may be more congruent with the production of socially serviceable goods and services than Veblen imagined. "Business" and "industry" may thus be less in conflict than the dichotomy suggests—yet this must remain a matter for empirical investigation rather than a priori assumption.

The neoclassicist's aim of avoiding the analysis of value judgments has been the main source of the problem of interpersonal comparisons. This, too, no doubt underlies the conventional view that the business-industry dichotomy is too ill defined, too narrow, and too insensitive to variation in individual needs to serve as an adequate measure of welfare. Of what value, then (if any), is the business-industry dichotomy for purposes of interpersonal comparability, and how adequate is it for purposes of distributive justice? In the Veblenian realm of human existence, the loss of well-being due to invidious comparison may well be grounds for the redistribution of wealth or income in the direction of more equality. Alternately, to shift the grounds of doctrinal authority to John Rawls, his notion of primary goods—goods that any person would need in order to carry out his or her life plan—seem more likely to be forthcoming in a society with more equality than one with less.

Veblen's "generic ends of life" rest on his belief that a conception of the elements that are important in making life good must be widely shared. He may seem merely to be making personal judgments about what makes a life better for the person who lives it; this strongly suggests that he believed some standards exist or can be developed for making judgments about the relationship between people's actual desires and what is really desirable. Moreover, there may be a difference between people's interests and what they are interested in. The whole range of issues that must be explored to adequately grasp the idea of "false consciousness," that is, lack of awareness of objective self-interest, lies outside our realm of inquiry here. However, Veblen clearly believed that certain things are generally intelligible as valuable and, furthermore, as valuable for any normal human. This suggests the efficacy of moving from interpersonal comparisons of well-being to collective, social aggregative, and cultural intrapersonal comparisons, which are less problematic. The consumption of some goods and services cannot plausibly be counted as part of well-being unless some standard or process of evaluation is articulated by which to measure their contribution to "fullness of life." A satisfactory account of human interests may be partially derived from actual preferences and desires, but Veblen suggests that the direction of explanation is not from individual desire to social value, but from social value to individual desire. To him, the term *social,* by its very nature, suggests equality and, when linked with the generic ends of life, both demand a high degree of equality of access to economic resources for their fullest realization.

Thus, Veblen's elevation of "industry" over "business" not only allowed him to express this belief, it also allowed him to argue that the link between efficiency and equity is very different than the so-called trade-off between the two as described in mainstream theory. If the aggregation of individual welfare does not necessarily lead to a maximal social welfare, then social efficiency depends on social equity, and the latter implies more equality. This is not a trade-off. Rather, it is one of the starting points for developing a radical institutionalism.

Of course, much more work needs to be done. The link or links between individual and social action are also problematic, for the two should coincide. Unfortunately, Veblen failed to adequately explore the range of overlap between the two concepts, as it occurs in a dynamic society. Such an exploration remains, perhaps, the single most important task for those working in the Veblenian tradition.

NOTES

* The author thanks Glen Atkinson, Mike Reed, and Bill Dugger for their critiques of his chapter. He gratefully acknowledges permission to quote from the correspondence of William Jaffe, given by his literary executor, Donald Walker.

1. In the summer of 1929 I went to Bonn and there had occasion to talk quite frequently with Professor Joseph Schumpeter. On one occasion he launched into a tirade against Veblen. He said he first saw Veblen at a meeting of the American Economic Association, and that Veblen, leaning against the wall near the threshold of a room, with a red scarf about him looked like a common *poseur*. Schumpeter added that he thought the distinction between making goods and making money only too obvious and utterly useless in economic analysis (William Jaffé to Joseph Dorfman, January 13, 1931, Dorfman Collection, Butler Library, Columbia University).

2. Reactions to Veblen's dichotomy between business and industry include David Riesman, *Thorstein Veblen: A Critical Interpretation* (New York: Charles Scribner's Sons, 1960), ch. 3; Lev Dobriansky, *Veblenism: A New Critique* (Washington, D.C.: Public Affairs Press, 1957), ch. 7; Douglas Dowd, ed., *Thorstein Veblen: A Critical Reappraisal* (Ithaca, N.Y.: Cornell University Press, 1958), chs. 10–11; Phillip A. O'Hara, "Veblen's Analysis of Business, Industry and the Limits of Capital," *History of Economics Review*, no. 20 (Summer 1993): 95–119, and "Marx, Veblen, and Modern Institutional Economics: Price and Dynamics" (Doctoral Dissertation, University of Newcastle, New South Wales, Australia, 1992). Further development of the Veblenian dichotomy is found in Clarence Ayres, *The Theory of Economic Progress* (Chapel Hill: University of North Carolina Press, 1944), chs. 6–10; David Hamilton, *Evolutionary Economics* (New Brunswick, New Jersey: Transaction Publishers, 1991); and Marc Tool, *The Discretionary Economy* (Santa Monica, Calif.: Goodyear Publishing Company, 1979), chs. 4–7.

3. See, for example, Marc Tool, "A Social Value Theory in Neoinstitutional Economics," *Journal of Economic Issues*, 11 (Dec. 1977): 827–28.

4. Concerning (3), it is important to note that, although much commentary and criticism have been devoted to the larger ceremonial-technological dichotomy, there has been less explication of the business-industry distinction, which is a subset thereof, and little textual exegesis of Veblen's 1901 article, "Industrial and Pecuniary Employments." This is surprising since this is the single most important statement Veblen made regarding the dichotomy. To the article, of course, must be added his analysis in *The Theory of Business Enterprise* (1904) and his rebuttal of John Cummings's review of *The Theory of the Leisure Class*. Although Veblen alludes to the distinction in his other writings, these are the most distinctive and detailed treatments of it, and it is primarily on them that this analysis will be based. It is important to note, however, that much analysis of the Veblenian distinction between business and industrial pursuits by other authors is buried inside texts that bear the title, "ceremonial-technological dichotomy."

See Veblen, "Industrial and Pecuniary Employments," Publications of the American Economic Association, Series 3 (1901): 190–235; Veblen, *The Theory of Business Enterprise* (New York: Charles Scribner's Sons, 1904), chs. 1–4; Veblen, "Mr. Cummings's Strictures on *The Theory of the Leisure Class*," *Journal of Political Economy*, 9 (Dec. 1899): 106–117.

5. Veblen, "Industrial and Pecuniary Employments," 204.

6. Veblen, "Mr. Cummings's Strictures," in *Essays in Our Changing Order* (New York: Augustus M. Kelley, 1964), p. 27.

7. Ibid.

8. In his still relevant critique of United States colleges and universities, *The Higher Learning in America* (New York: Augustus M. Kelley, 1965), Veblen comments:

The professional knowledge and skill of physicians, surgeons, dentists, pharmacists, agriculturists, engineers of all kinds, perhaps even of journalists, is of some use to the community at large, at the same time that it may be profitable to the bearers of it. The community has a substantial interest in the adequate training of these men, although it is not the intellectual interest that attaches to science and scholarship. But such is not the case with the training designed to give proficiency in business. No gain comes to the community at large from increasing the business proficiency of any number of its young men. There are already much too many of these businessmen, much too astute and proficient in their calling, for the common good. A higher average business efficiency simply raises activity and avidity in business to a higher average pitch of skill and fervour, with very little other material result than a redistribution of ownership; since business is occupied with the competitive acquisition of wealth, not with its production. It is only by a euphemistic metaphor that we are accustomed to speak of the businessmen as producers of goods. Gains due to such efficiency are differential gains only. They are a differential as against other businessmen on the one hand, and as against the rest of the community on the other hand (208).

9. Veblen, "Industrial and Pecuniary Employments," 190.

10. Ibid., 214.

11. Ibid., 215–16.

12. Ibid., 214–15.

13. Ibid., 216.

14. Ibid., 203–4.

15. Ibid., 206–7.

16. Ibid., 208.

17. Ibid., 223. J. M. Keynes wrote:

Of the maxims of orthodox finance none, surely is more anti-social than the fetish of liquidity, the doctrine that it is a positive virtue on the part of investment institutions to concentrate upon the holding of liquid securities. It forgets that there is no such thing as liquidity for the community as a whole. The social object of skilled investment should be to defeat the dark forces of time and ignorance which envelop our future. The actual practice of most skilled investment is to beat the gun. (Keynes, *The General Theory of Employment, Interest, and Money* [New York: Harcourt Brace and Company, 1936], 155).

18. Veblen, "Industrial and Pecuniary Employments," 209.

19. Ibid., pp. 209–10.

20. Ibid., 223.

21. Ibid., 224–5.

22. Alan Dyer, "Economic Theory as an Art Form," *Journal of Economic Issues*, 22 (Mar. 1988): 161.

23. See Veblen, "Industrial and Pecuniary Employments," 212.

24. See C. Wright Mills, "Man in the Middle: The Designer," in Irving L. Horowitz, ed., *Power, Politics and People* (New York: Oxford University Press, 1963), 374–86.

25. For a recent discussion of this issue, see Jon E. Elster and John Roemer, eds., *Interpersonal Comparisons of Well-Being* (New York: Cambridge University Press, 1991), 1–16.

26. See William D. Rowley, *M. L. Wilson and the Campaign for the Domestic Allotment* (Lincoln: University of Nebraska Press, 1970), 14–15.

27. See John E. Roemer, *Egalitarian Perspectives: Essays in Philosophical Economics* (Cambridge: Cambridge University Press, 1994), 66–67. See also, William M. Dugger and Howard Sherman, "Comparison of Marxism and Institutionalism," *Journal of Economic Issues*, 28 (Mar. 1994): 101–28.

28. John P. Diggins, *The Bard of Savagery: Thorstein Veblen and Modern Social Theory* (New York: Seabury Press, 1978), 128.

29. Dennis Smith, *The Chicago School: A Liberal Critique of Capitalism* (London: Macmillan Education, 1988), 55.

REFERENCES

Ayres, Clarence E. 1944. *The Theory of Economic Progress*. Chapel Hill: University of North Carolina Press.

Cummings, John. 1899. "The Theory of the Leisure Class." *Journal of Political Economy*, 7 (Sept.): 425–55.

Diggins, John P. 1978. *The Bard of Savagery: Thorstein Veblen and Modern Social Theory*. New York: Seabury Press.

Dobriansky, Lev. 1957. *Veblenism: A New Critique*. Washington, D.C.: Public Affairs Press.

Dowd, Douglas, ed. 1958. *Thorstein Veblen: A Critical Reappraisal*. Ithaca, N.Y.: Cornell University Press.

Dugger, William M. and Howard Sherman. 1994. "Comparison of Marxism and Institutionalism." *Journal of Economic Issues*, 28 (Mar.): 101–28.

Dyer, Alan. 1988. "Economic Theory as an Art Form." *Journal of Economic Issues*, 22 (Mar.): 157–66.

Elster, John E. and John Roemer, eds. 1991. *Interpersonal Comparisons of Well-Being*. New York: Cambridge University Press.

Hamilton, David. 1991. *Evolutionary Economics*. New Brunswick, New Jersey: Transaction Publishers.

Jaffe, William. Letter to Joseph Dorfman, January 13, 1931. Dorfman Collection, Butler Library, Columbia University. New York.

Keynes, John Maynard. 1936. *The General Theory of Employment, Interest, and Money*. New York: Harcourt Brace and Company.

Mills, C. Wright. 1963. "Man in the Middle: The Designer," In Irving L. Horowitz, ed. *Power, Politics and People*. New York: Oxford University Press, pp. 374–86.

O'Hara, Phillip A. 1992. "Marx, Veblen, and Modern Institutional Economics: Price and Dynamics." Doctoral Dissertation, University of Newcastle. Australia.

___. 1993. "Veblen's Analysis of Business, Industry and the Limits of Capital." *History of Economics Review*, 20 (Summer): 95–119.

Riesman, David. 1960. *Thorstein Veblen: A Critical Interpretation*. New York: Charles Scribner's Sons.

Roemer, John E. 1994. *Egalitarian Perspectives: Essays in Philosophical Economics*. Cambridge: Cambridge University Press.

Rowley, William D. 1970. *M. L. Wilson and the Campaign for the Domestic Allotment*. Lincoln: University of Nebraska Press.

Smith, Dennis. 1988. *The Chicago School: A Liberal Critique of Capitalism.* London: Macmillan Education.

Tool, Marc. 1977. "A Social Value Theory in Neoinstitutional Economics." *Journal of Economic Issues*, 11 (Dec.): 823–46.

____. 1979. *The Discretionary Economy.* Santa Monica, Calif.: Goodyear Publishing Company.

Veblen, Thorstein. 1899. "Mr. Cummings's Strictures on *The Theory of the Leisure Class.*" *Journal of Political Economy*, 9 (Dec.): 106–17.

____. 1901. "Industrial and Pecuniary Employments." Publications of the American Economic Association, Series 3: 190–235.

____. 1904. *The Theory of Business Enterprise.* New York: Charles Scribner's Sons.

____. [1934] 1964. *Essays In Our Changing Order.* Ed. by Leon Ardzrooni. New York: Augustus M. Kelley.

____. 1965. *The Higher Learning in America.* New York: Augustus M. Kelley.

2

Four Modes of Inequality

William M. Dugger

THE INEQUALITY TABLEAU

A mode of inequality is a social process whereby a powerful group of humans (top dogs) reaps benefits for itself at the expense of a less powerful group (underdogs). The process involves an institutionalized struggle over power, status, and wealth. Four modes of inequality will be discussed: (1) gender, (2) race, (3) class, and (4) nation. These do not include all of the ways in which humans take advantage of each other, but they do cover much of the ground. Moreover, the four modes overlap and reinforce each other.

Corresponding to each mode is a set of practices whereby the top dogs take advantage of the underdogs. These practices ensure that the top dogs win. Corresponding to each mode of inequality is also a set of enabling myths that culturally enforce the practices and "make the game seem fair" to both the top dogs and the underdogs. A focal point also exists for each mode of inequality. The focal point is a particular institution where the inequality resides—where the myths justifying it are learned and the practices realizing it actually take place. These focal points frequently change as the particular mode of inequality evolves. Moreover, corresponding to each mode is an antidote—a set of values, meanings, and beliefs—that can debunk the enabling myths. Inequality, then, is a whole complex of modes, practices, enabling myths, focal points, and antidotes. This complex does not reach a balance of forces. It is not an equilibrium system, but an interacting process of cumulative causation in which inequality either gets worse or better. Seldom, if ever, does it stay the same.

Values are central to inequality. They either rationalize it by making it seem fair and true, or they debunk it by pointing out its injustice and falsehood. We can pretend to be value neutral about inequality, but we never are.

Four Modes of Inequality Defined

Gender inequality is the domination of one gender by another. In our time and place (the twentieth century in the Western Hemisphere), men dominate women through a whole series of gendered practices. These practices are supported and justified by myths about female inferiority and male superiority. These myths are the substance of sexism. Sexist myths enable men to dominate women without feeling guilty and also enable women to be dominated without mass rebellion or suicide. The antidote to gender inequality is feminism.

Race inequality is practiced by one race discriminating against another. In our time and place, the most significant form is the discrimination of white Europeans against black Africans or other people of color. It is justified by myths about African, Asian, and Latin American inferiority and about European superiority. These myths are the substance of today's racism. Racist myths enable white Europeans to discriminate against non-European people of color without feeling guilty and also enable those people of color to adjust to their unfair treatment without fully realizing that it is unfair. The antidote to discrimination is civil rights.

Class inequality in capitalism is practiced through the exploitation of the workers by the capitalists. In Soviet communism, the workers were exploited by the nomenklatura. Class exploitation is supported by its own myths. In the West, the myths are about market efficiency, while in the East, the myths were formerly about the dictatorship of the proletariate. Class myths enable a powerful class to exploit a powerless class and are comparable to racist and sexist myths in terms of effect, if not in terms of content. The antidote to exploitation is economic democracy (see Dugger 1984).

Nation inequality is practiced through the predation of powerful nations on weak nations and is supported by jingoistic myths about national honor and foreign treachery. Jingoistic myths allow the members of powerful nations to take pride in the killing of the members of weak nations rather than feel shame. The antidote to national predation is internationalism. Table 2.1 summarizes all the modes, practices, myths, and antidotes.

Table 2.1
The Inequality Tableau

Modes	Practices	Myths	Antidotes
Gender	Domination	Sexism	Feminism
Race	Discrimination	Racism	Civil Rights
Class	Exploitation	Classism	Economic Democracy
Nation	Predation	Jingoism	Internationalism

FOUR MODES OF INEQUALITY EXPLAINED INSTITUTIONALLY

Mode of inequality refers to the way in which people are grouped for giving offense and for receiving it. The groups are separate and unequal. Individuals do not choose to join one group or the other, but rather are assigned to a particular group by the operation of law, tradition, and myth. Culture and coercion, not individual preference and choice, are the operative factors.

Grouping (1): The Class Mode of Inequality

When individuals are grouped into classes, the boundaries are based mainly on how they appropriate their incomes, but also on how large the incomes are. The upper class is composed of capitalists and people who have managed to appropriate large incomes for themselves. An exact number cannot be placed on just how large that income has to be, but the inexact nature of its boundary does not mean an upper class does not exist. It exists because its members have acquired and used differential economic advantages and have kept the lower strata from doing the same. The appropriation of large incomes can be done through the control of wealth or important services. Those who own or control industrial and financial capital—wealthy families, corporate executives, investment bankers, and the like—can use their capitalist position to enlarge their income. Such capitalists are the most powerful members of the upper class; they set its ideological tone and make it essentially a capitalist class. Those who control the delivery of financially important services—corporate lawyers, lobbyists, politicians, and the like—can also appropriate large incomes. The middle class is composed of the "wannabe" groups—those who want to appropriate large incomes but lack the differential advantage needed to do so. They are contenders but were born to the wrong parents; they were sent to the wrong schools, had access to the wrong social connections, or were steered into the wrong professions. Members of the lower class are not in contention, whether they themselves realize it or not. Enough class overlap and circulation between classes exists to allow a limited role for individual choice, merit, and luck. Nonetheless, membership in a particular class is determined primarily by what class a person is born into rather than that individual person's rise or fall (see Osberg 1984).

Although class is an economic category, it is also strongly influenced by cultural factors. The kind of school attended and the kind of learning that takes place there vary by class, as do family structures, religions, beliefs, values, and meanings. (For a conservative view of cultural factors and class, see Berger and Berger 1983. For a liberal view, see Jencks et al., 1972, 1979. For a radical view, see Green 1981; Harrington 1983.) All the basic institutions teach the youth of each class the values, beliefs, and meanings appropriate to their economic station in life. When the class role has been learned and accepted, the person will be well adjusted, perhaps even happy. When the class role is rejected, unhappiness and maladjustment result, and either a change in class will be attempted or a rebel will be made. (For further discussion see Moore 1978.)

Grouping (2): The Race Mode of Inequality

When individuals are grouped into races, the boundary between discriminating and discriminated groups is based on race, but race itself is as much a cultural heritage as it is a biological endowment. The particular form that the race mode of inequality takes in the United States will illustrate the point. (The classic work is Myrdal 1962.) "African American" is as much a cultural as a biological grouping. It does not necessarily include all people whose skin is black. Many people from India, Melanesia, and Sri Lanka are black, as are Native Australians. Many have their own problems and face their own injustices, but they are not in the racially discriminated group of African Americans. Even though the group of African Americans excludes many people whose skin is black, it also includes some people whose skin is white. People with white skins are African Americans if their ancestors were seized for slaves in Africa and forcibly transported to the Americas, where miscegenation and a whole myriad of laws, traditions, and myths forced generation after generation of, not only the dark-skinned, but also the fair-skinned, members of the group into an inferior position relative to "white" Europeans. Cultural learning, not genetics, was the principal factor operating throughout the period.

Grouping (3): The Gender Mode of Inequality

Females (those with ovaries) are assigned to the group called women and males (those with testicles) are assigned to the group called men. However, gender, like race, is as much cultural as it is biological. Female humans are taught to be women by their culture; male humans are taught to be men by their culture as well. What the assignees learn to become is determined by what the culture teaches them, not by their gonads. Humans with ovaries are expected to learn to be women. Humans with testicles are expected to learn to be men. That is, they learn how they are expected to behave in their assigned roles. Their genitals do not teach them; their culture does. (The classic is Mead 1949.) The males of today are expected to be superior to the females, and the females are expected to be inferior to the males.

Grouping (4): The Nation Mode of Inequality

When people are grouped into nations, arbitrary geopolitical boundaries separate the groups into the chosen people and the foreigners. Such groupings are also based on ethnic differences within individual nations, and can produce a considerable degree of inequality. However, when ethnic differences are combined with the power of the nation-state, an even more effective mode of inequality is formed. (Religion plays a role as well but will not be discussed in this chapter.) A nation is an area controlled by one state, where allegiance is to that state rather than another. Cultural and language differences may further differentiate the people in one state from those in another. Moreover, the controlling states may accentuate the differences through state education, state religion, and other forms of propoganda. The individuals who happen to find themselves identified as French, German, Italian, or Russian are not so by nature. They must be taught these identities. Since the nation mode of grouping people is particularly arbitrary, it relies very heavily on the teaching of alleged group differences. People must be taught that foreigners are untrustworthy, ignorant, brutal, and inferior. Only then can national leaders use their jingoism for supporting attacks against other nations or for mounting a defense against (imagined) attacks. Those members of the underlying population who do not accept their assigned roles in these jingoistic activities are exiled, ridiculed, imprisoned, or executed. A complex system of passports and identification papers keeps track of people and makes sure they are assigned to the "correct" national group—whether they want to be or not. Formidable security agencies are created by each nation to implement the groupings. Security agencies such as the former Soviet State Security Committee (KGB) and the U.S. Central Intelligence Agency (CIA) and Federal Bureau of Investigation (FBI) become focal points of nationalism.

FOUR PRACTICES OF INEQUALITY

The practices of inequality are interrelated forms of parasitic collective action. They cannot be reduced down to just one abstract practice without doing great damage to the multifaceted reality of inequality. The domination of women by men is really not the same as the exploitation of workers by capitalists, nor is the discrimination against African Americans by European Americans the same as the German invasion of Poland. Consequently, each practice will be discussed separately.

Practice (1): Domination

The domination of women by men has an institutionalized focal point in patriarchal societies—the family. An institution—and the family is no exception—is made up of people performing activities according to a set of rules that are justified by a set of values, beliefs, and meanings. As people perform their activities according to the rules, they internalize the values, beliefs, and meanings that justify the rules. Domination within the patriarchal family involves the male parent telling the female parent and her offspring (if any) how to conduct family activities. The patriarch exercises power over the other family members, assigning them most of the burdens and appropriating for himself most of the benefits of the family's activities. The patriarch enjoys liberties, and the other family members suffer exposure to the liberties. The patriarch appropriates most of the family status, wealth, and power. In full-blown patriarchy, the family becomes the extension of the patriarch's will. The other family members cannot own property or appropriate income in their own names; they cannot display status on their own behalves, nor exercise power to serve their own authentic wills.

Following the path of least resistance, as most of us do, the members of the family accept the rules that support the male parent's practices because they accept the values, beliefs, and meanings that support them. Male parents come to believe that they are the best judges of what is best for the other members of the family and that resistance to their will is not just inconvenient to them, but harmful for the family and immoral as well. Female parents come to believe that *family* means the patriarchal family only, and that no other types of families or meanings are possible. The female parent also learns to value her subservient role in patriarchy and to feel a real loss if deprived of it.

The values, beliefs, and meanings that support male domination within the family also spread to other social institutions. The acceptance of the subservient wife/mother role generalizes to the acceptance of a subservient worker role— including the acceptance of low-paid occupations or of lower pay for the same kind of work that males do. In the twentieth century, domination originating in the family has been picked up by a new and rising social control mechanism— bureaucracy. As women have moved into paid work outside the home, they have partially escaped the practices of domination within the home only to become enmeshed in the practices of domination within the modern bureaucracy, which now controls the workplace in both capitalist enterprises and government agencies. Access to the highest-paying jobs is controlled by a web of rules and traditions favoring males over females; so, too, is accesss to status and power within the workplace. Furthermore, if women turn from the family to the welfare agency instead of the workplace, the story is largely the same. State and federal welfare agencies control access to the welfare system through a web of rules and regulations formulated by males and based on the traditional roles of the patriarchal family.

Practice (2): Discrimination

I will focus on discrimination against African Americans. While the focal point for patriarchy begins with the family and the process of procreation, the focal point for discrimination began with slavery and the process of production. Although slavery varied from state to state and even from region to region within the same state, it always was supported by a racist culture in which Europeans were considered to be the superiors and Africans, the inferiors. The racist culture dehumanized Africans, turning them into property that could be bought and sold at will. Although the brutality of slavery varied, it always was coercive. Although the frequency of selling slaves varied, the owner's right to sell a human being as a commodity always was retained.

Agitation by whites for reform and resistance from slaves generally hardened the attitudes of slave owners and increased their coercive hold over their slaves.

Neither the slaves' resistance nor the abolitionists' moral outrage led to reform. Slavery was an either/or institution. It could not be reformed; it could only be abolished. It was not amenable to institutional adjustment. In this lies a lesson: incremental institutional adjustment, though desirable on its own merits, can lead to a hardening of inequality. Incremental institutional adjustment can act more like a vaccine against progress toward equality than a means of actually attaining equality. The Civil War finally ended slavery. (For further discussion, see Fogel and Engerman 1974; Genovese 1965, 1969; Hirshson 1962; Mellon 1988; Oates 1975; Stampp 1956; Low and Clift 1981, 756–96.)

Racism did not end with slavery; it has continued for 130 years. After reconstruction in the South, Jim Crow laws and sharecropping replaced slave codes and slavery itself. Now, however, instead of supporting slavery or sharecropping, racism supports a whole series of discriminatory practices diffused throughout the economy, society, and polity. In developments similar to those that are moving male domination over females out of the old focal point in the family and into the larger arena of the modern bureaucracy, the focal point for discrimination has moved, first out of slavery into sharecropping, and now out of sharecropping into bureaucracy. Now, educational bureaucracies control access to good education and training, while corporate and government bureaucracies control access to good jobs. Zoning laws, public housing bureaucracies, lending agent bureaucracies, and municipalities all control access to good housing. The bureaucratic rules and regulations are stacked against the African American in favor of the European American. The practice of discrimination has become institutionalized in the bureaucratic life of modern society. It has moved out of the production processes of the old agrarian South into the whole of society, where it is joined by male domination over females, upper class exploitation of the lower class, and the predation of the chosen people on foreigners.

Practice (3): Exploitation

The practice of class inequality is exploitation. Its focal point in capitalism is the hierarchical workplace, where owners hire workers and use them for producing commodities for a profit. The owners try to enlarge the flow of income that goes to them after all contractual costs are paid and after all costs that can be avoided are avoided (externalities). As in gender and race inequality, the practice of class inequality has become bureaucratized, and far more so than in the other modes of inequality. The production and sale of commodities for a profit is now organized by corporate bureaucracies. The income appropriated by the wage workers, middle managers, engineers, equity owners, and debt owners (rentier capital) is now the subject of bureaucratic rules, state regulations, court decisions, and continual struggle between different organizations and different hierarchical levels within organizations. The struggle is to obtain a differential economic advantage that will allow the appropriation of more income at the expense of those who have no such advantages. Such advantages are usually obtained through property ownership, but physicians, hospital administrators, lawyers, lobbyists, politicians, and even celebrities are also involved in the acquistion and use of differential economic advantages. The practices of exploitation are quite varied. Owners enlarge their incomes by pushing down wages and pushing up the prices of their products and by paying out higher dividends, interest, and rent to themselves. Chief executive officers of corporations enlarge their incomes by downsizing their companies and upsizing their own compensation packages. Physicians and hospital administrators charge exorbitant fees, perform unneeded services, and reap their rewards. Celebrities in the sports and entertainment fields push up their fees and salaries, endorsements, and such. We pay the higher ticket prices and wish that we could raise our "rates" as well. Lobbyists and politicians work out agreements between conflicting factions and pass new legislation that affects us all. Then they collect their fees for service rendered or leave public service for more lucrative private service, hoping the rest of us will not come to see whom they really serve.

Practice (4): Predation

The nation state is the focal point for predation, which is practiced through war and diplomacy. Favorable treatment is sought for the nation's elite groups of capitalist corporations and state bureaucracies (military or civilian). Successful predator nations build empires by forming shifting alliances with other predators, occupying opposing nations, subjecting opposing nations to unfavorable trade relations, or setting up puppet regimes within opposing nations.

Predation also allows the predatory apparatus of each state to extract status, power, and wealth from the underlying population of that state. The underlying population is induced to grant the state's predatory apparatus exceptional power in the name of defending the homeland. The liberties of citizens are reduced in the name of national security, and their exposure to arbitrary action by security officials is increased. Dissent becomes treason. Power is concentrated in the internal security apparatus and the external predatory apparatus. The status of the nation's predatory apparatus is increased by instilling in the underlying population the great importance of defending the homeland and of honoring those who do. Numerous medals and awards are granted to the national heroes as they fill up the cemeteries, hospitals, and prisons. The wealth of the nation's predatory apparatus is increased by inducing the underlying population to grant it exemplary taxing authority. (For further discussion see Melman 1983; Dumas 1986.)

Opposing predatory nations are busy doing the same thing. The activities of the one predatory apparatus gives the other predators stronger motivation to step up their own war preparations to a more feverish pitch. Each nation's predatory apparatus comes to serve as the reason for each other nation's predatory apparatus to expand itself. They are as much allies in their predation of their underlying populations as they are adversaries in their struggle against each other.

ENABLING MYTHS: THE CULTURAL SUPPORT OF INEQUALITY

Enabling myths are composed primarily of the stereotypes men believe about women, European Americans believe about African Americans, the upper class believes about the lower class, and the chosen people believe about foreigners. However, enabling myths are more than the stereotypes believed by the beneficiaries of inequality. Inequality must be justified, in the minds of both its victims and its beneficiaries. To avoid unrest among the victims, they must be taught that their treatment is not really unfair. To avoid guilty consciences among the beneficiaries—which is not nearly as important nor as difficult as avoiding unrest among the victims—the beneficiaries must be taught that their advantages are due them. Such learning is not resisted. It is easy to be convinced that one deserves all the good things that come one's way. Teaching acceptance to the victims is much harder and more important than teaching it to the beneficiaries, so it is the primary function of enabling myths. It is not easy to be convinced that one deserves all the bad things that come one's way.

Enabling myths also create "otherness" and this involves more than just instilling superiority in the top dogs and inferiority in the underdogs but also centrality and marginality For one to be superior, an "other" must be inferior. For one to be the center of things, an "other" must be on the margin. The enabling myths of sexism, for example, put males at the center of humanity and females on the margin. Simone de Beauvoir explained;

Thus humanity is male and man defines woman not in herself but as relative to him; she is not regarded as an autonomous being. ... She is defined and differentiated with respect to man and not he with reference to her; she is the incidental, the inessential as opposed to the essential. He is the Subject, he is the Absolute—she is the Other. (Beauvoir [1952] 1989, xxii–xxiii)

(1) Sexism: The Myths Supporting Gender Inequality

Sexist myths begin with the category of "otherness." Males are the ones; they are the center. Females are the others; they are the margin. Thus, when categorizing the human species we say "mankind" or "man." However, when we say "womankind" or "woman," we do not mean the human species. We mean women, the margin. Men are the categorically human; women are other. The justification for males dominating females begins here. Then it ranges far and wide. Public activities—those that yield wealth, status, and power—are the realm of men. Private activities—those that do not yield wealth, status, and power—are the realm of women. Men can speak better than women in public. Men are more intelligent and articulate. Men make better bosses. They are less emotional than women, more straightforward and honest in the pursuit of goals.

Women are too emotional and intuitive, less straightforward. Their place is in the home. Man's place is in the world. Women who internalize these myths find it easier to accept their narrowed role in life. Men who internalize these myths find it easier to keep women in their narrowed role, to exclude them with no regrets. Well-adjusted men and women may even succeed in putting the confined role of women on a pedestal, and idealizing it as the embodiment of feminine truth and beauty.

This feminine mystique is a myth about the proper role of woman (Friedan [1963] 1983). It contains positive inducements to reward women for accepting it—they are put on a pedestal, and raised to the height of feminine truth and beauty. The myth also contains negative sanctions (taboos) to punish women for violating it—they are put in the pit, and accused of being untrue to their femininity and ugly to boot. (Just three centuries ago, we burned such women as witches.)

(2) Racism: The Myths Supporting Race Discrimination

Like sexist myths, racist myths also begin with "otherness."   In the United States, literature refers to the writings of white Europeans; art means the works of white Europeans; culture, in short, means Greco-Roman culture. African writings are other; African art is other. Some exceptions exist: blues and jazz in music, and Pablo Picasso's adaptations of African art in painting and sculpture are notable. Nonetheless, in the United States, the African American is still *the other*, and the European is still *the one*.

From the foundation of otherness, the myths of racism spring forth. Racist beliefs, like the other enabling myths, are opportunistic. They serve a purpose, even though their propogation and acceptance need not be consciously opportunistic. Racial myths are resistant to evidence contradicting them. They exist in the realm of magic and superstition, not that of fact and experience (Myrdal 1962, 100). They are related directly to the otherness of the African American in the mind of the European American. Racial myths are rational in the sense that they serve the purpose of enabling "whites" to take advantage of "blacks." However, racial myths are also profoundly irrational in the sense that they are psychologically grounded in magic and in superstititious dread of the unknown, of the other.

(3) Classism: The Myths Supporting Class Exploitation

Classist myths are the most sophisticated of all, as they are layered. The first layer of class myths supports the denial of class exploitation, while the second layer of myths supports the belief that the capitalist/Western world is a free market system. The third layer supports the belief that a free market system is neutral with respect to class, and that it involves no class exploitation, but only individual competition, which results in benefits for all.

We are constantly aware of class and of our own class standing relative to others. However, while we constantly think in terms of class, we do not think in terms of class exploitation. One of the most profound discoveries of Thorstein Veblen was that Americans in the lower strata seldom think of the upper strata in the bitter terms of exploitation. Rather than feel resentment, those in the lower strata feel envy. They do not want to overthrow their exploiters. They want to move up into the higher strata themselves (Veblen [1899] 1975). Americans do not think straight when it comes to class because they do not think of it in terms of exploitation. (For further discussion, see DeMott 1991.)

The denial of class exploitation is supported by the belief that ours is a free market system. Beneficial market competition, not differential economic advantage, is believed to be the way in which our economy distributes income. Milton Friedman's two works for the general reader, *Capitalism and Freedom* (1962) and *Free to Choose* (with Rose Friedman; 1980), are the most popular representations of the myth of the market system. In the mythical world of these two popular books, free markets are those that are unfettered by government interference. In such markets, monopolies cannot exist for long, and so the freedom of the market becomes the foundation for the freedom of the polity and the society. Furthermore, in these free markets, individuals are "free to choose," not only what they will buy and what they will sell, but also how prosperous they will become. If they are thrifty, innovative, willing to take risks, and hard working, they can rise very far. No barriers hold them back, unless government interferes with their efforts or unions either keep them out of lucrative employment or take away their profits with exorbitant wages.

The Friedmans do qualify their market utopia. They add in a central bank that provides a framework of monetary stability by following a growth rate rule for the money stock, if we could just agree how to measure the money stock. They also add in a negative income tax to help the poor and maybe also an educational voucher, allegedly to help poor children. They even recognize the need for a limited court system—one that enforces the rules and makes sure that contracts are performed. Nonetheless, the market utopia they describe will benefit us all, provided we keep government interference at a minimum.

There is no class exploitation in the Friedmans' world; no gender domination, racial discrimination, or national predation—unless it is instigated by government interference. The Friedmans' utopia sounds very much like the utopia of Adam Smith, with his system of natural liberty. However, a major difference destroys the similarity. Smith's utopia was used to attack the tyranny of the monarchy's mercantilism. It was used by the underdogs of the time to push their way through the barriers erected by the top dogs of the time. It was used by the upstart merchants and mechanics to rise up against the resistance of the landed aristocracy and against the power of the great, royally-chartered, monopoly-granted, trading companies (Smith 1937; Dugger 1990). While Smith's utopia was used to defend the efforts of the upstarts, the Friedmans' utopia is used to attack the efforts of the upstarts. The upstarts of Smith's time were the merchants and mechanics, but they have grown rich and become established. They are no longer the underdogs but rather the top dogs. The upstarts of the Friedmans' time now must push against the former merchants and mechanics, who have become great retailing corporations, giant industrial conglomerates, and entrenched managerial and professional groups.

The upstarts of the Friedmans' time are women dominated by men, African Americans discriminated against by European Americans, workers and communities exploited by corporate capital, and foreign devils preyed upon by the predatory apparatus of powerful nations. Moreover, the way they push up against the top dogs is to call upon the state, particularly the welfare state, to aid them in their struggle. However, the Friedmans insist that the underdogs should not call for help, or try to improve their position through state aid. Instead, they should simply aid themselves by working harder, being smarter, and saving more. If they do not thrive, it is their own fault. They were not talented enough or did not work hard enough. If the victims of domination, discrimination, exploitation, and predation actually believe that, the top dogs are safe.

What a powerful enabling myth this is. It not only enables class inequality, it enables all the other forms of inequality as well. The wretched of the earth have only themselves to blame for their wretchedness. Here is another important intersection of the different modes of inequality. They are all enabled by the market utopian myth. In fact, the market utopian myth is so powerful that its pull became irresistible to even the former Soviet nomenklatura, who abandoned the myth of the dictatorship of the proletariat for the myth of the utopian market. No longer able to keep the former Soviet masses in their subservient places with the old myth, the nomenklatura adopted a new myth. The new propaganda is for free markets, while the reality involves reconstructed centers of differential economic advantage hidden by a new cover of darkness.

(4) Jingoism: The Myths Supporting National Predation

Jingoism supports national predation. In the United States, jingoism means that "Americans" are "the one" and foreigners, "the other." We are the ones with the manifest destiny. This belief has been with us for a very long time and needs little further discussion here (see Baritz 1985; Slotkin, 1985). Jingoism also involves denial and projection, which form an effective mechanism to justify attack and this requires further elaboration.

When the predatory apparatus of the United States attacks another nation, the attack is accompanied by a denial of our own hostile intentions and by projection of hostile intentions onto the nation being attacked. The best recent example of the denial-projection mechanism involved stories circulated in the United States about Libyan hit squads infiltrating the country with instructions to assasinate important U.S. leaders. We subsequently learned that the stories and other alleged hostilities were not true, but they did provide us with the opportunity to justify an air raid against Libya by projecting our own hostile intentions onto the Libyans (see Woodward 1987).

The denial and projection mechanism also allowed us to take a number of hostile actions against the Sandinista government in Nicaragua. It is the foundation of our great fear of international terrorism. We see Saddam Hussein of Iraq as being at the center of a vast network of terrorists who are poised for a myriad of attacks against the United States, both at home and abroad. (For further discussion of the "terrorism terror" see Perdue 1989; Herman and O'Sullivan 1990.)

Jingoism differs from the other enabling myths in a very important and tragic way. In gender, class, and race inequality the enabling myths of sexism, classism, and racism can be inculcated in their negative forms in the underdog groups. However, this is far less possible in nation inequality. Leaders of one nation are hard-pressed to convince the people of the opposing nation that they are inferior foreign devils, which makes the nation mode of inequality a particularly unstable and violent form. With the underdog groups harder to fool, inequality between nations requires more violence to enforce. Husbands have killed their wayward wives in patriarchal societies. European Americans have killed disrespectful African Americans, and capitalists have killed revolting workers. However, such killing does not occur on the same vast scale as it does in nation inequality. Indeed, "chosen peoples" (nations) have killed tens of millions of foreigners in the last century alone. It seems easier to kill foreigners than to pacify them with myths.

Enabling myths do four related things simultaneously: (1) they provide an opportunistic rationalization of privilege, (2) they create a superstitious dread of the unknown in the minds of the top dogs, (3) they create the otherness of the victim, and (4) they make it possible to deny that injustice occurs by encouraging the underdogs to blame themselves.

THE ANTIDOTES FOR INEQUALITY

Means of debunking myths are readily available. However, debunking specific myths is not enough because as long as the practices of inequality persist, innovative minds will create new myths to support them. The practices of inequality must be changed, and doing so will take more than just a change of heart. It takes collective action to change social practices. The adage that "you cannot legislate morality" is exactly wrong. In fact, you cannot change morality unless you legislate change in practices. Change the practices and the morals will follow. What people come to believe derives, in large part, from what they do (see Veblen 1919, 1–31, 32–55). Then, however, they use some of their beliefs to justify what they do. In the first instance, their beliefs come from their habits of life; beliefs are largely habitual constructs. Thus, to change the beliefs, the myths that support inequality, the practices of inequality must also be changed.

Inequality, then, must be attacked from two directions simultaneously. First, the irrational myths that support inequality must be debunked. This is the responsibility of the churches, the schools, the sciences, the arts, and the social movements.   Second, the actual practices of inequality must be transformed through collective action.   This is the responsibility of the unions, the professional associations, the corporate boards, the courts, the legislatures, and, again, the social movements. The following remarks deal with debunking the myths rather than changing the practices.

Debunking the Myths

Unfortunately, rumors of evil foreign intentions spring up eternally, so they must continually be investigated and the truth or falsehood of them exposed on a case-by-case basis. The only way to deal with them as they arise is to have faith and insist upon an open society, an aggressive press, and an informed citizenry.   Racist, sexist, and classist myths already have been debunked at length by numerous researchers. For my purposes here, only a brief discussion of the highlights of these debunking efforts is necessary.

With social Darwinism, enabling myths became "scientific."   Biological differences between the races and sexes were measured and listed by researchers of high standing in scientific circles.   One of the most infamous "scientific" myths supporting racism and sexism had to do with the allegedly biologically determined mental superiority of men over women and of the "white" race over the "black" race.   The biological determinists were avid bone collectors and skull measurers—rigorously mathematical and objective.   They created the "science" of craniometry.   The craniometricians "proved" that the white race was mentally superior to the black race and that men were mentally superior to women because the craniums of men were larger than those of women and the craniums of whites were larger than those of blacks. Of course, many of their measurements were inaccurate and their samples biased.   Nevertheless, their findings were accepted in wide university and scientific circles. However, when cranium size was finally related to body size, the results took a dramatic turn. Women were found to have larger craniums relative to their body size than men! Thus, the craniometricians lost heart, and face. How could they admit that women were actually more mentally advanced than men?   Of course, the craniometricians were men, and white ones at that. Moreover (needless to say), no evidence of any kind exists that can link mental ability to the size of the cranium of a healthy human of any color or sex (see Gould 1981; Montagu 1974; Ayres [1927] 1973).   These first biological determinists, who were supporters of racism and sexism, were eventually debunked by other, better scientists. However, a new crop of biological determinists has stepped into the cultural vacuum to conjure up deceptive bell curves in place of cranium sizes.

Although the keepers of the sacred truths of classism behave much like the biological determinists before them, the myths of classism have a very different origin. The market myth goes back to Adam Smith, in whose hands it was not an enabling myth. It did not justify the inequality of the status quo; instead, it attacked that inequality. The market myth now defends inequality, but it did not start out that way. The market myth's origin is noble, not base, so debunking it is much harder.

THE DYNAMICS OF INEQUALITY: CIRCULAR PROCESS

Inequality is not an equilibrium state but a circular process. Inequality either gets worse or better, but it does not reach an equilibrium. The continued practice of inequality strengthens the myths that support it, and the stronger myths then lend even greater support to the practice. The resulting circular process is not characterized by offsetting forces that reach a balance but by cumulative causation that continues to move an inegalitarian society toward more inequality or continues to move an egalitarian society toward more equality. The inequality process is a vicious circle, but the equality process is a virtuous circle. Both processes are cumulative, not offsetting.

The Vicious Circle

Collective action of the top dogs against the underdogs establishes the practices of inequality. White Europeans established the great Atlantic slave trade. Males established patriarchy; state leaders established the system of nation-states; and property holders established capitalism. They all did so through collective action. Then, the myths of each form of inequality strengthened the practices of inequality. White Europeans came to believe themselves racially superior to black Africans. Black Africans, who were trapped in slavery, were taught that they must adjust to it or perish. The practice of patriarchy strengthened sexist myths, and the sexist myths then strengthened the sexist practices. State leaders established nation-states. We learned that we were English or French or German and that the foreigners were plotting against us. This strengthened the hands of the state leaders as they extracted more income, status, and power from the underlying populations. They used their gains in foreign plots, teaching us the truth in jingoism. Feudal property holders pushed us off the commons and taught us to value their private property. We believed them and worked ever harder for them, hoping that we could save enough to get some property for ourselves. In each mode of inequality, parasitic practices are established through collective action, and then enabling myths make the practices seem legitimate. The practices then become more entrenched because of the myths, and the myths begin to seem like truths because of the practices. The process is circular.

The Virtuous Circle

If the vicious circle were all there is to the story, we humans would probably have destroyed ourselves long ago. However, there is more. Just as there is a vicious circle of inequality, there is a virtuous circle of equality. Collective action of the underdogs against the top dogs can put an end to the practices of inequality, albeit perhaps only to establish another set of parasitic practices whereby the old underdogs attack the old top dogs. The first become last and the last become first; the meek inherit the earth. Perhaps however, the practices of inequality can be replaced with the practices of equality. The possibility of a virtuous circle replacing the vicious circle is not that remote. The religious leaders of the American civil rights movement did not seek to replace white racism with black racism. Malcolm X became an enlightened antiracist, an egalitarian. Setting the example for the rest of us to follow, African-American collective action took the high road. African Americans took collective action against inequality and made considerable progress in eliminating racist practices and myths. Of course, much more needs to be done. Nevertheless, as racist practices were resisted by collective action and as racist myths were debunked, it became harder for white people to believe the myths and continue the practices. Thus, a virtuous circle was begun. Then, however, racial progress was interrupted, and then reversed by the Ronald Reagan administration and retrenchment. The vicious circle has replaced the virtuous, once again.

CONCLUDING REMARKS

This chapter supplied a simple vocabulary for describing inequality and suggested a dynamic framework of circular and cumulative causation for showing how the forces of inequality move in a reinforcing, rather than offsetting, fashion. The vocabulary includes the modes, practices, myths, focal points, and antidotes for inequality. A few examples and a bit of institutional context were provided to illustrate the concepts. The overall purpose was to help elucidate inequality and the different forms it takes, and to put the forms in an appropriate context. The treatment was introductory and exploratory, not exhaustive or definitive.

REFERENCES

Ayres, Clarence E. [1927] 1973. *Science: The False Messiah.* Clifton, N.J.: Augustus M. Kelley.

Baritz, Loren. 1985. *Backfire.* New York: William Morrow.

Beauvoir, Simone de. [1952] 1989. *The Second Sex.* Translated and edited by H. M. Parshley. New York: Random House.

Becker, Gary S. 1971. *The Economics of Discrimination.* 2d ed. Chicago: University of Chicago Press.

___. 1981. *A Treatise on the Family.* Cambridge: Harvard University Press.

Berger, Brigitte, and Peter L. Berger. 1983. *The War over the Family.* Garden City, N.Y.: Anchor Press/Doubleday.

Braverman, Harry. 1974. *Labor and Monopoly Capital.* New York: Monthly Review Press.

Coleman, Richard P., and Lee Rainwater, with Kent A. McClelland. 1978. *Social Standing in America.* New York: Basic Books.

DeMott, Benjamin. 1991. *The Imperial Middle.* New York: William Morrow.

Dugger, William M. 1984. "The Nature of Capital Accumulation and Technological Progress in the Modern Economy." *Journal of Economic Issues*, 18 (Sept.): 799–823.
___. 1989a. *Corporate Hegemony.* Westport, Conn.: Greenwood Press.
___. 1989b. "Instituted Process and Enabling Myth: The Two Faces of the Market." *Journal of Economic Issues*, 23 (June): 606–15.
___. ed. 1989c. *Radical Institutionalism.* Westport, Conn.: Greenwood Press.
___. 1990. "From Utopian Capitalism to the Dismal Science: The Effect of the French Revolution on Classical Economics." In Warren J. Samuels, ed., *Research in the History of Economic Thought and Methodology.* Vol. 8. Greenwich, Conn.: JAI Press, pp. 153–73.
Dumas, Lloyd Jeffry. 1986. *The Overburdened Economy.* Berkeley: University of California Press.
Fogel, Robert William, and Stanley L. Engerman. 1974. *Time on the Cross.* Boston: Little, Brown and Company.
Friedan, Betty. [1963] 1983. *The Feminine Mystique.* New York: Dell Publishing.
Friedman, Milton. 1962. *Capitalism and Freedom.* Chicago: University of Chicago Press.
Friedman, Milton, and Rose Friedman. 1980. *Free to Choose.* New York: Avon Books.
Genovese, Eugene D. 1965. *The Political Economy of Slavery.* New York: Pantheon.
___. 1969. *The World the Slaveholders Made.* New York: Vintage Books.
Gould, Stephen Jay. 1981. *The Mismeasure of Man.* New York: W. W. Norton.
Green, Philip. 1981. *The Pursuit of Inequality.* New York: Pantheon.
Hacker, Andrew. 1995. *Two Nations.* New York: Ballantine Books.
Harrington, Michael. 1983. *The Politics at God's Funeral.* New York: Holt, Rinehart and Winston.
Herman, Edward S., and Gerry O'Sullivan. 1990. *The "Terrorism" Network.* New York: Pantheon.
Hirshson, Stanley P. 1962. *Farewell to the Bloody Shirt.* Chicago: Quadrangle Books.
Jencks, Christopher, and Marshall Smith, Henry Acland, Mary Jo Bane, David Cohen, Herbert Gintis, Barbara Heyns, Stephan Michelson. 1972. *Inequality.* New York: Basic Books.
Jencks, Christopher, and Susan Bartlett, Mary Corcoran, James Crouse, David Eaglesfield, Gregory Jackson, Kent McClelland, Peter Mueser, Michael Olneck, Joseph Schwartz, Sherry Ward, Jill Williams. 1979. *Who Gets Ahead?* New York: Basic Books.
Low, W. Augustus, and Virgil A. Clift. 1981. *Encyclopedia of Black America.* New York: Da Capo Press.
Mead, Margaret. 1949. *Male and Female.* New York: Dell Publishing.
Mellon, James, ed. 1988. *Bullwhip Days.* New York: Avon Books.
Melman, Seymour. 1983. *Profits without Production.* New York: Alfred A. Knopf.
Montagu, Ashley. 1974. *The Natural Superiority of Women.* Rev. ed. New York: Macmillan Publishing Company.
Moore, Barrington, Jr. 1978. *Injustice: The Social Bases of Obedience and Revolt.* White Plains, N.Y.: M.E. Sharpe.
Myrdal, Gunnar. 1962. *An American Dilemma.* New York: Harper and Row.
Oates, Stephen B. 1975. *The Fires of Jubilee.* New York: Harper and Row.
Osberg, Lars. 1984. *Economic Inequality in the United States.* Armonk, N.Y.: M. E. Sharpe.

Perdue, William D. 1989. *Terrorism and the State.* New York: Praeger.

Slotkin, Richard. 1985. *The Fatal Environment.* New York: Atheneum.

Smith, Adam. 1937. *The Wealth of Nations.* Edited by Edwin Canaan. New York: Modern Library.

Stampp, Kenneth M. 1956. *The Peculiar Institution.* New York: Vintage Books.

Stanfield, J. Ron. 1982. "Toward a New Value Standard in Economics." *Economic Forum*, 13 (Fall): 67–85.

Veblen, Thorstein. [1899] 1975. *The Theory of the Leisure Class.* New York: Augustus M. Kelley.

___. 1919. *The Place of Science in Modern Civilization and Other Essays.* New York: B. W. Huebsch.

Woodward, Bob. 1987. *Veil.* New York: Simon and Schuster.

3

A Holistic–Evolutionary View of Racism, Sexism, and Class Inequality

Howard J. Sherman

INTRODUCTION

The methodology of radical institutionalism makes use of holism and an evolutionary outlook. This chapter begins by spelling out these approaches very briefly, and then seeing how they apply to three modes of inequality: class and exploitation, race and discrimination, and gender and discrimination. (For the radical literature on racism and sexism, see Deckard 1983; Reich 1980, and Sherman 1987.)

HOLISM

Neoclassical economics reduces all explanation to the factor of psychology. The key concept of utility is a subjective term, depending on the psychological values of each individual consumer. This approach ignores all social relations, social structures, and social institutions. If the analysis starts with given psychologies, then it cannot explain those psychologies or how they change.

At the other extreme is economic reductionism. Much of the now-dead Marxism of the Soviet era assumed that all explanation could be reduced to economic factors—though this was often denied in general rhetoric. Thus it was assumed that technology must change and that technological change will automatically change all social relations, social institutions, and psychological preferences. This theory can also be criticized as incomplete because there is no explanation for technological change: it is the beginning point and is not determined by anything else.

Radical institutionalists use a holistic approach, which begins with the whole matrix of social relations and institutions. In a holistic view it is impossible to begin from either psychology or economics and explain everything else in a one-way causation. Instead, the relations of society must be seen as a whole. Crime, for example, cannot simply be explained by deviant psychology but instead must be explained by the totality of social institutions and relationships. Institutions are composed of social relationships, so either term, institutions or relations, can be used interchangeably.

THE EVOLUTIONARY APPROACH

In most of its theoretical work, neoclassical economics is static, or comparative-static, that is, it compares two static-equilibrium situations.   It is assumed that all units maximize utility or profits and that this leads to an equilibrium situation. The job of economists is to tell government to stand aside and let the private economy reach equilibrium, which it will always do. History does not enter into this paradigm, and there is no theory of how society evolves.

Radical institutionalism has a complete theory of how the political economy evolves. It is a theory that tells us how society evolves, but not that it must evolve in a particular way or that some preordained "progress" will always occur. In this way it is different from the old dogmatic Soviet Marxism, which said that all societies must progress through slavery, feudalism, and capitalism untill they reach socialism. This theory of inevitable progress to socialism was a useful political tool for the Soviet Union, but it had no basis in reality.

By definition, radical institutionalists divide the economy into institutional and technical processes. The institutions include all human relationships in the processes of production and distribution. These institutions thus include under capitalism the work relationship of workers and bosses, the corporate structure, the trade unions, the whole financial process, and so forth. These relationships or processes can only be described for a single type of economy because evolution has witnessed various types of economies and will most likely witness many more in the future.   Thus, radical institutionalism must always be historically specific and must base its laws on the specific institutions of a specific society.

Veblen ridiculed neoclassical economics for assuming that the same theory could describe totally different types of economies. Radical institutionalists do not make that mistake. For example, different laws, processes, and relationships must be used to describe the economy of slavery in the old South as distinct from modern U.S. capitalism or the old Soviet political-economic system of dictatorship and central ownership. There are no eternal laws of economics.

There are regularities in the process of social change that we have observed to date.   What are these regularities?   First, a particular system of social relationships will help or hinder economic growth. For example, the structure of U.S. capitalism led to the Great Depression of the 1930s, thus holding back growth and technological change for ten years.

Second, in such a situation the tensions between frozen human relationships (institutions) and the desire for economic growth may lead to political movements for reform or revolution. In the 1930s, there were some movements for revolutionary change and an enormous movement for reform. Third, the newly dominant political ideas will change the political process. Thus, the ideas brought about by the Great Depression led to the New Deal. The New Deal government then brought about some vital reforms of the economic system. Fourth, the new economic institutions will then further change ideas. Living under the New Deal economic institutions, under which people take unemployment compensation and social security for granted, has further changed political thinking of the populace.

Thus, economic tensions may affect political movements and ideas. Political ideas and legal changes affect human economic relationships, which in turn affect technological change. In this sense, the radical institutionalist view of social evolution is holistic; it does not reduce the explanation of change to some single isolated factor but rather shows how the whole social matrix leads to change. Fifth, another social regularity lies in the fact that change always occurs over the resistance of vested interests. The only issue is the degree of violence in their reactions. For example, the slave owners' resistance to the peaceful end of slavery led directly to their secession and the Civil War.

INDIVIDUALIST VERSUS COLLECTIVIST METHODOLOGY

Closely tied to the psychological reductionism of neoclassical economics is its individualist methodology. This approach claims that all social explanation can, and must, be reduced to individual motivation. Neoclassical economists have attacked all of the macroeconomic concepts of Keynes on the basis that he fails to explain them in individual terms. However, this means that neoclassical economics assumes isolated, totally independent individuals as its beginning point. It cannot explain the behavior of these individuals except by assumption.

Since they base their argument on individuals and assume that all share an equal playing field, the concept of opposition between collective groups (or classes) is outside the neoclassicists' paradigm. There can be no concept of the exploitation of one group by another within a purely individualist paradigm. Some more moderate individualists admit the concept of class but have argued that people choose their class. This ignores the fact that people are part of given institutions—part of given class relations—and have no such choices. If an unemployed worker chooses to become a capitalist, he or she may choose to define himself or herself as a leisured individual rather than an unemployed individual but will still have no capital.

The individualist theory of Gary Becker (1957) says that it is wrong to speak of discrimination when racist and sexist attitudes are merely individual preferences (see Becker 1957, 5). The individualist theory of Milton Friedman says that capitalist competition automatically ends discrimination, so all wage differences between groups merely reflect the inferior productivity of some individuals to others (Friedman 1962, 108–18).

Radical institutionalists, on the contrary, have a collectivist methodology. This merely accepts the possibility that economists may say something useful about collectives, including groups and classes. Of course, it is a moderate, and not an extreme, collectivism. Some extreme collectivists have talked as if "the state," "the working class," or "the Serb nation" exists above and beyond all individuals. That is pure nonsense, and radical institutionalists are always ready to explain the actions of any group in terms of the individuals within it while noting that it may follow laws that are not easy to state merely as a summation of individuals. For example, Keynesians have noted that lower wages in a single firm may lead to increased employment in that firm because there will be a negligible effect on the consumer demand for that firm's products. However, if all firms lower wages, aggregate consumer demand will decline, reducing production and thereby reducing employment.

CLASS AND EXPLOITATION

In a consistent, but moderate, collectivist and holistic approach, each class may be defined by its relationship to other classes. One class may exploit another, that is, it may extract some of the work done by another class for itself. Thus, the slave owners of the U.S. South extracted profits from the labor of the slaves. That was an institution, a relationship, that permitted and assumed that kind of exploitation.

If a U.S. worker today is forced by U.S. institutions to produce more than her wage or salary, then she is exploited. This is the norm and not the exception because of the institutional conditions. First, there is the massive power of corporations, on which many institutionalists have commented so eloquently. Second, there is the weakness of the individual worker, who on the average has no savings or other resources. Furthermore, only a small percentage of U.S. workers are now in unions, and the unions have been weakened by well-financed ideological attack, legal attack, internal dissension, and changing circumstances.

Workers bargain with corporations against the backdrop of supply-and-demand conditions. Throughout the twentieth century (except for the two World Wars), the important condition in the labor market has been significant unemployment. The unemployment rate goes up in depressions and down in expansions, but it remains always at a high enough level to weaken the workers' bargaining power.

If all workers in the United States are exploited, and if they are the majority, why don't they make a greater effort to change the system? One reason is the use of wealth to control the information flow through the media, the educational system, and organized religion. What message do these institutions provide to the population? Their message includes many of what we might call enabling myths, which make it possible for the top dogs to (1) convince the underdogs that their position is justified by their own shortcomings and (2) to convince themselves and their allies that they really are worthy. To propagate an irrational myth may thus be a perfectly rational course for the ruling class.

The exploitation of one class by another is disguised and supported by several enabling myths. First, most Americans are led to believe that everyone is equal in the market, so we make equal exchanges, such as wages for work. If the exchanges are equal, then how can there be exploitation? As shown here, however, many exchanges are not on equal grounds, particularly the wage bargain between individual workers and giant corporations.   Second, in neoclassical economics it is assumed that the wage equals the marginal product of a worker. In popular terms, this is the dominant view that everyone is paid according to their product.   Thus, a low-paid worker must have low productivity, while a manager who is paid $3 million a year must be worth it. Consequently, the cause of low wages and poverty is inherent in the worker. Of course, however, most wealth in the United States is actually inherited, while most workers below the poverty line come from families below the poverty line, so there is no level playing field at birth.

Third, there is a myth that the economy operates by freely made decisions, meaning that unemployed workers have freely chosen unemployment. Alternatively, there are jobs for everyone but some people are lazy or inferior, so it is the individual unemployed worker who is a failure, not the system.

Fourth, a pervasive myth says that even if the economic system is at fault, all governments are corrupt and completely inefficient, so there is no way to change the situation. As a result, half the eligible voters do not vote, even in presidential elections. Those who do not vote tend to have a lower income, so those with the most to protest do not vote while most of the rest vote according to enabling myths.

The evolutionary aspect of radical institutionalism recognizes that the labor relation has differed in decisive fashion in various societies. The relation of slave to slave owner and of free worker to capitalist is similar only in that both types of workers are exploited and produce profit for another class. Otherwise they differ in every way and affect the rest of the institutions of society in very different ways.

RACE AND DISCRIMINATION

How has racism against African Americans evolved? For lack of space, only the African American minority is considered here.   Some excellent works on racism are Bonacich (1980), Boston (1988), and Reich (1980).

Racism under U.S. Slavery

Before the Civil War, the South had a slave mode of production. Almost all African Americans lived in the South on plantations as slaves. A minority of whites were slave owners, while the majority of southern whites were poor farmers. Racist attitudes and discrimination were the rule.

From an individualist viewpoint, individual racist attitudes are the cause of discrimination and of slavery. From the individualist view, therefore, racism is merely an irrational attitude, a view with the false premise that some groups are inferior to other groups. There appears to be a paradox here. The individualist view argues strongly that one can only understand society as a series of rational choices by individuals. However, if the average actor in society is rational, then why would the irrational attitude of racism arise and persist? This is a paradox of rationality that we must solve.

Whereas the individualist sequence runs from racial attitudes to slavery and discrimination, radical institutionalists use a *revised sequence*, that is, the cause of racism in this mode of production is slavery. One must begin with the institutions of slavery to understand why racism was pervasive. In the slave South, the attitudes of racism were promulgated by the political system, the educational system, and organized religion, as well as the small number of newspapers that existed. These institutions were dominated by the interests of the ruling slave owners—but why did they propagandize for this irrational ideology?

Racism may be called an enabling myth because it helps the powerful to exploit and oppress minorities and to feel justified in doing so. To propagate the irrational myth of racism may thus be perfectly rational for the ruling class. Let us examine this hypothesis.

Under slavery, it is obvious that the slave owners had a very strong interest in racist ideology. If everyone in the society believed that Africans were superior to whites, there would have been no excuse for enslaving them. (There would have been no excuse even if they were equals, as one does not enslave equals.) The Greeks believed that their slaves were not quite human. Aristotle says that it is given by nature that some people are suited to be masters and some to be slaves (Aristotle 1941, 1255). Similarly, throughout the South the white preachers all preached that Africans were inferior people. God gave the whites the burden of taking care of Africans, Christianizing them, and telling these simple folk what to do. Thus, the preachers told the world that slavery was in the interests of the slaves, that it was divinely ordained by God himself (not herself), and that it was a burden of Christian charity that white slave owners must bear. In reality, this irrational myth helped to maintain the exploitation of the slaves and the power of the slave owners.

Racism after the Civil War in Early Capitalism

After the Civil War, capitalist industrialists dominated the United States, but they left the South to white landowners, who were allowed to regain dominance by the use of force and violence. The violence continued with a remarkable number of lynchings all the way up to the 1950s. In this stage of capitalism, most African Americans remained as sharecroppers in the South under the domination of landowners, merchants, and moneylenders. Racist laws prevented African Americans from voting, from receiving a good education, and from integration with most of the economy. In 1890, 88 percent of all African Americans were still in agriculture or domestic service. In 1930, African

Americans were still 66 percent in agriculture and domestic service, and even in 1940, 75 percent of African Americans lived in the South, mostly in rural areas (see Baron 1985, 19).

Why did the irrational myth of racism persist after the Civil War and the disappearance of slavery? The answer is that racism is a wonderful justification for any kind of exploitation and oppression. It is an enabling myth that keeps the underdogs down and lets the rulers claim the purest motives. For example, in the 1890s populism spread like wildfire among the poor farmers and sharecroppers of the South. It threatened the establishment with the prospect of very radical governments. One defense was the conscious spread of racism, both in ideology and in institutionalized ways to keep people from voting. The result was that poor whites were split from African Americans and that very few poor of any race were able to vote in the South.

Thus the myth of racial inferiority and superiority helped the southern landowners from the 1870s till the 1950s to both hold political power and justify the high rate of exploitation of the African-American sharecroppers.

Racism since World War II

All this began to change during World War II when millions of African Americans moved to manufacturing jobs. By 1960, over 40 percent of African Americans lived in the North and 73 percent had jobs in manufacturing. The new economic environment allowed African Americans to organize into the civil rights movement. Under that pressure, the Supreme Court began to lift racial restrictions in 1954, and the Congress passed new civil rights acts in the early 1960s, removing the obstacles to voting and making job discrimination illegal. The result is formal equality under the law, which has resulted in a growing African-American middle class of managers and professionals. Most African Americans, however, remain in the lowest income categories, with twice the white rate of unemployment, a much higher rate of poverty, a much lower percentage with higher education, and a large majority with temporary, marginal jobs and no chance of advancement (see Baron 1985, 10–12).

The experience since the civil rights movement illustrates two points. First, there are limits to how far a myth can stand against reality. When the circumstances lead to conflict and the myth becomes transparently false, it will fail to stop an oppressed minority and will even fail to justify oppression in the eyes of some of the majority. Second, however, myths are hard to destroy, and the myth of racism retains power in the United States, especially among some sections of economically frustrated white males.

Why does the enabling myth of racism continue in the light of all the facts against it? Why does not every rational person see through this myth? The answer lies in part in the fact that the myth of racism is such a handy weapon for the ruling group that it is rational for them to perpetuate it. Racism helps the ruling class in several ways. First, it helps to allow apologists for business interests contend that African-American (and other minority) workers are poorly paid only because they are inferior workers.

Second, to the extent that white workers believe the racist myths, unions are weakened by excluding African-American workers or accepting them reluctantly and preventing them from having equal power in the union. White and African-American workers have frequently broken each others' strikes in the past, though they are now learning to work together. In the areas of strongest racism and weakest unions, such as the South, African-American workers' wages are very low; however, white workers' wages are almost as low in these areas. For this reason, capitalists gain from the prejudices of workers because their prejudice allows capitalists to divide and oppress them.

Third, the myth of racism is profitable to capitalists in its provision of a handy, but disposable, labor force. In a recession, a rational corporation will lay off African-American workers before white workers on the assumption that they will be unlikely to get permanent or better jobs elsewhere because of the discriminatory practices of other employers. Thus corporations can (and do) fire more African-American workers in each recession, only to easily hire them back in times of expansion. Corporations also gain by not having to pay the fringe benefits due workers who stay on the job for a longer time. Thus, the apparent irrationality of firing workers by race has a very rational basis in making profits.

Fourth, radicals maintain that a primary political function of the myth of racism is to find a scapegoat for all problems. For example, the white voter is told that the dirt and violence of the modern city are all due to African Americans. Similarly, Adolf Hitler told German workers that unemployment was all due to Jewish bankers, while the middle class was told that all the agitation was due to Jewish communists.

Fifth, another political effect of the myth of racism is to divide the oppressed so that the elite can rule. For example, few Americans are more oppressed or exploited than poor white southerners, yet they have usually fought against their natural allies, the African-American workers. Instead of allying with African Americans, poor whites have given political support to the wealthy white southerners who not only monopolize southern state and local politics but also wield disproportionate influence in Congress, where they hold key committee chairmanships and leadership positions by virtue of seniority. The same kind of divide-and-rule tactic is used in northern cities.

Sixth, racism (combined with jingoism) is also a particularly useful tool of foreign adventures against other countries. England especially has long used the strategy of divide and rule, pitting Hindu against Moslem in India, Jew against Arab in Israel, and Protestant against Catholic in Ireland. Moreover, the United States is quite willing to use the same tactic, pitting the Vietnamese against the Cambodian, and the Thai against the Laotian. Furthermore, "inferiority" (inherited or acquired) is still being given as an excuse for lack of development, where foreign exploitation is one of the real reasons.

Why do white racist attitudes persist? The first part of the answer lies in the six reasons cited here explaining why such an enabling myth is helpful to the ruling class. The second part of the answer lies in the control of the information flow by the ruling class. Whites are not born with attitudes of racial superiority. Rather, these attitudes are inculcated by society. They are given to children by the older generation in the family, and by the educational system (e.g., in stereotypes in textbooks), by the media (e.g., in stereotypes on television, and in newspapers, books, and magazines), and by political leaders.

GENDER AND DISCRIMINATION

Let us begin with the evolution of sexist discrimination, and then turn to the mechanism and enabling myths that support it.

Evolution of Sexist Discrimination

In most primitive societies, the women gather fruits and vegetables while the men hunt. Usually, the food supply contributed by women is more reliable than that contributed by men. It is not surprising, therefore, that the status of women and men is roughly equal in most primitive societies.

This situation changes dramatically with the introduction of slavery. Under slavery, male warriors conquer other groups and turn them into slaves, who become the property of the male slave owners. Male slaves do the heavy agricultural work, which is the basis of most slave societies. The male slave owners exploit the women slaves in both economic and sexual terms. It is common for the male slave owners to have several mistresses.

The wife of a slave owner is treated as property—but as very valuable property, especially if she is beautiful by the standards of that society (and standards of beauty can differ remarkably). As valuable property, she is often idolized in literature, but the reality is that she is kept isolated from other men, and from outside social and political processes, and is usually given little education. She is primarily a sexual object, who is kept pure to produce legitimate male heirs. Since the man may have sex as often as he wishes with slave women while his wife may receive the death penalty for sex with a slave, there is a blatant double standard. This general description of women under slavery applies equally to ancient Greece and Rome and to the southern United States before the Civil War, even though the specific forms of social life were different.

In the early western United States, men and women had to work together in isolated farms, both doing very hard work to survive. The result was a considerable degree of equality between the sexes. As capitalist industry became dominant in the United States in the last half of the nineteenth century, it brought increased equality to women in the South but a reduced degree of equality in the West. Among the working class, men and women both worked long hours but women's work was often at home, where she would cook and clean, take care of the children, and also sometimes do sewing or some other craft work that could be sold. Many working-class women worked in a factory and then came home to work many more hours. In the harsh conditions of early manufacturing, men often spent their checks on drink and came home to abuse their wives.

In the middle and capitalist classes, women did somewhat less work than women of the working class, but they still did an enormous amount of housework unless they were rich enough to have servants. The husband, however, was the one who owned property and business. Under the laws, as late as the 1870s all the income made by women automatically went to their husbands, women had no right to the property if there was a divorce, and they did not even have a right to keep their children if there was a divorce. Women had no right to vote, and were not supposed to have anything to do with politics. Women who worked got much lower wages than men, and most women received no education. While the subordination of women was much less absolute than under slavery, it was still very clear and taken for granted.

When industrialization and urbanization became widespread and there was greater affluence, women demanded greater rights. It took a hundred years of struggle to get the vote for women. It took many more years of struggle until laws were finally passed in the 1960s to guarantee equal wages and equal admission to education for women, laws that women are still fighting to enforce. Middle-class women have gotten closer to economic equality in some professional spheres, but the great mass of working women still work for lower wages than men.

The Enabling Myths of Sexism

Just as the ideology of racism relies on stereotypes of minorities, the ideology of sexism relies on stereotypes of women. For example, former Vice President Spiro Agnew, who was forced to resign because of his criminal activity, quipped, "Three things have been difficult to tame—the ocean, fools, and women. We may soon be able to tame the ocean; fools and women will take a little longer" (quoted in Amundsen 1971, 114). Napoleon Bonaparte said, "Nature intended women to be our slaves. ... [T]hey are our property, we are not theirs. ... What a mad idea to demand equality for women! ... Women are nothing but machines for producing children" (quoted in Morgan 1970, 2). Sexism is an enabling myth that serves to justify discrimination against the majority of human beings.

Economic discrimination against women includes lower wages for the same work and less promotion. The largest single cause of the wage gap, however, is the segregation that keeps women out of many high-paying occupations and pushes them into a few low-paying occupations. These low-paying occupations are then relatively overcrowded with the large supply of women workers forced into them, so the employers can continue to pay low wages. Thus most women workers are crowded into just a few occupational groups: clerical worker, retail trade salesworker, private household worker, high school and elementary school teacher, waitress, seamstress and stitcher, and nurse. Men, on the other hand, are spread out over a much wider range of occupations. At the other end of the spectrum, women are present in very small numbers in the high-paying occupations and professions.

A good example of segregation is the high-paying professional economist. Of the 11,842 members of the American Economic Association, only 145 are African Americans and only 1,752 are women (American Economic Association 1993).

The enabling myths that justify sexist discrimination are inculcated, not inherited. "Women are taught from the time they are children to play a serving role, to be docile and submissive" (Goldberg 1970, 35). Institutions that teach this to children include the family, the schools, the media, the church, corporations, and the government; these are institutions in which males are usually dominant. How do sexist myths and sexist discrimination affect the political and economic interests of different economic groups?

Neoclassical economists (like Friedman) contend that employers merely gain psychologically, while also incurring financial losses, from sex discrimination. On the contrary, the radical hypothesis is that employers, as well as conservative politicians, gain from sexism both in power and in profits.

How do employers make profit from the enabling myths of sexism? First, they use the myth of inferiority as an excuse to pay women lower wages. More important, sexist myths enable employers to divide male and female workers, making it more difficult to organize strong unions. In the United States one of every four men workers is unionized, as compared to only one of every seven women workers. The prejudice of union men is apparent in the fact that women constitute 20 percent of all union members but less than 1 percent of all union executive board members (Deckard 1983, 107). Furthermore, in the past, the myths of sexism caused unions to do little, if anything, for women's specific grievances. Some unions in earlier times even joined employers in agreements for lower wages and worse job categories for women, though some unions are now among the strongest defenders of women's rights.

Union men have often payed for their prejudices in broken unions and lower wages. Women will not fight for a union that ignores their needs. Because it reduces union bargaining strength, the myth of sexism causes lower wages for both men and women.

Second, as a result of sexist myths in occupations where most of the labor force is female, the pay is lower than average, even though the workers in many of those areas have higher than average qualifications (shown in more training and education). In many such occupations (such as librarians or bank tellers), women's education is far above the median of U.S. workers, but their wages are far below. The same is true of the men in these predominantly female occupations: their education is above, while their wages are below the average. A major reason for these results is that the myths of sexism are still dominant in the media and are still accepted by working men.

Third, in addition to weak unions, another reason for low wages in the predominantly female occupations is that women have few other economic options. Women are systematically excluded from other occupations and pushed into these. The myth in this case is that women are only suited for certain occupations, in spite of the reality that they now have role models in every profession. Such segregation causes overcrowding or oversupply in the areas where women are allowed to work, thus lowering wages in these jobs.

Fourth, the myth that glorifies housework can also be profitable. In the words of one male advertiser, "properly manipulated[,] ... American housewives can be given the sense of identity, purpose, creativity, the self-realization, even the sexual joy they lack—by the buying of things" (quoted in Friedan 1963, 199). Thus advertisers use the sexist ideology to instill "consumerism" in women. The sexist image of the good woman shows her in the kitchen surrounded by the very latest gadgets and the best cake mix, and made up with miracle cosmetics. Commercials imply that she is a failure if her floors are not the shiniest and her laundry not the whitest in the neighborhood. This myth, which is reinforced by constant images, helps business sell billions of dollars of useless (or even harmful) goods. Of course, due to the myths of advertising, conspicuous consumption is both a male and a female attribute.

Fifth, the myths of sexism are also profitable because they encourage and glorify women's unpaid work in the home. This unpaid work is crucial to the provision of the needed supply of labor. Housework is equivalent to about one-fourth of the gross domestic product (GDP), though it is not counted in the GDP. If business had to pay women in full to raise and clean and cook for the labor force, profits would be seriously reduced. The labor of women as housewives is vital to industry; there would be no labor force without it, yet it goes unpaid. Moreover, as a result of their dependent role in the sexist family, the teaching of religion, and stereotypes in the media, some women are socialized to be passive, submissive, and docile workers and may transmit these values to their children.

Sixth, important support for capitalist corporations comes from sexist myths that increase support for the political status quo. Much like racism, the myths of sexism are also used as a political divide-and-rule tactic. For example, former U.S. Secretary of the Treasury George Schultz blamed unemployment (and accompanying pressure for low wages) on the competition of women workers. Thus, conservative politicians try to make women a scapegoat for men's problems so that men will not see in women their natural ally against a system that oppresses them both.

Furthermore, gender issues supported by myths are used to divide any progressive movement. At the moment, the abortion issue is most prominent. The myth that has encouraged many men and women to be fanatics in opposition to abortion, and all women's rights by association, is that human beings are born at the instant of conception, and so abortion is murder. This is a myth manufactured purely by definition and religious authority. The antiabortion movement ignores all other murder and oppression, including the often miserable lives of children born to families living in poverty. Based on their mythology, their concern is for fetuses, and not living people, with results that are exceedingly harmful to poor women. These myths have also been used to pit the antiabortion movement against all progressive politics.

RELATIONS BETWEEN RACE, GENDER, AND CLASS

How does racism affect economics and class relations? In summary, the myth of racism helped support southern slave economic relations, the exploitation of sharecroppers, and the modern-day capitalist exploitation of minorities. The low pay of minority workers has meant much higher profits for corporations. Myths against minorities have helped weaken unions by dividing them. Myths against minorities have helped elect many reactionary, procorporation candidates by dividing the electorate.

How has sexism affected economics and class relations? In summary, for a long time sexist myths kept most women out of any paid job. Women worked very long hours every day and manufactured many things in the home, but they were not paid for their labor. When women did enter the workplace in great numbers, they were paid very poorly, partly because of sexist stereotypes. If women were all paid exactly the same as men, corporations would lose almost a third of their profits. Women have not only been paid less for the same job but have also been pushed into the worst jobs. Thus, sexism has resulted in a large subordinate group and has meant an overall greater exploitation of all employees. Furthermore, sexist prejudice has been used in various election campaigns, especially with reference to abortion but on other issues as well, to elect reactionary opponents of women, minorities, and labor.

Contrary to a simplistic economic reductionism, it is perfectly clear that racism and sexism have had enormous effects on class relations in the United States. Individualist social scientists interpret this to mean that individual prejudice causes discrimination and determines class relations to that extent, but they deny any effect of class on prejudice. From this analysis, it is clear that one cannot understand why certain enabling myths of racism and sexism arise and persist without understanding their basis in class interests. To understand these myths, one must revise the individualist sequence, from individual prejudice to class relations. Radical institutionalist must present in addition to the revised sequence, from class interests to individual prejudice. From a holistic view that envelopes the interactions of all of our social institutions, class structures, and individuals, our analysis has shown that racist and sexist myths affect class structure, but that class structure also explains the origins and persistence of these enabling myths. Moreover, our evolutionary analysis found that the nature of the myths, as well as the institutionalized discrimination, are different under different modes of production, such as slavery and feudalism.

In brief, racism, sexism, and class exploitation are all intimately tied together in a complex mosaic. All three aid the white, male part of the ruling class, and all three contribute to inequality. Individuals will be lower in the socioeconomic pyramid depending on whether they face one, two, or all three of these obstacles to equality.

REFERENCES

American Economic Association. 1993. *American Economic Review*, 83 (Dec.): 647.

Amundsen, Kirsten. 1971. *The Silent Majority.* Engelwood Cliffs, N.J.: Prentice Hall.

Aristotle. 1941. *The Basic Works of Aristotle.* Edited by Richard McKeon. New York: Random House.

Baron, Harold. 1985. "Racism Transformed." *Review of Radical Political Economics,* 17 (Fall): 10–33.

Becker, Gary S. 1957. *The Economics of Discrimination.* Chicago: University of Chicago Press.

Bonacich, Edna. 1980. "Class Approaches to Ethnicity and Race." *Insurgent Sociologist,* 10 (Fall): 9–24.

Boston, Thomas. 1988. *Race, Class, and Conservatism.* London: Allen and Unwin.

Deckard, Barbara Sinclair. 1983. *The Women's Movement.* New York: Harper and Row.

Friedan, Betty. 1963. *The Feminine Mystique.* New York: Dell Publishing.

Friedman, Milton. 1962. *Capitalism and Freedom.* Chicago: University of Chicago Press.

Goldberg, Marilyn. 1970. "The Economic Exploitation of Women." *Review of Radical Political Economics,* 3 (Spring): 1–18.

Morgan, Robin, ed. 1970. *Sisterhood Is Powerful.* New York: Vintage.

Reich, Michael. 1980. *Racial Inequality, Economic Theory, and Class Conflict.* Princeton, N.J.: Princeton University Press.

Sherman, Howard. 1987. *Foundations of Radical Political Economy.* New York: M. E. Sharpe.

4

Exploitation and Inequality

John E. Elliott

This chapter examines the concept of exploitation and its relationship to inequality. Exploitation thus interests us in two major ways: first, in its own right; and second, as both cause and effect of the inequality of wealth, power, and status in society.

MEANINGS OF "EXPLOITATION"

The term *exploitation* generally has three meanings: one, technical; the second, social; the third, ethical. The technical definition, as found in most dictionaries, is the efficacious use of something, as in the working of a mine, the cultivation of land, or the utilization of an oil field, or the combination of labor and machines so as to minimize costs. Let us call this "basic" exploitation (BE), because it occurs in all societies, both primitive ones in which the use of resources is sufficiently efficacious to merely reproduce society at a subsistence level and progressive ones wherein the use of resources is sufficiently productive to generate a surplus of labor and production above subsistence. BE is thus well-nigh universal.

The social definition, as found, for example, in the *Oxford Dictionary of the English Language*, focuses on a regime of "mastery or advantage" and the resultant use or manipulation of another person or persons for one's own benefit. Such advantageous use presupposes inequalities in wealth and power sufficient to establish mastery or domination by one person or group over others and alienation by those who are exploited from means of protecting themselves from exploitation. Because domination (and alienation) are normally incomplete, social exploitation may be reciprocal in varying degrees.

Social exploitation, defined in this way, may occur with or without the productive use of resources, that is, either with or without basic exploitation.

Marx aptly called the case where the two forms of exploitation commingle "primary exploitation taking place in the production process itself" (PE). Marx posited mastery over, and exploitation of, an (essentially propertyless) working class by an owning, capitalist class through the productive use of resources. Alternatively, a regime of mastery or advantage may occur apart from efficacious resource use. Because of his primary emphasis on production, Marx called this "secondary exploitation" (SE) (1967, 3: 609). One way in which "exploiters" can exercise mastery and advantage over "exploited" persons is through unequal talents and abilities in striking "sharp," shrewd bargains in the process of exchange. Another, classic mode of SE is monopolistic exploitation of buyers, which is characterized by above-competitive prices and below-competitive outputs, and by monopsonistic exploitation of sellers (e.g., workers), which is characterized by below-competitive prices of resources (e.g., wages) and below-competitive employment of inputs (e.g., labor). In contrast to PE, which involves both production and distribution, SE is a phenomenon that occurs purely in the realm of distribution and exchange.

A third, ethical definition of exploitation emphasizes taking selfish or unjust advantage of another person or persons. This third approach presumes (1) that exploitation, by definition, is wrongful, that is, that exploitation cannot be ethically neutral; and (2) that the sort of "wrong" embedded in exploitative processes is a kind of injustice. Thus, exploitation includes the injustice of a wrongful act in its very meaning. The notion of exploitation as definitionally wrongful is most obvious in regard to PE and SE. However, even in the "cool way" in which the term exploitation is used in regard to BE, something more is suggested than a "neutral description," because using people as if they were merely things or inanimate objects, "with no concern for their needs or wishes, is already heavily freighted with connotations of injustice" (Reiman 1989: 299-300).

It is common to find these definitions mixed together. Karl Marx was a paramount founding father figure in modern exploitation theory (see the essays by Brewer, Reeve, Cunliffe, and Carver in Brewer 1987.) Marx observed that economists sympathetic to the capitalist system of economy typically are unable to distinguish between the technical and natural process of the "exploitation of the machine by the workman" and the human and social process of the "exploitation of the workman by the machine" under a capitalist system of mastery and advantage (1967, 1: 443). Similarly, because exploitation is a passionate, value-laden word, it is common to fail to distinguish between social and ethical definitions. Thus, those who defend the existing social order are likely to deny the existence of social exploitation, indeed, even to eschew the very term, while social critics, especially egalitarians of various forms, typically are more likely to insist that "mastery and advantage" are ineluctable facts of social reality and that exploitation is not merely a word with which to beat capitalism over the head.

For example, conservatives believe that the actual state of social relationships in an industrially advanced capitalist economy are essentially just and that social change in the interest of justice requires only small and gradual reductions in inequality.   Conservatives characteristically (though not invariably) indict precapitalist social relations (e.g., slavery, serfdom) as exploitative, but regard capitalism as essentially nonexploitative.   Thus, Robert Nozick (1974), a prominent libertarian philosopher, asks: Would we really want to forbid labor–capital exchanges between consenting adults?

Liberals usually understand exploitation as treating people unjustly in terms of the norms and values of contemporary (capitalist) society, thus also conflating social and ethical exploitation to some extent.   Liberals believe that capitalism, as a politico-economic system, is basically just (and nonexploitative).   However, within the perception of an essentially just system, liberals identify significant enclaves or niches of social exploitation (for example, sweatshop labor, monopoly and monopsony, and so on), which they are prepared to designate as "exploitation" and propose to ameliorate through "welfare-liberal" reforms (Sterba 1992).

Radicals identify the actual state of society as departing substantially from the requirements of an ideal, just society, and they propound more fundamental and rapid changes in the pursuit of equality.   They are thus more likely to "see" exploitation as a social fact and to use its terminology, despite its value-impregnated character.

SOCIAL AND INSTITUTIONAL BASES OF EXPLOITATION

Many liberals and conservatives alike believe that capitalist society is fundamentally pluralist (Alford and Friedland 1985, pt. 1), that is, is comprised of individuals who find themselves pulled in several different directions by their numerous associations and interests.   Liberal–conservative models of society also typically posit an elitist component in their recognition that the "main role" in economic and political processes are assigned to "self-chosen groups of leaders," notably, top corporate executives, major corporate stockholders, and prominent politicians (Macpherson 1977, 77).   What prevents economic and political leaders from alienating, dominating, and exploiting ordinary workers, consumers, and citizens according to pluralist theory?   The answer is beguiling, albeit jarringly incongruent with social practice: competitive market processes foster equilibria between demands for, and supplies of, economic (and political) goods.   Under the auspices of competition, ostensible leaders adapt to market forces beyond their control.   Real suzereignty thus lies with consumers and citizens, and not with corporate CEOs, capitalist magnates, or political power brokers.

More precisely, under perfect competition, monopoly profits are excluded *ex definitione*. Pure economic profits, in general, would be eliminated in the long run.   If not, some workers, having ready access to credit under perfectly competitive assumptions, would exit from working-class status and compete away the profits by bidding up resource prices and bidding down prices of commodities. Supposing that the pace, intensity, and regularity of work, under a regime of perfect markets, is given and contractually specified in advance of production (a tacit assumption of what is called marginal productivity theory), then profit creation through management schemes to make workers labor longer, harder, more regularly, or more intensively are also ruled out. Full employment, established through competitive labor markets, would foster a robust demand for labor. High demand for labor, combined with easy reductions in labor supply and the associated establishment of new firms, would promote high real wages. Static equilibrium would preclude the creation of new pure economic profits through technological or other dynamic changes. Supposing that production and income creation are synchronized and that "time preference" is neutral between present and future, interest would tend to disappear (Schumpeter [1911] 1983, ch. 1). Abstracting from land rent, income would consist essentially of wages and depreciation, with industrial capitalists being reduced to living on managerial wages (Elliott 1995, 155).

By contrast to the liberal–conservative perspective, radicals often adopt a class perspective insofar as they focus on the social process of class relations, namely, the extraction of surplus labor and the appropriation of surplus output by a dominant capitalist class, and the provision of surplus labor and output by a nondominant working class (Wolff and Resnick 1987, 146; Resnick and Wolff 1987, 110). It is this proces of production and appropriation, under conditions of "uneven bargaining power" (Lutz 1995) or "unequal sovereignty" (Reiman 1989) that Marx called (primary) "exploitation." Insofar as PE is successful, it yields its "golden fruits" in the form of surplus values, which are translated into profits through competition. Subsumed under this fundamental or primary exploitation is the further subappropriation of portions of profit by financial and landed property owners in the form of, among other things, interest and rents (Wolff and Resnick 1987, 150).

Although Marx uses the language of the labor theory of value in his exposition, his theory of exploitation does not require such a theory

or even a theory of embodied labor time—merely a distinction between productive labour and mere ownership of productive resources. ... Marx's theory of exploitation proceeds from the notion of ownership of the means of production as non-work to the normative deduction that such owners, merely because they are owners, should not get the benefits of work done by others.(Carver 1987, 76)

Moreover, there is a strategic political element in Marx's notion of exploitation. It is the power associated with differential ownership of productive assets, "and the way that it is independent of collective control, which irks Marx, not simply the supposed advantage or disadvantage of an economic inequality in society" (Carver 1987, 78).

The radical image of industrially advanced, capitalist society abandons the demanding assumptions of the liberal-conservative perspective. Instead, economic (and political) leaders are conceived as a dominant class, which exercises substantially greater wealth and power than ordinary consumers, workers, and citizens. It should be noted that the class process does not invariably elicit pure economic profits for firms and their owners from the exploitation of labor. Some firms function poorly or even fall into bankruptcy. Under conditions of economic crisis and succeeding recession, many firms experience losses. In this event, the laborer "has been indeed exploited, but his exploitation has not been realized as such for the capitalist" (Marx 1967, 3: 244).

Under normal conditions, however, the operation of the class process results in positive profits, a phenomenon presumably discordant with long run, perfectly competitive, full employment static and stationary general equilibrium. One approach by which this discordancy can be removed is to modify these simplifying assumptions. First, modern industrial societies are characterized by differential ownership of productive assets. A relatively small number of owners do no substantial amount of work yet appropriate a significant portion of the output. A relatively large number of workers do virtually all the work, own no (or few) productive assets, and are largely alienated from meaningful control over work, production, appropriation, and disposition of surplus output, and other important public decision processes (Elliott 1995, 154).

Because of the extremely unequal distribution of the ownership of productive assets in society, substantial barriers exist to the transit of persons from working-class to capitalist or even small proprietary status, despite robust free (though not perfect) competition among firms. Differential ownership thus operates as a *de facto* class "monopoly" over the means of production and subsistence (Marx 1967, 1: 235). Although workers are juridically free to open new businesses and thereby to compete with established firms, they

typically lack the economic capacity, either in the form of savings or easy access to credit, to acquire the means of production (and sustenance) ... to do so or the business skills needed to successfully compete even if they were able somehow to acquire the required productive assets. Insofar as such impediments exist to fluid exit from the working class and free entry into competition as business proprietors, competition will result in a tendency toward equalization in profit rates among existing firms, but not necessarily to elimination of profits; and economic compulsion will force most workers, in order to obtain wage income, to sell their labor power to some capitalist employer or other, and thereby to continue to function as workers. (Elliott 1995, 155)

Even though workers are not tied to one employer, as under slavery or serfdom, to be a proletarian is to be dependent for employment and survival on some capitalist somewhere. Hence, the sale of the power or capacity to labor is "forced" despite its apparent free and voluntary contractual character (Cohen 1983).

Because the origin of the "forced" quality of the sale of labor power is the lack of economic independence associated with the ownership of productive assets, this first foundational element, in principle, is consonant with a fully employed economy. However, unemployment undoubtedly heightens this "force": the "existence of rationing makes a successful sale more urgent" (Dymski and Elliott 1989, 359). Recession and its associated unemployment is a (periodically) systemic feature of modern capitalist economy. Even during periods of prosperity, capitalist economies normally experience some amount of (involuntary) unemployment. By raising the degree of dependency of workers on employers, unemployment expands the inequality of bargaining power between them. Workers are reluctant to leave jobs and anxious to retain them (even if wages are lower than under full employment conditions) because they are uncertain whether they will be able to relocate with security. They are intensely desirous to obtain jobs, even at low pay and in unsatisfactory working conditions, because the existence of a sluggish job market places a premium on the security of obtaining work. There is thus also a familial similarity between unemployment as a cause of the (relative) benefits accruing to employers from unemployment and monopsony. Both are characterized by low wages and unemployment of labor, the former as a basis for PE, and the latter as a major source of SE.

Next, capitalism, by its nature, is a dynamic system, and not one in static and stationary equilibrium. Technologies, resource endowments, tastes, and markets all change because of the motivations and institutions of capitalist economy, and they change so as to generate positive profits under capitalist control. As Joseph Schumpeter once put it, even if surplus values were "impossible in perfect equilibrium, [they] . . . can be ever present because that equilibrium is never allowed to establish itself. They may always tend to vanish and yet be always there because they are constantly recreated" (1950, 28).

Finally, profits are more or less constantly recreated. On the one hand, working hours, like working conditions, are affected significantly by collective action, struggle, and legislation. Insofar as employers are successful in this struggle, being assisted by low working-class solidarity and such factors as "education, tradition, [and] habit" (Marx 1967, 1: 737), working hours will increase and workers will be employed more continuously and regularly, with expansionary effects on output and profits. On the other hand, the actual application of labor to the production process associated with any particular amount of labor power purchased is not typically specified in advance, either because "of a failure to fully detail the tasks of the agent hired or because productivity depends on an effort component of work which is inherently impossible to pre-determine" (Dymski and Elliott 1989, 359). Labor effort, in turn, depends on both market relations (e.g., sales and input availabilities) and intra-enterprise labor relations (e.g., worker satisfaction, the quality and character of management), and thus is highly uncertain, as emphasized by John Maynard Keynes (1936), Frank Knight (1921) and, more recently, Geoffrey M. Hodgson (1988). By the sale of their labor power, the workers submit, albeit grudgingly, to the political authority of the employer to control the work process (and the output coming from it). The labor process is thereby "contested" (Bowles 1985; Bowles and Edwards 1988), with capitalist employers and their managerial agents trying to extract as much actual labor from workers as possible, and workers trying to minimize such endeavors. Ex post output, and thereby potential profits, vary

positively with the employer's success in extracting labor effort and energy from labor power and, thus, with the efficacy of intra-enterprise domination, a phenomenon presumably absent under perfect competition and circumstances under which labor input-output relations are technically indistinguishable from those of other, non-human, resources.   Industrial domination, in turn, depends on such factors as managerial coordination and supervision, incentives systems, and stratagems to heighten workers' responsiveness to employers' commands, notably the threat of job loss and such cultural and ideological considerations as the character of workers' submissiveness, aggressiveness, and solidarity. (Elliott 1995, 156-57; see also Bowles and Gintis 1987)

The institutional and social bases of class exploitation under a capitalist system of property relations are such that workers are substantially alienated (i.e., separated) from the ownership and control of physical means of production and consumption, which instead is dominated by capitalists. This inequality in the domination of productive assets (DOPA) is sufficient to elicit secondary exploitation of worker-owned small businesses and workers' cooperatives by landlords and banks in the form of rents and interest, even in the absence of a labor market and capitalist domination of the workplace.

These property relations, together with capitalist market exchange relations, compel workers to sell their labor power to capitalist employers and enable the latter to dominate over the purchase of labor power. This extends the process of labor exploitation into PE based on DOPA, the "forced" sale of labor power, and unemployment, on the one hand, and various means for the extraction of actual labor from labor power, as explained previously. Consequently, workers also are alienated from the products they have produced, capitalist employers exercise dominion over the disposition of products and the appropriation of products, and the realm of "mastery and advantage" is extended to incorporate the appropriation of profits from primary and secondary exploitation.

EXPLOITATION AND INEQUALITY

Let us now identify more explicitly the main connecting linkages between the processes of labor exploitation and inequality. The key to these connecting linkages is that exploitation (together with alienation and domination) serves both as cause and effect. As Marx put it in his early writings on alienation ([1844] 1964, 131), capitalist property relations are both the "means by which labor is alienated" and the "product, the necessary result, of alienated labor." In *Capital*, he writes: the "capitalist system presupposes the complete separation of the labourers from all property in the means by which they can realize their labour. As soon as capitalist production is on its own legs, it not only maintains this separation, but produces it on a continually extending scale" (Marx 1967, 1: 712).   Capitalism thus reproduces itself in the process of producing and distributing products. At the end of the production cycle, the worker produces products in the form of capital, "an alien power that dominates and exploits him," while the capitalist reproduces labor power itself, separated from the products needed for its sustenance. "This incessant reproduction is the *sine qua non* of capitalist production" (Marx 1967, 1: 571).

Of course, this stark and passionate nineteenth-century language needs to be tempered in the light of social practice on the eve of the twenty-first century. Millions of small businesses exist in the United States, for example, in which workers are simultaneously owners and individually appropriate their own surplus products (after paying interest, rent, taxes, and so on). Workers' cooperatives, which are rising in number, also provide a (collective) alternative to capitalist firms. Labor unions exercise a countervailing force, stronger or weaker from country to country, to capitalist appropriation and, in combination with safety and other legislation, temper employers' power over hours and working conditions as well as wages. Monetary and fiscal policies, on balance, probably tilt capitalist economies in the direction of closer approximation to full employment, thereby enhancing labor's bargaining power in its negotiations with capital.

Despite these important qualifications, however, there is no question that in our day, as in that of Adam Smith, the economic and political power of business firms is generally stronger than that of workers. Given inequality in bargaining power between employers and workers, wages tend to be lower than they otherwise would be. Adam Smith, founding father of modern political economy, elucidated several elements in the contestation between capital and labor that continue to be applicable today. According to him, wages depend on the contract made between workers and "masters" (employers),

whose interests are by no means the same. The workmen desire to get as much, the masters to give as little as possible. The former are disposed to combine in order to raise, the latter in order to lower the wages of labour. It is not, however, difficult to foresee which of the two parties must, upon all ordinary occasions, have the advantgage in the dispute and force the other into a compliance with their terms. The masters, being fewer in number, can combine much more easily. (Smith [1776] 1976, 74)

Moreover, "wealth," said Smith,

is power. ... The power which [wealth] immediately and directly conveys ... is the power of purchasing; a certain command over all the labour, or over all the produce of labour which is then in the market. ... In all such [labor] disputes the master can hold out much longer. ... In the long-run, the workman may be as necessary to his master as his master is to him, but the necessity is not so immediate. (Smith [1776] 1976, 35, 74–75)

It also seems equally clear that inequality in the distribution of wealth is a fundamental cause of differential power. Finally, inequality in the distribution of productive assets and politico-economic power is a foundational element in the system of "mastery and advantage," which we have called "exploitation," and thereby in the distribution of income, which is one of the major benefits (to capitalists) from exploitation. Through income inequality, the appropriation of society's surplus labor and surplus product takes the concrete form of industrial profits, rents, and interest (and taxes, which fund governmental programs, which in turn support and nurture business enterprise).

These unequally distributed benefits from differential wealth and power then provide the further bases for thousands of concrete acts of investment and capital accumulation, which continually extend the scope of the capital–labor relationship.   The magnitude of the interconnected processes of alienation, domination, and exploitation thus expand simultaneously with the growth of economic activity generally.

It should be noted that the exploitation of labor, and the inequalities of wealth, power, and income associated with it, may be, but need not necessarily be, accompanied by absolute poverty for the general body of the working population.   During periods of rapid growth, especially as the economy approaches full employment, increasing demand for labor tends to raise wages. However, this does not negate wage labor as a system of exploitation, any more than feeding slaves well will abolish slavery. "The rise of wages therefore is confined within limits that not only leave intact the foundations of the capitalistic system, but also secure its reproduction on an expanding scale" (Marx 1967, 1: 620).

In closing, we should note that labor exploitation is linked with inequality in race and gender as well as class. We shall not comment here on race and gender issues per se. However, while racial and sexual inequalities form an integral constituent in class exploitation theory, they are anomalies in class harmony theory. In the dominant neoclassical paradigm of perfect competition, (class harmony in the long run) inequality by race and sex is puzzling. If we suppose, for example, that the physical productivity of males and females (and of whites and African Americans) is essentially the same in a given instance, the payment of differential wages is economically inefficient and therefore less profitable than the payment of equal wages. Presumably, and barring the operation of irrational elements, perfectly competitive markets would tend to eliminate wage (and other) differences in long-run equilibrium.

Examined from the perspective of the enterprise as a locus of politico-economic power, however, the paying of differential wages has a rationale. It serves as a means to cement an alliance between employers, on the one hand, and white, male employees on the other. Paying relatively higher wages (but not necessarily absolutely higher than those that would prevail under perfect competition) for a chosen group is also a means to secure labor peace and the minimization of strikes, insofar, for example, as the favored group plays a dominant role in an affiliated labor union. Thus, racial and gender inequality may serve as a rational part of a class strategy of divide and conquer among constituent elements of workers.

62   Basic Approaches

REFERENCES

Alford, Robert R., and Roger Friedland. 1985. *Powers of Theory: Capitalism, Democracy, and the State.* New York: Cambridge University Press.

Bowles, Samuel. 1985. "The Production Process in a Competitive Economy: Walrasian, Neo-Hobbesian, and Marxian Models." *American Economic Review,* 75, no. 1: 16–36.

Bowles, Samuel, and Richard Edwards. 1988. "Contested Exchange: Political Economy and Modern Economic Theory." *American Economic Review,* 78, no. 2: 145–50.

Bowles, Samuel, and Herbert Gintis. 1987. *Democracy and Capitalism.* New York: Basic Books.

Brewer, John D. 1987. "The Scottish Enlightenment." In Andrew Reeve, ed., *Modern Theories of Exploitation.* Beverly Hills, Calif.: Sage, 6–29.

Carver, Terrell. 1987. "Marx's Political Theory of Exploitation." In Andrew Reeve, ed., *Modern Theories of Exploitation.* Beverly Hills, Calif.: Sage, 68–79.

Cohen, G. A. 1983. "The Structure of Proletarian Unfreedom." *Philosophy and Public Affairs,* 12: 3–33.

Cunliffe, John. 1987. "A Mutualist Theory of Exploitation." In Andrew Reeve, ed., *Modern Theories of Exploitation.* Beverly Hills, Calif.: Sage,: 53–67.

Dymski, Gary A., and John E. Elliott. 1989. "Roemer vs. Marx: Should Anyone Be Interested in Exploitation?" In Robert Ware and Kai Nielsen, ed., *Analyzing Marxism.* Calgary, Canada: University of Calgary Press: 333–74.

Elliott, John E. 1995. "Comment on Anthony Brewer, 'A Minor Post-Ricardian? Marx as an Economist.'" *History of Political Economy,* 27, no. 1 (Spring): 147–58.

Hodgson, Geoffrey M. 1988. "Production versus Allocation in Economic Theory or Marx After Keynes and Knight." Working paper, Newcastle upon Tyne, U.K.

Keynes, John Maynard. 1936. *The General Theory of Employment, Interest, and Money.* New York: Harcourt Brace and Co.

Knight, Frank. 1921. *Risk, Uncertainty, and Profit.* Boston: Houghton Mifflin.

Lutz, Mark A. 1995. "[Book review of *Property and Contract in Economics* by David P. Ellerman]." *Review of Social Economy,* 53, no. 1 (Spring): 141–47.

Macpherson, C. B. 1977. *The Life and Times of Liberal Democracy.* New York: Oxford University Press.

Marx, Karl. [1844] 1964. "Economic and Philosophical Manuscripts." In Tom Bottomore, ed., *Karl Marx: Early Works.* New York: McGraw-Hill.

___. *Capital.* Vols. 1, 3. 1967. New York: International Publishers.

Nozick, Robert. 1974. *Anarchy, State, and Utopia.* Cambridge: Harvard University Press.

Reeve, Andrew. 1987. "Thomas Hodgskin and John Bray." In Andrew Reeve, ed., *Modern Theories of Exploitation.* Beverly Hills, Calif.: Sage: 30–52.

Reiman, Jefrey. 1989. "An Alternative to 'Distributive' Marxism: Further Thoughts on Roemer, Cohen, and Exploitation." In Robert Ware and Kai Nielsen, eds., *Analyzing Marxism.* Calgary, Canada: University of Calgary Press: 299–331.

Resnick, Stephen A., and Richard D. Wolff. 1987. *Knowledge and Class: A Marxian Critique of Political Economy.* Chicago: University of Chicago Press.

Schumpeter, Joseph A. [1911] 1983. *Theory of Economic Development.* New York: Transaction Press.

___. 1950. *Capitalism, Socialism, and Democracy.* New York: Harper.

Smith, Adam. [1776] 1976. *An Inquiry into the Nature and Causes of the Wealth of Nations.* Chicago: University of Chicago Press.
Sterba, James P. 1992. *Justice: Alternative Perspectives.* Belmont, Wash.: Wadsworth.
Wolff, Richard D., and Stephen A. Resnick. 1987. *Economics: Marxian versus Neoclassical.* Baltimore, Md.: Johns Hopkins University Press.

5

Taxation without Representation: Reconstructing Marx's Theory of Capitalist Exploitation

James Devine

This chapter presents a robust reconstruction of Marx's theory of capitalist exploitation, eschewing both his jargon and Marxology, and using largely mainstream language. However, my effort contrasts with that of Roemer (1982), who tries to fit Marxian conclusions onto the Procrustean bed of mainstream theory. Instead, it stresses that concepts and theories developed by Marx can be restated in mainstream terms only as long as key points of disagreement are noted. Perhaps the term that generates the most important disagreement is the concept of exploitation.

The word *exploitation* necessarily has a normative content. However, since the aim of clarifying the theory is positive, I use Makhijani's (1992) phrase, "taxation without representation," as summarizing the word's normative side. Just as taxation is based on coercion, capitalist exploitation is based on "institutional coercion," involving both macro-level capitalist *supremacy* (the worker's proletarianization) and the micro-level *subjection* of labor by capital. Allowing this coercion to persist is workers' conscious *submission*, but capitalist exploitation is not the same as taxation: the coercion that allows it to persist is different from the force used by the state and can work in a decentralized way. Further, unlike most coercion, capitalist "taxation" can encourage the growth of production.

For Marx, other economic systems, such as feudalism and slavery, are "exploitative." However, the only concern here is capitalism. This chapter starts with mainstream views of exploitation, in contrast to Marx's vision. Next, Marx's theory is introduced. Using Dymski and Elliott's (1989) terms, this theory centers on *primary* exploitation, the creation of a surplus product. Finally, the theory of *secondary* (merely redistributive) exploitation is explained and the chapter is summarized.

THE MAINSTREAM AND MARX

For all authors, exploitation is a persistent economic relationship, and therefore not simple theft. Further, my dictionary sees it as "an unjust or improper use of another person for one's own profit" (*Webster's Ninth New Collegiate Dictionary*, 1991, 438). Mainstream economists see exploitation as "improper" because it goes against the public interest. Of the three mainstream perspectives, the neoclassicals dominate: exploitation is market failure, deviation of the world from an ideal vision of capitalism. The exploiter is a monopsonist or monopolist; a hired agent who uses asymmetric information to exploit the principal; or a free rider in the production of public goods. However, in a second view, exploitation can coexist with "perfect" markets: given a special position in society, a group can gain a scarcity rent, even though they serve no reasonable purpose: while George (1879) pointed to landowners, Keynes (1936) saw rentiers as fitting this picture. Roemer (1982) extends this conception to include the entire capitalist class. The third view weds imperfections with a stress on exploiters as a segment of society. The Friedmans (1980) see the government as exploitative, a rent-seeking monopoly run by special interest groups, and regularly interfering with markets.

Marx's theory combines aspects of the mainstream visions, but uses a different methodology. First, while neoclassicals see economics as concerning the allocation of scarce resources, Marx adds the notion that society produces a surplus product (Obrinsky, 1983), an aggregate output exceeding costs of production so that the average product of labor (APL) net of materials costs exceeds the wage rate. This surplus corresponds to the *surplus labor* done by workers to produce the surplus product. Under capitalism, surplus labor appears in money form as surplus value (property income), which is divided among profits, interest, rent, much of taxes, and the salaries of top managers.

Marx's second relevant deviation from the mainstream is his institutionalism: the societal process is more than atomistic agents' decisions under natural conditions. Many constraints are artificial, benefiting groups that fight to preserve them. These institutions shape individual preferences and actions. Though continually recreated by people, institutions take on a life of their own, at once alienated from, and molding, individual wills.

Nowadays, capitalism is a central institution of this sort. Whereas the mainstream sees exploitation either as a disease curable even under capitalism or as a natural part of the human condition, Marx saw it as essential to that institution and to be abolished with it: "the production of surplus-value ... is the specific end and aim, the sum and substance of capitalist production" ([1867] 1967, 298). The mainstream types of exploitation are relatively secondary.

Third, Marx rejected the politics/economics distinction as artificial. The split between the "state" and the "economy" arose, he believed, only with capitalism. Further, Marx saw "politics"—including conflictual relations among people— not only in the state sphere, but also inside the capitalist firm.

MARX'S THEORY

Though the current presentation is a reaction to Roemer, this is not the place to criticize his work (cf. Devine and Dymski 1989, 1991). It should suffice here to say that his theory suffers from a conflation of the "primary" exploitation by industrial capitalists, production of a surplus, and the "secondary," redistributional, exploitation by rentiers (paralleling Wolff and Resnick's, 1987, 146–51, distinction between "fundamental" and "subsumed" class processes).

To Marx, the exploitation story centered on a representative capitalist laying out money (M) to buy commodities (C), which are then used to get more money (M'). The issue is why $M' > M$ on the macrosocietal level. Profits from "buying low and selling high" are seen as mere redistributions (secondary exploitation) that cancel out on the macro level and are so ignored ([1867] 1967, ch. 5).

To understand what is at stake, examine profit theory in light of neoclassical theory. (Marx's exploitation theory *is* his profit theory.) As Obrinsky (1983, chs. 4, 11) showed, this theory has largely involved the unexplained or undertheorized assumption that profits are positive. The existence of profits— and of property income in general—has usually been a nonproblem. For many years, neoclassicals explained property income, profits, or interest (which were almost always conflated) using an aggregate production function: the profit (interest) rate equaled the marginal product of "capital." That this was an "explanation" indicates the low priority put on the problem: it is equivalent to simply assuming that profits exist, since the social role of owning capital goods (which evokes a flow of property income) is not justified by the goods themselves. This theory collapsed when Sraffa (1960) demolished the aggregate production function. Among sophisticated neoclassicals, it has been replaced by general equilibrium theory.

A better response has been to develop a micro theory of profits. For the individual capitalist, "normal" profits are a given, representing income needed to justify staying in the industry (with supernormal, "economic," profits adding to zero on the macro level). Still needed is a theory of why such profits exceed zero. One answer is to equate normal profits with interest that could be earned on alternative uses of a capitalist's assets, since the capitalist could decide to leave "real" production.

However, this poses the question of why the interest rate (i) is positive. Here a graph is drawn showing an individual's intertemporal choice between current consumption and future income. The individual's choice is shown by the intertemporal budget line's tangency with the highest indifference curve feasible and to the intertemporal production possibilities frontier below it. Often, the graph is assumed to apply equally at the micro and macro levels—or the macro/micro issue is not addressed.

Marx's theory of primary exploitation aimed to explain why the intertemporal production possibilities frontier *for the economy as a whole* has a slope such that i can exceed zero, in order that one individual can earn interest without that gain simply being a redistribution from another individual. (He was explaining capitalism, not piracy and not philanthropy.) Marx went beyond explaining why i > zero, to help us understand all other types of property income, emphasizing the rate of *profit* (r, total property income divided by capital). Then, if r > zero can be explained, i > 0 follows.

Marx's surplus problematic explains how capitalist institutions create and over time reproduce a steep ppf that constrains choice, leaving the issue of the actual choice made as secondary: in his ([1867] 1967, ch. 24, s. 3) discussion of the abstinence theory, for example, the choice of how much surplus to accumulate is subordinate to the actual existence of a surplus; abstinence alone does not explain why $r \geq i$ > zero.

Consider another etiology of surplus, which brings up a second issue, the form in which surplus appears under capitalism. Imagine an independent producer working hard now, and taking advantage of natural possibilities to produce a surplus in the future. Assuming a surplus is actually produced, there is, as yet, no exploitation or profit in the capitalist sense. Marx's exploitation excludes such concepts as the self-employed producer "exploiting herself": exploitation is a relationship between people. To understand it, it must be discovered how someone can capture the proprietor's surplus and also motivate her to continue to produce it (so that this is not simply theft). This explained, then the intertemporal ppf will be such that $r \geq i$ > zero for capitalists or moneylenders rather than simply for the proprietor.

The Austrian school, among others, has a completely different answer: a surplus arises and i > zero (usually equated with r > zero) due to "roundaboutness," as when wine improves with age, so that "waiting" or "abstinence" is rewarded with profit. Others suggest that "risk taking," technology, or "entrepreneurship" produce profits. A critique of these theories is beyond this chapter's scope (but see Obrinsky 1983), but one example suffices to show that the mainstream factors explaining profit are necessary, but not sufficient, at the macro level.

A professional poker player uses equipment, takes risks, delays gratification, engages in strategic behavior, tries new tricks and tactics (innovates), owns tools (e.g. marked cards), cheats, and earns large winnings—and can even do so repeatedly. However, no surplus results from such behavior; the gambler's winnings are simply redistributions from others, with no new production occurring. The poker player is not a capitalist. Thus, the mainstream factors might be necessary for an individual to receive profits, but they are far from sufficient for these winnings not to be pure redistributions. We need to understand the societal conditions that allow the risk taker (and others) to get a profit without being a mere thief or bunko artist.

PRIMARY EXPLOITATION

To explain the production of surplus that shows up as profit received by nonworkers, Marx's theory adds involuntary elements to Roemer's purely voluntary exploitation. Since this coercion is part of the capitalist social structure, it fits with Marx's institutionalism. However, not all of the story involves coercion: an individual can make a profit (secondary exploitation) without participating directly in the production of surplus value (primary exploitation), just as a holder of treasury bonds can garner interest without participating in the state's forcible extraction of taxes. Secondary exploiters might be seen as recipients of "stolen goods" resulting from primary exploitation.

Institutional coercion's role can be understood by first examining capital's macro-supremacy and then its micro-subjection of labor.

Supremacy

Marx emphasized "the so-called primitive accumulation" ([1867] 1967, chs. 27–33), the violent historical creation of the "fundamental conditions of capitalist production." Under these conditions, workers are "free in a double sense" in that "neither they themselves form part … of the means of production, as in the case of slaves … nor do the means of production belong to them, as in the case of peasant-proprietors" ([1867] 1967, 714). This capitalist supremacy (workers' proletarianization) is more profound than Roemer's capitalist "dominance" in that, not only do workers lack control over the capital goods, but their own income-producing assets are insufficient to provide them with a livelihood for any extended period. They are thus forced by their social circumstance to work for the capitalist class, no matter how unpleasant the job: "the laborer purchases the right to work for his own livelihood only by paying for it in surplus-labor" (Marx [1867] 1967, 515).

1. The two aspects of workers' freedom help produce the reserve army of unemployed labor. First, freedom from bondage allows this army to exist: there is no joblessness under slavery (for example) since the slave owner strives to use his property as intensively as possible. Second, workers lack access, not only to the means of production, but also to consumption goods, which they can get only by working for capitalists. Since they have nowhere else to work for their livelihoods (unlike in Roemer's models), the only alternative is to be unemployed (though this conclusion will be moderated later in the chapter). Marx discusses Wakefield's theory that in land-rich colonies, it is necessary to forcibly keep workers from the frontier if profits are to be garnered by hiring them ([1867] 1967, ch. 33).

The ability of workers to quit or to reject job offers (part of the first kind of freedom) does not equate the marginal disutility of worktime to the wage rate. Instead, the former is equated to the marginal disutility of becoming jobless, or roughly, the cost of job loss (COJL), a concept developed by Weisskopf, Bowles, and Gordon (1983). Labor's mobility tends to equalize wages and working conditions between sectors. However, absent alternatives to working for capitalists, even complete equalization does not abolish the capitalist supremacy that allows exploitation.

2. Other ways exist to avoid working for the capitalists besides going to the frontier, but are quite limited. Going into business for one's self is very difficult without sufficient assets and the ability to diversify one's investments. Workers lack that ability by definition (cf. Bowles and Edwards 1993, 130). There *is* a constant flux of workers into the self-employed petty bourgeoisie (and a trickle of these that become full-scale capitalists), but there is also a constant reflux into the working class as enterprises fail. Though some move between class positions, the class structure itself remains, leaving the vast majority where they started.

The difficulty of a worker going into business persists in part because of the competition from capitalist firms, which can benefit more easily from economies of scale and scope. At the same time, unemployment keeps the wages low, making it extremely difficult for workers to get sufficient income to save enough for the initial investment needed to go into business: saving for retirement or consumer durables such as houses is difficult enough. Since this blocks their ability to earn income for saving from their own businesses, they face a vicious circle.

Another place to get subsistence is from the state. But unemployment insurance benefits and other welfare state programs are paid for by redistributions from employed workers, as analyses of the incidence of payroll taxes indicate. The actual benefits are historically contingent, based on struggles: politicians and social scientists work to make sure that welfare state programs do not undermine the "incentive to work" for capitalists. Absent a strong counterpressure from working people, as in Western Europe after World War II, these programs seldom represent a viable alternative to selling labor power to the capitalists. For the United States, Tonak (1987) and Miller (1989) both found that state programs helping workers were more than paid for by taxes on wages for 1952 to 1985.

Yet another option is to live off one's peers. Even though this encourages conflicts, extended families, communities, and labor unions can and do provide (privatized) unemployment insurance. However, this simply emphasizes the redistributive nature of that insurance. Crime is another possible source of unemployed workers' livelihood, but it mostly represents a redistribution from other workers (whose incomes are limited by the reserve army of unemployed): the main victims of "street crime" are the poor.

3. Open unemployment (as measured in the United States) is less important than the more general phenomenon of the COJL. In many underdeveloped countries, there is almost no open unemployment: almost all propertyless people who can work have jobs, no matter how pathetic. However, the large gap between wages in the capitalist sector and the income earned from petty trading, street hustling, crime, and the like (and the nonexistence of unemployment insurance, etc.) imposes a large COJL on workers in the capitalist sector (cf. Schor 1987, 175). Even without open unemployment, perhaps the only thing worse than being exploited by a capitalist is *not* being exploited by one. A formal description helps us summarize:

$$\text{COJL} = C(U, W\text{gap}) \text{ where } C(0, 0) = 0 \tag{1}$$

where C is a positive function of both the open unemployment rate (U) and Wgap, the gap between the wage earned working for the capitalists and alternatives such as street hustling and the dole. Now suppose that there exists a minimum COJL (Cmin) necessary to result in an adequate profit rate (from a capitalist viewpoint). At this Cmin, U and Wgap substitute for each other in providing an adequate COJL. In the "first world," the Wgap is minimal but U is positive, while in the "third world," U is minimal and Wgap is large. Note the difference with Roemer's models, where it is possible for U and Wgap to both equal zero, so that the COJL is zero.

4. Before turning to alternatives to the COJL, Marx's theory must be completed. What *preserves* COJL $\geq$ Cmin over time? To avoid functionalism—the view that something exists simply because it helps the capitalists—more is needed. If the COJL's persistence can be explained, so, too, can the difficulties of workers going into business or providing privatized unemployment insurance, since a high COJL makes these difficult. The story also helps us understand the limits on welfare state measures.

In Roemer's model, workers' abundance relative to capital goods is abolished automatically (and with it, profits and exploitation) if capitalists follow market incentives and invest their profits in scarce capital goods. Marx's solution is simple here, because his theory of exploitation is so different. For Roemer, profits are quasirents. For Marx, while these goods' scarcity is not denied, the receipt of profits is not simply based on this alone. Instead, profits are akin to a tax that capitalists can impose because they control the growth process, including the pace and nature of investment and technical change.

Suppose that $C < C$min, or that this situation is anticipated soon, threatening a profit squeeze as workers are more able to push for high wages, cut back on work intensity, or even go into business for themselves. The capitalists' control over investment decisions means that they can, and will, cut investment spending (and the economy's growth rate) when profits are so threatened; this "capital strike" restores the profit-boosting situation of high unemployment by depressing the economy (cf. Marx [1867] 1967, 619; Goodwin 1967). No conspiracy is needed: profit squeezes hit all capitalists to varying degrees, encouraging a certain unity of purpose.

This theory presumes that capitalists cannot simply mark-up money wage costs: when Marx wrote, the gold standard prevented such a passing-on of costs. Today, competition faced by individual capitalists and by nations on the world market prevent complete passing-on, at least in the short run. But in a modern economy with fiat and credit money, the short-term profit squeeze could encourage accelerating inflation instead of recession (cf. Bowles and Boyer 1990). Central banks' vehement opposition to inflation (reflecting the power of property owners) encourages recession, reproducing Marx's classic scenario in a politicized form. Even without this opposition, accelerating inflation eventually encourages recession that reestablishes a COJL adequate to preserve profits.

This theory differs from that of Bowles and Gintis (1990a, 1990b; 1993) and Devine and Dymski (1991), who stressed the origins of the COJL from purely microeconomic behavior, in essence, the payment of "efficiency wages." While the idea that managers manipulate wage payments in order to motivate workers by raising the COJL is mostly reasonable and can cause unemployment by interaction with other non-Walrasian elements of the economy (cf. Devine, 1993a), the emphasis below is on the macroeconomically created COJL. In the spirit of Marx's presentation, the role of "imperfections" is largely ignored.

Threatened by high wages or low work effort, capitalists can also institute labor-saving technological change (Marx [1867] 1967, ch. 25, s. 2), while seeking new supplies of labor power at home and abroad. Indeed, they are driven to seek ways to replace labor power by the competitive battle amongst capitalists and the possibility that wages will rise in the future. Further, they may use the state, as when capitalists push the state to change immigration laws to import "guest workers" in times when labor power is scarce.

Governments are sites for intraclass competition and interclass conflict, and need not always serve the capitalist class interests. However, a government that attempts to lower the COJL has to face the limits created by the profit squeeze/capital strike and capitalist control over technological change. If a government promotes true full employment or institutes programs seen as undermining profitability (even if they are not truly so), eventually investment will stagnate or capital will flee to more profitable shores. This induces recession or increased inflation, falling tax revenues, foreign exchange problems, and/or long-term productivity-growth stagnation. These undermine popular support for the government and either push it out of office or to change its policies (cf. Kalecki [1943] 1971; Block [1977] 1984; Lindblom, 1982). "Automatic destabilization" cases include those against Salvador Allende in Chile and Francois Mitterand in France.

5. However, the receipt of profits is not *guaranteed* by the capitalist control of investment and technological change, since capitalists can get themselves into serious crises, such as the Great Depression, when unemployment became "too large" and hurt the realization of profits (cf. Devine, 1994). Further, workers can revolt or pressure the state in a way that lowers this tax. However, in "normal" (noncrisis) times, capitalists receive positive profits, because crises are typically not as severe as the Depression and workers compete against each other. Developing the latter point, workers often side with "their" employers in the battle of competition, or with "their" nations in international competition, in hopes of getting benefits. This divides and rules them as a class, legitimating the system and preserving capital's supremacy over time.

The existence of exploitation is partly based on workers' conscious submission, so we should turn to the possibility of a social-democratic contract that can substitute for the COJL: workers might accept exploitation in exchange for a relatively good deal in terms of the distribution of benefits (Bowles and Edwards 1993, 136, 144). Capitalists put up with this situation because of the security that the contract provides.

This possibility is based on interpretations of the history of Sweden and similar countries; to some extent, this kind of contract has also existed in the "primary labor markets" of the rest of the capitalist world. In these cases, the type of consent based on the COJL and divide and rule is replaced in part by a more democratic and popular form of legitimation. Taxation begins to edge toward being "taxation with representation" and to stop being exploitation in a normative sense.

However, such a "social contract" is partial, conditional, and temporary. It is partial because it excludes many workers, either those who produce imported inputs or the "guest workers" who do menial tasks within the nation (and are exported during bad times). Even if democratic legitimation applied in Sweden or the primary labor markets, the divide-and-rule type of legitimation still applies for capitalism as a whole.

It is conditional because as soon as the social-democratic contract stops being profitable to the capitalists, capital strike will result or capital will flee to areas that constrain profit seeking less. This implies that the contract is temporary: the normal globalization of capitalism means that greater opportunities for capital flight arise, so that the contract becomes more likely to break down.

Alternatively, the social democratic system could be transformed into socialism through the abolition of capitalism. Not only has this never happened, but it seems unlikely. The social-democratic contract was won as a compromise because of the strong organization and socialist consciousness of workers pushing for something even better. However, social democracy itself is built on the subordination of this organization and consciousness to compromise, and so slowly undermines the possibility of future working-class victories.

In the current global economy, most of the old social-democratic programs are under attack and are falling apart, while primary labor markets are shrinking. This suggests a return to relying on the COJL and divide and rule in order to preserve exploitation. However, the possibility of a social democracy, at least a temporary one, cannot be denied in the far or intermediate future.

Fascism is a second alternative within capitalism to the COJL: state violence can be wielded to directly force people to work (cf. Kalecki [1943], 1971). This type of exploitation is relatively transparent and needs no profound analysis. However, just as with slavery, fascist rule seems inadequate for promoting high-quality work, productivity growth, and the like, since forced labor is usually poor labor. A fascist economy would not do very well in market competition with nonfascist capitalist powers, and so tends toward autarchy and military competition. The societal imposition of a COJL on workers seems to be a more "efficient" way of promoting capitalist accumulation. The fascist solution has been imposed only in situations in which capitalist social and property relations were threatened.

In sum, exploitation's existence requires societal impetus on workers to "pay their taxes" to the capitalist class, where the COJL is a substitute for the direct application of force or conscious consent in allowing these revenues to be received. Turn next to the *impact* of this type of societal pressure on the actual production of surplus on the micro level.

Subjection

The pressure to "pay taxes" need not cause the actual production of surplus; similarly, capital's supremacy is only part of the story, being necessary but not sufficient. The "anarchy in the social division of labor," namely, the unplanned and relatively harmonious cooperation of industries and firms through the market (in the absence of fascism or social-democratic planning) is complemented by "despotism in the workshop" (Marx [1867] 1967, 356). This subjection of labor by capital is instrumental coercion (threats of firing, etc.), referring to the direct capitalist rule *in production*, as opposed to voluntary exchange (the Roemer story): the coercer can impose a significant cost on the coercee for not complying with his wishes. COJL $\geq$ Cmin makes employers' threats credible.

1. Capital's supremacy cannot be sufficient, since it does not explain the existence of surplus: capitalists could use their macro-societal power to induce a pure redistribution that reduces the standard of living and/or net worth of workers. This would make capitalists like the kleptocratic elite seen in extreme libertarian statements about government, extorting taxes in order to waste them on luxury, war, and further tax collection, and steadily depressing peoples' standard of living and/or net worth. This is also similar to Marx's vision of precapitalist usury, which "impoverishes the mode of production, paralyzes the productive forces instead of developing them, and at the same time perpetuates these miserable conditions in which the social productivity of labor is not developed." ([1894] 1967, 596).

This degenerates into a stationary state, thus differing qualitatively from the capitalist exploitation that Marx explained; instead it can produce new real assets rather than simply redistributing them from others.

To rule out this purely redistributive, and thus self-limiting, exploitation theory and to define and thus understand the production of surplus, some standard of comparison is needed. Marx assumed that the workers are paid enough to reproduce themselves as a class over time (according to the culturally based and historically determined subsistence level). This captures the fact that workers' needs are more than just a matter of subjective wants; they are a matter of survival, not just physically but as human beings in society. If paid at subsistence, they need not reduce net worth to survive.

Marx stated the micro-etiology of exploitation as follows: surplus is produced if the work-day exceeds the value of labor power (VLP), which is the socially necessary, abstract worktime required to produce the daily wage determined by the subsistence level. Workers are exploited *despite* being paid the VLP, which is the standard defining nonexploitation. This complements the assumption that capitalists do not simply profit at each others' expense; in other words, the focus is on the macro creation of surplus rather than mere redistribution of a given product.

As seems appropriate nowadays, we will use an hour rather than a day as the unit for which workers are paid: the value of an hour of labor power equals the amount of socially necessary, abstract labor time needed to produce the hourly real wage. So the VLP is the real wage (RW) for an hour of labor power divided by the average output produced by the labor done during an hour of labor power hired (output per hour hired, the APL).

To use modern language, avoid further reference to the VLP and allude to RW and APL alone. Marx's issue can be restated as whether or not APL > RW. In turn, the APL is explained by the following tautology:

$$APL = (output/labor\ done)(labor\ done/labor\text{-}power\ sold) = q\,e \qquad (2)$$

where q is the effectiveness of labor done and e is the intensity of labor or the "degree of effort" (cf. Devine and Reich 1981). The ability of the capitalists to extract a surplus and exploit workers thus depends on technology and management systems, plus the ability of capitalists to depress wages.

Initially, changes in q (reflecting current technology and management systems) are largely ignored. Given this, the production of surplus depends on managers' ability to evoke sufficient effort from workers. The issue of technical change is addressed in paragraph (5).

Many have criticized Marx's assumption of the exogenously given RW. Instead, Friedman (1977, 267–9), Lebowitz (1992, 119–20), and others argue that RW is the product of endogenous class struggle. To assure generality, therefore, go beyond Marx to consider the case in which wages are set by steadily changing social needs and class struggle in the context set by the supply of and demand for labor power—and can change in response to exploitation.

Marx's micro-theory of exploitation is not dependent on the fixed RW. In the Marx/Goodwin theory, wages are the "dependent variable" ([1867] 1967, 620) rather than the independent variable that they were earlier, in *Capital*. The reserve army "confines the field of action of this law (of supply and demand for labor power) within the limits absolutely convenient to the activity of exploitation and to the domination of capital" ([1867] 1967, 639). That is, the cycle, labor-saving technical change, and the like ensure that profit squeezes are abolished.

2. Now assume RW constant, with its current value determined by what was received in the previous year (roughly, their customary standard of living, as in Bowles and Edwards 1993, ch. 4). Given this assumption, return to the issue of how the capitalists can succeed in getting more out than they put in to hire workers during this period. Marx's answer is simple: workers are not paid for the actual labor they *do* but instead for the cost of bringing themselves (their labor power) to work; their actual labor has no price on the market because it is not marketed. Further, they labor more intensively than necessary to exceed the

labor needed to produce the RW, while the capitalists can capture the benefits of management systems and technology that raises labor's effectiveness.

This theory is not contradicted by marginal productivity theory (assuming it to be valid). A profit maximizing capitalist equates the marginal productivity of hiring labor-power to the RW, which is the price of labor power. However, the wage is not *determined* by the marginal product of labor (MPL). Rather, as far as a competitive capitalist is concerned, labor-power market conditions (the COJL) determine the wage; then, the capitalist determines employment given that wage. Even if the RW is constant, the COJL helps to determine the degree of effort, the amount of labor done, and thus the marginal productivity of an hour of labor power hired.

3. Given the coercion allowed by the COJL, a central question is why it is that workers get paid for providing labor power rather than labor. Workers sell their time on the market and it is that time (labor power) that has a price; once they have struck a deal, they are under the capitalist's authority, and their product is the latter's property. The social relations within the workplace are distinctly nonmarket in character, involving much more than individual exchanges.

Recent research fits with Marx's vision: as Williamson (1975), Gintis (1976), and others explain, most jobs involve more than hiring an individual to do a single and simple task: complete contingent futures contracts between employer and employee are impossible. This fact's general acceptance has encouraged economists to increasingly distinguish between "labor sold" and "services rendered" and to worry about the principal/agent (P/A) problem. With the workers as agents and the capitalist as principal, the latter must discover how to get the agent to work hard in the real world of asymmetric information. Otherwise, embezzlers will steal from their bosses while slackers and petty bureaucrats will impede operations, making them unprofitable. Without dictatorial supervision, in the Marxian view, no profits will be received since inadequate amounts of work will be done to do more than pay for the wages.

Skillman (1995) argues that the P/A problem does not add anything significant to exploitation theory; rather than explaining why profits are *positive*, dictatorial supervision explains only why profits are *higher* than with self-supervised workers organized through markets. However, this argument that subjection is merely epiphenomenal misses the limitations of the neoclassical P/A literature. The neoclassical P/A article starts with a totally hypothetical "full information" Pareto-optimal economy and then introduces asymmetric information. However, Marx's standard for comparison in his exploitation theory is not the Paretian ideal, but rather a nonexploitative ideal of simple commodity production (posited by economists of his time). Marx, like others of his era, would have considered the notion of perfect information to be irrelevant. More importantly, the neoclassical view simply avoids the theoretical issue of the origins of surplus. If anything, its existence in the full-information model is implicitly assumed, with P/A problems leading to the imperfect realization of these profits. Though on the technical level, P/A models are unobjectionable, to explain positive profits we cannot start by assuming what we are trying to explain.

Skillman's (1995) effort follows the neoclassical pattern, except that he explains profits' existence with Roemer's "full information" theory. However, Roemer's theory simply assumes that APL > RW, while the scarcity of capital goods is insufficient to explain the actual production of surplus as opposed to the mere redistribution of an already-produced surplus. We need the more complete picture of institutional coercion to explain the existence of profits.

In fact, the P/A problem undermines Roemer's models, which lack any way to enforce contracts. Though the state is implicitly assumed to do the job, it lacks the resources (including information) needed to enforce each and every contract, even if it were possible to fully specify contracts ahead of time. State enforcement is thus, at most, complementary to the efforts of the contract enforcers whom capitalists hire or mechanisms that they use (including the COJL) to ensure contract compliance. Without the subjection of labor, contract compliance breaks down.

In sum, if we are trying to explain, rather than presume, the existence of a surplus, the P/A problem stops being an example of "inefficiency" defined relative to an imagined ideal but rather becomes a conflict over the amount of production—a variable.

4. Let us turn to an important practical concern that goes beyond the P/A problem and limits the effectiveness of such individual solutions to the problem as "bonding" (as happens with individual contractors) and the paying of efficiency wages to individuals. Since work occurs in groups, there are so many interdependencies—externalities *within* the workplace—amongst the various workers and their work that it is extremely difficult if not impossible to separate out the contributions of individual workers in the "team."

Alchian and Demsetz (1972) see the capitalist as a supervisor, who "monitors" the teams' inputs and outputs to avoid "shirking." The capitalist receives the "residual" gained through such monitoring. However, these authors do not note the fact that this residual accrues to the capitalist, not simply because of any supervision, but also because of ownership rights. With different ownership rights, the residual might be received by (for example) a workers' cooperative, in which workers supervise each other. Even given capitalist property rights, Alchian and Demsetz miss the way in which the reserve army of labor (and the COJL) allow the employer to threaten workers to get them to work in order to produce a surplus.

The collective nature of work suggests that workers have group interests (the production of collective goods, such as a leisurely pace of work) that conflict with the goal of the capitalist manager. This differs from Williamson (1975) or Stiglitz (1975), for whom the capitalist/manager and workers share a single collective good. However, these authors' vision is not totally wrong: while there exists a basic conflict of interests between capitalists and workers, in many cases, workers (fearing unemployment and hoping for raises) and their employers ally against the employers' competitors.

In view of the common conflict between profits and the workers' collective good, however, the capitalist tries to encourage the free-rider problem among workers, in order to divide and rule his employees (Marglin 1974; Devine and Reich 1981). Friedman (1977) and Edwards (1979) both emphasize the need for organized management systems to control workers, usually incorporating the divide-and-rule principle. In this vision, the capitalist control of production is more than simply a matter of setting up an incentive system and enforcing it; rather, it is a (micro) political problem, involving both potential and actual conflicts of interest. In this management relationship, the submission that was necessary to the perpetuation of supremacy is also needed to reproduce subjection over time. A rebellious workforce willing to throw spanners in the works or go on wildcat strikes will not allow subjection or exploitation.

In response to all this, the case of piece rates is often mentioned as a counterexample. However, as noted in Mathewson (1931) and Devine and Reich (1981), the payment of piece wages is very limited in application and, further, does not prevent political problems. Besides the problem of actually isolating an individual's contribution to the total product, one problem with market-like piece rates is that the *quality* of the pieces is impossible to contract ahead of time. Another is that workers band together to prevent the downward adjustment of piece rates that so often happens when they work harder. Unlike competitive farmers, who face a somewhat similar situation, workers find it relatively easy to do so because they often work together in a single workplace and thus find it easier to communicate and cooperate with each other, even if that cooperation is tacit while on the job. Both these considerations indicate that in addition to the piece rate, workers must submit to the authority of the employer. Piece rates and capitalist management/control systems are complements rather than substitutes.

5. As Marx realized, real wages may not be low enough (given technology, and thus the effectiveness of labor) to actually allow for exploitation to occur. Given the absolute limits set by *physical* subsistence needs, it may be impossible to reduce the RW. Increases in the intensity of labor may simply induce a higher cost of reproducing labor power, thus preventing the creation of a surplus. With undeveloped forces of production, therefore, it is quite possible that the degree of exploitation will be extremely low or even zero (Marx [1867] 1967, 511).

However, once capitalism takes hold of the production process—what Marx called the *real* subjection of labor by capital—it promotes growth in labor productivity, thus helping to assure the reproduction of exploitation over time. This real subjection is more stringent than mere supervision (formal subjection): it involves the capitalist control over technology and its introduction on the micro level. Capitalists are no longer dealing with workers who bring their own tools and knowledge to work (as with many craft workers even today, as in the construction industry); instead, they are replacing their own machinery with new and different types of capitalist-owned machinery and are monopolizing the technical knowledge developed by hired scientists and engineers.

Under real subjection, the capitalists can install the technology they want, one which raises the effectiveness of labor (q) without directly causing increases in real wages. Such labor-saving technological change also helps create a reserve army of labor (technological unemployment) and the economies of scale and scope that block workers' entrance into business.

Once established, the normal production of surplus can then be (for the capitalist) the basis for a virtuous circle of accumulation and the creation of further profits, even in the face of rising wages. After the initial stage, in which more overt force may be needed, the somewhat automatic Marx/Goodwin cycle and labor-saving technical change can make sure that wages do not rise too much to allow the production of profits, since the real subjection of labor implies that the capitalist controls investment and technical change. Such control is not present if production simply involves workers deploying their own tools.

At the same time, automation and similar techniques are used to lower the skill content of the work process, taking control away from craft workers (cf. Braverman 1974). In the end, workers may be relatively skilled, but both the machines and the knowledge are supplied by the capitalists or their institutions (such as technical schools) so that workers have no special advantage arising from their individual attributes. Unlike many craft workers in the building trades, for whom the ownership of skills and tools conveys certain advantages even in the absence of a union, under the real subjection of labor by capital, workers must band together to resist capital or to bargain collectively.

Despite the introduction of machinery and the deskilling of craft-based labor, exploitation remains a political problem at the micro-level. Even "unskilled" workers can devise ways to block the introduction of new machinery or to undermine its effectiveness if the capitalist has not solved the political problem. This can be done either via collective action (unions, wildcat strikes, etc.) by some subset of workers who manage to find a strategic location in the management structure (such as a bottleneck in the assembly line), or even by sabotage. Submission is still needed for exploitation to be reproduced over time.

6. Subjection is necessary but not sufficient; it is *complementary* to capitalist supremacy. First, subjection depends on supremacy, the lack of workers' options besides working for capitalists; the COJL gives subjection its force. In turn, capital's supremacy involves capitalist control over both investment and the introduction of new technology.

Completing the circle, these types of control require subjection. In an imaginary economy totally organized by self-employed craft workers using their own tools and knowledge, capitalists would have no direct control over real investment or technological change. If there were no COJL, the craft workers would face no disadvantage vis-a-vis contractors and bankers, so the latter could not force their decisions concerning investment and technology. With no direct control by capitalists over the workplace, there would be no way to get the craft workers to produce a surplus or to hand it over to the capitalists.

Secondary Exploitation

The six mainstream kinds of exploitation sketched out as pure cases represent "secondary exploitation." However, important "impure" cases exist, which are either mixed with and/or contribute to primary exploitation. Consequently, the simple case of "all exploitation arises out of industrial production" needs to be modified. Even so, primary exploitation sets the context in which secondary exploitation occurs.

1. Some capitalists—monopolists—have special positions that prevent the entry of competitors, meaning that their profit rate exceeds the average for the economy as a whole; they receive "super profits." Others—monopsonists—have workforces with a restricted ability to seek jobs elsewhere and are able to pay lower wages than on average, allowing the capitalists to "super exploit," to participate in exploitation more than others. In the latter case, if capital mobility is unblocked, the monopsonist will not receive an above-average profit rate in notional equilibrium, as other capitalists rush in to take advantage of below-average wages. However, it is possible that monopolistic and monopsonistic privilege are combined (as with the company town), in which case the company will receive super profits.

Unless the monopoly or monopsony is extremely important in the economy as a whole (which seems unlikely, given the magnitude of world capitalism), it will not affect the over all degree of exploitation. If this is unchanged, the monopolist or monopsonist will gain super profits only from other capitalists, who receive subnormal profits.

If these phenomena are extremely important to the operations of the economy, the capitalist economy has a significant admixture of feudalism or some other form of overt servitude, such as fascism. If these phenomena are the normal way in which business is operated, then they should raise the overall degree of exploitation, though it may hurt the long-term growth of labor productivity.

2. The P/A theory of exploitation has three levels. First, capitalist agents, such as the top managers of firms, are able to capture part of societal surplus in the form of exalted salaries, perks, stock options, and/or embezzlements, thus reducing the incomes of stock owners and creditors and getting more than justified from these principals' perspective. Their ability to do so depends on the primary exploitation of the direct producers. Though they may use their power in a way that limits the size of the surplus produced, that course will undermine their income in the long run.

Second, from the point of view of these managers, the members of the workforce are the agents. The latter can refuse to produce a surplus product. Further, if we use the customary standard of living to define the RW and, given the APL, the surplus product, workers can capture part of the latter by pushing to earn more than their customary level. This represents a central part of subjection, namely, the constant political problems that it involves.

Workers are sometimes seen as earning "employment rents," which some see as the exploitation of capitalists by workers. However, this is looking at matters backwards. Workers fear the COJL and thus produce a surplus, after which they may be able to win back some of the surplus that they created. They are not the exploiters.

Third, individual workers can gain at each others' expense. While such "opportunism" (Williamson 1975) can benefit individual workers in an "exploitative" way, this competition among workers (if kept within bounds) also divides and rules the workforce and encourages the production of profit: the back-stabbers in "office politics" can help the managers and owners by motivating workers to work hard to rise in the hierarchy rather than fight to attain collective goals. To management, such behavior must be kept within limits; doing so is part of the political problem that capitalist exploiters must face.

3. The free-rider problem is best explained in terms of a specific case, that of the destruction of nature and the exploitation of future generations. It is part of a Marxian theory of competition. In their efforts to survive the competitive battle, capitalists actively seek to internalize external benefits and externalize internal costs, often in innovative and highly creative ways that demonstrate an ability to plan ahead and delay gratification in the name of profit cf. (Hunt 1980; Devine 1993b). The successful development of new ways to dump costs on others can give a company a competitive advantage and temporary super profits that can be capitalized, allowing for further growth. Of course, on the macro-level, this behavior can eventually lead to the destruction of the natural conditions allowing capitalist exploitation to exist. However, a competitive capitalist cannot act on such knowledge. In other words, the free-rider problem is part and parcel of the way in which freely competitive capitalism works.

4. Just as for George, Marx saw the land-owning class as crucial. For both, landowners capture some surplus because they control scarce gifts from nature. The major difference is that George, having a different theory of profits, stressed a basic harmony between the urban classes. For Marx, on the other hand, landowners are able to grab a part of the aggregate surplus value, representing a redistribution from industrial capital, where surplus value is produced.

The landowner may also be an industrial capitalist (hiring farm workers to harvest the crop, etc.) In this "impure" case, the landowner is contributing to the aggregate surplus value. Further, the extent to which workers are landowners themselves (rather than being pure proletarians) limits the degree to which they can be exploited by normal capitalist means.

5. Marx's attitude toward rentiers was similar to that of Keynes, without sharing the latter's admiration of the entrepreneurs (industrial capitalists). The rentiers gain a share of the societal surplus value in the form of interest from their control of loanable money capital. However, industrial capitalists are the ones who induce the workers to produce the surplus in the first place. For Marx, unlike for Roemer, the rentier's pure money lending does not create the basis for the receipt of property income.

Of course, there exist cases of <u>impure</u> money lending, as when a loan-shark forces a worker to work hard and long. However, the loan-shark is not a rentier but instead shares some characteristics of an industrial capitalist, namely, the direct participation in the subjection of labor. As the P/A literature on banking points out, much money lending shares this characteristic (to varying degrees): the loaners ration credit, snoop into prospective debtors' personal lives, and impose conditions concerning collateral and the like (cf. Mishkin 1992: 171–78).

Given capitalist supremacy, namely, the threat of the COJL and the absence of alternatives—this type of behavior might induce an "I owe, I owe, so it's off to work I go" response on the part of workers, complementing the industrial capitalist's subjection, which (if common enough) raises the aggregate degree of exploitation. Without supremacy, the dependence of workers on industrial capitalists for their livelihood, however, the money lenders' hold over workers would be nil. Again, it is clear that the institutional coercion of labor is central to the exploitation story.

Even many or most of the independent producers living on the edges of capitalism (the petty bourgeoisie and home workers) are subject to capital's supremacy. In the extreme, they own neither the means of production (including raw materials) nor the means of subsistence (or have very limited access to these) and must gain access to them through the agency of the capitalists. These workers may not even own the homes in which they work and may be borrowing money to finance consumption. They are also threatened by the existence of the reserve army, as a merchant can "fire" home workers and hire replacements. They may also be competing in product markets with wage workers operating much more advanced equipment (i.e., with low-cost commodities produced under conditions of the subjection of labor by capital). Of course, some independent producers are not in this kind of bind: these are not exploited and instead are on the edge of joining the capitalist class.

6. The final theory of exploitation centers on the role of the state. Contrary to the popular image of Marx as a super-statist, he was hostile to the state, striving for its "withering away" (cf. Draper, 1977–90). In Marxian theory, the state is central to the existence of both supremacy and subjection over labor, since it helps create and preserve capitalist property rights. Under feudalism and other precapitalist modes of exploitation, the use of armed force (a characteristic role of the modern state) is inseparable from the "economic" relations between the lord and the serf: the former simultaneously collects rent and taxes, two incomes that cannot be separated. However, under nineteenth-century capitalism there was a societal division of labor between those sectors "monopolizing the legitimate use of force" (Weber [1918] 1946) and those that engage in purely economic activity. Taxes on capital may be seen as partly a matter of redistribution of surplus value to the state in return for services rendered to the capitalist class.

The state can also use its force in order to raise the degree of exploitation, as under fascism, or may emulate capitalists by directly engaging in production, as with state capitalism (e.g., the U.S. Tennessee Valley Authority). To some extent the modern welfare state (like social democracy) contributes to the production of surplus value by legitimating capitalism and its social relations. In these cases, the societal division of labor is fuzzy compared to classical liberal capitalism, so that taxes are not simply a deduction from (redistribution of) surplus value.

On the other hand, the state is "relatively autonomous": that is, it is not under complete capitalist control and does not always serve the interests of the capitalist class. It might serve only a fraction of that class, or there may be a P/A problem, this time with the state bureaucracy as the agent. As the Friedmans would be the first to point out, the state may go "too far" in the collection of taxes, feathering the government bureaucrats' nests with no obvious benefit to the capitalists or anyone else besides these parasites.

Third, and finally, the working class's political activity can (and sometimes does) succeed in winning benefits from the state in excess of the taxes they pay. While this also contributes to the system's legitimation and, as noted above, can thus raise the amount of surplus produced, to some extent workers can reduce the surplus left over for capitalists. In fact, these two effects may work together (as it has in Sweden for decades), where the state works to both increase the surplus through legitimation and decrease the surplus via distribution to workers, without hurting, and perhaps actually helping profits. In the end, however, as argued, social democracy cannot escape the laws of motion of capitalism.

CONCLUSION

The point of this chapter is to reconstruct Marx's theory of exploitation in modern terms, applying his surplus problematic, institutionalist perspective, and political-economic vision. The most profound type of exploitation—the one explained by Marx—involved, not simply the redistribution of existing assets, but the creation of new ones. The basic theory is both macro- and micro-institutional, and involves coercion. Exploitation might be likened to taxation without representation.

Whereas Roemer's effort to summarize Marx's positive theory of the capitalist exploitation of labor in a Walrasian framework severely limits the role of politics, this summary defense of Marx's theory is profoundly politicized on the complementary macro and micro levels. Nonarmed coercion based on the threat of costly job loss and the dictatorial rule of the workplace by the capitalist, including the real subjection of labor, the ability to revolutionize production by introducing new technology, form the microeconomic basis for exploitation. On the macro-level, the exclusion of workers from producing for themselves using the gifts of nature and the products of their labor (the means of production) creates the cost of job loss and the conditions allowing microeconomic subjection. Finally, there must be ideological submission by workers, in whose eyes capital's institutional coercion of labor must be legitimated if it is to continue. Further, severe economic crises must be avoided. As fits with Marx's emphasis on the nature of capitalism as historically limited, the persistence of exploitation is not *guaranteed*.

The discussion of secondary exploitation leads to the conclusion that the institutions allowing purely redistributive exploitation can be mixed up with and can sometimes even reinforce the production of surplus value.

Though it goes far beyond Marx's methodological framework, Roemer's *normative* definition (1982, 194) cannot be avoided. Any kind of criticism of "capitalist exploitation" seems somewhat futile if there exists no alternative, not only non capitalist but non exploitative, way of organizing production beyond reversions to precapitalist modes of production or to Stalinist economics. Given the importance of conscious consent, this is not just an academic matter: the absence of an alternative is clearly one of the factors that legitimates capitalist exploitation and allows its perpetuation.

REFERENCES

Alchian, Armen, and Harold Demsetz. 1972. "Production, Information Costs and Economic Organization." *American Economic Review,* 62, no. 5 (Dec.): 777–95.

Block, Fred. [1977] 1984. "The Ruling Class Does Not Rule: Notes on the Marxist Theory of the State." In Thomas Ferguson and Joel Rogers, eds., *The Political Economy: Readings in the Politics and Economics of American Public Policy.* Armonk, N.Y.: M. E. Sharpe, 32–46.

Bowles, Samuel, and Robert Boyer. 1990. "Labor Discipline and Aggregate Demand: A Macroeconomic Model." *American Economics Review,* 78, no. 2 (May): 395–400.

Bowles, Samuel, and Richard Edwards. 1993. *Understanding Capitalism.* 2nd ed. New York: Harper Collins.

Bowles, Samuel, and Herbert Gintis. 1990a. "Contested Exchange: New Microfoundations for the Political Economy of Capitalism." *Politics and Society,* 18, no. 2: 165–222.

___. 1990b. "Reply to Our Critics." *Politics and Society,* 18, no. 2: 293–315.

___. 1993. "The Revenge of Homo Economicus: Contested Exchange and the Revival of Political Economy." *Journal of Economic Perspectives,* 7, no 1 (Winter): 83–102.

Braverman, Harry. 1974. *Labor and Monopoly Capital.* New York: Monthly Review Press.

Devine, James. 1993a. "Microfoundations and Methodology in Modeling Capitalism." *Review of Radical Political Economics,* 25, no. 3: 51–59.

___. 1993b. "The Law of Value and Marxian Political Ecology." In Jesse Vorst, Ross Dobson, and Ron Fletcher, eds., *Red on Green: Evolving Ecological Socialism.* Winnipeg/Halifax, Canada: Society for Socialist Studies, 133–54.

___. 1994. "The Causes of the 1929–33 Great Collapse: A Marxian Interpretation." *Research in Political Economy,* Vol. 14: 119–94.

Devine, James, and Gary Dymski. 1989. "Roemer's Theory of Capitalist Exploitation: The Contradictions of Walrasian Marxism." *Review of Radical Political Economics,* 21, no. 3: 13–17.

___. 1991. "Roemer's General Theory Is a Special Case: The Limits of Walrasian Marxism." *Economics and Philosophy,* 7, no. 2 (Oct.): 235–75.

___. 1992. "Walrasian Marxism Once Again." *Economics and Philosophy,* 8, no. 1 (April): 157–62.

Devine, James, and Michael Reich. 1981. "The Microeconomics of Conflict and Hierarchy in Capitalist Production." *Review of Radical Political Economics,* 12, no. 4: 27–45.

Draper, Hal. 1977, 1978, 1986, 1990. *Karl Marx's Theory of Revolution.* 4 vols. New York: Monthly Review Press.

Dymski, Gary A., and John E. Elliott. 1989. "Should *Anyone* Be Interested in Exploitation?" *Canadian Journal of Philosophy,* supp. vol. 15: 333–74.

Edwards, Richard. 1979. *Contested Terrain: The Transformation of the Workplace in the Twentieth Century.* New York: Basic Books.

Friedman, Andrew L. 1977. *Industry and Labor: Class Struggle at Work and Monopoly Capitalism.* London: Macmillan.

Friedman, Milton, and Rose Friedman. 1980. *Free to Choose: A Personal Statement.* New York: Harcourt, Brace, Jovanovich.

George, Henry. [1879] 1942. *Progress and Poverty.* New York: Robert Schalkenbach Foundation.

Gintis, Herbert. 1976. "The Nature of Labor Exchange and the Theory of Capitalist Production." *Review of Radical Political Economics,* 8, no. 2 (Summer): 36–54.

Goodwin, Richard M. [1967] 1972. "A Growth Cycle." In E. K. Hunt and Jesse Schwartz, eds. *A Critique of Economic Theory.* Harmondsworth, UK: Penguin, 442–49.

Hunt, E. K. 1980. "A Radical Critique of Welfare Economics." In Ed Nell, ed., *Growth, Profits, and Property.* Cambridge: Cambridge University Press, 239–9.

Kalecki, Michal. [1943] 1971. "Political Aspects of Full Employment." In *Selected Essays on the Dynamics of the Capitalist Economy.* Cambridge: Cambridge University Press, 138–45.

Keynes, John Maynard. 1936. *The General Theory of Employment, Interest, and Money.* New York: Harcourt, Brace and Co.

Lebowitz, Michael. 1992. *Beyond Capital: Marx's Political Economy of the Working Class.* New York: St. Martin's.

Lindblom, Charles E. 1982. "The Market as Prison." In Thomas Ferguson and Joel Rogers, eds., *The Political Economy: Readings in the Politics and Economics of American Public Policy.* Armonk, N.Y.: M. E. Sharpe, 3–11.

Makhijani, Arjun. 1992. *From Global Capitalism to Economic Justice.* New York: Apex Press for the Council of International and Public Affairs.

Marglin, Steven. 1974. "What Do Bosses Do?" The Origins and Functions of Hierarchy in Capitalist Production." *Review of Radical Political Economics,* 6, no. 2: 33–60.

Marx, Karl. [1867, 1885, 1894] 1967. *Capital.* Vols. 1–3. Edited by Friedrich Engels. New York: International Publishers.

___. [1891] 1992. "Critique of the Gotha Program." In Robert Tucker, ed., *The Marx-Engels Reader.* 2d ed. New York: Norton, 525–41.

Mathewson, Stanley. 1931. *Restriction of Output among Unorganized Workers.* New York: Viking.

Miller, John. 1989. "Social Wage or Social Profit? The Net Social Wage and the Welfare State." *Review of Radical Political Economics,* 21 (Fall): 82–90.

Mishkin, Frederic S. 1992. *The Economics of Money, Banking, and Financial Markets.* 3d ed. New York: HarperCollins.

Obrinsky, Mark. 1983. *Profit Theory and Capitalism.* Philadelphia: University of Pennsylvania Press.

Roemer, John. 1982. *A General Theory of Exploitation and Class.* Cambridge: Harvard University Press.

Schor, Juliet. 1987. "Class Struggle and the Macroeconomy: The Cost of Job Loss." In Robert Cherry, Christine D'Onofrio, Cigdem Kurdas, Thomas R. Michl, Fred Moseley, and Michele I. Naples, eds., *The Imperiled Economy, Book I: Macroeconomics from a Left Perspective.* New York: Union for Radical Political Economics.

Skillman, Gilbert L. 1995. "Ne Hic Saltaveris!: Marx's Positive Theory of Exploitation After Roemer." *Economics and Philosophy,* 4 (Oct.): 309–31.

Sraffa, Piero. 1960. *Production of Commodities by Means of Commodities.* Cambridge: Cambridge University Press.

Stiglitz, Joseph. 1975. "Incentives, Risk and Information: Notes Toward a Theory of Hierarchy." *Bell Journal of Economics,* 6, no. 2 (Autumn): 552–79.

Tonak, E. Ahmet. 1987. "The U.S. Welfare State and the Working Class, 1952–1980." *Review of Radical Political Economics,* 19, no. 1 (Spring): 47–72.

Weber, Max. [1918] 1946. "Politics as a Vocation." In H. H. Gerth, and C. Wright Mills, eds., *From Max Weber: Essays in Sociology.* New York: Oxford University Press, 77–128.

Weisskopf, Thomas, Samuel Bowles, and David M. Gordon. 1983. "Hearts and Minds: A Social Model of U.S. Productivity Growth." *Brookings Papers on Economic Activity.* no. 2: 381–441.

Williamson, Oliver E. 1975. *Markets and Hierarchies: Analysis and Antitrust Implications.* New York: The Free Press.

Wolff, Richard D., and Stephen A. Resnick. 1987. *Economics: Marxian versus Neoclassical.* Baltimore, Md.: Johns Hopkins University Press.

6

Seen through a Glass Darkly: Competing Views of Equality and Inequality in Economic Thought

Edythe S. Miller

Schools of economic thought differ sharply in their analyses of the nature and causes of economic inequality. The conflicting interpretations follow closely from incompatible foundational principles and assumptions underlying the analytic structures; that is, they follow from inconsonant impressions of reality. The "scientific" theoretical tools and ideational constructs of the disparate schools of thought are themselves informed and colored by, and in turn inform and color, a distinctive cultural perspective and comprehension of reality.

This is not to suggest that reality exists only in the perception of it. To the contrary, it is a statement both of the existence of an external reality and of the contention that it is consciousness of the facts of reality, comprised not only of states of being but also of underlying causative and structural factors, that permits us to gain insight into economic conditions. Among the facts perceived differently are those related to inequality and power.

The orthodox, or neoclassical, school tends to deny, excuse, ignore, or downplay the existence of inequality and power. In contrast, the institutionalist school has always been concerned with inequality in its various manifestations, the varieties of invidious differentiation that often fuel it, the public policies that sustain it, and the patterns of dominance that control its arrangement. The different perceptions are due to fundamental divergencies in underlying philosophy and methods of analysis, in other words, to a clash of visions.

ORTHODOX AND INSTITUTIONAL PATTERNS OF THOUGHT

Orthodox schools of economics are based on concepts of individualism, rationality, and maximization and see economic actors essentially as passive reactors to pecuniary stimuli. Institutionalism, in contrast, sees humans as essentially social beings, both creations and creators of, as well as active participants in, the economic and social milieus. Moreover, institutional economics sees human motivation as multifaceted rather than singular, and as containing both rational and irrational aspects. Where the mainstream of economics denies the very existence of power, thereby rejecting the prospects of exploitative action, institutionalism sees power as pervasive in the society.

Neoclassical schools of economics posit efficiency as the goal of all economic endeavor, even as it is maintained that efficiency is a means rather than an end, and as it is denied that economics should have any part in the determination of ends. Moreover, because neoclassicism views resources as scarce and thinks in individualistic terms, it defines efficiency in individualist, allocative terms. Institutionalism, while viewing efficiency as an appropriate objective, looks to instrumental efficiency—a social concept that includes a large equity component—rather than allocative efficiency as a goal.

Institutionalism does not perceive a world of scarce resources. In contrast, it sees a world in which the once useless matter of existence successively becomes useful by virtue of new technologies and understandings opening up new means of defining and using resources. It sees a world, however, in which waste is sanctioned by limitations placed upon output to maintain price, tolerance of preventable unemployment, employment of individuals at less than potential, and denial of participation because of invidious attitudes toward members of specific groups. These tendencies are not diminished by the lip service given efficiency by orthodox economics; rather, if anything, they are magnified by it.

It is clear that the orthodox and institutionalist schools have disparate definitions of efficiency and inefficiency. Where the former sees efficiency as a matter of moving around the pieces on the chessboard of production, the latter defines inefficiency in terms of waste of human resources tolerated as a result of dominant economic belief. Moreover, while neoclassicism advances its view of efficiency as a value free concept and, indeed, claims to eschew valuing as an appropriate role for economics, goal setting is perceived by institutionalism as an appropriate, and indeed, unavoidable task of economics. Means and ends are viewed as interactive and unitary: the means chosen unavoidably influence the ends achieved, while ends become means in succeeding phases of activity. Moreover, institutionalism apprehends the individualism posited as a guidepost and beacon by neoclassicism as a morally imposed norm, and its view of economics as neutral as itself a value-laden judgment.

Orthodoxy accepts only a very limited role for government (or, for that matter, for any collectivity), seeing its appropriate role as no more than that of police officer, umpire, or at most, protector of individual rights. Institutionalism holds that there are important and necessary social tasks that require collective action and that their neglect often will have perverse and mischievous effects for the social and economic whole.

In other words, institutionalism sees economics as a problem solving science. In defining problems and assessing outcomes, it advocates the use of trial-and-error techniques to determine if perceived solutions to problems are appropriate, and adequate, to the task at hand. It sees economics as normative: value judgments neither can, nor should, be avoided. In defining problems and assessing outcomes, it advocates the use of democratic methods based in methods of experimentation and respect for differences of opinion. It sees learning and doing as unitary and interrelated: understanding and dealing with problems requires hands-on involvement with underlying causes and their manifestations (Lawson 1994, 512–14; Miller 1995).

Crucially, in its analysis, orthodoxy relies upon a hypothetico-deductive method, sometimes supplemented by crude empiricism. In the former mode, it reasons a priori from antecedent principle to logically consistent conclusion. Knowledge is viewed as a reflection of external antecedent reality and underlying principle given from outside the system (Rorty 1979, 10). That is, learning is perceived as cognizance of a natural order of things that is discoverable only a priori through logical reasoning (Miller 1990, 723–24). In the latter mode, it looks to the isolated event for confirmation.

The process relies upon formalistic, highly mathematized models, based in patterns of static equilibria. Of necessity, important and relevant factors are excluded from analysis. If anything, the system prides itself upon its use of a small number of unrealistic assumptions (the use of Occam's razor, or explaining much by little). Neoclassicism sees regularity in economic affairs. Therefore, economics is viewed as capable of prediction, and prediction is taken as its appropriate aim.

However, it should be emphasized that the simplifying assumptions that initially are utilized for purposes of analytical facility and clarity end up as belief. The ideal is misconstrued as the real. For example, the existence of a competitive market is accepted both as abstraction and actuality. The utilization by producers of the marginal tools of microeconomics is accepted as dictum as well as example. Homo economicus, the hero of all orthodox stories, is seen not simply as symbol, but as fact.

Moreover, in the orthodox view, if there is deviation from some of the conditions included as part of these models, acting "as if" the anomalies did not exist will achieve desired results (for an early statement of the as-if proposition, see Friedman 1953, 20–21). Thus there are proposals in which treatments applicable to the orthodox ideal of, say, a competitive market are proposed for application to a contrary set of circumstances. For example, contestability theory suggests that the application of competitive tools such as open entry in a tightly oligopolistic market will achieve competitive results; the theory of the "natural" rate of unemployment twists definitions to fit a view of the world (the prevalence of full employment) dictated by the ideal. In a Procrustean process, the world is trimmed to fit the models. This would not really matter all that much—it would remain a matter of fanciful pastime—except for the fact that what starts out as simplifying assumption and turns into belief, ends up as guide to action—and this may be very harmful indeed.

The individualist focus of the neoclassical paradigm posits the individual transaction, expressed through the private market, as the central economic fact and the appropriate focus of analysis. That is, orthodoxy proposes the individual bargain and contract as both ideal and norm. It acknowledges certain exceptions but views them as rare and, for the most part, trivial. Policy departures, therefore, require justification. The burden of proof and persuasion lies with those who argue from an alternative perspective. The framework is contractarian and voluntaristic. Individuals bargain until they reach a mutually satisfactory result. Transactions are negotiated by individuals of equal power pursuing private, selfish ends. The norm and standard is the model of the perfectly competitive market. Market activity is apprehended as consensual. The imposition of outside rules or authority is viewed as unnecessary and mischievous, except under narrowly specified, anomalous conditions. As opposed to the consensuality of the individual transaction, government is seen as coercive. Private bargain and contract result in mutual benefit, for if it were not so, the parties would not have entered into agreement. The existence of power disparities is ignored.

On the question of the relative status of employer and employee, for example, it is claimed: "The relationship of each team member to the *owner* of the firm ... is simply a 'quid pro quo' contract. Each makes a purchase and sale. The employee 'orders' the ... [employer] to pay him money in the same sense that the employer directs the ... [employee] to perform certain acts" (Alchian and Demsetz 1972, 783, emphasis in original).

Institutionalism, in contrast, takes the real world as its text, often using a case study or a pattern-modeling and story-telling (Wilber 1978) approach. It is evolutionary and processual, eschewing equilibrium analysis. It sees little, if any, regularity in economic life. It takes as its purpose, not prediction, but rather explanation in causal terms, which is required for the adjustment of structure to increase the responsiveness of the process to human needs.

While institutionalism does not dismiss individual exchange activities as matters of interest, it sees individuals as essentially interrelated and interdependent rather than independent and reactive. It envisions a positive role for collective, social action in solving the various problems confronting society. Many of the structural factors underlying the problems examined by institutional economists have to do with disparities of power, inequalities of status and condition, and the permutations and effects of privilege in its myriad forms.

EXTENSIONS AND VARIATIONS OF NEOCLASSICAL ECONOMICS

The works of the many "new" schools of economics that are prominently on display in the "acceptable" academic journals and the academy—for example, transaction cost economics (the so-called new institutional economics), the public choice school, the revealed preference school, the rational expectations school, and even the new Keynesianism (or, to use Joan Robinson's apt description, "bastard Keynesianism")—are little more than neoclassicism dressed in new, if rather threadbare, clothing (Robinson 1981, 34–35). Some of the assumptions and precepts of neoclassicism (for example, perfect rationality and perfect certainty) are relaxed, others (for example, utility maximization) are fuzzed up to a degree, but the philosophic core remains intact. Description advances in terms of the self-interested individual; individual exchange is the major area of interest; voluntarism and contractualism are the preferred modes of activity; and the market the only appropriate area of endeavor. Government involvement—indeed, collective action of any kind—are beyond the pale.

I have previously made this point in regard to transactions cost theory (Miller 1993). In fact, both Ronald Coase and Oliver Williamson, who are among its major formulators, have pointed out that transactions economics should be viewed, not as an alternative, but as an extension and complement to standard theory (Coase 1991a, 48; Williamson 1975, 1; Miller 1993, 1043).

Coase is especially clear on this point, emphasizing that the orthodox economic principles—principles of competition and profit maximization, of the equality of prices and costs, of consumer sovereignty—that he initially had learned continues to nourish his work. Of particular importance is the teaching he absorbed, as part of his academic mother's milk, so to speak, about the potential harmfulness of government activity and regulation. Government, in his view, most frequently promotes a monopoly organization rather than a competitive one and itself often serves special, and not general, interests (Coase 1991b, 37–38; Miller 1993, 1042–43).

Indeed, while certain of the assumptions of orthodoxy are loosened (for example, "bounded rationality" is substituted for the unqualified variety), the public policy prescriptions of the "new economics" are virtually identical to those of the old. The theory of contract that it explicates is held to be applicable to any type of transaction; social control of almost any type is rejected, while power disparities are ignored (Miller 1993, 1051–52).

The other "new" economic schools are similarly reliant upon aspects of individualism, rationality, and maximization. Rationality is sometimes qualified as bounded rationality. Maximization may be somewhat altered in form, but it remains an abiding principle. Thus, while profit maximization remains the motivator of producers, utility maximization sometimes is transformed into, for example, revealed preferences or need fulfillment. Through it all, however, the focus on individualism and individual market exchange remains.

The utilization of revealed preference, as opposed to utility maximization, came about at least partly as a result of a certain amount of discomfort with aspects of utility—for example, its ambiguity and immeasurability. Utility cannot be seen, it cannot be felt, it is difficult to describe and, worst of all, it cannot be quantified. An additional sticking point, of course, is the perceived inability to make interpersonal comparisons of utilities. Preferences, on the other hand, are viewed as visible, they are made evident through the choices people make in the market. One can look to that choice, then—a discernible fact— rather than to underlying preferences for economic analysis. As with its forebear, revealed preference is apprehended as contractual and voluntaristic.

Institutionalism perceives a continuous back-and-forth flow between the individual and the social, and among individuals, which unavoidably influences individual desire and its expression. It looks, therefore, to the origin of wants, often finding it in social factors such as emulation and socialization. Wants are viewed as often learned or acquired.

Mainstream economics, in contrast, sees a one-way flow, perceives social utility as the sum of individual utilities, and views utility or preference as innate to individuals. The focus of analysis is upon the interaction of the forces of supply and demand in the market. Outcomes are the result solely of supply and demand considerations. The factors that underlie these forces, such as preferences and technological change, are taken as given or exogenous or else have applied to them the ceteris paribus principle. That is, analysis proceeds on the basis of immediate market effect rather than underlying explanatory cause.

Moreover, specific inferences are drawn from the preferences revealed through market results. Thus, it is said that people "choose" lower-paid work because it is less risky or because it involves less responsibility; they "choose" part-time work or abstinence from the labor market because of the value placed on leisure. Women "choose" not to work because they desire to spend time at home with their children or in household management.

Similarly, income distribution is viewed as solely the outcome of factors of supply and demand. That is, the price received for one's labor is perceived as a result of free choices made about training that determine skill level, as well as about work and the marginal productivity of the laborer. Inequality is assumed to have individualistic causes (Clark 1995, 4–5). Matters extraneous to the model, such as the influence of family background or ascribed social roles on these "free" choices, are ignored. Also overlooked is the prevalence and influence of labor unions, except insofar as they are viewed as impediments to the free operation of market forces.

Institutional economists long have pointed out, in contrast, that production is essentially a cooperative endeavor and that it is impossible to isolate the individual contributions of the separate factors. In fact, economists have recognized—and dismissed—at least since the time of John Stuart Mill that the distribution of income is strictly a matter of social discretion rather than one of scientific economic law.

So in thrall are mainstream economists to the orthodox perspective, that even some formulations that attempt to include in analysis such factors as altruism and sympathy rely upon an individualistic model. Thus, it is contended that an individual utility function may include an interest in, or concern for, the well-being of others (Hausman and McPherson 1993, 686–87). Even most such treatments, however, fail to grasp the inseparability of the individual and the social, and the extent to which the social permeates and conditions individual preference and behavior.

The case made for competitive markets by mainstream economics is cloaked in a rationale of efficient allocation. Underlying it, however, is an argument for individual freedom (Hausman and McPherson 1993, 675). It is interesting how often the term *freedom* appears in the lexicon of economics—free private enterprise, free markets, freedom of contract, and so on. These, of course, are moral judgments. They ignore the extent to which individual actions are sensitive to social stricture and customary mode of thought and to the important distinction between "freedom from" (the simple absence of restraint) and "freedom to" (the ability, frequently dependent upon a supportive economic and social network, to maximize individual interaction and connectivity, and fulfillment of potential).

For example, Amartya Sen points out that the priority given by the public choice school to procedural over consequence based methods is illustrated in its view of the role of government. The public choice school believes that the role of government is to maintain a framework of rules under which individuals have maximum freedom to pursue their private interests, rather than that of advancing a general public interest (Sen 1995, 11). The view expressed is indistinguishable from that of the mainstream generally.

POLICY APPLICATIONS

The distinctive theoretical frameworks that typify the analyses of the different schools of economics carries over into every applied field of specialization. Moreover, analysis in virtually every subspecialty has important implications for questions of equality, inequality, and power.

I should point out that it is important to understand the foundations and implications of the orthodox perspective, despite its inapplicability to real-world problems, primarily for two reasons. First, it is important because there is an increasing tendency to define as narrowly economic all manner of sweeping public policy questions. Broad policy issues involving, among many others, the nation's educational system, its health and medical system, inner-city decline, race and gender discrimination, and the plight of the emerging nations of Eastern Europe all are seen as narrowly technical and as amenable to standard market analysis.

One result of this view of things is that when it comes to the implementation of programs to address these issues, the orthodox position is by far the most popular, if not, indeed, the only one that carries weight and influence with contemporary policy makers. For solutions to these pressing general problems, which are viewed as narrowly technical, the policy makers turn to the experts in economics. Experts accepted as credible are those who have received recognition—the Nobel laureates, those who publish in "reputable" journals, those on the faculties of the prestigious universities. These are the establishment economists. They are invariably drawn from orthodoxy. Their solutions almost without exception are market oriented, tilted toward economic "efficiency" and "neutrality" and toward strategies of laissez-faire. If we care about how our world is being tended, these positions require critical scrutiny.

In addition, it is important to recognize the role played by prevailing doctrine in legitimizing and encouraging particular behaviors. When the dominant orthodoxy maintains that persons are motivated purely by rational self-interest, the self-seeking behaviors of individuals are both justified and encouraged, in turn validating the theory. The belief that all markets are competitive or, in any event, will yield competitive results if only restraints are removed justifies current policies of deregulation. The wholesale removal of restraints in itself lends credence to the view that all markets are competitive. In other words, orthodox approaches both identify what is recognized as genuine scholarship and help shape popular attitudes and behavior (for example, by defining what activities "count" as "work").

Indeed, it is part of the genius of the prevailing system of thought that it leads many of its victims to conclude that they are, instead, its beneficiaries. Thorstein Veblen long ago noted the importance of emulation as a motive force in the economy. It is an aspect of American economic history that a true European type class system never developed in this country. The lack of class consciousness resulted in individuals of the lowest reaches believing they could achieve the highest realms. Moreover, the privileged were not afflicted with dreary notions of the responsibilities of *noblesse oblige.*

This carries through to popular attitudes about the oppressiveness of all government activity. Moreover, the view of government as but one among many competing interests further diminishes respect for it (McKenna, Wade, and Zannoni 1988, 221). Even many of those who stand most clearly to benefit from services the delivery of which (given current attitudes about public debts and deficits) is dependent upon taxes, as well as those who are not disadvantaged by a progressive tax system, see taxes as burdensome and intrusive, as a fallout of nonstop persuasion to that effect. A converse of this that has much the same effect is that of observers (of both genders) who see womens' lower status as a privileged state. There is an identification of the private interest of the powerful with a public one, and the belief by even the most disadvantaged that it works to their advantage.

Consequently, when we repeatedly are advised that government action serves only to burden the most productive members of society and that the imposition of taxes results only in obstruction, we are happy to believe it and to vote into office those who will relieve us (and the economy) of this perceived unnecessary ordeal. A tilt of fiscal policy toward the privileged, in the name of increased opportunity for the lower echelons, reinforces a bias toward the powerful as benefactors of the economy: they are the providers of its jobs and economic development.

The very definition of equality as equal opportunity (see Tool, this volume), is based upon a concept of freedom strictly as "freedom from" and reinforces the view that status is accounted for solely by individual traits. If external restraints are removed, the argument runs, the race will go to the fleet of foot. This ignores the impediments to fleet-footedness imposed by such factors as lack of family connections, inherited wealth, reserved family slots at prestigious universities, and invidious attitudes toward members of specific groups, to say nothing of the elevated self-image promoted by such matters.

At the same time, because the theoretical framework underlying the prescribed policies ignores the reality of power and inequality, their programmatic approaches actually compound that reality. Policies that "get government off our backs" (for example, a diminution in the use of macro tools, a substitution of monetary for fiscal policy because monetary policy is perceived as more "neutral," the weakening of programs that sustain the most vulnerable members of society, deregulation of oligopoly) promise to increase the power of the most powerful, and lessen that of the least.

The emphasis upon the role of orthodox economic thought in legitimizing existing patterns of power and privilege should not be understood as a contention that the dominant economic wisdom is the sole cause of the acceptance of current beliefs and practices. Clearly, the yield would not have been so abundant if the seed had not been cast on fertile ground.

The intellectual history of the United States reveals alternating cycles of acceptance of conflicting ideals of equality and liberty (indeed, of contrasting definitions of equality) and of conflicting attitudes about the desirability of government activity. There is little doubt, for example, that in the western United States, where ideals and romantic notions of individualism were probably as strong as any, the government nevertheless played a very active, and welcome, role in development. Nevertheless, "rugged individualism" survives as a romantic ideal. The accomplishment of establishment economics was not to play the sole role in achieving acceptance of this belief set, but to provide it an academic gloss, that is, the intellectual cover that authenticates and grants legitimacy.

It is important to recognize that when it comes to the applied fields, the policy recommendations of orthodoxy are all of a piece. In each practical application, and irrespective of the realities of power in the field, orthodox recommendations are based on assumptions of free markets. Almost without exception, their recommendations run along laissez-faire lines, arguing for more rather than less market orientation, and for lesser rather than greater government involvement. It carries no little irony that this is achieved in the name of ethical neutrality.

This is true irrespective of whether the questions involve issues of the regulation of business monopoly and oligopoly, of tax and expenditure policy, of welfare policy, of labor policy, or of race and gender discrimination; that is, in total disregard of the nature of the subject matter. Orthodox economists survey the economic and social landscape and observe free markets as far as the eye can see.

Institutional economists, in contrast, seek to tailor solutions to the nature of the problem. They recognize, first of all, that the market is an economic symbol, rather than a concrete physical reality. It is not a locale peopled by real human beings and stocked with real commodities. The concept of the market is highly metaphorical. Moreover, the allegory may or may not be reflected in real life. Thus, the arena within which real world economic activities take place may be relatively unfettered or it may be restrained by power and dominance of various kinds. This lack of uniformity and the variability of what is assumed constant in orthodox theory is one of the bases for institutionalist advocacy of experimentation to test the usefulness and appropriateness of recommended policies.

The standard employed by institutionalists in assessing policy is human betterment, a concept that is admittedly value laden. The criterion of human betterment is identified with the goal of shaping a social design that is hospitable to the maximum fulfillment of the potential of its citizens, with particular attention to the requirements of the most vulnerable, a course not necessarily disadvantageous to the presently powerful, if they would but see it. The approach advocated will not provide ready-made answers to all conceivable problems, as does the orthodox paradigm. Institutionalism does not envision this as an option because it confronts a more complex world than does orthodoxy. The criterion of human betterment is advanced, not to provide consistent and universal answers, but in an attempt to set the parameters of the debate.

Thus, the neoclassical model presents a vision of reality in which individual achievement knows no bounds. Free markets permit unfettered individual movement up the employment and status ladders. The system recognizes no ceilings (glass or otherwise) to achievement other than those imposed by such individual traits as sloth and lack of industry. It recognizes the infrequent occurrence of "natural" barriers that prevent the efficient operation of market forces. In the industrial organization and so-called welfare economics literature, these are most often identified with economies of scale and the production of a narrowly defined class of public goods, and they are assumed to be a minor and diminishing factor in the economy. These barriers to the free operation of markets are characterized as market imperfections or market flaws, terms that in themselves imply the existence of an otherwise perfect, or near perfect, market. However, institutionalism perceives a very different set of facts.

For example, a recent book by Wallace Peterson details the relative deterioration, over the past two decades, of economic conditions in the United States. The decline includes decreases in the real incomes of workers, stagnation in family incomes, and declines in the growth of productivity. He contrasts this with the growth and expanding expectations that characterized the immediate post-World War II era (Peterson 1994).

Peterson notes the contemporary fixation on free markets as a solution to all problems. He points out that the private market is socially created, and that it could not exist without the existing system of property law and contracts, a system that is socially created and enforced (Peterson 1995, 4). Giving an ironic twist to the concept, he points to current market failures in our economy: the failure to achieve full employment, the decreasing quality of jobs and the income they provide, the deteriorating distribution of income. There is not, it need hardly be noted, anything "natural" about these market failures; they are humanly created and could be socially cured.

Harry Trebing often has detailed in public utility industries (for example, Trebing 1995) existing incentives, and configurations, for price discrimination, cross subsidization, and risk shifting, along with patterns of market dominance, high profits, the exploitation of strategic advantage, and the inequitable distribution of burdens and benefits. These traits of exploitative pricing and market control are intensified by the current antigovernment fervor and increased deregulation. Neoclassical rationalizations to the contrary notwithstanding, contemporary patterns will damage economic viability. There is no denying, however, that the potential for increasing market power inherent in current trends has not diminished the enthusiasm for supplanting economic regulation and weakening social control in these industries.

These differences in foundational principle and practical application between institutional and orthodox thought are not confined to the examples mentioned here. Indeed, they are equally applicable to each subspecialty and problem area in economics.

CONCLUSION

Orthodox economics envisions a world in which isolated self-interested individuals seek maximum pecuniary advantage, thereby inadvertently causing a net social gain. It recognizes no public interest distinguishable from the aggregation of individual gains. It describes the economy by means of formal mathematized models, based upon logical deduction from a priori principles, and it sees its role as prediction—not explanation, and definitely not remediation. Its vision of reality is one in which persons of equal attributes bargain to reach mutually propitious positions, netting a social gain. It perceives individual action favorably, because it sees it as consensual. It views collective action as perverse because it is, by definition, coercive.

Policy positions flow ineluctably from this sole perspective. Without exception, and regardless of circumstance, neoclassicism argues for maximum individual latitude and minimal, limited government. It contends for the provision of information in preference to the setting of standards. Irrespective of the presence or absence of various manifestations of dominance and privilege and of market imperfections (of both the traditional and nontraditional variety), mainstream economics interprets all circumstances as confirming its own view of the world. Above all, orthodoxy sees a world in which tangible power does not exist. The view is of a system malleable to the application of standard economic remedies. Government controls are to be removed, and market forces are to be allowed to determine results. If this creates hardships for persons, well then, it is only a short-run phenomenon. In the long run, and on the average, the best of all possible worlds will come to pass.

The interpretation of real world facts that run counter to a vision of reality as confirmation of that vision is a condition denominated by psychologists as cognitive dissonance. It conceives a world consonant with cherished prejudice, irrespective of brute, irreducible facts. Orthodox economics seems to be in a permanent and unyielding state of cognitive dissonance. It is a perspective that institutional economics consistently has challenged by reference to real world realities.

In conclusion, I feel that one omission on my part merits some explanation. It may have received some notice that, despite the fact that this chapter is part of a collection devoted to radical institutional perspectives, my inquiry into interpretations of inequality in neoclassical and institutional economics does not once employ the phrase "radical institutionalism." This has not been a matter precisely of coincidence. It is because, despite earnest effort, I am not at all clear about what radical institutionalism is or how it differs from the unqualified variety. My admittedly incomplete scrutiny reveals primarily, if not, indeed, exclusively, similarities between radical and nonradical institutionalism in both perspective and method. Nor does the distinction seem to serve any particular purpose, having the appearance of a classic case of a distinction without a difference. That is, the distinction between traditional and radical institutionalism (if I may be permitted the use of an oxymoron as well as a redundancy, respectively) seems to me to be both unclear and pointless.

To an extent, however, the last comment involves a bit of hyperbole. In truth, institutionalism is both radical and conservative. It is radical in that it presents a vision that is the converse of the traditional philosophy that has been the polestar of mainstream economics from the time of its inception. As such, it is new and fresh and disdainful of ruling authority.

It is important, however, to recognize a contrary characteristic of institutionalism in the aspect that speaks to methods and patterns of institutional change. J. Fagg Foster identifies as one of his "fundamental principles of economics" that of minimal dislocation (Foster 1981, 941–42). He describes this as specifying that institutional adjustments must be capable of integration into prevailing institutional patterns that are not viewed as problematic by the community; that is, that the adjustments must be unlikely to disrupt the institutions not apprehended as troublesome. This is an element of the democratic character of institutionalism. In a sense, it is also representative of its conservative nature.

In truth, institutionalism is neither radical nor conservative. Yet, in a sense, it is both. It is part of its incisiveness and integrity that it follows no controlling path.

REFERENCES

Alchian, Armen A., and Harold Demsetz. 1972 "Production, Information Costs, and Economic Organization." *American Economic Review,* 62, no. 5 (Dec.): 777–95.
Clark, Charles M. A. 1995. "Legitimizing Inequality: Some Recent Attempts at Explaining Rising Inequality [mimeo]." Paper presented at the annual meetings of the Association for Evolutionary Economics, January, Washington, D.C.
Coase, Ronald. 1991a. "The Nature of the Firm: Meaning." In Oliver E. Williamson and Sidney G. Winter, eds., *The Nature of the Firm: Origins, Evolution, and Development.* New York and Oxford: Oxford University Press, 48–60.

___. 1991b. "The Nature of the Firm: Origin." In Oliver E. Williamson and Sidney G. Winter, eds., *The Nature of the Firm: Origins, Evolution, and Development.* New York and Oxford: Oxford University Press, 34–47.

Foster, J. Fagg. 1981. "The Fundamental Principles of Economics." *Journal of Economic Issues,* 15 (Dec): 937–42.

Friedman, Milton. 1953. "The Methodology of Positive Economics." In *Essays in Positive Economics.* Chicago: University of Chicago Press, 3–43.

Hausman, Daniel M., and Michael S. McPherson. 1993. "Taking Ethics Seriously: Economics and Contemporary Moral Philosophy." *Journal of Economic Literature,* 31 (June): 671–731.

Lawson, Tony. 1994. "The Nature of Post–Keynesianism and Its Links to Other Traditions." *Journal of Post Keynesian Economics,* 16 (Summer): 503–38.

McKenna, Edward, Maurice Wade and Diane Zannoni. 1988. "Keynes, Rawls, Uncertainty, and the Liberal Theory of the State." *Economics and Philosophy,* 4 (Oct.): 221–41.

Miller, Edythe S. 1990. "Economic Efficiency, the Economics Discipline, and the 'Affected-With-A-Public-Interest' Concept." *Journal of Economic Issues,* 24 (Sept.): 719–32.

___. 1993. "The Economic Imagination and Public Policy: Orthodoxy Discovers the Corporation." *Journal of Economic Issues,* 27 (Dec.): 1041–58.

___. 1995. "Institutional Economics and Eternal Verities [mimeo]." Paper presented at the annual meetings of the Association for Institutional Thought, April, Oakland, Calif.

Peterson, Wallace C. 1994. *The Silent Depression: The Fate of the American Dream.* New York: W. W. Norton.

___. 1995. "Institutions and Institutionalism: Crisis and Opportunity [mimeo]." Speech at the J. Fagg Foster Award Ceremony, University of Denver, April, Denver, Colo.

Robinson, Joan. 1981. "The Age of Growth." In *What Are the Questions? and Other Essays.* Armonk, New York: M. E. Sharpe, 33–42.

Rorty, Richard. 1979. *Philosophy and the Mirror of Nature.* Princeton, N. J.: Princeton University Press.

Sen, Amartya. 1995. "Rationality and Social Choice." *American Economic Review,* 85 (Mar.): 1–24.

Tool, Marc R. 1996. "Choose Equality [mimeo]." Reprinted in William M. Dugger, ed., *Inequality: Radical Institutionalist Perspectives on Race, Gender, Class, and Nation.* Westport, Conn.: Greenwood Press.

Trebing, Harry. 1995 "Structural Change and the Future of Regulation." *Land Economics, 71* (Aug): 401–14.

Wilber, Charles K., with Robert S. Harrison. 1978. "The Methodological Basis of Institutional Economics: Pattern Model, Storytelling and Holism." *Journal of Economic Issues,* 12 (Mar.): 61–89.

Williamson, Oliver E. 1975. *Markets and Hierarchies: Analysis and Antitrust Implications.* New York: The Free Press.

Part II

CRISIS OF THE WELFARE STATE

7

Choose Equality

Marc R. Tool

The maxim, "Choose equality and flee greed," originated with the Greek, Menander (Arnold 1949, 574). In this chapter, it appears as an emotive admonition, an ethical dilemma, a social imperative, an economic necessity, and finally, a political agenda. This maxim was used by Professor John C. Livingston as the summarizing construct for the closing pages of *Fair Game?* (1979)—his insufficiently heralded treatise on affirmative action and the reduction of racial inequality. Livingston offered some thirteen persuasive reasons for choosing equality. The purpose of this chapter is to extend and apply his arguments concerning why and how a community should follow the maxim, "Choose equality and flee greed." In particular, the normative underpinnings for the construct of equality are addressed. Put analytically, the intent is to embed the instrumental theory of social value (Tool 1986, 33–84) in the normative maxim of "Choose equality." The conviction that drives this inquiry is that a further consideration of the meaning and significance of equality may encourage scholars and others to develop more fully, and employ instrumentally, their reflective and creative capabilities in conflict resolution and social problem solving. This is an advocacy essay in neoinstitutional political economics that builds, in part, on the Livingston contribution, including in particular his critiques of meritocratic efficiency and its corollary, equality of opportunity.

DIMENSIONS OF THE MAXIM

The "choose equality" maxim implies an *emotive admonition* because it fuels a continuing and vigorous public debate between egalitarian and antiegalitarian contenders over affirmative action, sexual harassment, administration of justice, antidiscrimination laws, immigration controls, and the like. Over the last three decades particularly, charges and countercharges of discrimination and reverse discrimination have punctuated impassioned arguments over institutional adjustments addressed to egalitarian goals (Green 1981; Letwin 1983; Sowell 1994). Neoinstitutionalists urge egalitarian policies and programs. The social pressures to pursue or reject equality are at issue. The "choose equality" maxim implies an *ethical dilemma* as individuals confront their own attitudes and actions toward, for example, gay rights, interracial marriages, gender denigration, and religious intolerance, on the one hand; and, more generally, their advocacy of particular social and economic policies, on the other. What ethical tenets—what principles of social value—apply, and what is their source of validation? Ethical relativists defer to cultural and community standards and customs; to each, his or her own. Values are relative to person and context. Ethical absolutists defer, in contrast, to religious canons, philosophic "truths," or ethnic dicta as criteria. These are given, formalistic, and generally not amenable to normative challenge or evidential inquiry. Instrumental value theory is neither ethically relative nor ethically absolute (Tool 1986, 285–89); it locates ethical premises in the social process and instrumental inquiry about that process (Tool 1993, 120–31). It is the underlying normative philosophy reflected in this essay. Neoinstitutionalists are pragmatic instrumentalists (Bush 1993). The ethical meaning of equality is at issue.

The "choose equality" maxim implies a *social imperative* as it compels the acknowledgment of the impact of invidious discrimination on individual self-images and morale and on social conceptions of family, class, and caste. The use of differences of race, gender, ancestry, ethnicity, age, stature, power, wealth, and the like (to categorically demean individuals and groups, routinely promote hierarchical placement, and systematically reduce discretion), generates inequality. The failure to "choose equality" generates inter- and intra-group conflicts, destroys community, and makes problem resolution difficult, if not impossible. Neoinstitutionalists promote noninvidiousness in all participatory contexts. The psychic and social impact of inequality is at issue.

The "choose equality" maxim implies and acknowledges an *economic necessity* to reduce the horrendous personal and social costs of discriminatory inequality, as reflected in the maldistribution of income, wasted resources, undeveloped and underutilized talent and capacities, destructive internecine conflict over income shares, and related impediments to the provisioning process (Rogers 1982; Osberg 1984). Included as well are inequitable advantages generated for the wealthy and powerful in tax codes and entitlements provided by governments (Stern 1973; Peterson 1991, 57–94). Neoinstitutionalists seek reductions in the degree of economic inequality. The productive and distributive impact of inequality is at issue.

The "choose equality" maxim implies, finally, a *political agenda* because it imposes questions on the community at large of "who chooses" and "what is chosen." It implies as well a governance system in which the "choosers" are democratically selected and held accountable. The locus and use of political control over policy is typically the controlling determination in reshaping beliefs and behaviors concerning equity and equality. Political discretion typically reflects the possession of de facto economic power (Verba and Oren 1985). All the policy measures providing or promoting participatory involvement— illustratively, educational access, affirmative action, equal employment opportunities, removal of restrictive covenants, income maintenance programs, and progressive taxation—are institutional innovations promoting equality that were generated by political judgments and actions (Schwartz 1983). Democratic ends-in-view require democratic means for their realization. Antiegalitarians view such measures as "excessive coercion" (Bauer 1983, 360–82). Neoinstitutionalists insist on democratic determination of participatory and distributional policies. The political quest for equality is at issue.

MEANINGS OF EQUALITY

The analytical consideration of equality and inequality requires some clarification of meanings and usages. Four meanings of equality are introduced: the first two are incompatible with instrumental value theory, while the latter two are compatible.

Equality as sameness or identity of persons is, of course, denied by common knowledge and ordinary experience. Individuals are biologically and culturally unique. No two persons have identical genetic ancestry, cultural conditioning, physical stature, intellectual potential, or actual experiences. Authoritarian advocates of inequality have long seized on this referential meaning to undergird their invidious claims to deference and dominion. The quest for instrumentally warranted equality does not presume identity or equivalence of power, status, treatment, or income. "Equality means the absence of artificial and arbitrary barriers. It does not, of course cannot, mean the absence of individual differences, physical, mental, or even social" (Ayres 1961, 187). Equality, rather, is a condition in which individuals' uniqueness of capacity and learning are socially supported and develop instrumentally to guide their exercise of discretion in shaping and ensuring participation.

Equality of opportunity, at first hearing, sounds remarkably persuasive. Here equality is presumed to refer to a condition where everyone has an equal chance to compete; talent, guile, drive and luck will produce a winner who survives. As "almost the official theory today" (Schaar 1964, 870), the equality of opportunity construct implies a competitive scramble of equally positioned individuals who emerge from a common starting gate and race competitively to maximize their respective inherently unequal capabilities and opportunities. "To the victor belong the spoils." Critical is the presumption, in the vernacular of the day, of a "level playing field." As subsequent analysis will explore at some length, equality of opportunity is a recipe to enhance inequalities.

Equality as an antecedent human right, is addressed in the U.S. Declaration of Independence: "All men are created equal ... they are endowed by their Creator with certain inalienable rights ... among these are life, liberty and the pursuit of happiness" (Commager 1948, 1: 100). "In a society that regards life as a competitive racetrack [the Revolutionary philosophers] warned, the vices of avarice and ambition will be legitimized and fostered" (Livingston 1979, 202). "Men are capable of embracing the ethic of equality, but 'where avarice and ambition beat up for recruits, too many are prone to enlist.'" (perhaps Livingston's favorite quote, from John Taylor, in Livingston 1979, 205). The founders' vision of equality was "categorically opposed to the idea of opportunity to compete for scarce prizes. It was an affirmation of fraternity and human solidarity, as well as of individual moral autonomy, not a celebration of a society that offers the main chance to the man on the make" (Taylor, in Livingston 1979, 208). The Declaration affirms the right to be and to belong (Schaar 1970, 151), but neither its warrant nor its significance depends on a metaphysical origin in nature or God. It affirms that persons, simply as human beings, should be accorded developmental and involvement options without invidiously discriminatory denials. Membership in the human community per se connotes, not sameness, but participatory access and the discretionary dignity accorded by that access (cf., Gilbert 1991, 61–72). However, the nature of that participation must itself be warranted by instrumental value judgments.

Equality as achieved results is warranted when participation and distribution, as outcomes, are such as to fully facilitate the instrumental involvement of all members of the community. However, equality of results does not necessarily connote equivalence or identity. The quest is not for what Fagg Foster called "equational justice" (Tool 1986, 126–34), a balance of efforts and rewards, of pleasure and pain, or of cost and benefit; neither is it the pursuit of equal income shares, as G. B. Shaw once recommended (1928, 19). The quest, rather, is for achieved outcomes that, acknowledging differential capacities, instrumental needs, and developmental potential, enhance the community's ability to embrace and support the development of each member. *Equivalence* in substantive realization is not required, but gross disparities of achieved results grounded in status, wealth, and coercive power, for example, are not "required" either. Indeed, such disparities serve as stimuli to inquiry into the equitability of achieved outcomes.

In sum, the following analysis abandons equality as sameness, critiques equality of opportunity, supports equality as a human right, and recommends the achievement of greater equality as instrumentally warranted outcomes.

STRUCTURE OF THE CHAPTER

In the hope and expectation that *emotive admonitions* may be modified by the discussion in the remainder of the essay, I will forgo their further specific consideration here. I turn then in Part 2 to the *ethical dilemma* by giving brief consideration to instrumental social value theory, in contradistinction to utility value in *this* context. In Part 3 the *social imperative* is addressed by incorporating and adapting Livingston's treatment of meritocracy and efficiency and his assessment of equality of opportunity. In Part 4 the *economic necessity* of equality is considered by exploring concepts of personal and social cost.

Finally, in Part 5, a *political agenda* is proposed that points direction and considers institutional adjustments to permit us more regularly to "choose equality."

THE ETHICAL DILEMMA: SOCIAL VALUE THEORY

In social inquiry, ethical principles function as criteria in the appraisal of participatory contributions of individuals as reflected in their inherent and developmental capabilities and behavior. The basic question is this: Which appraisals of judgment and conduct threaten or destroy the opportunity for individuals to be treated equitably, to experience the "equality of being and belonging" (Schaar 1970, 151)? The application of such ethical tenets is intended to define the extent and character of participation for individuals in the social process generally. Value theory explains the character and grounding of such ethical principles, which may guide individual conduct as well as direct social change. Three kinds of social value theory of particular pertinence in this chapter are ethical absolutism, ethical relativism, and ethical (pragmatic) instrumentalism (Bush 1993, 59–107).

Ethical Absolutism

Ethical absolutist affirmations of ethical tenets are rooted in particular philosophic, cultural, and religious traditions and are accepted and defended as articles of faith or belief. They are perceived as a priori principles of anterior and external origin. They are neither the product, nor the continuing object, of empirically grounded inquiry. Interpretative variations, which engender rivalries and schisms, are not uncommon. In whatever form, these ethical tenets are presumed to have universal and continuing relevance and applicability. They are not necessarily grounded in demonstrable evidence or experience. Examples would include biblical dicta concerning homosexuals, papal encyclicals defining female roles and participation, fascist pronouncements denigrating race and ethnicity, conservative affirmations of the natural sanctity of private ownership, and culturally embedded conventions elevating and sustaining family, clan, class, and caste.

Ethical Relativism

Ethical relativist admonitions are normatively ambivalent; they both claim and disclaim ethical tenets in inquiry. Taking the latter claim first, the insistence is, for example, that economics is a positive (and not a normative) science. "Economics is a science of means; it does not prescribe ends" (Posner 1983, 350). "Economics deals with the ascertainable facts; ethics with valuations and obligations" (Robbins 1952, 148). Value judgments reflecting ethical tenets are allegedly outside the universe of discourse of economists.

The former claim is reflected in the classical and neoclassical traditions of economic inquiry in the acknowledgment of the omnipresence of normative facets of inquiry. Bentham's classical "hedonistic calculus" embodying the pleasure principle is familiar (Bentham quoted in Mitchell 1967, 171–234). Contemporary neoclassicists make extensive and continuing use of the Paretian optimum as their only admitted ethical premise. (Alexander quoted in Hook 1967, 107–111). Common to each is the underlying utility theory of social value. For classicists, including Marx, labor was the measure of value; for neoclassicists, price is the measure. The ethical ought is to maximize utility, satisfy tastes and preferences, and make someone better off with out making anyone worse off, where "betterness" is referenced in utility (cardinal or ordinal). Wants, tastes, preferences, and the referent for being better off are all given, anterior to inquiry. Their substantive content is typically excluded from inquiry. In consequence, utility based judgments are ethically relative.

Ethically relative judgments, then, are rooted in the utility meaning of social value. Utility value theorists sometimes admit (but do not explain) the cultural emergence of that which satisfies. Such admissions do not impinge on their analytical models. They consider the free market system to be the most efficient instrument through which the maximization of utility, as measured by price, occurs. The efficient operation of this unfettered market system is both the ethically warranted, and the politically pursued, judgmental approach.

However, are unfettered markets really blind to color, indifferent to gender, and ambivalent to the character of preferences? Not really: to mention only one reservation, market participation is dependent on prior access to money income and credit. Where race, gender, class, caste, and ethnicity, for example, define or delimit individual access to money income, they specify the extent and character of market involvement; the market system, in fact, reflects and affirms the invidious use of human differences. Utility value theory cannot speak to the *character* of preferences. Its ethical relativism often screens from obvious view ethically absolute preferences for racism, chauvinism, and elitism. In its reinforcement of invidious distinctions, the unfettered market is not *amoral*, it is *immoral*.

Pragmatic Instrumentalism

Instrumental value theory offers a markedly divergent response to the task of creating and employing ethical premises as criteria of judgment. It is neither ethically absolute nor ethically relative; it is the normative vehicle for analysis of the meaning and significance of choosing equality.

The instrumental value principle encompasses the following criterion: do or choose "that which provides for the continuity of human life and the noninvidious recreation of community through the [creation and] use of knowledge" (Tool [1979] 1985, 293). Operative normative tenets include coevolutionary continuity, noninvidious relations, community enhancement, and warranted knowledge dependency. Elsewhere, various aspects of this social value theory have been explored (Tool 1986, 1993; Bush 1988, 1993; Hickerson 1988). Bush, in particular, augments the theory by providing a derivative concept of "progressive" change. Institutional change is progressive "when, for a given fund of knowledge, ceremonial patterns of behavior are displaced by instrumental patterns of behavior" (1988, 151). Since ceremonial patterns are reflected in the invidious use of distinctions among people and since such invidious judgments are the source of most inequalities and inequities, progress depends on the continuing erosion of ceremonial/invidious assessments and their replacement with instrumentally warranted judgments. For our purposes then, *choosing equality is a necessary condition to generate and sustain social and economic progress.*

The ethical dimensions of the instrumental value principle of immediate concern here are the constructs of "invidious judgments" and "recreation of community." Veblen used the term *invidious* "in a technical sense as describing a comparison of persons with a view to rating and grading them in respect of relative worth or value—in an aesthetic or moral sense. ... An invidious comparison is a process of valuation of persons in respect of worth" (Veblen 1934, 34). Choosing equality requires an ethic that provides for progressive reduction of the use of invidious measures of relative worth.

The recreation of community is served by recognition and response to the inescapable interdependencies of all human communities and the continuing need to adjust institutional regularities. The denigrative impairment of any part cripples the community generally. The denial of health care to any segment, for example, threatens the larger community both financially and physically. Earlier I wrote:

Democratic equality refers to a condition in which, through participatory (choice-making) involvement of all persons, "the being and belonging"—hence the dignity—of each member is affirmed. The affirmation is precisely that "advantages"—political prerogatives, real income, communal responsibilities, educational access—shall be shared, not based on indexes of who is deserving, or by application of [invidious] evaluative principles, but on the basis of mutuality, interdependence and common humanity. ([1979] 1985, 326)

The instrumentally warranted ethical judgment of "choose equality" affirms conceptions of human worth and dignity.

THE SOCIAL IMPERATIVE: THE LIVINGSTON LEGACY

The invidious use of distinctions among persons—race, gender, class, caste, ethnicity, age, power, wealth—has the effect on individuals of eroding self-worth and motivations, generating intergroup conflict, impairing the development of warranted knowledge, and wasting human and material resources. To "choose equality" is to acknowledge the continuing presence of such impediments and to urge their progressive removal. I turn now to contributions of Livingston for insights with which to address this responsibility.

Livingston's *Fair Game?*

To set the context, I offer some brief comments about the Livingston volume as such. The proximate task of *Fair Game?* was to provide a philosophic and analytical undergirding for the program of affirmative action as a corrective for race-grounded denial of access to education and employment for persons of color. The Supreme Court's decision in the *Bakke* case concerning admission to the University of California at Davis medical school provided a timely and pertinent universe of discourse on the basic issues (*Bakke v. Regents of the University of California*, 18 Cal. 3d 34 [1976]; cited in Livingston 1979, 273). Affirmative action, originating in the 1960s, "was designed to produce the group results required by the doctrine of equal opportunity, based on the assumption of racial equality." It was, and is, a policy "in the struggle for racial justice" (Livingston 1979, 10).

In the first half of the work, Livingston deals directly and insightfully with the pros and cons of affirmative action. The case *against* affirmative action is formidable and thought to be associated with democratic values. That "anti" case is, allegedly "pro-equality, grounded in the Constitution, against discrimination and prejudice, mindful of past injuries, protective of private freedom against governmental intervention, and rooted in a commitment to equal opportunity and the rule of merit" (1979, 28). The basic proposition in the argument against affirmative action "is that discrimination on the basis of race is unjust, and that when such discrimination is reflected in law or public policy it is unconstitutional as well" (29). Livingston unravels the confusion in these arguments relating to the distinction between racial quotas and goals (19–27), to charges of reverse discrimination (48–63), to claims that affirmative action is demeaning to its beneficiaries (64–71), and to constitutional questions of equal protection (81–114), among others. In each case he demonstrates that affirmative action is not the enemy of democratic goals but a necessary instrument for their realization. His arguments may be extended to encompass affirmative action to address issues of gender discrimination if appropriate attention is paid to the differences between race discrimination and gender domination.

In the second half of this work, Livingston moves from the particulars of affirmative action to a more general consideration of the philosophical premises that ground equality and to analytical approaches that facilitate its conceptual reformulation. He returns to the particulars of the earlier pages for illustrative material as needed. For our purposes, I wish to call attention to two foci of his more inclusive analysis: (a) his critique of social efficiency and meritocracy and (b) his critique of the corollary, equality of opportunity.

Meritocracy and Efficiency

For Livingston, meritocracy "describes a technocratic and bureaucratic social order in which individuals occupy places in a hierarchy of income, status, and power that they have earned exclusively on the basis of their demonstrated individual abilities" (1979, 18). Indeed, their "differential status and differential income" constitute the incentives that stimulates the appearance of an "elite of talents." The ideological sources of meritocracy lie more with social Darwinism than with Jeffersonian democracy (122). As Julian Huxley put it: "Our new idea-system must jettison the democratic myth of equality: human beings are not born equal in gifts or potentialities, and human progress stems largely from their inequality" (quoted in Livingston 1979, 123). For the older view of equality that "everybody could be somebody" meritocrats insist (in words of Mark Hanan) that "when everybody is somebody, nobody is anybody" (quoted in Livingston 1979, 123).

Contemporary meritocracy assumes a "radical, natural inequality among men," a belief in a "trickle-down process" of elitist support for the many (noblesse oblige), a faith that real merit is reflected in "social position, wealth and power," a "commitment to efficiency and economic growth as highest social goals," an insistence on "law and order as the basis for social stability," and a contention that "equality is a thin veil for the malignant envy of the masses." At bottom is the insistence that elite status is after all "achieved rather than ascribed" (1979, 124–25).

Contemporary meritocracy differs from the Darwinian tradition in two respects, however. First, where the older view presumed a broad spectrum of talents culminating in money making, to which most could, with effort, aspire, the newer view narrows merit to an "intellectual aptitude" or "brain power" (1979, 129). "Meritocracy means opportunity for the intellectually gifted few." It is "a bald doctrine of 'every man in his place'"(131). Second, where the Darwinists assumed a natural competitive selection process from which emerged the fittest individuals, modern meritocracy's elites are "self-chosen, having been co-opted into elite status by the previously existing elites" (133).

Livingston summarizes the point: "Meritocracy does not seek to justify the inequities of the existing order; it simply overlooks them. It ignores the inequalities of opportunity that lead to economic inequalities just as it neglects the heritage of injustice that handicaps racial minorities"(133).

From an instrumentalist perspective, the meritocratic position cannot be sustained as a defense for inequality of access, status, income, or power. The whole of its case rests on forms of invidious discrimination—the use of measured intellect to define elites and to denigrate those who, allegedly because of race, ancestry, gender, social and economic status, lack "intellectual aptitude." The effect is to diminish and impair the full development of all persons in the community. Returning to the categorical characteristics of contemporary meritocracy, the following critical observations are offered:

There is a demonstrable difference among persons on all manner of indices of stature, temperament, developmental potential (both physical and intellectual), cultural backgrounds, and more. How much is hereditarily given and how much is culturally developed is a continuing subject of the nature-nurture inquiry. However, the concept of "natural talents" (e.g., "intellectual aptitude") is no more than an area of potential development. People are largely a product of culture. Even IQs are amenable to enhancement. Absent recognition and development, and "natural talents" are stillborn. Capacities for reflection, organization, manipulative skills, artistic expression, and physical prowess emerge as cultural developments of genetic potentials. In sum, "merit," however defined, is a cultural product and a response to prior institutional judgments. Instrumental judgments to identify and support talents of all sorts erode all claims to meritocracy.

The presumption of a trickle-down process, "through which the superior talents of a few make possible a bearable life for the many" (Livingston, 1979 124), is without foundation. Evidence will not support any such claim. For example: income distribution by quintiles remains remarkably constant and inequitable over time. Indeed, most recent data indicate increasing inequality (Peterson 1994, 98–110). Elites are largely self-perpetuating through family, corporate, and bureaucratic structures. Where invidious discrimination on race and gender has been reduced, it appears to have been engendered by direct legislative and judicial intervention and direction.

The claim that real merit is reflected in existing social position, wealth, and power is a conjectural, self-serving cliché. There is no competitive market mechanism sifting and sorting to ensure that only the competent gain access to elitist membership. Moreover, it is difficult to regard the political system as accomplishing this goal, although it is sometimes attempted. Since self-identification and one's sense of one's own significance are tied typically to positions of peer recognition, wealth, and power, then vociferous defenses for, and perpetuations of, elitist status are merely invidious, and not instrumental, affirmations. The possession and use of power over others is itself a major conditioner of subsequent belief and conduct.

Efficiency and economic growth are conventional claims to meritocratic significance, but the normative dimensions are ignored. Does meritocratic efficiency sustain existing power systems or ensure the wider generation and distribution of real income? Economic growth is of what character, and on whose behalf is it being generated? Whose economic interests are really being served? When these questions are addressed and appraised with criteria from instrumental value theory, the claims of meritocrats for antiegalitarian measures to perpetuate elitist rule become unpersuasive.

The deference to law and order of meritocrats, is in large part, a posture to ensure the perpetuation of the status quo and the existing positions of power and wealth of those so identified. The maintenance of public order is essential in any democratic society, of course, but any spillover effects that convert this legitimate concern into a means to sustain loci of unaccountable control perpetuate inequality.

Envy by the masses of meritocrats probably does exist. Veblen's attribution of emulation suggests as much (1934). The propensity of the poor to play lotteries in the hopes of making a financial leap into the circles of the wealthy is also suggestive. However, the envy (and anger) are more likely fueled by an absence of career ladders, the presence of gender and race discrimination, the intimidation of the resourceless, and the denigrative absence of personal and social status. The quest for greater equality is not a thin veil of malignancy but a concern to achieve the right to be and to belong in the larger community.

Equality of Opportunity

The foregoing exploration of meritocracy is of course one aspect of equality of opportunity—the "master American myth of competitive inequality." It is the "magic formula by which the rhetoric of democracy is made to serve the substance of the aristocratic ideal" (Livingston 1957, 223). It is the vehicle through which "careers open to talents, the achievement ethic, the efficacy of competition, [and] the reconciliation of equality and liberty" are realized (Livingston 1973, 55). It does not argue that "*everyone* can be rich, powerful and famous;" it argues that "*anyone* can be." Competitive inequality means "success evaluated in terms of the failure of others; and wealth, power, and fame defined by the relative poverty, powerlessness, and invisibility of the losers" (Livingston 1979, 21). Again, equality of opportunity in fact means competitive inequality. In the words of John Schaar, the doctrine

asserts that each man should have equal rights and opportunities to develop his own talents and virtues and that there should be equal rewards for equal performances. It recognizes that inequalities among men on virtually every trait or characteristic are obvious and ineradicable, and it does not oppose differential evaluations of those differences. (Schaar 1970, 136)

What value theory informs the "differential evaluations"?—ethical relativism?

The defense of equality of opportunity—the right to engage in competitive inequality—is vulnerable to five fatal analytical and empirical challenges. First, the notion that competitors start even, and then begin to demonstrate their inequalities is, of course, a fraud. The analog of a starting gate for a competitive race does not apply. As Bellamy argued, economic equality is the necessary precondition for equality of opportunity. For the competitive struggle to be called, "without mockery, a fair test of the qualities of the contestants" it would be essential "to equalize their educational equipment, early advantages, and economic or money backing" (quoted in Livingston 1979, 125). As Livingston put it elsewhere, "those without boots have extraordinary difficulty lifting themselves by their bootstraps"(1979, 155). *The alleged competitive race advantages the already advantaged.* The playing field is never level in the sense of an even start: advantages rooted in money, power, education, position, discretion, ancestry, ethnicity, and more determine who gets on the field and with what competitive instruments.

Second, once one has started on a competitive struggle for place, recognition, and income, inequalities still prevail. There is routine bureaucratic resistance to competitors coming from below. The system, public and private, works to protect those who have already arrived. "America is committed ... to an achievement ethic. But as a national ideal it is honored in our rhetoric and systematically sabotaged in our practices. America, despite our rhetoric, is a tenured society" (Livingston 1973, 59–60). Tenure, as institutionalized security of employment in one form or another, is not limited to educators; it is sought by board directors, union members, civil servants, bureaucratic administrators, and CEOs, among others.

Third, in the meritocratic view of equal opportunity, there is a confusion of merit with worth. There is an inversion of private and public perceptions. In Livingston's words

Invidious judgments of groups, inherently social in the nature and impact, are relegated to the private realm of individual conscience. At the same time, judgments of the relative worth of individuals, made on the basis of their imputed intellectual value to society, become public. The genius of the Declaration of Independence was to make the universal equality of human worth a public principle. (1979, 155)

Meritocratic "true believers" erode the Declaration premise. On their terms "properly private judgments of the merits of others are elevated into a public standard for judging their relative worth, and the properly public standard of equal human worth dissolves into individual preferences. Inequality becomes the public principle" (155–56).

Fourth, the presumption that free competitive markets provide equality of opportunity rests on an ideological illusion about the nature of actual markets. The presumption that talent, drive, pluck, and luck will give each participant economic opportunity ignores the realities of institutionalized markets. Actual markets are, typically, institutional complexes comprised of habits and routines (Hodgson, 1988 123–38). As neoinstitutionalists consistently reconfirm, markets are behavioral and attitudinal structures that are created and managed to accomplish specific purposes of negotiated exchanging, market sharing, administered pricing, and status generating outcomes (Tool 1995, 47–92). Rules regarding participants' admission and conduct are prescribed and proscribed. This habituated institutional fabric both limits and expands options. Markets do not necessarily reward commensurate with talent and effort. The invidious use of race and gender distinctions, for example, knocks the rungs out of career ladders (e.g., "glass ceilings"); indeed, they often preclude access to any such ladders. Insider "old boy" networking, family ties, union rules, legal shelters and perquisites, wage patterns and contours, and financial incentives, among others all shape and pattern career paths. Cultural backgrounds, lingual skills, computer competencies, college degrees, and the like formally define and delimit access.

Accordingly, claims to equality of opportunity in any particular context, where talent, effort, pluck and luck are presumed to win out in a competitive scramble on "a level playing field," are at best a rarity, and more likely a screen or cover for the realities of institutionalized power and its use, which is often for invidious purposes. Although "Americans never accepted the idea of social hierarchy based on natural inequalities" (Livingston 1979, 149), they have been conditioned to pretend that equality of opportunity existed and that it precluded an increasing dominion by a social and financial elite (Peterson 1994, 93–128). The contrary is the case; equality of opportunity is not the rule. As Schaar observes:

The doctrine of equality of opportunity, which in its origins was a rather nervous attempt to forestall moral criticisms of a competitive and inequalitarian society while retaining the fiction of moral equality, now ironically magnifies the natural differences among men by policies based on an ostensibly equalitarian rationale. The doctrine of equal opportunity, social policies and institutions based on it ... all conspire ... to produce more and more inequality. (Schaar 1970, 139)

Fifth, and finally, equality of opportunity as a construct of guidance or an end sought is normatively, and hence morally, barren and without credence. It is equality of opportunity to do what? There appears to me to be a studied avoidance of posing the question of what kinds of consequences are presumed to occur where equality of opportunity is pursued. Those who emerge from the competitive scramble are presumed to have "merit." Membership in the victorious elite, however, is not enough to warrant instrumental accolades. The fact of possession of power, wealth, and status is no testament to its legitimacy. The social value theory of neoinstitutionalists permits a sorting out and assessment of the consequences invoked in competitive struggles for position and power. On its face, given the drive for power and wealth, most such efforts will have only, or mainly, an invidious warrant. Instrumentally warranted behavior is not impossible for elites, but it is difficult. The simple drive to retain the identity of, and membership in, the elite, however identified, suppresses instrumentally warranted behavior addressed to problem solving. Moreover, equality of opportunity, as Schaar has shown, is incompatible with the democratic ethic (Schaar 1970, 142–46). It reinforces the status quo, generates invidious divisions, encourages hierarchies, and delimits discretion. Finally, it leads, says Schaar, "to moral arrogance on the part of the winners and to the taking of moral holidays by the losers" (151). The possession of wealth and power by winners is an automatic invidious index of merit; aspirations to emulate such conduct by the losers compromises their social morality as well. Winners and losers become coconspirators against a democratic and humane social order in which human worth is assumed and accepted and human merit may be developed and applied instrumentally. Being and belonging are not at issue; rather, continuously at issue is the creation of a noninvidious community.

THE ECONOMIC NECESSITY: SOCIAL COSTS OF INEQUALITY

The pursuit of equality, I have suggested, is also an economic necessity and, as we shall see, a political agenda. Equality is an economic necessity because its absence generates an enormous array of differing sorts of social costs: Individuals are denied access, participation, and skill enhancement; the social order is denied productivity, growth, and stability.

Neoinstitutionalists reject social cost notions rooted in utilitarian constructs of neoclassical orthodoxy, such as the irksome expenditure of effort (labor), painful abstention from consumption (saving), and cost-benefit evaluations in pursuit of Paretian optimality (better-offness). From a neoinstitutionalist perspective, social costs are real costs that "refer to the destructive consequences to individuals, their social order, their environmental and ecological systems and their ideational and material resources of invidious and ceremonial judgments that impair or impede the social and provisioning processes" (Tool 1995, 144). Social costs sometimes also arise from a corollary tenet: the "underdevelopment of, and/or the failure to apply, instrumentally-warranted reasoning and judgments as provided and refined by the current state of reliable knowledge" (121). Here the effort is to apply instrumental analysis to the recognition, reduction and/or removal of social costs so identified. There are enormous social costs of inequality to individuals and to the social order generally. Given the present constraints, we can mention only a few.

Social Costs of Inequality to Individuals

The invidious use of human differences to deny, arrest, or reduce the flow of money income to individuals, whether as earned income or grants, generates an immediate crisis for most who are affected. Given the present levels of economic specialization and consequential interdependence, nearly all the material means of life must be purchased in markets managed by discretionary and empowered agents. Money income provides the general tickets for participation in the exchange process. Ordinary buyers face, but have little impact on, administered prices.

Pecuniary consequences of low or reduced levels of money income, and/or discontinuity in its flow, produce a continuing economic trauma for perhaps the lower two-fifths of the community, who must try to cope with needs that frequently exceed their capacity to fulfill. The degree of inequality in income receipt in the United States is indicated by the fact that families in the lowest fifth receive about 10 percent of that of the highest fifth. The top 5 percent of families receive significantly more income than the bottom 40 percent of families (Peterson 1994, 100–101).

And the inequities are increasing. In a recent paper L. Randall Wray provided a striking summary:

Since 1973, real weekly wages have been falling at nearly 1% per year. The poverty rate stopped falling and rose for nearly all groups except the elderly. Depending on the measure used, between 3/4 and 4/5 of all Americans have a lower standard of living now than in 1973. We've had 4 official recessions and increasingly severe financial crises occur more frequently. The pace of deterioration increased dramatically during the 1980s. Wealth is now as unequally distributed as in 1929 ... and the bottom 60% now has a smaller share of income than in 1947. During Reagan's Springtime in America, half of all new jobs paid less than the poverty line. More than 10% of the population is now on food stamps—a record. ... The problem is concentrated among the young, less educated, minority and female-headed households. Currently, 12 million people live on less than half the official poverty line—3/5 of those are in families headed by women—and forty percent of all the poor are children. (1995, 2)

Actual or relatively shrinking money income, for the majority in our society, means lowered nutrition, less access to health care, more meager housing, critically diminished support for children, and frequently increased social strife and disorder. Extensive interruption of even that flow of income precludes, in addition, making home mortgage or rental payments, maintaining insurance coverages, providing educational support for children, and securing medical care (except for emergency room visits).

Does this extensive and increasing inequality of income receipts reflect recourse to invidious and ceremonial judgments? What part, for example, does discrimination based on gender and race play in generating and sustaining such inequities? No definitive answer is possible here, but indicative is the fact that women, comparably employed, earn a scant two-thirds the income of men; while blacks, comparably employed, earn some four-fifths of whites (Osberg 1984, 115). Also indicative is the fact that in 1990, the poverty rate for whites was about 11 percent; comparable rates were, for blacks, 32 percent, for Hispanics, 28 percent, and for female, single parents, 37 percent (Peterson 1994, 134). That invidious judgments contribute to inequality is a certainty, although the magnitude of that contribution cannot be established here.

Nonpecuniary consequences of income flow impairment from invidious discrimination and from other sources of social costs are also severe, but perhaps less easily observed. With un- or underemployment, there occurs an erosion of workers' skills and capabilities. Unused manipulative and cognitive capacities erode; the learning of new approaches and techniques is shelved. Mental and emotional instability is often substantial and disabling. An erosion of a sense of self-worth is common, while habituated characterizations of self are shaken or shattered (Furey [1975] 1981, 110–11; Ginsburg 1983, 85–107). Instrumentally warranted status in the community is threatened. Supportive parenting becomes increasingly difficult and children experience spillover effects of family instability, abuse, and depression. Invidious discrimination even on continuing jobs can produce similar pathological consequences. Invidious discrimination illustratively is reflected in racial bias in contracting, gender-defined dead-end jobs in bureaucracies, and ethnic job assignments in garment making, hand-labor farming, and domestic service.

The social costs to the individuals and their families of inequality of income distribution, as well as of the invidious discrimination that contributes to such inequality, are extensive, and in large part obvious. Any such summary roster would include loss or deprivation of the following:

minimal material means	motivation and drive
health care	sense of community
adequate care for children	emotional stability
creative stimuli	intra-family stability
emotional support of community	instrumentally warranted status
skilled productive capabilities	sense of self-worth

Social Costs of Inequality to the Community

Social costs for the community at large generated by invidiously and ceremonially warranted policies and judgments are partly, but not wholly, the simple aggregate of impairments experienced by individuals. A brief recasting will be helpful in anticipating the following political agenda to "choose equality." However, it bears repeating to say that, given existing levels of high and growing interdependence, whatever significantly cripples any segment of a community, cripples the whole community to that degree. Moreover, the crippling from invidious discrimination is a substantial causative factor in any attempt to account for the existence and continuance of poverty. Reducing poverty requires that the discriminatory aspects of the current economic system be addressed directly. Social costs for the community, reflecting invidiously and ceremonially warranted judgments generating inequalities of income and position, are illustratively considered in the four following topical areas:

Income and employment. Underutilization of the labor force is a social cost. *Having a job at a decent wage matters*, not only for the individuals affected, but for the economy at large. "Over most of this century, scholars have been estimating income and real product losses from unemployment. The decade of the Great Depression including a period during which one-quarter of the labor force was involuntarily unemployed, evidently deprived the United States community of the equivalent of one to two years of production at end-of-decade output levels" (Tool 1995, 149). *Any* level of unemployment, over perhaps a 1 to 2 percent frictional level, must be assumed to be generating economic waste and social cost. The difference in income and output between nearly full employment and the insidious and invidious (neoclassically inspired) "natural rate" of unemployment (6 to 7 percent) is not trivial (Peterson 1994, 230).

The maintenance and expansion of aggregate demand is the primary stimulus to investment spending and economic growth. However, the pursuit of this goal is repeatedly sabotaged by real or contrived fears of inflation. In the hassle over the Phillips Curve—the alleged trade-off between inflation and employment (Piore [1978] 1981, 69–79; Peterson 1988, 464–84)—whose interests really are primary? The anti-inflationary pursuit of high interest rates and tight money serves the pecuniary and ceremonial interests of the financial community. The pursuit of full employment serves the instrumental interests of the underclass as well as the community at large. There is no necessary trade off. Moreover, inflation, if experienced, can be contained sufficiently by incomes policies and direct controls over administered pricing.

Productivity. Discriminatory inequality impinges adversely on the economy's capacity to produce, and will generate social costs. Since productivity is a consequence of the development and application of warranted knowledge as technology to processes of producing and distributing environmentally acceptable goods and services, any invidious intrusion on, or impairment of, those who develop and apply that knowledge are generating social costs. The character of production is also at issue. If productivity is directed, for example, to the production of "Veblen goods" (status and ceremony oriented), or to excessive military goods (power oriented), the underclass (bottom 40 percent) is ill served. Their concerns for affordable housing, environmentally safe neighborhoods, quality education for children, and the like are given a low priority.

Health Care. The present complex structure providing health care in the United States is dramatically inequitable and produces major social costs. Urban areas are much better served than rural areas. The availability and quality of care for the underclass are much less extensive than that for the middle and upper classes. Although one dollar in seven is spent on health care in the United States, some 40 million people—some 15 percent of the total—are without health insurance (*Economic Report of the President, 1994* 1994, 133). Often coverage is tied to a job; if the job ends, so does the health care coverage. While the quality of care is high for those who can afford full fee-for-service coverage, the underclass, except for the elderly, are poorly and underserved. They remain inadequately addressed despite efforts by the Bill Clinton Administration in 1994. The organized power bases of the pharmaceutical houses, hospital associations, private insurance carriers, and medical practitioners, each identifying its interests as those of the public, have, through pressures on Congress, so far prevented the development of a universal care system. Efforts of organized health care providers to retain their power bases constitute ceremonially warranted influence on policy making. Such efforts are contributing to the rising pecuniary and social costs of health care. Finally, the failures in the present system to place *preventive* care as the highest priority permit the social costs of needless impairment (real pain and suffering) and delayed treatment to soar. The social cost of lost productive work and shortened lives from somewhat preventable disease (smoking and lung cancer, obesity and heart disease, sexual conduct and AIDS) is enormous, by any standard. If preventive practices were to become commonplace, demands for treatment obviously would be significantly reduced. The use of preventive vaccines is now generally accepted. The same sense of pertinence and significance must be expanded across the spectrum of medical care.

Education. The clichés that affirm that a nation's future resides with its children and that education is the basic determinant of civilized life, however hackneyed, remain largely correct. "Choosing equality" means that "all individuals should have the opportunity and support to develop their inherent and acquired capabilities (reflective and behavioral) to the fullest extent possible" (Tool 1995, 147). It follows that any "institutional structures and behaviors that deprive children and adults of educational access, and invidiously discriminate in ways that negate the educational experience, generate social costs" (147). Perhaps the basic responsibility of those who educate is to help students of any age, color, or ancestry to develop the capacity "to think critically and coherently over the entire range of their experience" (Foster, quoted in Tool 1995, 147). Social costs arise with every failure to assist students to develop their cognitive, lingual, and manipulative skills to the fullest extent possible. Deprivation can be prevented with open access and budgetary support. Discrimination can be prevented by noninvidious ordering of educational experience. They soar with the failure to provide competent and challenging education; social costs soar with elitist participatory programming and invidiously differential funding.

In these illustrative ways, social costs generated by mind sets and conduct that affirm inequality on invidious or ceremonial grounds substantially diminish the ability and the capacity of the economy efficiently to generate and equably to distribute real income.

A POLITICAL AGENDA TO PROMOTE EQUALITY

Having briefly explored the social costs attributable to our collective failures fully to "choose equality," it is now appropriate to address "what should be done." What sort of political agenda for changes in institutional structure can be suggested that give promise of addressing the real problems of social and economic inequality? Three observations set the context for discussion. First, to "choose equality" is, and must be, largely a matter of making public policy. Governments are the central vehicles through which a community redefines the structure and functions of its social order, its institutional fabric. Nongovernmental bodies and groups can, of course, contribute significantly, but it is governments that have the powers, finally, of mandamus and injunction, and thus must remain as primary centers of deliberation and decision making. Those holding power must be held accountable through democratic strictures and structures that specify who may gain that power and how it may be used. Legitimacy is generated by de facto accountability.

Second, policy proposals to "choose equality" must here be limited to a terse identification of, and comments on, national-level policy. Appropriate, yet similar, policies for smaller jurisdictions will vary with time and circumstance.

Third, the agenda drawn here is intended only to point the direction and suggest examples of instrumentally warranted institutional adjustments. Political feasibility of what is proposed cannot be explored here. That must be considered in a specific time, place, and context. Moreover, it is probable that large segments of the "conservative" political community would vigorously oppose these proposals. That opposition is, politically speaking, of interest and importance, but it should not be permitted to compromise the fundamental argument being made to "choose equality." The latter's credibility does not derive from its "political correctness." The inquiry task is to make arguments and proposals that will stimulate public discussion and social action. The policy suggestions here address many of the areas of concern already discussed.

Income

Goal. The goal is to reduce the extent of inequality of income distribution.

Policies. (1) Increase the minimum wage to levels meeting the official poverty line and tie subsequent changes to that income level as the basic support level. (2) Revamp the personal income tax structure as follows: retain the recently augmented earned income tax credit for low-income families. Eliminate (by phases) virtually all deductions and tax expenditures (subsidies) from the tax code. Identically tax *all* income, *from whatever source*, that accrues to individuals as wages, salaries, tips, pensions, social security, interest, dividends, capital gains, rental payments, "golden parachutes," and the like. Tax such income at moderately progressive rates with a cap of 40 to 50 percent on highest incomes (cf. Peterson 1995, 15–16). Remove all tax-avoidance and tax-evasion options (loopholes) that can be identified.

Employment

Goal. The goal is to ensure that everyone who wants a job has one and that it pays a living wage.

Policies. (1) Enact legislation that *guarantees* employment for all adult citizens at reasonable wages without regard to invidious distinctions. Those not able to find employment in the private sector, would be provided employment in the public sector. This makes access to employment a human right to be fulfilled by government, as proposed (but not passed) in the Humphrey-Hawkins Bill in the 1970s (Ginsburg 1983, 63–78). (2) Since gender and race discrimination evidently still persist in gaining access to employment, affirmative action programs will continue to be needed for another decade or two. (As this is written, heavy pressure is developing among conservatives and others to scrap these programs at the federal and state levels.) (3) Through legislation, bring the Federal Reserve Board of Governors under continuing political accountability so that rising employment will not be undercut by inflation-fearing bankers raising interest rates. (4) Create local and national development banks to generate the credit needed to finance the rebuilding the national infrastructure

(Peterson 1994, 206–11). (5) Although, given guaranteed employment, the need for it will be reduced, revamp the national "safety net" to ensure that those unable to work are able to live at a level no lower than the poverty line and as much above it as resources permit.

Productivity

Goal. The goal is to restore and expand levels of productivity in the economy.

Policies. (1) Generate a comprehensive and continuing program for training and retraining workers in all productive areas seeking new employees. Here is an area for public and private coordination and cooperation, including funding. (2) Involve workers in a continuing problem centered interchange with production managers, design specialists, and technicians jointly to pursue the creation and instrumental application of current and new knowledge in production routines. (3) Continue and extend public subsidization of the growth of warranted knowledge in universities and research centers. (4) Prioritize public spending options on investment employing instrumental criteria. Shift the character of production to enhance the life process (e.g., fast trains take priority over space stations). (5) Restore a significant excise tax on private expenditures on "Veblen goods" and services (conspicuous consumption).

Health Care

Goal. The goal is to ensure full access to high quality health care for all citizens.

Policies. (1) Treat access to quality health care as a basic human right available to all members of the community, without invidious regard to income, status, or condition. This means a system providing universal coverage. (No one would lose coverage by changing jobs or locations.) (2) Introduce a single-payer system with the national government as the main disburser of payments. Economies of scale, reduction of redundancies, and technical efficiency are all available. (3) Organized health care providers (hospitals, medical practitioners, pharmaceutical firms et al.) must be subjected to negotiated and continuing cost controls. (4) Prochoice (not proabortion) must continue to be the national policy. The termination of pregnancies should not be denied on financial, religious, or other ceremonial grounds. Expand effective educational programs to forestall unwanted teen pregnancies.

Education

Goal. The goal is to assist every person to develop their latent abilities to think critically and coherently, create imaginatively, integrate socially, communicate effectively, and participate noninvidiously in the communities of which they are members.

Policies. (1) Place the *education and welfare of children* as or priority in the use of the nation's resources, without invidious regard ethnicity, gender, or race. To cherish, nourish, and support the development of children should take second place to no other nationa (2) Develop more extended programs to enhance the quality and resp ...ty of parenting to provide, as much as possible, threat-free, supportive, and stimulative childhoods. (3) Early childhood education (K–4) is critically important in determining subsequent development. Monetary, facility, and teaching support priorities should be placed here (with small classes and dedicated teachers). Comprehensive expansion of the Head Start program is one option to consider. (4) Educational infrastructure is critically run down. We should launch a major, well-funded, national restoration and expansion project to rebuild educational institutions. Its magnitude should rival the superhighway building programs of the 1950s and 1960s. (5) Generate incentives to bring the nation's brightest and most committed young people into the teaching profession and treat them as professionals once they are engaged. (6) Reintroduce a civilian equivalent of the earlier Government Issue (G.I.) Bills (which educated a generation of the nation's young people) to ensure that any young person who can benefit from the experience can have access to higher education, technical training, or other productive preparation (Bush 1986, 37–41). Public support should be provided sufficient to permit her or him to continue so long as reasonable progress is being made.

A CONCLUDING COMMENT

Professor Livingston concluded his *Fair Game* by urging his readers to "choose equality" in order to "flee greed," "find moral meaning in personal and social experience," generate political legitimacy, foster compassion, escape from competitive denigration, provide "the precondition for individuality," "maximize initiative and creative effort," promote "genuine mutuality," secure praise of equals, salvage the democratic perspective, escape "the arrogance of the 'talented' elite," and "regain control over our own destinies" (1979, 214–27). I join in these admonitions and suggest the following as addenda.

To "choose equality" is to choose a habit of mind and a mode of public conduct that affirms the inherent *worth* of each person. It implies the obligation to develop our own capacities for instrumental thought and behavior and to assist others in similar endeavors.

To "choose equality" is to give "equal opportunity" a whole new referential content that abandons its connotative role as an aristocratic ideal and embeds in it the normative recognition that *noninvidiousness* is its legitimate, democratic meaning and a condition of its realization.

To "choose equality" is to abandon the conventional and conservative rhetoric about meritocratic models, "level playing fields," hierarchies of talents, competitive races to enhance inequalities, and condescending attitudes toward poverty and the poor.

To "choose equality" is not only to affirm the worth of each person but to recognize that only through social action as public policy can the potential instrumental merit of people be assured and acknowledged. I am suggesting that "worthiness" implies, among other things, the human rights to be and to belong, to work at meaningful pay, to have unfettered access to health care, and to become as fully trained and educated as our interests and abilities will permit.

To "choose equality" is to be on the side of normatively credible "angels"—in other words, of democratic social and economic reformers.

REFERENCES

Alexander, Sidney S. 1967. "Human Values and Economists' Values." In Sidney Hook, ed., *Human Values and Economic Policy*. New York: New York University Press, 101–16.

Arnold, Matthew. 1949. *The Portable Matthew Arnold.* New York: Viking Press.

Ayres, Clarence E. 1961. *Towards a Reasonable Society.* Austin: University of Texas Press.

Bauer, Peter. 1983. "The Grail of Equality." In William Letwin, ed., *Against Equality.* London: Macmillan Press.

Bush, Paul D. 1986. "On the Concept of Ceremonial Encapsulation." *Review of Institutional Thought*, 3 (Dec.): 25–45.

___. 1988. "The Theory of Institutional Change." In Marc R. Tool, ed., *Evolutionary Economics I: Foundations of Institutional Thought.* Armonk, N.Y.: M. E. Sharpe, 125–66.

___. 1993. "The Methodology of Institutional Economics: A Pragmatic Instrumentalist Perspective." In Marc R. Tool, ed., *Institutional Economics: Theory, Method, Policy.* Boston: Kluwer Academic Publishers, 59–107.

Commager, Henry Steel, ed. 1948. *Documents of American History.* Vols. 1, 2. New York: Appleton-Century-Crofts.

Economic Report of the President, 1994. 1994. Washington, D. C.: U. S. Government Printing Office.

Furey, Edward B. [1975] 1981. "The Fear, the Numbing Fear." *New York Times.* Reprinted in David C. Colander, ed., *Solutions to Unemployment.* New York: Harcourt, Brace, Jovanovich, 110–11.

Gilbert, Richard S. 1991. *How Much Do We Deserve? An Inquiry in Distributive Justice.* Lanham, N.Y.: University Press of America.

Ginsburg, Helen. 1983. *Full Employment and Public Policy: The United States and Sweden.* Lexington, Mass.: D. C. Heath.

Green, Philip. 1981. *The Pursuit of Inequality.* New York: Pantheon Books.

Hickerson, Steven R. 1988. "Instrumental Valuation: The Normative Compass of Institutional Economics." In Marc R. Tool, ed., *Evolutionary Economics I: Foundations of Institutional Thought.* Armonk, N.Y.: M. E. Sharpe, 167–93.

Hodgson, Geoffrey M. 1988. *Economics and Institutions.* Cambridge: Polity Press.

Letwin, William, ed. 1983. *Against Equality.* London: Macmillan Press.

Livingston, John C. 1957. "Alexander Hamilton and the American Tradition." *Midwest Journal of Political Science*, 1 (Nov.): 209–24.

___. 1973. "Tenure Everyone?" In Bardwell L. Smith, ed., *The Tenure Debate*. San Francisco: Jossey-Bass, 54–73.

___. 1979. *Fair Game? Inequality and Affirmative Action*. San Francisco: W. H. Freeman and Company.

Mitchell, Wesley C. 1967. "Jeremy Bentham and the Utilitarian Creed." In *Types of Economic Theory I*. New York: Augustus M. Kelley, 171–234.

Osberg, Lars. 1984. *Economic Inequality in the United States*. Armonk, N.Y.: M. E. Sharpe.

Peterson, Wallace C. 1988. *Income, Employment & Economic Growth*. 6th ed., New York: W. W. Norton.

___. 1991. *Transfer Spending, Taxes, and the American Welfare State*. Boston: Kluwer Academic Publishers.

___. 1994. *The Silent Depression: The Fate of the American Dream*. New York: W. W. Norton.

___. 1995. "Silent Depression: Cause, Consequences, and Cure." Paper presented at meetings of the Association for Evolutionary Economics, January, Washington, D.C.

Piore, Michael J. [1978] 1981. "Unemployment and Inflation: An Alternative View." *Challenge*, May/June; Reprinted in David C. Colander, ed., *Solutions to Unemployment*. New York: Harcourt, Brace, Jovanovich, 69–79.

Posner, Richard A. 1983. "Economic Justice and the Economist." In Willam Letwin, ed., *Against Equality*. London: Macmillan Press, 345–59.

Robbins, Lionel 1952. *The Nature and Significance of Economic Science*. 2d ed., London: Macmillan and Co.

Rogers, Harrell R., Jr. 1982. *The Cost of Human Neglect*. Armonk, N.Y.: M. E. Sharpe.

Schaar, John H. 1964. "Some Ways of Thinking About Equality." *Journal of Politics*, 26: 867–95.

___. 1970. "Equality of Opportunity and Beyond." In Anthony de Crespigny, and Alan Wertheimer, eds., *Contemporary Political Theory*. New York: Atherton Press, 135–53.

Schwartz, John E. 1983. *America's Hidden Success: A Reassessment of Twenty Years of Public Policy*. New York: W. W. Norton.

Shaw, George Bernard. 1928. *The Intelligent Woman's Guide to Socialism and Capitalism*. New York: Brentano's Publishers.

Sowell, Thomas. 1994. *Race and Culture*. New York: Basic Books.

Stern, Philip M. 1973. *The Rape of the Taxpayer*. New York: Random House.

Tool, Marc R. [1979] 1985. *The Discretionary Economy: A Normative Theory of Political Economy*. Boulder, Colo.: Westview Press.

___. 1986. *Essays in Social Value Theory: A Neoinstitutionalist Contribution*. Armonk, N.Y.: M. E. Sharpe.

___. 1993. "The Theory of Instrumental Value: Extensions, Clarifications." In M. R. Tool, ed., *Institutional Economics: Theory, Method, Policy*. Boston: Kluwer Academic Publishers, 119–59.

___. 1995. *Pricing, Valuation and Systems: Essays in Neoinstitutional Economics*. Aldershot, U.K.: Edward Elgar Publishing.

United States. *Economic Report of the President 1994*. 1994. Washington, D.C.: U.S. Government Printing Office.

Veblen, Thorstein B. 1934. *The Theory of the Leisure Class*. New York: Modern Library.

Verba, Sidney, and Garry R. Oren. 1985. *Equality in America: Elite Values in Politics and Economics*. Cambridge: Harvard University Press.

Wray, L. Randall. 1995. "A New Year's Keynesian Wish: Advice to Clinton in the Aftermath of November 1994." Paper presented at meetings of the Association for Evolutionary Economics, January, Washington D.C.

8

Reconstructing the Welfare State in the Aftermath of the Great Capitalist Restoration

*James Ronald Stanfield and
Jacqueline Bloom Stanfield*

The Great Capitalist Restoration that began with the Margaret Thatcher and Ronald Reagan administrations has now spread through much of the world. Retrenchment in the name of the hallowed truths of the nineteenth century has spread from its Anglo-Saxon roots to New Zealand, Australia, France, and elsewhere. The third way models of social democracy in Scandinavia have not gone untouched by this movement. Of late, Japan and the former Federal Republic of Germany have begun to feel the squeeze from global retrenchment. The restoration also includes the transition to capitalism in the former planned economies and the installation of capitalist public and private financial foundations in the emerging market economies. Everywhere one looks it seems that the social structure of capitalist accumulation is being restored.

However, amid the fanfare and celebration, the forgotten problematic of late capitalist society remains. Economic vulnerability and deprivation grow amid the replanted roots of capitalist accumulation. A "silent depression" has engulfed the American economy at least, seriously eroding the economic footing of family life (Peterson 1995; see also Schor 1991; Abelda 1992; Amott 1993). Ecological destruction expands along with the mystified income and product measures of economic success. Social and ecological dislocation breed despair and violence.

These and other problems persist and will require remedy when the fool's gold dust of complacent celebration settles once again. With the apparent collapse for the foreseeable future of revolutionary socialism, the welfare state becomes even more definitely the systematic response to these problems. Apparently, "the more successful capitalisms of tomorrow will be those that address the difficulties of the present period— … internationalization of capital, … inflation, … social and ecological vulnerability to technological disruption—

by new structures that utilize the state in various ways" (Heilbroner 1985, 203). Hence, the need to comprehend the nature of the welfare state becomes even more pressing (J. R. Stanfield 1979, chs. 5, 6; 1995, ch. 9). However, as the problems mount, the political economic establishment continues its myopic celebration of its own greed (Thurow 1992; see also Galbraith 1992) in the face of its enervating gridlock.

These problems and the languishing force of leadership under political economic stalemate in the industrial democracies is compelling evidence of comprehensive cultural lag. Nowhere is this more apparent than in America, where the deteriorating social landscape and decaying infrastructure have long been evident. The neglect of the logic of reform (J. R. Stanfield 1986, ch. 5) by those in power steadily exacerbates an urgently precarious social economic situation. The Galbraithian (1958) formulation of cultural lag as a persistent social imbalance between private and public goods becomes all the more evident in this era of gridlocked government. Along with a growing social imbalance, such a stalemate of political economic forces raises the specter of authoritative resolution, as described by Hayek (1944) and Polanyi ([1944] 1957) with respect to interwar Europe.

In the present chapter, we suggest that the comprehension, and therefore the conscious reconstruction, of the welfare state requires an evolutionary, holistic understanding of the social economy and its complex interactions. Family and gender relationships must be understood in light of the economic process, and political competition must be cognizant of myriad interactions that require more than passing and occasional reference in political economic discourse. We suggest an outline of the sort of comprehensive, long-view analysis that we believe to be necessary to eschew the comfort of rhetorical stereotypes and confront the debilitating problematic of late capitalism.

The first section reviews the institutional adjustment focus of the American institutional economists. The second suggests that a nurturance gap besets American society in particular and a world dominated by the social structure of accumulation in general. The third section outlines our hypothesis on the roots of the nurturance gap. The concluding section briefly traces some of the implications of our argument.

CULTURAL LAG AND INSTITUTIONAL ADJUSTMENT

Institutional economics conceives *the* economic problem to be the continuous adjustment or reconstruction of economic institutions. Technological and social changes disrupt the established ways and means by which people make a living and order their existence, necessitating adaptation. Cultural continuity must be a factor in evaluating and shaping economic performance because the basic purpose of the economy is to provision and encourage, and not to obstruct or distort, the development of individual personalities. The nurturant functions of family life are especially important to individual development and cultural continuity.

Discontinuities in adaptation emerge because the process of identifying and implementing progressive institutional adjustment faces severe obstacles. Habitual ways and means are buttressed by the power of inertia. Institutional adjustment means redistribution of power so to remove instituted barriers to individual participation in political economic processes.   Very often these barriers represent the protective apparatus for entrenched invidious distinctions of relative rank or status.   Since considerable institutional or cultural lag will always exist, the task of ideological reviewing and institutional reform is a permanent aspect of the political economic process.

Recent changes in gender and family relations provide a compelling example of institutional lag.   The concern for the effects of technological and social changes on the American family have long been matters of scholarly concern (Levitan and Belous 1981; Yorburg 1983). The changes in gender and family relations have been accelerating in the past few decades, fundamentally altering family structure and the role of women in society (McNall and McNall 1992). Of especial import has been the dramatic rise in the participation of women in the paid labor force, declining economic dependence of women on men, somewhat more egalitarian gender relations within marriage (Yorburg 1983), and the increase in single adults living alone (McCrate 1987).

The women's movement has become a more or less permanent force in the social landscape.   Wartime employment led to an increasing number of women who questioned traditional gender roles (Deckard 1983) and pressed for the eradication of social barriers to women's participation in political economic processes.   Women began to acquire the education and skills necessary to compete for better jobs.   Technological changes such as more reliable contraceptive devices and labor-saving household appliances and processed goods also increased the capacity of women to participate in the paid labor force.

Postwar economic trends contributed to the dramatic increase in women's participation in the paid labor force.   The quarter-century boom to 1970 increased demand in the pink-collar occupations (those dominated by women) and generated labor shortages in other fields that were not the traditional parvenu of women. Along with the changing social relations between the genders, which increased women's responsibilities for supporting themselves and their children, the stagnant real wage in the American economy since the 1970s has added considerable economic stress and induced more intensive recourse of women to the paid labor force (Abelda 1992; Schor 1991; Amott 1993).   These changes have been mixed blessings for couples undergoing role strain (J. B. Stanfield 1985, 1996) and for women who have all too frequently worked the "second shift" (Hochschild 1989) because the growth rate of more equal sharing of domestic labor has been much slower than that of more equal participation in the paid labor force.

The common definition of the family is an ideological holdover in that it defines the family in terms of its past patriarchal structure, in which each adult in the family fulfilled a traditional role oriented toward the birth and rearing of children (Parsons and Bales 1955). This mentality persists in the Bureau of the Census (United States Bureau of the Census 1989, 25) definition of the family "as a householder and one or more other persons living in the same household who are related to the householder by birth, marriage, or adoption." However, there have emerged numerous alternative living arrangements that fulfill the companionate nurturant function (J. B. Stanfield 1992, 1996; McNall and McNall 1992). It would seem that any structurally oriented definition is likely to lag behind social change and neglect many arrangements by which people seek to fulfill the nurturant function of the family ("The Family" 1987; Fine 1993).

Hampered by such obsolete definitions, the recent family values discussion has neglected the most basic question of whether families lack values or time and resources. Poverty is degrading, and economic insecurity undermines family cohesion. The facts seem to suggest that no fundamental change in family values has occurred that matches in significance the rising level of economic stress in our consumeristic society (Stanfield and Stanfield 1980; Schor 1991; Abelda 1992; Amott 1993; Peterson 1995). Alongside wage stagnation, the social safety net for the maintenance of family functions has also been eroded in the era of Capitalist Restoration.

Galbraithian (1958) social imbalance constitutes cultural lag. As gender and family relations have changed, new profit opportunities have emerged and have led to the provision of new private goods in food processing, service industries, catalog sales, and household technology. However, government response to changing gender and family relations has been slow, so the provision of new public goods has lagged behind the provision of new private goods. As a result, poverty is becoming feminized, and its incidence is accelerating at its most tragic and destructive locus—children (Peterson 1987; Northrup 1990; Stanfield 1992). Not only the obsolete antigovernment market mentality but also the patriarchal culture is at work in this regard. Measures designed to protect the income of male breadwinners—unemployment compensation, workers's compensation, social security payments, and mandated union representation—do not necessarily augment the income of women and children not living with a male. Even if the income of the male breadwinner is protected, he may or may not share it with his wife and children.

Class exploitation, race discrimination, and national predation are significant pathologies. Nevertheless, only the concept of patriarchy (gender domination) can account for the curiously dualized welfare system in the United States (Pearce 1990; Peterson and Petersen [1993] 1994). Women and children who have lost the income provided by the death, disability, or retirement of a male earner receive higher income and benefits than those who are without a male earner because of desertion, divorce, or single parenthood. However, women in both categories face the same obstacles to earning income in the market; women and children in both categories have similar economic needs. Nothing distinguishes the two groups except their relationship to men. Clearly, policies are needed that focus on the specific employment and income constraints faced by women.

THE NURTURANCE GAP

To nurture is to sustain, to care for, to promote the growth and development of, to rear, to educate or train. Much of this activity is performed within relationships that induce nurturing labor without an immediate calculation of economic significance. However, this activity is of vital economic significance. Human beings require nurturance as individuals, and their social relationships must be sustained by nurturing interaction. Social reproduction requires that a new generation be nurtured to maturity with the ability to sustain intimate relations and participate in social processes. The need for nurturance to sustain social reproduction continues throughout the life cycle. Adults as well as children require dignity and loving attendance to their elemental needs. A functioning social order requires a sense of connection or social bonding that must be continuously reinstituted.

The nurturance gap is the breakdown of this dynamic function of nurturing human individuals capable of cooperative social relationships. In the present American case, we see evidence of this breakdown in the loss of childhood, intimacy, dignity, and civility.

Children experience extended financial, emotional, and social dependence on adults. The requisite adult support is too often not forthcoming, given poverty, single-parent families, and dual-earning couples. In 1987 child care was a wrenching personal problem facing millions of American families (Wallis 1987), and in 1995, with more than 60 percent of mothers with children under age 5 being in the paid labor force child care continues to be a personal problem. Some parents have solved the child care dilemma by giving their children the awesome responsibility of coming home alone. These children are referred to as latchkey children. They carry a house key with them to school, arrive home from school before the parent(s) return from work, and care for themselves. The latchkey phenomenon is part of present-day ethnography. From 1970 to 1991, single parent-families increased from 10 to 24 percent of families with children (Lewen [1992] 1994). Notwithstanding the ongoing debate as to whether single-parent or same-sex families can effectively socialize a new generation, we seek to build on the argument that adults who suffer inadequate financial resources and severe time constraints are unable to be the necessary nurturing force in children's lives. We contend that a functional or process conception of the family, rather than a structural one, is needed to assess this and other issues (Stanfield 1992; Lanciaux 1989; Zimmerman 1988). In other words, the process orientation in the definition of family involves a dynamic view, which argues that family functions should not be tied to the traditional patriarchal family structure.

All too often, single parent families are headed by women who possess limited earning capacity. Thus, poverty begins harming the young before they are even born (Cook and Brown 1994). Government programs such as Aid to Families with Dependent Children do not support these female-headed single parent families above a subsistence level. Poverty continues to harm the young after they are born. The 1994 Carnegie report (Carnegie Task Force on Meeting the Needs of Young Children 1994) identifies a quiet crisis that exists in the United States. The quiet crisis refers to the increasing number of children under the age of six who are living in poverty. The report makes two points about young children living in poverty. First, one in four infants and toddlers (about 3 million children out of 12 million children) under the age of three live in families earning below the federal poverty level. The second point is that while the number of children under six increased by less than 10 percent between 1971 and 1991, the number of poor children under six increased by more than 60 percent. A significant number of these children living in poverty are also living in single-parent households, the majority of which are female headed.

Loss of intimacy between individuals is a second component of the nurturance gap. An increasing number of singles, a decline of quality time for couples, and domestic violence characterize the loss of intimacy. In addition to the rapidly growing number of single-parent families, there is a growing number of single-person families, consisting of an individual who lives alone. This singleton way of life differs slightly from the married way of life. The major difference is that the singleton does not automatically have someone at home with whom to share time, thoughts, experiences, and desires. That is, there is no one at home with whom intimacy is guaranteed.

Even those adults who do form unions with others are likely to experience a loss of intimacy. As our society has become increasingly complex, with individuals encountering growing numbers of role obligations and experiencing increasing role strain (Goode 1960), quality time together for couples decreases. Both partners in a relationship are forced to participate in the labor force just to make ends meet; and if they are working at minimum wage jobs, they do not make ends meet—they live in poverty. If they are lucky, they work the same hours. If they work different hours, they may greet each other at the garage door as one leaves and the other returns home. In either case, there is little time to spend together, and certain household responsibilities remain (i.e., cleaning, paying bills, caring for dependents, etc.).

A third major characteristic of the loss of intimacy is domestic violence. This includes violence against women, against children, and to a much lesser extent, violence against men. Women tend to stay in relationships with men who are violent toward them for several reasons, and a cycle of violence ranging from loving moments to physical violence in abusive relationships has been well documented (Gelles 1995). Two startling statistics about domestic violence are that in any given year, 10 percent of American women are beaten by a man with whom they are intimately involved (Smith 1993), and that 50 percent of spousal homicides occur in households where the police have been called multiple times for domestic violence (Spurlock and Robinowitz 1990). The cycle of violence persists because women feel that they lack the means to adequately support themselves and their children (Okin 1989) and because typically, the women have low self-esteem, have been threatened with death if they leave, and often feel they have no place to go. Generally, when domestic violence begins to be aimed at their children, women finally become emotionally strong enough to leave the abusive relationship. Children who are abused or who observe violence between their parents are much more likely to participate in domestic violence themselves, either as a perpetrator or victim of battering or as an abuser of children (Smith 1993). Both men and women are violent toward each other, and both are as likely to kill. The difference is in how the violence is perpetrated. Men are more likely to use physical force to overpower a woman, while women are more likely to use a deadly weapon against an abusive spouse or partner. This increased number of singles, the loss of time together, and domestic violence together characterize the loss of intimacy, which is a major component of the nurturance gap.

The nurturance gap spans the human life cycle from childhood to old age. A loss of dignity also characterizes the nurturance gap, as interactions between and with the elderly diminish and as the elderly find themselves isolated, whether living in affluence or poverty, independently or in nursing homes. As the twenty-first century approaches, the number of older Americans will swell as the baby boomers of the twentieth century age. In 1995, the first wave of baby boomers reaches the age of 50. Some of the elderly (and soon to be elderly) are financially fortunate, having saved and planned wisely for their retirement years. This group is able to maintain their homes or to move into retirement communities with other people their own age. Moving into retirement communities, however, reduces intergenerational interactions and isolates the elderly. Another group of elderly is not so financially fortunate and often finds itself in the same position of poverty as single parent-families (Haley 1994). The care that this less-fortunate group receives is highly variable. Because of their financial status, they are solely dependent on Medicare for the coverage of their health care. In many cases, medical doctors do not accept Medicare patients because the reimbursement level is so low, and as a result the elderly delay seeking medical care. Those who are no longer able to live alone and care for themselves often find themselves in nursing homes that are understaffed and offer substandard care. The media is ripe with stories of neglected, overly sedated, bedridden elderly persons living in nursing homes under unsanitary conditions. This is not the dignified existence to which our older generation is entitled. Level of living is determined by level of income for all people.

Poverty is tragic; there is no one who "deserves" to be poor. There is no dignity in poverty; to being old, homeless, eating from soup lines, and depending on others for care. Poverty is just as disastrous and destructive for the elderly as for other age groups in society.

The fourth component of the nurturance gap is the loss of civility. Civility refers to respect, manners, and common courtesy, and the loss of civility means the declining nature of these (i.e., disrespect for others). A simple example illustrates the loss of civility. The simple acts of accepting or declining an invitation, of saying thank you or excuse me, have all but vanished from our social life (Cashnelli 1994). The loss of civility is obvious in other aspects of daily life as well. People driving in cars yell obscenities out the windows. Disputes over parking places are settled with guns. Elderly people are not offered seats on public transportation. Telemarketers telephone at all hours of the day and evening. This loss of civility arises because children are not taught these basic social skills. Instead, they oftentimes learn their social skills from violent and disrespectful television shows.

THE MARKET MENTALITY AND THE SOCIAL ECONOMY

Prior to the rise of the modern economy, the traditional family was largely self-sufficient in terms of its daily economic requirements. The bulk of production was carried out within domestic relationships. This was the case even for the American frontier family, despite the commercial economy elsewhere in the country. Gender roles in domestic production were sharply defined and reflected in socialization and education. With the rise to dominance of the commodity production economy, industrialization, and urbanization, productive functions steadily shifted to specialized productive institutions.

The altered functions of the family affected the internal character of family life. The family evolved from an extended kinship system for instituting a wide range of productive activities to a nuclear family with more specific socioeconomic functions. With this evolution to the modern companionate family (Burgess 1926; Burgess and Locke 1945), intimate contact and nurturance rose in proportion to the totality of family functions. In the companionate family, although they remain significant, material production activities have fallen dramatically in proportion to procreation and affection functions.

The commodity production organization of much material reproduction continues to impact kinship relations. The disembedded market economy tends to dominate other aspects of culture (Polanyi [1944] 1957; see also Stanfield 1986, ch. 4). Our argument may seem to imply that Polanyi's *protective response* is losing out in its struggle with the exchange economy. The protective response is the collective intervention in market relationships by which society reasserts reciprocity and the primacy of society (Polanyi [1944] 1957; see also Stanfield 1986). But it may be instead that we are at the threshold of a dramatic extension of the protective response if the political economy recognizes the nurturance gap and acts collectively to furnish the functional equivalents of the family structure.

The market mentality places obsessive emphasis upon pecuniary values and the efficiency and growth of commodity production, and it explicitly resorts to invidious distinction as an incentive. Invidious bargaining behavior and mobility in pursuit of economic interests are of critical importance to pecuniary success. The incessant pursuit of individual advantage necessarily leads to a universal wariness that undermines social bonds of trust and empathy. The lesser one's constraints by emotional affinities of one kind or another, the greater one's mobility. Time pressures reinforce the effects of bargaining and mobility.

Under this unremitting pressure, social relationships yield space. The extent of reciprocity is restricted, and kinship obligations become limited to one's immediate family; evidently the continuity of the nuclear family itself is in doubt in the American case. The sense of community and *civitas* is also eroded because public-mindedness is based on reciprocal expectation. In short, declining reciprocity implies a decline in the "spontaneous conformity" on which social order is based (Lowe 1988). Spontaneous conformity is institutionalized by reciprocity in that one conforms because one expects others to do likewise.

The erosion of spontaneous conformity increases transaction costs and undermines social structure in various ways. Exchange relations require more scrutiny in specification and compliance. Litigation and collection actions rise. Police activity becomes more pervasive. Moral hazard becomes more pronounced. Intimate relationships are damaged. Nurturing labor is instituted by transactions governed by spontaneous conformity to a code of interpersonal obligation and concern for significant others. The intimacy required for the continuity of interpersonal obligation takes time in that it must be continuously reinstituted by successive reciprocal acts of caring and concern.

Patriarchy sustained nurturing labor within the marital relation, but the attack on patriarchy along with rising economic stress have drastically altered its scope (McCrate 1992; J. B. Stanfield 1985, 1992, 1996). In the tension between patriarchal and market forces, nurturing labor has become more expensive, both with improved market opportunities for women and with rising economic stress (Albelda 1992; Schor 1991). Apparently, the income effect of the falling real wage is stronger than the substitution effect. People seem to have increased rather than reduced paid labor force participation with the declining real wage in order to maintain the household's standard of living.

Redistributive transactions are an evident aspect of the modern public sector, but they are not well understood. To those enamored of the market mentality, they are inherently unproductive, being pursued for reasons of equity at the expense of diminished (exchange) efficiency. However, redistributive transactions are important in integrating the division of labor within the kinship and political sectors of any economy. Moreover, since they operate alongside reciprocity to sustain social connection, such transactions are necessary to the cooperation accomplished through exchange transactions. Without cultural, social, and diplomatic bonds, there could be no exchange, only conquest and defeat.

A comprehensive transactional analysis of the economic process must recognize that reciprocal and redistributive transactions play a significant role in the integration of the division of labor. Such transactions are not usefully viewed as imperfect exchanges but rather require analysis on their own terms because they are placed in the social structure in a very different fashion than exchange. A comprehensive economic analysis must consider the significant wealth and real income that is produced within nonexchange relationships.

CONCLUSION: RECONSTRUCTION OF THE WELFARE STATE

Improved family policy requires a more dynamic, process-oriented definition of the family that is focused upon the function rather than the structure of family life (Zimmerman 1988; Lanciaux 1989; Stanfield 1992). The companionate, nurturant function is inherent in adult relationships as well as in the rearing of children.   Important production of goods and services for direct household consumption occurs in the household.   The concept of *leisure* needs to be relieved of its passive connotation lest we sacrifice socially vital activities in the interest of increasing pecuniarily measured productivity and income.

Improved discourse on family policy can only occur if the obsolete patriarchal and market mentalities are abandoned. The patriarchal mentality impedes the necessary process-oriented conception of the family as an ongoing social arrangement composed of people who are committed to meeting each other's psychological, social, and physical needs (Stanfield 1992; Zimmermann 1988). This process-oriented definition addresses the many things that families do and includes all the varieties of family life that might exist. Policymakers using this definition can direct their energies toward developing policy relevant to social problems rather than debating platitudes about the morality of family structure. This should allow a clarification of the problems and alternatives involved in the family policy area and separate the views of those who want to design family policy to support family functions from those who seek a morally oriented regulation of behavior (Aldous and Dumon 1991). The moral regulation tactic is further evidence of the heldover patriarchal culture that generated the dualized-income support system.

The family policy discourse should comprise the examination of social policy in terms of its impacts on families from a multicultural perspective. Given the residual effects of patriarchy, one specific aim of family policy should be to finance the empowerment of women and children so to directly confront socially structured gender inequality. This will require more adequately funded, better constructed programs to aid families with dependent children, as well as measures to abet women in the acquisition of marketable skills, in securing employment and compensation commensurate with these skills, and in balancing the demands of child care and employment. Parental leave; family allowances; expanded earned income and child care tax credits; subsidized, high-quality child care; national health insurance; and flex-time work arrangements are examples of policies that should be highly placed on the policy agenda.

The market mentality is also a resolute barrier to the needed social change. Leisure connotes the condition of not earning an income. Its passive nuance stems from the utilitarian view of consumption as passive activity in comparison with the activity of work. The truth, of course, is that leisure time contains productive activities that are as vital to the standard of living as those instituted within the paid labor force. Transactions instituted within reciprocal and redistributive relationships require an even-handed discussion with exchange transactions within a comprehensive model of the social economy. The bias that only exchange transactions are productive must be overcome. It must be recognized that state transfers to finance the reproduction of family life with dignity and opportunity comprise productive transactions that integrate the division of labor that is requisite for the continuity of life. Similarly, reciprocal relationships that institute nurturing labor contain productive transactions, notwithstanding their absence from quantitative calculations of gross national product and national income. For the American social economy at the present time, the most pressing issue is the adjustment of political economic institutions to the reality of changing family and gender relations. The deterioration in the life chances of children is an ominous harbinger of future social decay and lagging productivity. The increased dualization of individual life chances between those reared in families with or without a male present is a cause for concern, not only in its own right, given the wasted potential and avoidable misery endured, but also because of the ever-present reality of violence and social unrest that it breeds. The growing despair and anger of those confronted by the loss of dignity, intimacy, and civility further fan the incendiary frustration of social erosion.

The institutional adjustment that is needed to reverse this decline must have as one of its key foci the empowerment of women and children without regard to their relationships to males. This empowerment must be financial, since finance is the power system of the commodity production economy. The requisite adjustment must also comprise a multicultural appraisal of a complex society in need of social bonds refashioned on new premises in order to offer new premises and new responsibilities. Much of the family values debate, with its atavistic moralizing about the decline of the traditional family, is a lamentable waste of time in the face of the increasing urgency of instituting an effective response to the economic and social challenges at the close of the twentieth century.

REFERENCES

Albelda, R. 1992. "Whose Values, Which Families?" *Dollars and Sense.* no. 182 (Dec.): 6–9.

Aldous, Joan, and Wilfried Dumon. 1991. "Family Policy in the 1980s: Controversy and Consensus." In Alan Booth, ed., *Contemporary Families: Looking Forward, Looking Back.* Minneapolis, Minn.: National Council on Family Relations, 466–81.

Amott, Teresa. 1993. *Caught in the Crisis.* New York: Monthly Review Press.

Burgess, E., and H. J. Locke. 1945. *The Family from Institution to Companionship.* New York: American Book.

Burgess, Ernest. 1926. "The Family as a Unity of Interacting Personalities." *The Family,* 7: 1: 3–9.

Carnegie Task Force on Meeting the Needs of Young Children. 1994. [Report of the Carnegie Task Force on Meeting the Needs of Young Children]. New York: Carnegie Corporation.

Cashnelli, Toni. 1994. "RSVP? Do It Now." *Coloradoan,* Nov. 17, B1.

Cook, John T., and J. Larry Brown. 1994. *Two Americas: Comparisons of U.S. Child Poverty in Rural, Inner City and Suburban Areas.* Medford, Mass.: Center on Hunger, Poverty and Nutrition Policy.

Deckard, B. S. 1983. *The Women's Movement.* New York: Harper and Row.

Fine, M. A. 1993. "Current Approaches to Understanding Family Diversity." *Family Relations, 42: 235–37.*

Galbraith, J. K. 1958. *The Affluent Society.* Boston: Houghton-Mifflin.

___. 1992. *The Culture of Contentment.* Boston: Houghton-Mifflin.

Gelles, Richard J. 1995. *Contemporary Families: A Sociological View.* Thousand Oaks, Calif.: Sage Publications.

Goode, William. 1960. "A Theory of Role Strain." *American Sociological Review, 25: 483–96.*

Haley, Dan. 1994. "Pushed to the Edge by Poverty." *Coloradoan,* Nov. 24, A1.

Hayek, F. A. 1944. *The Road to Serfdom.* Chicago: University of Chicago.

Heilbroner, R. L. 1985. *The Nature and Logic of Capitalism.* New York: Norton.

Hochschild, A. R., with A. Machung. 1989. *The Second Shift: Working Parents and the Revolution at Home.* New York: Viking.

Lanciaux, Bernadette. 1989. "The Role of the State in the Family." In W. M. Dugger and W. T. Waller, Jr., eds., *The Stratified State: Radical Institutional Theories of Participation and Duality.* Armonk, New York: M. E. Sharpe, 195–215.

Lewen, Tamar. [1992] 1994. "Rise in Single Parents Is Reshaping America." *New York Times,* Oct. 5. Reprinted in Prentice Hall, *Themes of the Times: Sociology,* 18.

Levitan, S. A. and R. Belous. 1981. *What's Happening to the American Family?* Baltimore: John's Hopkins University Press.

Lowe, A. 1988. *Has Freedom a Future?* New York: Praeger.

McCrate, E. 1987. "Trade, Merger, and Employment." *Review of Radical Political Economy.* 19, no. 1: 73–89.

___. 1992. "Accounting for the Slowdown in the Divorce Rate in the 1990s: A Bargaining Perspective." *Review of Social Economy, 50 (Winter): 404–19.*

McNall, Scott, and Sally A. McNall. 1992. *Sociology.* Englewood Cliffs, N. J.: Prentice Hall.

Northrup, E. M. 1990. "The Feminization of Poverty: The Demographic Factor and the Composition of Economic Growth." *Journal of Economic Issues,* 24 (Mar.): 145–60.

Okin, S. 1989. *Justice, Gender, and the Family.* New York: Basic Books.

Parsons, Talcott, and Robert F. Bales. 1955. *Family Socialization and Interaction Process.* New York: Free Press.

Pearce, D. 1990. "Welfare Is Not *for* Women: Why the War on Poverty Cannot Conquer the Feminization of Poverty." In L. Gordon, ed., *Women the State and Welfare.* Madison: University of Wisconsin Press, 265–79.

Peterson, J. 1987. "The Feminization of Poverty." *Journal of Economic Issues,* 21 (Mar.): 329–37.

Peterson, J. L. and C. D. Petersen. [1993] 1994. "Single Mother Families and the Dual Welfare State." *Review of Social Economy,.* 52 (Fall): 314–38.

Peterson, W. C. 1995. *Silent Depression.* New York: Norton.

Polanyi, K. [1944] 1957. *The Great Transformation.* New York: Rinehart. Reprint. Boston: Beacon.

Schor, J. B. 1991. *The Overworked American: The Unexpected Decline of Leisure.* New York: Basic Books.

Smith, P. 1993. *Feminist Jurisprudence.* New York: Oxford University Press.

Spurlock, J., and C. Robinowitz. 1990. *Women's Progress: Promises and Problems.* New York: Plenum Press.

Stanfield, Jacqueline B. 1985. "Research on Wife/mother Role Strain in Dual-career Families." *American Journal of Economics and Sociology,* 44, no. 3: 355–63.

___. 1992. "Family Policy in America: A Continuing Controversy." *Review of Social Economy,* 50 (Winter): 420–31.

___. 1996. *Married with Careers: Coping with Role Strain.* Brookfield, Vt: Avebury Press.

Stanfield, J. R. 1979. *Economic Thought and Social Change.* Carbondale, Il.: Southern Illinois University Press.

___. 1983. "The Institutional Crisis of the Corporate-Welfare State." *International Journal of Social Economics,* 10, nos. 6–7: 45–66.

___. 1986. *The Economic Thought of Karl Polanyi.* London: Macmillan Press. New York: St. Martin's Press.

___. 1995. *Economics, Power, and Culture: Essays in the Development of Radical Institutionalism.* London: Macmillan.

Stanfield, J. R., and Jacqueline. B. Stanfield. 1980. "Consumption in Contemporary Capitalism: The Backward Art of Living." *Journal of Economic Issues,* 14 (June): 437–50.

"The Family Changes Shape." 1987. *USA Today,* Apr. 13.

Thurow, L. 1992. *Head to Head.* New York: William Morrow.

United States Bureau of the Census. *Earnings of Married Couple Families: 1987.* 1989. Current Population Reports, Series P-60, No. 165. Washington, D.C.: U. S. Government Printing Office.

Wallis, Claudia. 1987. "The Child Care Dilemma." *Time,* June 22, 54–60.

Yorburg, B. 1983. *Families and Societies: Survival or Extinction.* New York: Columbia University Press.

Zimmerman, Shirley L. 1988. *Understanding Family Policy: Theoretical Approaches.* Beverly Hills, Calif.: Sage Publications.

9

Social Provisioning and Inequality: Women and the Dual Welfare State

Janice Peterson

"Welfare reform" is once again at the top of the national policy agenda. From President Bill Clinton's campaign promises to "end welfare as we know it," to the Republican Party's "Contract with America," programs that provide income support to the poor are under attack. The program that receives the most attention is Aid to Families with Dependent Children (AFDC), which provides cash assistance primarily to poor, single-mother families. While the various "welfare reform" proposals differ in important ways, they all threaten the economic security and well-being of one of our society's most vulnerable populations.

The Clinton administration's welfare reform proposal, for example, stresses the placement of a time limit on the receipt of AFDC benefits ("two years and you're out"), to be accompanied by workfare programs and promises of increased job training, services, and efforts to "make work pay" (Amott 1994; Haveman and Scholz 1994–95). The "Personal Responsibility Act" of the "Contract with America" calls for time limits and new work requirements for AFDC, in addition to new eligibility restrictions (such as the denial of aid to young, unmarried mothers) and a reduction in the federal government's role in financing and administering the program (Bloom et al. 1994).

While these proposals are being presented by their supporters (and many critics) as radical departures from previous social welfare policy—and do call for significant changes—many of the underlying themes are not particularly new and instead reflect the long-standing race-, gender-, and class-based inequalities that permeate American society. The purpose of this chapter is to examine how these various modes of inequality have shaped the development of the U.S. welfare state and how the structure of the U.S. welfare state has, in turn, operated to institute and reinforce social and economic inequality.

Radical institutionalism, with its emphasis on values, myths, and power, provides a useful starting point for this investigation. The first section presents a radical institutionalist view of the welfare state, situating its role in the processes of social provisioning that define the economy. In the second section, the contradictory nature of state action will be examined through a discussion of the dualistic structure of the U.S. welfare state and the implications of this structure for the goals of equality and economic security. The third section concludes with a discussion of the implications of the dual welfare state for the current "welfare reform" debate.

RADICAL INSTITUTIONALISM AND THE WELFARE STATE

Social Provisioning, Equality, and Economic Security

Radical institutionalist views on the welfare state have their roots in the definition of economics found in institutional political economy. Institutionalists reject the notion that economics is merely the study of individual choices made in order to cope with some acultural notion of scarcity. Economics is defined as the study of social provisioning—the processes by which societies secure the material goods and services necessary to maintain and reproduce themselves. The purpose of such economic inquiry is to provide the tools to actively guide these processes to outcomes that promote the full participation of all individuals and the noninvidious recreation of community (Dugger 1989, 126; Waller 1992, 153).

In this framework, inequality is not something that can be explained away in terms of inappropriate individual choices and scarcity. Rather, inequality is the result of institutional processes based in invidious distinction and sustained by enabling myths, and it must be approached as an issue of status and power (Dugger 1989, 11). Inequality distorts the process of social provisioning and limits social and economic participation. Thus, equality is a fundamental goal of radical institutionalism. It is not viewed as a luxury to be pursued after the economy has reached prosperity; instead, it is viewed as "an essential element to progress" (Dugger 1989, 11).

The pursuit of social and economic equality requires economic security as a primary outcome of the social provisioning process. Economic security is necessary for the pursuit of other goals; it is necessary for the full participation of all individuals in a meaningful way (Waller 1992, 158). Radical institutionalism views economic security as "being the result of ongoing social/cultural processes, not as a consequence of individual efficacy" (Waller 1992, 156). Thus, radical institutionalists reject individualistic explanations of economic insecurity, arguing that it is a systemic problem requiring a collective response.

The Welfare State

Institutionalists argue that the state, through its definition and enforcement of the working rules, defines the economy and legitimizes the power relationships, institutions, and beliefs that shape economic outcomes (Samuels 1989). Thus, the state is intimately involved in the process of social provisioning and has a necessary role to play in the provision of economic security and the pursuit of equality. Government policies most closely associated with these goals are those of the "welfare state"—"the use of the power of the central government to protect people from the income loss inherent in industrial society ... and to provide a minimum standard of economic well-being for all citizens, irrespective of circumstances" (Peterson 1985, 602).

Radical institutionalists also stress that the relationship between the state and the economy is a complex and often contradictory one. The contradictory nature of state action reflects the fact that the state both defines and is defined by the status quo distribution of power (Samuels 1989, 431). Through its policies, the state may provide a vehicle for the amelioration of social and economic problems at the same time that it supports that status quo and resists change.

The structure and development of the U.S. welfare state reflects this contradiction. On one hand, the welfare state is a response to the insecurities introduced by machine technology and market capitalism (Hamilton 1984). However, the state's response to such insecurity has not been the same for all groups in society. The determination of whose interests will count and how they will be served has been shaped by class interests, gender norms, and racism.

Thus, while the U.S. welfare state has altered private market outcomes and provided economic security for many, it has also instituted various forms of inequality. As Gosta Esping-Anderson has argued, "The welfare state is not just a mechanism that intervenes in, and possibly corrects, the structure of inequality; it is, in its own right, a system of stratification" (quoted in Quadagno 1994, 8). In the United States, this system of stratification is manifested in the "dual welfare state"—the two-tiered system of income support that has shaped social welfare policy through this century.

THE DUAL WELFARE STATE AND INEQUALITY

The Dual Welfare State and the Meaning of *Welfare*

The defining feature of the U.S. welfare state is the distinction between social insurance and public assistance income transfers. Social insurance and public assistance programs provide benefits of different degrees of adequacy and coverage to different groups in society, creating a dualistic, two-tiered system with: "a top layer of increasingly generous and politically legitimated social insurance programs and a bottom layer of politically vulnerable programs aimed at the poor" (Weir, Orloff, and Skocpol 1988, 297).

This structure limits the welfare state's potential for progressive redistribution, by essentially "helping most the people who need it the least" (Gordon 1994, 6). Those individuals most likely to have access to the primary-tier, social insurance programs are also the ones most likely to receive private pensions, sick leave, and health insurance. Public spending on the poor through public assistance has consistently been much smaller in magnitude than social insurance spending. Thus, any redistributive gains that may have been offered to the poor through public assistance have been offset by the superior benefits to the middle and upper-working classes through social insurance (Gordon 1994, 300).

In addition, the hierarchical structure of the welfare state fosters the enabling myths that legitimize various forms of inequality. Although "income support" includes both types of programs, Americans "make a sharp conceptual and evaluative distinction" between public assistance and social insurance programs (Skocpol 1988, 296). Linda Gordon argues that the contemporary, pejorative meaning of *welfare* derives from this distinction, which: "labels only some programs 'welfare' and understands others to be in a different category" (Gordon 1994, 1). Public assistance programs are considered *welfare*; social insurance programs are not.

This distinction has been particularly important, and damaging, in the evolution of the AFDC program: the perverse tendency of our welfare system to deepen inequality has been particularly pronounced in the case of AFDC. The stigmas of "welfare" and of single motherhood intersect; hostility to the poor and hostility to the deviant family forms reinforce each other. The resentment undercuts political support for the program, and benefits fall farther behind inflation. The resulting immiseration makes poor single mothers even more needy and less politically attractive. (Gordon 1994, 6)

Thus, evolution of the AFDC program in the context of the dual welfare state—its evolution and characteristics as welfare—provides an important perspective on today's welfare reform discussions.

The Roots of the Dual Welfare State

The dual welfare state grew out of the social reforms of the Progressive Era. The income support programs of the Progressive Era were structured by the concerns and ideologies of their time. Of particular importance was the ideology of "separate spheres" and the assumption of the "family wage." This ideology prescribed very different economic roles for men and women—"the breadwinner/father and the economically dependent, domestic wife/mother" (Gordon 1994, 7). Although this was never a particularly accurate description of many families, the gender, race, and class norms contained in this ideology shaped social welfare policy through the structure of programs and the exclusionary practices of welfare administrators.

Two state-level Progressive Era programs—Mother's Pensions and Workmen's Compensation (both enacted in 1911)—provided the early models for public assistance and social insurance. While both programs attempted to address the increased economic insecurity associated with the evolution of industrial capitalism, they represented very different approaches to public provisioning—one primarily focused on women, the other primarily focused on men.

Workmen's Compensation was the first social insurance program, introducing the notion of collective responsibility for the insecurity and risks imposed on individuals in an industrial society (Hamilton 1984, 147). It was specifically designed to protect workers and their families from income loss due to disability or death in industrial accidents (Silverberg 1985, 2; Polakow 1993, 53). The workers actually served by this program were predominantly white—the "criteria for eligible labor" excluded both domestic workers and agricultural labor, thus excluding the majority of black workers (Polakow 1993, 55).

Mother's Pensions were designed to aid poor children in families that had lost their male breadwinner. There was concern that, left without the financial support of a husband, mothers could not adequately perform their childrearing duties. It was argued that if these mothers entered the labor force, their children would lack the supervision and guidance necessary to become productive citizens (Silverberg 1985, 4; Katz 1986, 113–29; Abramovitz 1988, 190–94). Mother's Pensions set an important precedent through its provision of public "outdoor" (noninstitutionalized) aid to poor women and children in the United States (Katz 1986, 128–29).

The characteristics of Mother's Pension's also set the pattern for future welfare programs. Even among its supporters, there was concern about the "pauperizing tendencies" of such public aid. This concern was addressed by providing benefits to "deserving mothers" only and keeping such benefits extremely low (Gordon 1994, 49–52). Administrators of the program distinguished between "deserving" and "undeserving" mothers on the basis of their adherence to (class- and race-defined) gender norms and notions of "moral behavior." "Suitable home" requirements were used to exclude many of the women who needed aid the most. The vast majority of Mother's Pension recipients were white and widowed (Nelson 1990, 141–42; Polakow 1993, 55; Gordon 1994, 46, 50–52; Sidel 1986, 83).

The differences between the two programs reflect the fundamental differences between social insurance and welfare. The eligibility and decision rules in Mother's Pensions were not as standardized and automatic as those used in Workmen's Compensation. The behavior of Mother's Pensions recipients was considered in their continued eligibility, while the behavior of Workmen's Compensation recipients was not (Nelson, 1990, 141–142; Polakow, 1993, 55; Gordon 1994, 46). Exclusion on the basis of race, however, was a characteristic shared by both. This established important patterns that would be replicated in the federal legislation that followed.

The Construction of the Dual Welfare State

The widespread economic insecurity of the Great Depression challenged traditional explanations of poverty that focused on individual causes and promoted private solutions. The Social Security Act of 1935 firmly established the role of the federal government in the provision of economic security and broke the traditional reliance on private charity and local aid. The act established a system of income support that has improved the standard of living of many Americans.

At the same time, the Social Security Act instituted the dualistic structure of the U.S. welfare state, carefully distinguishing between social insurance (Old Age Insurance and Unemployment Compensation) and public assistance (Aid to Dependent Children, Old Age Assistance, and Aid to the Blind) programs. This nourished existing social divisions and created new ones, increasing the relative poverty of those ineligible for social insurance. The tendency of this division to foster inequality was strengthened by two major omissions from the Social Security Act, public jobs and medical insurance (Gordon 1994, 302).

The social insurance programs were constructed as the core of the Social Security Act. They extended the philosophy behind the earlier Workmen's Compensation programs, stressing the systemic insecurity of industrial market capitalism and the need for the public to assist the victims of such insecurities in a dignified manner (Gordon 1994, 149). Social Security administrators sought to build legitimacy and public support for the social insurance programs by distinguishing them from the public assistance programs (see, for example, Gordon 1994, 145–46, 283; Weir, Orloff, and Skocpol 1988, 287).

Unlike public assistance, the social insurance programs were not directed at the poor, but sought to protect the incomes of wage earners and prevent them from falling into poverty. Thus, "one of social insurance's selling points was its benefits to all classes" (Gordon 1994, 150). The social insurance programs of the Social Security Act did not, however, provide economic security to all workers. The focus on the interruption of wages as the central problem led to the neglect of the "working poor" and those who were not wage earners, such as small businessmen and farmers (Gordon 1994, 179). In addition, the definition of covered occupations worked to exclude many female and black wage earners.

The social insurance programs assumed traditional gender roles and the family wage. Thus, it was assumed that women would benefit from social insurance as the economic dependents of wage-earning males (Gordon 1994, 179). In addition, the occupations covered, as well as the type of employment history and wage levels required for eligibility, excluded many women wage earners from these programs (Quadagno 1994, 157; Abramovitz 1988, 250).

Race and class interests also entered directly into the structure of social insurance programs, through the exclusion of the agricultural and domestic service occupations—the primary sources of employment for blacks at that time (Scokpol 1988, 303) These occupations were excluded as part of a political compromise to secure the support of key southern Congressmen, who "opposed any program that would grant cash directly to black workers, because direct cash could undermine the entire foundation of the plantation economy" (Quadagno 1994, 21). Thus, the majority of black workers were excluded from the economic security offered by the core programs of the Social Security Act (Quadagno 1994, 21, 157; Abramovitz 1988, 250; Gordon 1994, 276; Katz 1986, 244).

The family wage ideology also influenced the development of the public assistance programs, particularly Aid to Dependent Children (ADC). Like Mother's Pensions, the ADC program reflected the concern that single mothers, if forced to support themselves through wage labor, could not adequately nurture and supervise their children (Abramovitz 1988, 315). ADC was designed to "benefit women directly when male wage earners failed them, but did not encourage women's independence from men" (Gordon 1994, 180).

As with the social insurance programs, the passage of the public assistance programs required political compromise. In the case of ADC, the most significant compromise was the sacrifice of federal standards. State and local control in determining eligibility requirements and benefit levels meant "that blacks in the South could be deprived of adequate welfare assistance," reducing the threat to Southern low-wage industries and agriculture (Skocpol 1988, 303). Southern welfare administrators typically "could see no reason why the employable Negro mother should not continue her usually sketchy labor ... they had always gotten along" (Gordon 1994, 296). Thus, while ADC was supported by arguments of the importance of motherhood, many women (particularly women of color) continued to be viewed as low-wage workers.

Lack of federal control also encouraged continuing reliance on the "suitable home" requirements contained in Mother's Pensions. This allowed ADC administrators to remove any mothers from the program if their behavior was considered "immoral or unfit." The "suitable home" rules were more concerned with controlling the behavior of ADC recipients than protecting the well-being of children, and were disproportionately applied to black families (Miller 1990, 33–34; Gordon 1994, 275–76).

Like the supporters of Mother's Pensions before them, proponents of ADC stressed that it was a program for "deserving mothers" only. State and local control of the program gave ADC officials a great deal of discretion in determining who fit this criteria. Initially, the majority of ADC recipients were white widows (Abramovitz 1988, 315). The 1939 amendments to the Social Security Act established Survivor's Insurance (SI), a social insurance program providing benefits for the widows and children of men covered by the Old Age Insurance program. As the white widows of industrial workers shifted from ADC to SI, the ADC population became increasingly stigmatized (Quadagno 1994, 119–20). This extended the stratification in the welfare state, creating a dual-income support system for single mother families (see, for example, Peterson and Petersen 1994).

The Limitations of the Dual Welfare State

The structure of public provisioning instituted by the Social Security Act guided and constrained all social welfare policy that has followed. Nowhere have the limits of this structure been "more telling than among black Americans" (Weir, Orloff, and Scokpol 1988, 297). The racially segregated welfare state and inequitable treatment of black Americans was challenged by the Civil Rights Movement of the 1960s.

Lyndon Johnson's War on Poverty, launched in response to the Civil Rights movement, was an attempt to address the economic needs of black Americans by adding a "new layer of programs especially targeted for the poor" (Weir, Orloff, and Scokpol 1988, 305). The designers of the War on Poverty believed that economic growth would allow for the continued expansion of the social insurance programs that benefited the white middle class at the same time that new antipoverty programs were established. The hope was that these new programs (such as Food Stamps, subsidized housing, and Medicaid) would "overcome racial divisions by eliminating poverty once and for all" (Weir, Orloff, and Scokpol 1988, 305).

Ultimately, the designers of the War on Poverty were trapped by the structure of the dual welfare state and did little to alter its basic structure. The new poverty programs further entrenched the hierarchical structure of social provision inherited from the Social Security Act (Weir, Orloff, and Scokpol 1988, 298; Katz 1986, 255). While the War on Poverty sought to extend equal opportunity to all Americans, it failed to address the most important needs: "social programs for managing the labor market and supporting the needs of service sector workers" (Quadagno 1994, 12–13). Thus the War on Poverty did "little for the working poor and for women in the expanding service sector" (Quadagno 1994, 12–13).

The experience of the War on Poverty also illustrates the centrality of race in American social welfare policy. Jill Quadagno argues that many of the programs of the War on Poverty did have the potential to address racial inequities and promote racial equality, which is why they ultimately fostered opposition leading to the backlash against the welfare state in the 1980s and 1990s (Quadagno 1994, 155). Thus, racism is critical to understanding the context of current welfare reform discussions: "An anti-government ideology has generated most antagonism to the welfare state when it has been associated with racial issues" (Quadagno 1994, 196).

Since the War on Poverty, discussions of "welfare" have been focused on AFDC and the question of whether single mothers should be "regarded primarily as 'workers' or as 'mothers' for the purposes of income support" (Evans 1992, 378–79). The continuing debate on this topic reflects the contradictory relationship between women (particularly single mothers) and the welfare state. The Social Security Act aided women as mothers not workers, despite the economic realities that denied exclusive domesticity to many women. Changes in the structure of the economy and the roles of women in the decades following the Social Security Act made this even more destructive. The welfare state has consistently failed to address the needs of women wage earners, creating a situation where many working mothers (single and married) have "faced two bad choices—employment or 'welfare,' both on inferior terms" (Gordon 1994, 301).

Work incentives and work requirements have come to dominate notions of welfare reform, beginning with the 1967 Social Security amendments, continuing through the 1988 Family Support Act, and setting the tone for current discussions. The emphasis on moving poor single mothers into the workplace is particularly strong in the United States, reflecting (among other things) the importance of race in American social welfare policy and the categorical nature of the U.S. income support system (see, for example, Evans 1992). The failure of work programs to achieve the desired reduction in the AFDC caseload has contributed to public dissatisfaction with the program.

Implications for Welfare Reform

There are several characteristics that define AFDC as a secondary-tier welfare program. In terms of the current welfare reform discussion, the following are particularly important:

1. Meager benefits—the monthly AFDC benefit for a family of three in the median state is $366 (Bloom et al. 1994, 55).
2. Stigma—the receipt of welfare has always been highly stigmatized. "Welfare mothers" are the new national scapegoats, and have been declared responsible for a multitude of social and economic problems.
3. Behavioral Requirements—from "morals testing" to work requirements, eligibility and receipt of AFDC has always been conditional on recipient's behavior.
4. State and Local Control—the AFDC program has always had a high degree of state and local control in comparison with primary-tier programs, such as Old Age Insurance. Moreover, state and local control have worked to accentuate the first three characteristics.

The general policy conclusion that arises from the literature on the dual welfare state is that these characteristics are not desirable and instead contribute to the poverty of single mothers and their children. Any real welfare reform, therefore, should seek to eliminate these characteristics and reduce the stratification in social welfare policy. The current proposals promise to do the opposite—capping and limiting benefits, increasing the behavioral content of eligibility requirements, and increasing state and local control of welfare programs.

An examination of the history of the U.S. social welfare policy highlights several important omissions that have accentuated the structural inequities of the dual welfare state. Lack of attention to job creation and the provision of full employment, lack of programs to address the problems of low-wage labor faced by the "working poor," lack of programs to aid working parents (particularly mothers), and lack of a national health care plan have limited the benefits of the welfare state to many Americans. More progressive approaches to welfare reform seek to address these omissions by focusing attention on strengthening low-wage labor markets and the provision of services required by working parents (see, for example, Haveman and Scholz 1994–95, 8–9; Bergmann and Hartmann 1994).

A progressive approach to welfare reform—one concerned with eliminating poverty versus merely reducing caseloads—must recognize that the problems faced by welfare recipients go beyond the welfare system. As Chris Tilly and Randy Albelda argue, "The solution must be more comprehensive than simply reforming that system. What we need is a set of thorough changes in the relations among work, family and income" (Tilly and Albelda 1994, 9). Tilly and Albelda propose the following (1994, 9–10):

1. Provide supports (such as universal health coverage and child care) for low wage workers.
2. Use the power and resources of the federal government to create jobs.
3. Make work pay by changing taxes and government assistance programs.
4. Make work pay by shoring up wages and private benefits.
5. Make a serious commitment to lifelong education and training.
6. Build flexibility into the workplace.
7. Mend the safety net, recognizing the insecurity of the market system.

In attempting to reform welfare, it is necessary to respond to the *realities* of the lives of welfare recipients, not the welfare myths that reinforce inequality. It is critical to acknowledge that welfare exists as a small part of a much larger system of income support—a system that reflects and reinforces serious social and economic divisions. These inequalities—within the welfare state and across society—must be addressed as part of welfare reform. True welfare reform requires serious attention to economic inequality, civil rights, and the problems of racism and sexism.

William Waller has argued that in addition to the provision of a minimal level of real income, economic security involves "continually providing opportunities for individuals to participate more fully in the economic activity of society in a meaningful way" (Waller 1992, 157). This provides a radical institutionalist principle to guide our examinations of welfare reform. True reform will require that the welfare state explicitly address the goal of equality and work toward the end of the "noninvidious recreation of community" (Tool 1979, 293).

REFERENCES

Abramovitz, Mimi. 1988. *Regulating the Lives of Women: Social Welfare Policy from Colonial Times to the Present.* Boston: South End Press.
Amott, Teresa. 1994. "The War on Welfare: Clinton's Carrots and Sticks," *Dollars and Sense,* Nov./Dec., 12–17.

Bergmann, Barbara, and Heidi Hartmann. 1994. "A Welfare Reform Based on Help for Working Parents [mimeo]." Economists' Policy Group for Women's Issues, Washington, D.C.

Bloom, Dan, Sharon Parrott, Isaac Shapiro, and David Super. 1994. *The Personal Responsibility Act: An Analysis.* Washington, D.C.: Center for Budget and Policy Priorities.

Dugger, William M. 1989. *Radical Institutionalism: Contemporary Voices.* Westport, Conn.: Greenwood Press.

Evans, Patricia. 1992. "Targeting Single Mothers for Employment: Comparisons from the United States, Britain, and Canada," *Social Service Review,* 66 (Sept.): 378–98.

Gordon, Linda. 1994. *Pitied But Not Entitled: Single Mothers and the History of Welfare.* New York: Free Press.

Hamilton, David. 1984. "The Myth is Not the Reality: Income Maintenance and Welfare," *Journal of Economic Issues,* 18 (Mar.): 143–58.

Haveman, Robert, and John Karl Scholz. 1994–1995. "The Clinton Welfare Plan: Will It End Poverty as We Know It?" *Focus,* 16 (Winter): 1–9.

Katz, Michael. 1986. *In the Shadow of the Poor House: A Social History of Welfare in America.* New York: Basic Books.

Miller, Dorothy. 1990. *Women and Social Welfare: A Feminist Analysis.* New York: Praeger.

Nelson, Barbara. 1990. "The Origins of the Two-Channel Welfare State: Workmen's Compensation and Mothers' Aid." In Linda Gordon, ed. *Women, the State and Welfare.* Madison: University of Wisconsin Press, 123–51.

Peterson, Janice, and Carol Petersen. 1994. "Single Mother Families and the Dual Welfare State." *Review of Social Economy,* 52 (Fall): 314–38.

Peterson, Wallace. 1985. "The U.S. 'Welfare State' and the Conservative Counterrevolution," *Journal of Economic Issues,* 19 (Sept.): 601–41.

Polakow, Valerie. 1993. *Lives on the Edge: Single Mothers and Their Children in the Other America.* Chicago: University of Chicago Press.

Quadagno, Jill. 1994. *The Color of Welfare: How Racism Undermined the War on Poverty.* New York: Oxford University Press.

Samuels, Warren. 1989. "Some Fundamentals on the Economic Role of the Government." *Journal of Economic Issues,* 23 (June): 427–33.

Sidel, Ruth. 1986. *Women and Children Last: The Plight of Poor Women in Affluent America.* New York: Viking.

Silverberg, Helene. 1985. "Private Mothers and Public Policy: Women, Welfare and the State." *The Cornell Journal of Social Relations,* 18 (Spring): 1–12.

Skocpol, Theda. 1988. "The Limits of the New Deal System and the Roots of Contemporary Welfare Dilemmas." In Margaret Weir, Ann Orloff and Theda Skocpol, eds., *The Politics of Social Welfare Policy in the United States.* Princeton, N.J.: Princeton University Press, 293–311.

Tilly, Chris, and Randy Albelda. 1994. "It's Not Working: Why Many Single Mothers Can't Work Their Way Out of Poverty." *Dollars and Sense,* Nov./Dec., 8–10.

Tool, Marc R. 1979. *The Discretionary Economy.* Santa Monica, Calif.: Goodyear.

Waller, William. 1992. "Economic Security and the State." In William Dugger and William Waller, eds., *The Stratified State: Radical Institutionalist Theories of Participation and Duality.* Armonk, N.Y.: M. E. Sharpe, 153–71.

Weir, Margaret, Ann Orloff, and Theda Skocpol, eds. 1988. *The Politics of Social Welfare Policy in the United States.* Princeton, N.J.: Princeton University Press, 293–311.

10

Inequality and Government

Zahid Shariff

This chapter does two things. The first part ("The Role of Government") identifies the unit and level of government with the greatest potential for reducing income inequalities. The issue has some significance because the number of governments operating in the United States is presently more than 85,000 (United States 1994a, 1). The second part ("Political and Institutional Dynamic") explains the forces that produce the conclusion reached in the first part. Some final thoughts are in the conclusion.

THE ROLE OF GOVERNMENT

Fiscal Outcomes

As is now widely accepted, government intervention is virtually impossible to locate with some certainty (or, for that matter, completely factored out) for the simple reason that it is so pervasive. The free market economy is itself created by government and indeed could not exist without the very considerable continuing support of tax-supported institutions (Pitelis 1993).

Nevertheless, attempts that can only be called valiant have been made to determine the aggregative impact of fiscal decisions of the thousands of governments. The well-known studies show mixed results (Gillespie 1965; Musgrave, Case, and Leonard 1974; Reynolds and Somlensky 1977). More recently, the efforts of the federal government to reduce income inequality have weakened. The fiscal effects of the Ronald Reagan years are not in doubt: income inequalities have increased (Pechman 1985; see also Phillips 1990). Crucial problems common to virtually all of these and similar studies have to do with the absence of any consensus concerning the values to be attributed to such major variables as the incidence of taxes (particularly those on business and property), allocation of benefits (particularly for defense and highways), and the cost of general government.

Government Revenues. The most powerful influence on income inequalities in the revenue structures is the choice of taxes levied.   In this regard, progressivity is clearly most pronounced in federal government.   Since 1945, more than 40 percent of federal revenues have come from the personal income tax; presently they contribute 44 percent (United States 1995, 23–24).   That is very considerably higher than is to be found in any other government in the United States.   Even the Reagan administration's changes reduced, but did not eliminate, the progressivity of that tax (Pechman 1985).   To a very limited extent, Clinton's first budget restored the lost progressivity.

In addition to the personal income tax, the federal government collects social security taxes.   They are regressive and their contribution to federal revenues has increased from 16 percent in 1960 to 37 percent in 1995.   Corporate tax meanwhile has dropped from 23 to 10 percent over the same period of time (United States 1995), but determined efforts have not yielded reliable conclusions about who actually pays it.

In the case of state and local governments, income tax has never contributed more than 10 percent of state and local taxes, and its marginal rate rarely reaches the federal level (United States 1994c, 302).

Changes in income tax sometimes bump into other fiscal realities and produce complex results.   Recently in New Jersey, for instance, Governor Christine Todd Whitman claimed credit for reducing income tax by 30 percent over a two-year period; in reality, that yielded an average income tax saving of $40, while the property tax soared, on the average, by $170 (Herbert 1995).   State and local governments collect revenues from other sources than income as well.   The major categories for 1992 (the last year for which figures are available) are provided in Table 10.1.

Table 10.1
Sources of State and Local Government Revenues, in Billions

REVENUE SOURCE	DOLLARS
Income tax	115
Property tax	178
Sales tax	196
Corporate tax	24
Other taxes	42
Utility and liquor stores	62

Source: United States (1994c), 302.

Overall, state and local taxes are decisively regressive.   Recent state tax and/or spending limitations have probably reinforced that regressivity. Furthermore, all state and local taxes on income, real estate, and personal property are deductible for federal tax purposes, which reduces the progressivity of the federal income tax.

Government Spending

Social security, disability, and medical costs consume about half of total federal spending, and outlays for defense and interest take up another third. The rest is spent on general government and grants to state and local governments. Allocating benefits of these expenditures to different income classes is a nightmarish task. In some cases, as in defense, the principle of indivisibility leads to one conclusion, whereas the distribution of that benefit in accordance with one's income or wealth leads to quite another. Leaving aside, in addition, the functional benefits of poverty for the nonpoor (Gintis 1994), the overall proportion of such outlays, even by conventional standards, are not high compared to Canada and Western European countries. The United States. Congressional Budget Office projections for means-tested programs for fiscal year 1995 are summarized in Table 10.2. The total for such programs amounts to about 12 percent of the federal budget. Of that, $73 billion (or a little more than 2 percent) is allocated for poverty, and another $73 billion is for the elderly in need. About half of the total is for the medical needs of the poor.

Table 10.2
Federal Funding for Means-Tested Programs, in Billions

MEANS-TESTED PROGRAM	DOLLARS
AFDC*	17
Food stamps	25
Supplementary security**	27
Housing assistance	27
Medicaid	90
Head start	4
TOTAL	190

Source: United States (1994b), 42.
*AFDC is Aid to Families with Dependent Children.
**This is for elderly Americans with low incomes or disabilities.

At the state and local levels, the kinds, variety, and volume of public spending are even more confusing. The difficulties of allocating spending, through these governments' highly imaginative categories, to various income groups require (in some ways), even more tedious, as well as imaginative, study than at the federal level. State and local governments in 1992 spent $154 billion dollars, out of their total expenditures of $1,147 billion, on public welfare (United States 1994c, 302). That amounts to about 10 percent, but even that small a portion is largely funded through grants from the federal government. In the absence of federal willingness to pay half or more of such costs, as it does presently, it is entirely unclear what the level of local support would be. Cuts in federal funding have not been made up by such governments; average welfare benefits now are considerably lower in constant dollars than they were more than ten years ago. On the other hand, public highways, parks, beaches, libraries, higher education, forests, summer camps, museums, and golf courses, all of which are financed to a greater extent by the state and local governments' own resources, are generally known to be used by the nonpoor more frequently than the poor.

Fiscal Mismatch

Public spending takes place, not only by different governments, but also through various transfer mechanisms. Funds tend to flow from the national to subnational units of government, with varying degrees of conditions attached. Since the needs of the units and their financial resources are often not equally matched, national governments attempt to reduce the extent of that mismatch; that is called *fiscal equalization*. A study of four federal systems (Australia, Canada, Germany, and the United States) by the Advisory Commission on Intergovernmental Relations (ACIR), concluded:

Thus, it seems clear that the United States is less committed to equalizing resources than are the other three federal systems studied. Yet equalization is by no means absent from the field of U.S. intergovernmental relations, where the General Revenue Sharing program constitutes the major vehicle to achieve this objective. This program provides aid to more than 38,000 units of general government, and as the ACIR's and other studies have noted, the assistance does successfully transfer resources in an equalizing manner, with greater amounts being provided to the less fiscally able jurisdictions. In addition to General Revenue Sharing, a number of categorical aid programs have formulas that include measures of fiscal ability to distribute aid for specific purposes. (1981, 98)

Fiscal equalization is not only important in federal states, it takes place in unitary states as well. In Japan, for instance, it is pursued through local allocation grants (Ishi 1993, 267–81), and 17.5 percent of the 1994 budget was set aside for that purpose (Asahi Shimbun 1995).

Unfortunately, it is precisely those fiscal arrangements that generate the pressure for fiscal equalization that declined during the Reagan administration: General Revenue Sharing disappeared, many categorical grants were consolidated, grant funding was reduced, and block grants took their place. Fiscal equalization by the U.S. government was not impressive in comparison with other federal systems; that is now true even in relation to its own past.

Public Policies. In the distribution of incomes, fiscal measures played a major role, but other influences were also at work. It was the strong base furnished by the momentum of President Franklin Roosevelt's public policy commitments that eventually reduced or eliminated for many the impediments to escaping from low incomes; they, too, were responsible for reducing inequality among income groups.

During and after World War II, a number of race-, gender-, and class-related developments at the federal level increased the incomes of millions who had been shut out of many occupations, and trapped in low-paying jobs or at the bottom rungs of hierarchies. Frequently repeated charges concerning "failures" of governmental programs during the 1960s and 1970s overlook the considerable achievements in these areas (Levitan and Taggart 1976); it may even be that their relative effectiveness has been threatening enough to induce these denunciations. Many barriers or exclusions were lifted, and well-established patterns of neglect, eliminated. The opening up of opportunities for persons of color, women, and the poor had demonstrable effects. For instance, "about 22 percent of the population had cash incomes below the poverty line in 1959. The poverty rate dropped rapidly to 11 percent in 1973" (Rivlin 1992, 48). Poverty among the elderly was dramatically reduced by the changes in Social Security benefits. Furthermore, in 1939 the per capita income of blacks was only 39 percent of white income, but by 1971, it was 57 percent. The poverty rate dropped rapidly for blacks, although it remained far above the rate for whites (Rivlin 1992, 49). In virtually all these cases, the federal role was crucial in opening up opportunities for those who were discriminated against or were vulnerable to some other form of predation.

The overall effect of the fiscal and public policies of the federal government was to reduce income inequalities. In the past, federal achievements were greater. In view of that record, of the dynamic that produces that result, and of the resources and instruments at its disposal, the federal government clearly has the greatest potential for reducing inequalities.

POLITICAL AND INSTITUTIONAL DYNAMIC

The conclusion drawn here—that it is the federal government that has the greatest potential for reducing income inequalities—prepares the ground for asking why that is so. What are the forces that help produce that result? Some of the answers are found, I believe, in exploring the preference for local action and the political and institutional dynamic that often propels the federal government in progressive directions.

The Appeal of State and Local Governments

The attractiveness of state and local political units is based on perceptions that are steeped in history and repeated regularly in political rhetoric. Since they are so well known, a quick listing will suffice. Preference for a stronger role for states and localities is often based on one or a combination of four basic arguments. They are, first, that such governments are closer to citizens than the federal government. That, in, turn, is linked to such notions as their (a) natural or organic character, (b) consensus decision-making (as opposed to partisan clashes in larger governments), (c) ability to offer an authentic sense of community or fellowship, (d) potential for checking the authority of a distant federal government, and (e) responsiveness to the needs of citizens, as well as their "empowerment."

The second argument is that the transfer costs of sending revenue to Washington, D.C., and then getting some of it back involves unnecessary costs. The metaphor of "leaky buckets" has been employed in this context (Okun 1975). The holes in the bucket represent administrative costs as well as the imposition of federal priorities unsuited to local needs.

Third, when the prospects for change through community action are not feasible or not quick enough, individuals are said to have the ability to move to other political jurisdictions that have more compatible priorities. This is sometimes described as "voting with one's feet." Keeping alive "exit" as an option (Hirschman 1970) expands individual freedom by requiring the devolution of power to numerous political units and limiting it at the national level.

Finally, the multiplicity of governmental units as they wrestle with various efforts to comply with the citizens' preferences come up with a variety of policy and implementation designs. These are seen as "experiments" and the state and local governments are applauded as "laboratories for change." Local action, it is argued, should precede federal initiative.

Any review and evaluation of these arguments must acknowledge their long history and continuing popularity. A true national role for the federal government in centralizing and harmonizing domestic policies, other than waging war, has been accepted only reluctantly in the United States, whereas support for decentralized power is voiced from both ends of the political spectrum.

The notion that local and state governments are closer and more responsive to people is part of the standard political rhetoric, but it has very little basis in reality. The proportion of Americans who vote for state and local representatives and officials is remarkably low. Press and Fournier reviewed the relevant evidence and came to this conclusion: "About 50 to 55 percent of potential voters participate in presidential elections compared to an average of 45 percent in governors' races and 25 percent in mayoral elections" (1990, 131). Voters' information about the powers and terms of office correspond to these figures. As for the organic or natural basis for local units of government, it is perhaps appropriate to recall that the United States is a "settler" nation. As such, it is an "unnatural" or "rational" enterprise that not only involved the conquest of pre-settler groups, but also the self-interested construction of a whole set of new institutions that favored the settlers. The boundaries of governmental jurisdictions were consciously drawn; they were not "lost in the dim mist of history," as organic or natural entities are often thought to be. Furthermore, the absence of partisan politics may indeed represent consensus, or it may, just as likely, represent the thwarting of dissent. Consensus politics at the local level (it is rarely practiced at the state level) may also be maintained by resorting to exclusionary practices that keep out certain kinds of people, and their opinions.

The "leaky buckets" are based on a number of unexamined assumptions. The leaks, Okun argued, are not the result only of transportation to federal government and back, they also are the bureaucratic costs of programs. However, closer examination suggests that these costs are high when the service provided is labor intensive (e.g., defense and health) or the distrust of the "customer" is very high (e.g., welfare).   When, on the other hand, the "customer" is held in high esteem and is trusted—as is the case when predominantly high-income earning individuals derive their governmental benefits through tax expenditures—the bureaucratic cost (that is to say the extent of scrutiny for possible abuse or fraud) suddenly shrinks. Bigger leaks may represent class, gender, and race issues, and not some neutral notions of efficiency (Shariff 1990).

"Voting with one's feet" and "laboratories for change" may be taken up together.   Some unique local practices have indeed emerged in local jurisdictions and so have innovations that have later been adopted at the federal level. In other cases, their significance is limited; they may even produce some perverse results. Mobility and experimentation are based on the view that the range of options should be expanded or maintained to meet the diverse needs of people. Consider that range for a moment. At one point, the range of options eagerly sought for included the continuation of some free and some slave states. A costly war settled that question; as a consequence, the range of options was certainly narrowed for some, but it dramatically expanded the rudimentary elements of freedom for millions of others.   What should be the limits of sacrifice on the part of some to enable the freedom of others? The answers to that question turn on the perennial issues of class, race, and gender. Sweeping all that under the rubric (rug) of diversity, or freedom, or experimentation is at least confusing, if it is not also disingenuous.   The ability to indulge one's prejudices as readily as in the past has indeed been reduced; but that has also increased the freedom of others to feel secure. Travel from one area to another, or "shopping for a community," no longer provides the variations it once did. Recreating opportunities for such "experimentation" for some spells terror for others.

Political and Institutional Dynamic

Revealing the seamy side and contradictions of the appeal for decentralized government is an important part of an explanation for federal government's potential for reducing inequalities, but there is more to it. Other forces, some structural and some social, are also at work.

Punishing Success. The problems facing most citizens are less likely now to be ones that can effectively be addressed at the local level. Moreover, when heroic local effort does, in some cases, produce positive results, its effects are often tragic.   Let us assume that an area's government is able to reduce pollution, poverty, homelessness, and racial, gender, and class discrimination. These changes will lead to predictable results: more people will move in, services will be stretched beyond their limits, and businesses will consider locating elsewhere as their tax burdens increase and their political influence is reduced. For these reasons, local successes rarely go unpunished.

Political Competition. As the federal government "returns power to states and localities" (a chorus presently being sung by both major political parties) two consequences are noticeable. First, competition among states and cities for jobs becomes intensified. The kind and extent of subsidies provided are of no small consequence; they are offered in the form of tax abatement, infrastructure development, environmental waivers, and even special labor contracts, and they run into hundreds of millions of dollars. The granting of such subsidies poses at least three major problems: (a) often no new jobs are, in fact, created; jobs are only moved around; (b) even when they are created, the price tag is high: incentives of $100,000 for each job moved or created are not unheard of (Fiordalisi 1989); (c) diversity among political jurisdictions is reduced as their incentive packages begin to look similar; and a more generalized fear focuses political debate increasingly on making the state or city attractive for the existing businesses to stay and for others to move in. Fear of capital strike already hangs over many politicians, a situation that Lindblom (1977) perceptibly called the "priveleged position of business." How far will such competition pull down other values—environmental protection, support for families and communities, reduction of income inequalities—is not known in advance, but the trend toward "downward harmonization" is unmistakable. What this competition puts in place is a structure of rewards and penalties that channels resources in some directions without clearly identifying the interests that suffer and those that benefit. Cost-benefit analysis, alas, is insisted on only when the federal regulation of business or spending on social programs is involved. Competition for jobs erodes certain values, reduces diversity among governmental units, and increases political interference in market forces; cost-benefit analysis is often not applicable in such contexts. (Carefully selecting a methodological tool to serve ideological purposes is now a well-established practice; it is frequently reinforced by insisting that the tool is neutral.) Conservatives often take a stand against the reduction of diversity and intervention in market forces, but here they quickly abandon them in support of their class interests.

Second, pressuring local governments to resolve the problems that manifest themselves within their borders creates a self-reinforcing dynamic. As poor localities become less attractive, those who can exit, do, further diminishing the pool of common resources. In this segmented world, the urban poor grow increasingly distant from the suburban majority (Weir 1994, 338). The relative ease with which governments can be formed, a phenomenon "often praised as the essence of American democracy, provides powerful incentives for the well-off to form separate political jurisdictions" (Weir, 1994, 339). Reich (1992) commented on the propensity of the affluent "symbolic analysts" to secede from the rest of the nation. This was noted, too, by Bellah et al. (1986), who referrred to the emergence of enclaves among the well-off to secure a sense of community within and some distance from the rest. Moreover, Kozol (1992) provided a moving account of how this is practised by business interests around St. Louis, Missouri. Abandoning the poor, both physically and politically, is both the cause and the effect of the newly discovered virtue of decentralization (sometimes also called "empowering the poor").

Electoral System. Smaller-area governments tend to have smaller constituencies. From such constituencies (i.e., electoral districts), which are characterized by single member, simple-plurality electoral systems, as McConnell (1966) has persuasively argued, emerges a definition of public interest that is parochial and narrow. Larger electoral districts, on the other hand, generally reflect the aggregation of diverse interests, and produce policies that are broader and more inclusive (including, for instance, income redistribution). That may explain why progress on such basic issues as race, gender, and class have their origins more frequently in federal government and why states and local governments have frequently remained so recalcitrant. It may also provide a clue for understanding the presence of a progressive revenue base at the federal level and a regressive one at the subnational levels.

Too Many Governments. In addition to the electoral process, there is another unique feature of the United States to take into account. Compared to European countries, the

American government asks its citizens to vote far more often. While the typical European voter may be called upon to cast two or three ballots in a four-year period, many Americans are faced with a dozen or more separate elections in the space of four years. Furthermore Americans are expected to vote for a much wider range of political offices. With one elected official for about every 500 citizens, and elections held somewhere every week, it is no wonder that it is difficult to get Americans to the polls. In contrast, local, regional, and even national elections in Europe and Japan normally consist of casting a single ballot for a single office; the extensive list of elective offices and long ballots common to American elections are unknown in Western Europe and Japan. (Dalton and Wattenberg 1993, 210–11)

Even if the subnational governments acquire greater authority and resources, there are so many of them that expecting citizens to be both informed and active participants in them is highly unrealistic. "Too much democracy" thus defeats the general public interest. The presence of a very large number of governments controlled by even larger numbers of public officials elected overwhelmingly from small, single-member electoral districts tends to fragment public power, a result that is further reinforced by dividing the executive authority of governments. The prospects of pursuing a broad, diverse, and inclusive public interest is consequently beyond the reach of citizens most of the time. The fact that such an arrangement, paradoxically enough, emerged in an ad hoc fashion often in a populist (or antielitist) spirit makes its contemporary functions more difficult to unmask and its rhetoric more difficult to resist. Dominant interests that might be threatened by the coalescing of forces around such issues as income distribution or environmental protection are reassured and, ironically, the relatively weaker groups that seek to aggregate their resources by operating in larger electoral districts are called "elitists." This is a uniquely American way to support the privileged by fragmenting the forces that might threaten their interests. What was once called the divide and rule strategy now comes wrapped in the dominant interests' Orwellian language of returning power to small and responsive governments; amazingly, those daring to resist such efforts become centralizing elitists.

Curbing Discrimination. It is now even more fashionable than before to condemn the federal bureaucracy for both aggrandizement and inefficiency. This is a safe ploy; bureaucracy is now virtually everyone's favorite whipping boy. Leaving aside the factual and conceptual errors in such an attack (they are explored by Downs and Larkey 1986; Goodsell 1994; and Shariff 1981), the interests behind the vilification need to be considered. It is hard to believe that the administration of food stamps and school lunches will be any less bureaucratic or efficient under the aegis of the state government than it was under the federal government. Actually, the federal involvement in the distribution of those benefits even now is highly limited. What "the feds" represent through their oversight functions with regard to categorical grants, for instance, is, first, an attempt at fiscal equalization; second, an effort to reduce the diversion of funds for other purposes (block grants increase that danger); and, third, an opportunity to struggle against discriminatory practices. Some doubt, or even suspicion, may be justified about those who attack bureaucracy but do not reveal nonbureaucratic methods of delivering public services nor guarantee that the abuses that prevailed before the feds got involved will not reemerge.

Returning Power to Subnational Governments. It may be argued that when the federal "balance" has been restored—namely, when federal government does less and subnational governments do more—disparities in political participation as well as policy outcomes will also decrease. That appears unlikely in view of the considerations discussed here. Restoring such "balance" (or "returning power to the people") is more likely to increase income inequalities, not enhance participation in subnational governments.

Unfortunately, even some authors who are not willing to condone discrimnatory behavior continue to have faith in the initiatives of subnational governments. Two recent examples might be mentioned. Wiebe (1995) states that vigorous and egalitarian democracy of the nineteenth century, despite its imperfections, was lamentably replaced by the corporate consolidation of power and the expansion of a distant, centralized, and administrative state in the present century. He supports "guerilla politics" to return power to local communities. Perhaps the federal government could have thwarted these developments in the twentieth century (however unlikely such a possibility might be), but that could not have occurred to any significant degree without some communal and/or workers' control over local economic resources. Paradoxically enough, he has very little to say about workers' control or economic democracy. Nor does he confront the contradiction between his disdain for the modern culture of individual rights, on the one hand, and the ability of local communities to deny those rights to major groups (persons of color, women, and gays) and exclude them from participation, on the other. These were not unheard-of practices, as he is well aware, in his nineteenth-century "democracy." Also ignored are the efforts in the twentieth century by those distant hierarchical structures to enforce some elementary rules in local participation, without which nineteenth-century democracy was viewed by perhaps the majority of the residents then as a hoax.

And now even Alice Rivlin (1992) has recently joined the ranks of those who seek a new federal-state "balance." She calls it "dividing the job." She proposes transferring such functions to the states as public investments to increase productivity, and the elimination of most federal programs in "education, housing, highways, social services, economic development, and job training" (Rivlin 1992, 17). She is aware of the fear that "the state will neglect the less fortunate, particularly by retreating from federal efforts to improve the life chances of poor children. The fear has some basis, but poor and minority young people will not be left out if states play an aggressive role in economic development" (Rivlin 1992, 122).

That "if" represents a huge unexamined assumption. Her faith seems to based, in part, on some governmental reforms in states such as shorter ballots and longer terms of office of governors. Of course, no reforms have taken place in important economic areas such as the strengthening of unions at the state level through the repeal of so-called right to work laws.

The issue, however, is not the reforms undertaken by the states as much as it is the structural and political dynamic that initially produced the defense of states' rights as a cover for abusing persons of color and neglecting the poor. The reforms introduced in the states do not relieve the fear that such states' rights will not emerge again to accomplish racist and sexist goals. The question that the supporters of states' rights have not adequately answered in the past (nor are they able to do so adequately now) is this: why were some interests—of which race, gender, class, poverty, and environment will come readily to mind—neglected in subnational governments in the first place? In the present American context, why do increased states' rights seem to come at the expense of decreased individual rights?

When taken into account by themselves, each of these considerations are significant enough, but when viewed together, their force is overwhelming. Even if we were to be persuaded that the distinct dangers associated with subnational governments of the past, for some plausible reason, no longer existed, the incentives for new or similar dangers to return are now provided by the heightened competition among governmental jurisdictions for jobs. Such moral hazard manifests itself, in particular, in the "devolution" of governmental powers, especially when they are combined with the increased competition for jobs; it represents a powerful threat to many of the cherished values associated with decency in North America and Western Europe.

CONCLUSION

The federal government is only one of many governments that operate in the United States. However, it is the largest, and is likely to remain so. Subnational governments, too, will persist in the future. The issue raised here is not whether the latter should have any part in the governance of the country. They have, and it is indeed important; there are enough characteristics of any area and population that are sufficiently different to require flexibility and local initiative. When the objective is reducing income inequalities, however, they have been an instrument for thwarting progress, and that, too, is unlikely to change. Conservatives' resistance to reducing inequalities will be translated, in part, into support for the subnational governments; that is quite consistent with their opposition in the past to the civil rights agenda by eagerly supporting states' rights. Seeking substantive goals through procedural means is a well-established political tactic.

It is true that change at the local and state levels is possible and that errors made there are likely to inflict harm on fewer people. Such a self-correcting, incrementalist approach has to be viewed in the light of opportunities lost while waiting for a new policy initiative to gradually work its way through the states before it eventually becomes acceptable at the federal level. The contest here is between the danger avoided and the opening seized. Waiting for the future to arrive, if the problems have not disappeared in the meantime, ostensibly has the virtue of patience, but in reality serves the interests of those who are handsomely rewarded by inaction. Others whose patience requires sacrifice and whose immediacy of needs sets them apart may be entitled to a different view. In any case, federal government is not incapable of correcting its errors through the extensively used method of amending existing legislation, explicitly limiting the duration for which a new policy will remain in force (sunset legislation), formulating and amending executive orders of the presidents or regulations by the agencies, and deliberately designed experiments (for example, to test responses of welfare recipients to a variety of stimuli). In addition to its other characteristics, federal action also economizes effort.

While devolution mania grips the national imagination, globalization introduces its own pressures. Hancock, Logue, and Schiller (1991, 342) wrote: "An increasingly globalized and deregulated market for goods and services has prompted a transfer in the institutionalized loci of political power from national government to regional centers. The most relevant is ... the European Community" (1991, 342). While the United States induces and recognizes such changes, on the one hand, it strengthens subnational governments and restricts the federal role, on the other. These are contradictory moves that are more likely to induce paralysis than build the organizational capacity to cope with change. The pursuit of such conflicting goals is also expected to exacerbate income inequalities.

REFERENCES

Asahi Shimbun. 1995. *Japan Almanac 1995.* Tokyo: Toppan.

Bellah, Robert, Richard Madsen, William M. Sullivan, Ann Swidler, and Steven M. Tipton. 1986. *Habits of the Heart.* New York: Perennial Press.

Dalton, Russell J., and Martin P. Wattenberg. 1993. "The Not So Simple Act of Voting." In Ada W. Finifter, ed., *Political Science: The State of the Discipline II.* Washington, D.C.: The American Political Science Association, 193–218.

Downs, George W., and Patrick D. Larkey. 1986. *The Search for Government Efficiency.* New York: Random House.

Dugger, William M. 1984. *An Alternative to Economic Retrenchment.* New York: Petrocelli.

Fiordalisi, Georgina. 1989. "Did Kentucky Pay Too Much for Toyota Plant? *City and State,* June 19, 9–11.

Gillespie, W. Irwin. 1965. "Effect of Public Expenditures on the Distribution of Income." In Richard Musgrave, ed., *Essays in Fiscal Federalism.* Washington, D.C.: Brookings Institution, 122–86.

Gintis, Herbert. 1994. "Positive Functions of the Undeserving Poor: Uses of the Underclass in America." *Politics and Society,* 22 (Sep.): 269–83.

Goodsell, Charles T. 1994. *The Case for Bureaucracy.* 3d. ed. Chatham, N.J.: Chatham Publishers.

Hancock, M. Donald, John Logue, and Bernt Schiller. 1991. "Conclusion: Managing Modern Capitalism: Unanticipated Consequences and Prospects." In M. Donald Hancock, John Logue, and Bernt Schiller, eds., *Managing Modern Capitalism.* New York: Praeger, 341–50.

Herbert, Bob. 1995. "The Shell Game." *New York Times.* Feb. 1.

Hirschman, Albert O. 1970. *Exit, Voice and Loyalty.* Cambridge: Harvard University Press.

Ishi, Hiromitsu. 1993. *The Japanese Tax System.* 2d. ed. Oxford, U.K.: Clarendon Press.

Kozol, Jonathan. 1992. *Savage Inequalities.* New York: Harper Perennial.

Levitan, Sar A., and Robert Taggart. 1976. *The Promise of Greatness.* Cambridge: Harvard University Press.

Lindblom, Charles. 1977. *Politics and Markets.* New York: Basic Books.

McConnell, Grant. 1966. *Private Power and American Democracy.* New York: Vintage Books.

Musgrave, Richard A., Karl E. Case, and Herman Leonard. 1974. "The Distribution of Fiscal Burdens and Benefits." *Public Finance Quarterly,* 2 (July): 259–311.

Okun, Arthur M. 1975. *Equality and Efficiency.* Washington, D.C.: Brookings Institution.

Pechman, Joseph A. 1985. *Who Paid the Taxes, 1965–85?* Washington, D.C.: Brookings Institution.

Phillips, Kevin. 1990. *The Politics of Rich and Poor.* New York: Random House.

Pitelas, Christos. 1993. *Market and Non-Market Hierarchies.* Cambridge: Blackwell.

Press, Charles, and Robert Fournier. 1990. *State and Community Government Federal System.* New York: Harper Collins.

Reich, Robert B. 1992. *The Work of Nations.* New York: Vintage.

Reynolds, Morgan, and Eugene Somlensky. 1977. *Public Expenditures, Taxes, and the Distribution of Income.* New York: Academic Press.

Rivlin, Alice. 1992. *Reviving the American Dream.* Washington, D.C.: Brookings Institution.

Shariff, Zahid. 1981. "Contemporary Challenges to Public Administration." *Social Science Quarterly,* 62 (Sept.): 555–68.

___. 1990. "Bureaucracy and Trust." Paper presented at the annual conference of the Public Administration Theory Network, Los Angeles, Calif.

United States. Advisory Commission on Intergovernmental Relations. 1981. *Comparative Federalism: Australia, Canada, The United States, and West Germany.* Washington, D.C.: Advisory Commission on Intergovernmental Relations.

___. Bureau of the Census. 1994a. *Census of Governments.* Vol. 1, no. 1. Washington, D.C.: Government Printing Office.

___. 1994b. *Statistical Abstract of the United States.* Washington, D.C.: U.S. Government Printing Press.

___. 1994c. *The Economic and Budget Outlook: Fiscal Years 1995–1999.* Washington, D.C.: Government Printing Office.

___. Office of Management and Budget. 1995. *Budget of the United States Government: Historical Tables.* Washington, D.C.

Weir, Margaret. 1994. "Urban Poverty and Defensive Localism." *Dissent,* Summer, 337–42.

Wiebe, Robert H. 1995. *Self-Rule.* Chicago: University of Chicago Press.

Part III

INTERNATIONAL CONTEXTS

11

East Meets West: Dewey, Gandhi, and Instrumental Equality for the Twenty-First Century

Doug Brown

> A time is coming when those who are in the mad rush today of multiplying their wants, vainly thinking that they add to the real substance, real knowledge of the world, will retrace their steps and say: "what have we done?"
>
> Mahatma Gandhi

Like Gandhi, and as the twentieth century is about to close, many have begun to ask, "what have we done?" However, even more to the point and more alarmingly, people the world over are beginning to ask, "what is happening to us?" The difference between these two questions concerns the issue of "who controls." There is a growing sense today that whether one is living comfortably in the First World or wretchedly in the Third World, everyone shares the feeling that fear and insecurity define our lives. Increasingly, people feel that no one is in control. Some, including radical institutionalists and other reflective souls, suggest that perhaps it is the new global capitalism, as a system, that is in control. The following discussion of John Dewey, Mohandas (Mahatma) Gandhi, and equality has to do with regaining social and democratic control over a new type of global capitalism that threatens human and biospheric sustainability and creates a dangerous level of "dysfunctional inequality."

As a result of the current global transformation of capitalism, the issues of sustainability and inequality are now also global in character. Even in the 1980s, the Bruntland Commission assembled to announce the impending global environmental and human sustainability crisis. (The Bruntland Commission was sponsored by the United Nations and it is the first to address the paradox that it is the Third World nations' poverty that drives them, out of desperation, to overuse their environments. As a result, the Bruntland Report was also the first to discuss the concept of sustainable development.) It asked us "to move away from our preoccupation with our own nation and recognize the internationalism that our ecological common future thrusts upon us" (Milbrath 1989, 324). Whether or not we will think of these issues in a global manner, gain control over the new global economy, rescue sustainability, and create not only social justice but "instrumental equality," remains to be seen. As Bill Dugger suggests in his chapter in this volume, the question is whether or not we can create a "virtuous circle of equality." My purpose here is not to suggest that we will. However, premised upon the fact that we should try, I want to offer an interpretive framework for situating the discussion of the world's inequality. There is no escaping the fact that inequality will be at the top of political and economic agendas in the next century. We need to shape the philosophical and social context in which the world's people argue about inequality and equality. That context is one of globalism and is derived from the requirements of sustainability. Perhaps institutionalists must become "global ecoinstitutionalists."

The logic of what follows is straightforward: (1) the globalization of capitalism is a reality; (2) this transformation threatens human and biospheric sustainability; (3) the magnitude of the global inequality that results from this process is so severe that it undermines sustainability; consequently, (4) we must move toward the realization of a new, postcapitalist global economy that assures sustainability in part through forms of economic and political redistribution. The vision and the interpretive framework in which to direct the redistribution I would label "instrumental equality." Thus, sustainability requires us to pass beyond today's dysfunctional inequality and achieve an instrumental equality.

How do John Dewey and Mahatma Gandhi fit into this? Dewey and Gandhi were contemporaries, and both wrote and acted in the twentieth century in ways that are suggestive of how to achieve sustainability for the twenty-first century. Their ideas complement each other.

Additionally, for the benefit of developing a global institutionalist perspective, Gandhi is a powerful figure whose ideas situated in Eastern philosophy dovetail remarkably well with twentieth-century Western institutionalism. Dewey's pragmatism and instrumentalism provide the *method* of sustainability for the next century, while Gandhi's philosophy provides the *culture* of sustainability. Each provides something different, but their ideas converge around the principle of instrumental equality. In a sustainable, global economy, inequality is pathological.

Both embraced in this past century the need for sustainability in the next. John Dewey helped articulate and expand the philosophical foundations of institutional economics as a method of inquiry into how to promote and enlarge human discretion so that humans are free in nature and not enslaved by it. Mahatma Gandhi worked toward building a world in which the distribution of wealth would be consistent with men and women acting as trustees instead of owners and as partners instead of masters. Both Dewey and Gandhi, moreover, had a tremendous faith in the ability of people to learn how to live justly, equitably, and sustainably, and both believed that the "virtuous circle of equality" was achievable. In spite of the immediate problems both faced, each was a long-run optimist.

THE GLOBALIZATION OF CAPITALISM

The new global economy has an unnerving, laissez-faire character to it. Some call it the "New Leviathan;" others call it postmodern capitalism, the globalization of production, "unorganized capitalism," and the "regime of flexible accumulation" (see Ross and Trachte 1990; Lash and Urry 1987; Harvey 1989; Dicken 1992). Not only is this global restructuring a reality that most accept, but people and governments everywhere are reacting with fear and alarm. It is a "multipolar system" and, as Peter Dicken suggests;

an era of *turbulance and volatility* in which economic life in general is being restructured and reorganized both rapidly and fundamentally. We live in a world of increasing complexity, interconnectedness and volatility; a world in which the lives and livelihoods of every one of us are bound up with processes operating at a global scale. (Dicken 1992, 1)

Moreover, as Ross and Trachte state, "Its individual agents, global firms, and financial institutions, are not sovereigns but severely constrained competitors committed to the *economic* war of each against all" (Ross and Trachte 1990, 2).

The global economic war of each against all has not only unnerved us, but it has shaken our twentieth-century foundations, decentered our existence, and destroyed our confidence in ourselves and our institutions. *Postmodernism* is the term that lays claim to the examination of these cultural shocks. The globalization of capitalism has created a culture shock yielding psychic fragmentation, growing diversity, disintegration, and the eclipse of belief in universal truths and objective knowledge. The human ship has lost its moorings at the close of the century; not only that, but it is adrift around an earth island threatened with volcanic eruption. Human and biospheric sustainability are at risk.

THE CRISIS OF SUSTAINABILITY

Capitalism as an economic system is most likely sustainable. Of course, the human cost may be incredible, but this is not the way to phrase the question. It is whether or not humankind, within a global network of complex ecosystems (the biosphere), is viable on the basis of globalized capitalism. As Sandra Postel of the Worldwatch Institute stated: "The pace and scale of degradation that started about mid-century—and continues today—is historically new. The central conundrum ... is now too apparent: population and economies grow exponentially, but the natural resources that support them do not" (Postel 1994, 3; see also Milbrath 1989, 12; Schor 1992, 165; Hardin 1968).

These changes raise the issue of sustainability. Postel says that "the earth's environmental assets are now insufficient to sustain both our present patterns of economic activity and the life-support systems we depend on" (Postel 1994, 4). Moreover, "There is no substitute for the assimilative capacity of the biosphere"

(Dryzek 1994, 178). These facts notwithstanding, what about the condition of the world's poor, whose material needs are also imperative? As Lester Milbrath contends,

There simply are too few resources and there is too little waste-absorbing capacity in the biosphere to support economic growth of the magnitute needed to bring all, or even most, of the LDC's [less-developed countries] up to the current standard of living of the MDC's[more-developed countries]. Even if we found the resources for a spurt in economic growth, the inevitable increase in carbon dioxide levels would stimulate such swift climate change that all national economies would plunge into catastrophic economic decline. (Milbrath 1989, 325)

One conclusion surfaces from this discussion: global capitalism as a wealth-producing system has not faced this problem until now. Moreover, it is not simply profits, markets, money, and trade that is the problem. It is the very logic of the system that is counter to sustainability. As Arjun Makhijani argues, "It does not require detailed theoretical development to note that the transformations which human activites are making in the environment from the local to the global are generally in a direction which is opposite of that of sustainability" (Makhijani 1992, 145; see also Ekins, Hillman, and Hutchison 1992, 50; Milbrath 1989, 38).

Capitalism is a "driven system." It is insatiable: the drive for profits is endless, as is the appetite of the world's consumers. As Joel Kassiola suggests, "We have a policy of unlimited and continuous economic growth with a normative basis of industrial materialism producing a citizen with infinite desires created by the very process that is supposed to satisfy them but cannot" (Kassiola 1990, 144). It is the logic of the system that is the ultimate obstacle to sustainability. Kassiola calls this the "industrial drive for self-infinitization" (1990, 183).

The *logic* of the market rules; it is no longer a case of market magic. James O'Connor states that there are no agencies or governmental bodies in advanced nations today working toward the creation of a sustainable capitalism. Moreover, "The idea of an ecological capitalism, or sustainable capitalism, has not even been coherently theorized, not to speak of becoming embodied in an institutional infrastructure" (O'Connor 1994, 168).

With what are we left? A crisis of sustainability resulting from a new global economy based upon the logic of insatiability. As Dewey said, "In consequence, man has suffered the impact of an enormously enlarged control of physical energies without any corresponding ability to control hinmself and his own affairs" (Dewey 1994, 248). What's more, we are now faced with a type of dysfunctional inequality. Robert Kaplan, in an issue of the *Atlantic Monthly*, wrote a tremendously powerful, but frightening, piece outlining a very real possibility:

It is time to understand "the environment" for what it is: *the* national-security issue of the early twenty-first century. The political and strategic impact of surging populations, spreading disease, deforestation and soil erosion, water depletion, air pollution, and possibly, rising sea levels in critical, overcrowded regions like the Nile Delta and Bangladesh—developments that will prompt mass migrations and, in turn, incite group conflicts—will be the core foreign policy challenge from which most others will ultimately emanate, arousing the public and uniting assorted interests left over from the Cold War. (Kaplan 1994, 58)

DYSFUNCTIONAL INEQUALITY

Business Week recently published a special issue entitled *21st Century Capitalism,* in which editor Stephen Shepard commented that in the twenty-first century, "for many people, life will be immeasurably better. But as skill-driven markets realign the globe, the gap between the haves and have nots will widen, and that could have disastrous consequences" (Shepard 1994, 8). Dysfunctional inequality speaks to these disastrous consequences. Kaplan contends:

We are entering a bifurcated world. Part of the globe is inhabited by Hegel's and Fukuyama's Last Man, healthy, well fed, and pampered by technology. The other, larger, part is inhabited by Hobbe's First Man, condemned to a life that is "poor, nasty, brutish, and short." Although both parts will be threatened by environmental stress, the Last Man will be able to master it; the First Man will not. (Kaplan 1994, 60)

Additionally, the trend in the new global economy is toward worsening inequality. In 1960 the richest 20 percent had 70 percent of global income; now they claim 83 percent. Likewise the poorest 20 percent had 2.3 percent of global income in 1960, but by 1989 their share dropped to 1.4 percent (Postel 1994, 5). The 1994 United Nations *Human Development Report* states:

The income disparity between the richest 20% and the poorest 20% of the world's population has doubled over the past three decades, where one-fourth of humanity is unable to meet its basic human needs and where the rich nations are consuming four-fifths of humanity's natural capital without being obliged to pay for it. The concept of one world and one planet simply cannot emerge from an unequal world. (United Nations Development Program 1994, 21)

In a world of 5.3 billion people, the richest 1 billion have 60 times the income of the poorest billion (United Nations 1994, 2). It is also predicted that 95 percent of the world's population growth over the next 50 years (from 5.3 billion to 9.5 billion), will be in the poorest regions of the world (Kaplan 1994, 59). As Makhijani argues, with a "culture of limitless greed, the wealthy are right to be afraid" (Makhijani 1992, 151).

This is a type of inequality that Dewey understood: "Special privilege always induces a standpat and reactionary attitude on the part of those who have it; in the end it usually provokes a blind rage of destruction on the part of those who suffer from it" (Dewey 1994, 192). What was Gandhi's view? "But today," said Gandhi, "the situation is so tragic that on the one hand there are people who roll in pomp and luxury and on the other there are people who do not have enough clothes to cover their bodies and who live on the brink of starvation" (Gandhi 1990, 346). All the foregoing suggests the need for a less driven system in which there is global redistribution towards an instrumental equality. This appears to be a precondition for twenty-first century sustainability.

INSTRUMENTAL EQUALITY

Without this type of redistribution, Kaplan is perhaps correct to assert that: "A large number of people on this planet, to whom the comfort and stability of a middle-class life is utterly unknown, find war and barracks existence a step up rather than a step down" (Kaplan 1994, 72). From the institutionalist perspective, including Dewey's instrumentalism, sustainability is the ends-in-view, while equality is the means. Gandhi would surely agree.

Instrumental equality is a concept—a vision. It has to be operationalized, as well. As a vision, I would also call it "diverse equality" or perhaps "Zen equality." It must draw on what is common in, and for, all people. This is essential. Equality finds its validation in that which all people have in common. As James O'Connor states, "We need to scrutinize critically all time-worn political formulae and develop an ecumenical spirit, and to celebrate our commonalities or 'new commons' as well as our differences" (O'Connor 1994, 173).

However, with the postmodern cultural shakedown, most of the world is preoccupied with differences among us, rather than what we have in common. One cannot help but observe that globally there is an identity crisis occurring in which people are becoming fixated on carving out their own new identities by emphasizing how each is different from the other. The world's sustainability demands a measure of instrumental equality, yet its people insist on preserving their diversity, their uniqueness, and their individuality.

There is an obvious tension here that is not easily reconciled. Diverse, or instrumental, equality implies the "elimination of inequality in all its different forms and the building of a truly democratic society. It also implies the right to be different and the idea that difference shall not constitute a basis for inequality" (Brecher, Childs, and Cutler 1993, xvii). Diverse equality is a type of equality that requires a fully democratic and socially just economy. It is one in which life chances and the means to life are reasonably equal. It does, I believe, suggest a greater shift towards equality of outcome, not merely equality of opportunity. However, equality of outcome can also mean equality of means in the basic pursuit of life. Diversity is encouraged so long as it does not undermine the equality of means. We become equally free to pursue our uniqueness within a fundamental equality of means. How would this vision be operationalized and what would the culture it requires look like? Dewey and Gandhi provide some help.

DEWEY'S CONTRIBUTION

Dewey provides us with a *method* to guide humanity and its debate over sustainability and equality in the next century. With the announcement of postmodern critiques of nineteenth-century Enlightenment philosophy, the teleological "grand narrative" social theories have been largely undermined (see Lyotard 1984; Rorty 1979, 1990; West 1988; Foucault 1980, 1986; Brown 1991, 1992). The modernist beliefs in eternal and universal truths, in representationalism, in "covering law" theories, in the spectator theory of knowledge, and in a "God's eye view" of human reality have been debunked. However, this process of postmodern deconstruction was carried out by Dewey early on. In Dewey's *Quest for Certainty* and *Reconstruction in Philosophy,* he anticipated the postmodernist critique a half-century later, clearly proving himself ahead of his time. As Cornel West suggests:

The recent revival of pragmatism provides a timely intellectual background for the most urgent problem of our post-modern moment. That is a complex cluster of questions and queries regarding the meaning and value of democracy. No other modern philosophical tradition has grappled with the various dimensions of this problem more than that of American pragmatism. (West 1993, 32; see also Rorty 1990)

Dewey's pragmatism and instrumentalism, along with the methods and traditions of institutionalism carried on today with the work of Marc Tool, among others, is a way out of the "moral agnosticism" and "walking nihilism" that postmodernism seems to imply. Dewey's effort to combat both objectivism in the old Enlightenment philosophies and relativism inherent in today's postmodernism is pioneering. It is his contribution of embracing experimentalism and democratic methods that we must use to get us into the next century and beyond. As E. E. Liebhafsky explained:

The significance of institutional economics lies in its recognition that any belief not supported by experimental evidence is tenuous and in its analysis of change as a process in which everything is tentative. Rather than seeking final truths, institutional economists seek knowledge to shape institutional change through operational concepts permitting problem solving in reality. Accomplishment of their purpose ... is not possible within the framework of an analysis in which natural forces are deduced to lead to the values inherent in an ideal. (Liebhafsky 1993, 750)

Following Mill and Peirce, Dewey has led the way in the twentieth century in outlining a means for discovering a sustainable society. In 1948, the same year that Gandhi was killed, Dewey wrote an updated preface to the 1920 edition of *Reconstruction in Philosophy*. This statement is prophetic because it seems to anticipate both the postmodern cultural crisis and the crisis of global capitalism and sustainability:

Today Reconstruction of Philosophy is a more suitable title than Reconstruction in Philosophy. For the intervening events have sharply defined, have brought to a head, the basic postulate of the text: namely, that the distinctive office, problems and subject matter of philosophy grow out of the stresses and strains in the community life in which a given form of philosophy arises, and that, accordingly, its specific problems vary with the changes in human life that are always going on and that at times constitute a crisis and a turning point in human history. (Dewey [1920] 1948, v–vi)

I suspect that as the century closes, increasing numbers of those who have waded through the postmodern critiques and are not content to "leave things as they are," as Wittgenstein believed all philosophy was condemned to do, will gravitate toward the American tradition of pragmatism. It is scientific reasoning based on democratic norms and experimental behaviors and is our tool to operationalize a sustainable planet.

Finally, Dewey was a believer in equality, but he believed in diversity as well. Of equality he said, "It does not mean sameness; it is not to be understood quantitatively, an interpretation which always ends in ideas of external and mechanical equality" (Dewey 1994, 190). Thus, given the requirements of sustainability and the equality it demands, Dewey says, "The problem of constructing a new individuality consonant with the objective conditions under which we live is the deepest problem of our times" (Dewey 1994, 253). The problem of constructing a new individuality compatible with sustainability is where Gandhi's contribution enters. Gandhi offered a culture of sustainability to go along with Dewey's method of discovery.

GANDHI'S CONTRIBUTION

Clearly Dewey, the academic philosopher, and Gandhi, the political activist, shared a common set of values and beliefs. They witnessed the world in the first half of the twentieth century in much the same way, albeit from different geographic and cultural locations. Gandhi wrote voluminously, but mostly in the form of correspondence. His one book on economics, *Hind Swaraj* (1938), is a critique of neoclassical economics that can be considered institutionalist in character.   However, more important for institutionalism and American pragmatism is the subtitle of his autobiography (published in 1948 shortly before his death): *The Story of My Experiments with Truth* (Gandhi 1948). Gandhi shared with Dewey the belief in experimentalism. In this sense, he was a pragmatist.

However, to understand the culture of a sustainable twenty-first century economy, one must understand Gandhi's concept of truth. Unlike Dewey, Gandhi had a notion of truth that was in many respects static, immutable, and eternal.   Truth, for Gandhi, was discovered through selflessness, not self-sacrifice. However, truth is not simply the pursuit of selfless behavior, but the idea that the world would actually work—that it would be a just, nonviolent, and sustainable world—if people pursued the right amount of selflessness. The trick, and thus the "experimentalism," concerns discovering the proper, or necessary, amount of self-restraint such that a sustainable and just society can be realized. How and in what fashion must society constrain the individual/the self in order to create justice, equality, and sustainability? Of course, here is where Dewey's method of pragmatism helps to discover the way and operationalize the necessary amount of selflessness. We use democracy and the scientific method as applied to human affairs to figure out how much self-constraining must be done.

Thus, Gandhi's pursuit of Truth led him to believe that capitalism was not the solution (see Dasgupta 1989; Hempel 1989). Capitalism is a system that sanctifies the self and elevates the individual and individuality to a sacred status. Gandhi knew that such a system was exploitative, violent, unjust, inequitable, and ultimately unsustainable. For him, what was needed was to harness the "self."

Harnessing the self meant transcending the consumerist culture of capitalism—its drivenness, its infinite pursuit of self-aggrandizement and insatiability. Gandhi knew also that the purpose of capitalism is not justice, not equality, not security, and clearly not sustainability. Its purpose is the maximization of wealth with the hope and expectation of its defenders that everything else that is important in life will somehow work out. Gandhi stated:

Western nations today are groaning under the heel of the monster-god of materialism. Their moral growth has become stunted ... in so far as we have made the modern materialistic craze our goal, in so far are we going downhill in the path of progress. I hold that economic progress in the sense I have put it is antagonistic to real progress. (Gandhi 1990, 97)

Gandhi saw capitalism as the unlimited self-pursuit of the "multiplication of wants," yet he also believed, like Dewey, that people were capable of getting a grip on their behavior if they understood the need to do so (Gandhi 1990, 378).

One of Gandhi's best statements on the culture of sustainability and what people need to do to actually get a grip on their lives is the following. He asks the question, "From what will the masses be delivered?" He then observes that most would like to have the status of capitalists, yet this is only possible by violence. Capitalism, for Gandhi, is an extremely violent system because of its exploitative logic, which is directed at both people and nature. He then suggests that people should reject the "evils of capital" and that

If they would revise the viewpoint of capital, they would strive to attain a juster distribution of the products of labour. This immediately takes us to contentment and simplicity, voluntarily adopted. Under the new outlook multiplicity of material wants will not be the aim of life, the aim will be rather their restriction consistently with comfort. We shall cease to think of getting what we can, but we shall decline to receive what all cannot get. (Gandhi 1990, 107)

The principle of Zen equality, that is, what I have called instrumental or diverse equality, is also implicit in Gandhi's maxim. Gandhi likened the relationship of individuality to society to that of a drop of water in the ocean. The individual as a unique and self-actualizing being can only flourish in the context of a just, equal and sustainable society. The pursuit of self and diversity must be constrained by the requirements of sustainability and justice—Gandhi's truth:

Individuality is and is not even as each drop in the ocean is an individual and is not. It is not because apart from the ocean it has no existence. It is because the ocean has no existence, if the drop has not, i.e., has no individuality. They are beautifully interdependent. (Gandhi 1990, 173–4)

This is the cultural context for sustainability within which we can pursue diverse equality.

CONCLUSION

Gandhi's cultural consciousness for sustainability is postcapitalist, postconsumerist, and characterized by simplicity, justice, democracy, and equality. There is virtually nothing in Gandhi's economics with which institutionalists and Dewey would take issue, with the possible exception of one very Eastern principle—the pursuit of selflessness.

The individual in capitalist, Western society is overrated, according to Gandhi. Of course, institutionalists, particularly Veblen, would agree to the extent that it is the overrated concept of the self that leads in part to invidious, status-seeking behavior as well as to consumerism, "more is better," and the "good life is the 'goods' life." Dewey and Gandhi would agree that sustainability in the next century requires radical change. It requires instrumental equality along with justice, democracy, and "getting simple"—and "getting simple" requires a postcapitalist global economy that is not "driven" or based on "getting ahead." If it is going to be "driven" at all, it should be driven by the desire for virtue rather than that for "self-infinitization." Using Dewey's method and Gandhi's culture will provide the best tools for creating the "virtuous circle of equality" and a sustainable world in the twenty-first century.

REFERENCES

Best, Steven, and Douglas Kellner. 1991. *Postmodern Theory: Critical Interrogations.* New York: Guilford Publications.
Brecher, Jeremy, John Brown Childs, and Jill Cutler, eds. 1993. *Global Visions: Beyond the New World Order.* Boston: South End Press.

Brown, Doug. 1991. "An Institutionalist Look at Postmodernism." *Journal of Economic Issues*, 25 (Dec.): 1089–1104.

___. 1992. "Doing Social Economics in a Postmodern World." *Review of Social Economy*, 50 (Winter): 383–403.

Dasgupta, Sugata. 1989. "The Core of Gandhi's Social and Economic Thought." In John Hick and Lamont Hempel, eds., *Gandhi's Significance for Today*. New York: St. Martin's Press, 189–202.

Dewey, John. [1920] 1948. *Reconstruction in Philosophy*. Boston: Beacon Press.

___. [1929] 1960. *The Quest for Certainty: A Study of the Relation of Knowledge and Action*. New York: Capricorn Books, G. P. Putnam's Sons.

___. 1994. *The Moral Writings of John Dewey*. James Gouinlock, editor. Amherst, N.Y.: Prometheus Books.

Dicken Peter. 1992. *Global Shift: The Internationalization of Economic Activity*. New York: Guilford Publications.

Dryzek, John. 1994. "Ecology and Discursive Democracy: Beyond Liberal Capitalism and the Administrative State." In Martin O'Connor, ed., *Is Capitalism Sustainable?* New York: Guilford Press, 175–97.

Ekins, Paul, Mayer Hillman, and Robert Hutchison. 1992. *Green Economics*. New York: Doubleday.

Foucault, Michel. 1980. *Power/Knowledge*. Colin Gordon, editor. New York: Pantheon.

___. 1986. "Of Other Spaces." *Diacritics*, 16, (Spring): 22–26.

Gandhi, M. K. 1938. *Hind Swaraj*. Ahmedabad, India: Navajivan.

___. 1948. *Gandhi's Autobiography: The Story of My Experiments with Truth*. Washington, D.C.: Public Affairs Press.

___. 1990. *The Essential Writings of Mahatma Gandhi*. Raghavan Iyer, editor. New York: Oxford University Press.

Hardin, Garrett. 1968. "The Tragedy of the Commons." *Science*, 162 (Dec. 13): 1243–48.

Harvey, David. 1989. *The Condition of Postmodernity: An Enquiry into the Origins of Cultural Change*. Cambridge: Basil Blackwell.

___. 1991. "Flexibility: Threat or Opportunity." *Socialist Review*, 21 (Jan.): 65–78.

Hempel, Lamont. 1989. "Introduction to Part III." In John Hick and Lamont Hempel, eds., *Gandhi's Significance For Today*. New York: St Martin's Press, 185–88.

Kaplan, Robert. 1994. "The Coming Anarchy," *The Atlantic Monthly*, 273, no. 2 (Feb.): 44–76.

Kassiola, Joel Jay. 1990. *The Death of Industrial Civilization: The Limits to Economic Growth and the Repoliticization of Advanced Industrial Society*. Albany: State University of New York Press.

Lash, Scott, and John Urry. 1987. *The End of Organized Capitalism*. Madison: University of Wisconsin Press.

Liebhafsky, E. E. 1993. "The Influence of Charles Sanders Peirce on Institutional Economics." *Journal of Economic Issues*, 27 (Sept.): 741–54.

Lyotard, Jean-Francois. 1984. *The Postmodern Condition: A Report on Knowledge*. Minneapolis: University of Minnesota Press.

Makhijani, Arjun. 1992. *From Global Capitalism to Economic Justice*. New York: Apex Press.

Milbrath, Lester W. 1989. *Envisioning a Sustainable Society: Learning Our Way Out*. Albany: State University of New York Press.

O'Connor, James. 1994. "Is Sustainable Capitalism Possible?" In Martin O'Connor, ed., *Is Capitalism Sustainable?* New York: Guilford Press, 152–75.

O'Connor, Martin. 1994. "Introduction: Liberate, Accumulate--and Bust?" In Martin O'Connor, ed., *Is Capitalism Sustainable?* New York: Guilford Press, 1–36.

Postel, Sandra. 1994. "Carrying Capacity: Earth's Bottom Line." In Worldwatch Institute, ed., *State of the World 1994: A Worldwatch Institute Report on Progress toward a Sustainable Society.* New York: W. W. Norton, 3–21.

Rorty, Richard. 1979. *Philosophy and the Mirror of Nature.* Princeton, N.J: Princeton University Press.

___. 1990. "Pragmatism as Anti-Representationalism." In John P. Murphy, ed., *Pragmatism: From Peirce to Davidson.* Boulder, Colo.: Westview Press, 1–6.

Ross, Robert, and Kent Trachte. 1990. *Global Capitalism: The New Leviathan.* Albany: State University of New York Press.

Schor, Juliet. 1992. *The Overworked American: The Unexpected Decline of Leisure.* New York: HarperCollins.

Shepard, Stephen B., ed. 1994, Nov. *Business Week Special Issue: 21st Century Capitalism.* New York: McGraw-Hill.

United Nations Development Program. 1994. *Human Development Report 1994.* New York: Oxford University Press.

West, Cornel. 1988. "Interview with Cornel West." In Andrew Ross, ed., *Universal Abandon: The Politics of Postmodernism.* Minneapolis: University of Minnesota Press, 126–30.

___. 1993. *Prophetic Thought in Postmodern Times.* Monroe, Me.: Common Courage Press.

Wittgenstein, Lugwig. 1965. *Philosophical Investigations.* New York: Macmillan Publishing.

12

International Inequality and the Economic Process

Brent McClintock

International economic relations are marked by inequality. Contemporary neoclassical trade and development theory, based as it is in nonevolutionary, noninstitutional methodology, does not address the power relations and inequality between nations and peoples. It treats economic growth, development, and trade as the outcome of given factor endowments, property rights, and (largely unexplained) technological change rather than as the result of evolving technology and institutional adjustment that redistributes power between economic groups. In the neoclassical view, efficiency conditions and income distribution are largely seen as the outcomes of the logic of the market system and the ad hoc, often ill-fated, interventions of the state.

Institutional economics can contribute toward the development of a more realistic theory of the international economy which would incorporate the following. First, economic theory must analyze the polarizing tendencies of market-based trade and development rather than the convergence myth propagated by mainstream theory. Second, the analysis of collective action with an international context requires a theory of the nation-state and the emerging supranational quasistate which incorporates both the state's repressive and integrative roles. Third, the interaction of technology and institutions in a given cultural context leads to path-dependent development which may or may not generate greater economic growth and equality. The task of human society at the end of the twentieth century is how to encourage cultural pluralism in economic and political affairs without a breakdown in international relations. Necessarily, world society must construct supranational governance institutions that promote fairer trade and finance, redistribute world resources, and ensure full participation for all in economic and political processes.

THE PROBLEM OF INTERNATIONAL ECONOMIC INEQUALITY

The divergence in economic performance between societies is a relatively recent phenomenon if one takes a very long-run perspective on the human experience. Simon Kuznets, Paul Bairoch, and others have observed that it is only in the last 200 to 300 years that there has been great divergence in economic growth rates (Kuznets 1966, 68–69). In 1750, a time when most societies were still largely precapitalist, today's developed and less developed countries (LDCs) had similar gross national product (GNP) per capita levels (Bairoch 1982, 162–63). With the advent of capitalism and the rapid technological change embodied in the Industrial Revolution, European societies underwent accelerated economic growth much beyond that of other regions of the world (Jones 1981). By 1980, GNP per capita levels in the developed nations were more than seven times those of the LDCs as a group. Hence, one fact to be explained is how convergence and polarization between societies have contributed to international equality and inequality.

Today, the income distribution is wider in the United States and the United Kingdom than any time since the 1930s (*Economist* 1994, 19). After narrowing between the 1930s and 1960s as a consequence of sustained economic growth and the redistributive policies of the welfare state, income distribution widened again. Tax cuts for the rich, social welfare expenditure cuts, market deregulation, and a slowdown in productivity growth were some of the forces causing greater income inequality. Rising inequality, albeit somewhat milder, has also been observed over the course of the 1980s in 12 out of 17 of the Organization for Economic Cooperation and Development (OECD) developed countries (Fieleke 1994; OECD 1993).

Meanwhile, the plight of the poor in the LDCs remains grim. Between 1980 and 1992, low- to middle-income LDCs posted annual economic growth averaging 0.8 percent, while high-income economies averaged an annual growth of 2.3 percent (World Bank 1994, 162–63). Clearly, the economic gap between rich and poor nations has widened since 1980. Measures of income inequality in LDCs are notoriously difficult to make, so it is perhaps better to look at more direct indicators of social welfare like infant mortality and life expectancy. Citizens of the lowest income LDCs have a 20 percent shorter life expectancy than those in industrial economies (World Bank 1994). Infant mortality rates more than halved in low income LDCs between 1960 and 1992. This is progress, but far too slow compared to that made in high-income economies. While the infant mortality rate in LDCs was five times higher than the rate in high-income economies in 1960, it had risen to ten times the rate in high-income economies by 1992 (World Bank 1994). Of course, this is not a systematic analysis but is indicative of the large gaps that continue to persist between the world's rich and poor.

The social and economic dilemmas posed by greater polarization between developed and less developed nations have resulted in increased international tensions between countries in the north and south. Rising industrialization in some LDCs and the reduction of trade barriers through the General Agreement on Tariffs and Trade have contributed to rapid import penetration in the developed nations. Manufactured imports from LDCs rose from 5 percent of total imports for developed nations in 1970 to nearly 14 percent by 1990 (Fieleke 1994, 10). While this meant rising employment and incomes for the LDCs, the changing pattern of trade contributed to abrupt structural change in many of the northern nations. Deindustrialization reduced the relative profitability of labor-intensive manufacturing in the north and shaved up to 4 percent off the share of manufacturing in total employment (Wood 1994, 191–212). Increased global competition, technological change, and changing state policies combined to raise inequality and mass unemployment in the north. The burden fell particularly heavily on lower-skilled workers, who faced lower wage growth and a loss of employment.

These, then, are the circumstances in which societies find themselves in the international economy at the end of the twentieth century. How well does mainstream or neoclassical economics explain long-run economic growth, economic convergence and polarization, and the nature of international economic equality or inequality?

CONVERGENCE OR POLARIZATION? THE CONVENTIONAL WISDOM

The Neoclassical Growth Model

The neoclassical economic growth model hypothesizes that output growth is the result of increases in the quantity of resources such as capital, labor, and natural resources, along with qualitative improvements in these factors of production brought about by technological innovation (Solow 1956). The key driving force in economic growth in the neoclassical view is increases in the nation's capital stock financed out of aggregate savings. In this model, which was first developed by Robert Solow, technological change is estimated as a residual contribution to economic growth. Innovation is an exogenous variable in the theory, which means within the model, that technology improves in some unexplained way.

Using the Solow model, neoclassical economics predicts that over the long run, gross domestic product (GDP) and productivity growth rates between countries will converge. The chain of causation in this theory of economic convergence commences when some country or countries with an initial advantage in technological and resource endowments experience faster productivity and GDP growth than other nations with fewer resources and poorer technology. These "leader" nations tap into their accumulated stock of technology, resulting initially in economic divergence. Since the benefits of applying this stock of innovations are great, "follower" nations will be eager to acquire and absorb technologies in order to boost their own productivity and income growth.

Convergence theory suggests that it is possible for "follower" nations to catch up with leaders through technology transfers leading to rapid improvements in productivity. The "catch-up" hypothesis emphasizes the technological gap between leaders and followers, predicting that followers will be able to leapfrog to the adoption and diffusion of innovations at the leading edge of science and technology. This is made possible, according to the neoclassical model, because technology is assumed to be a public good and to be highly mobile internationally. Leader nations, while still continuing to innovate, find that their physical capital is aging in terms of the technology embodied in their capital so their productivity growth rate slows. As the technology gap narrows, the growth potential of the followers converges toward that of the leaders.

Has economic convergence taken place? The evidence does not support the neoclassical model's prediction. De Long, Abramovitz and others, when testing for convergence between industrial countries, have found divergence appeared as likely an outcome as convergence (De Long 1988; Abramovitz 1986). When shorter time periods were analyzed, it was discovered that income per capita had diverged between 1870 and 1950 for 16 industrial countries (Abramovitz 1986). Some degree of convergence took place between 1950 and 1973; however, there seems to have been some slowing in the rate of convergence after 1973. When LDCs were added to convergence studies, Romer concluded there was no tendency for LDCs as a group to experience faster GDP growth rates than developed countries, which would be necessary to lead to convergence after 1950 (Romer 1994).

The New Growth, or Endogenous Growth, Theory

Increasingly, it was realized that neoclassical growth theory could not explain economic reality. It could not explain the failure of the LDCs to catch up to the leading nations of the industrial world, and part of that difficulty lay in its lack of a workable theory of technology. This led to the emergence of the new, or endogenous, growth theory in the 1980s.

Endogenous growth theory explores the reasons why output grows at a faster rate than if technology were treated as contributing to growth from outside the economic process (Romer 1986, 1990; Lucas 1988; Rebelo 1991; Grossman and Helpman 1991). To treat technology as endogenous means invention and innovation occur because of decisions by individuals and organizations in the production process (primarily by firms and the state) to engage in research and development as the economy grows. "Learning by doing" as production expands and making improvements in education and training are seen to result in a faster rate of accumulation of physical and human capital, which in turn contribute to higher economic growth rates.

What distinguishes the new growth theory from earlier neoclassical growth theory? First, technological change is treated as partly endogenous, whereas in the Solow model it is largely left unexplained. Second, technology is no longer seen as a pure public good which is nonrival and nonexcludable in consumption. Instead, much knowledge, while nonrival in consumption, is excludable. In many instances it is possible for knowledge producers to enforce property rights to knowledge by excluding others from its use, as through the use of patents, copyrights, and licensing. Third, because of excludability, firms have the ability to exert market power and extract monopoly rents as they exploit their technologies in the production process. Consequently, new growth theory tends to assume a monopolistic-competition market structure. Fourth, individual firms create positive externalities or spillovers for other firms in the innovation and production processes, generating increasing returns to scale at the aggregate level. These increasing returns contribute to a faster economic growth rate. Finally, unlike previous neoclassical models, new growth theory incorporates more international technological interdependence within its framework (Grossman and Helpman 1991, 1994). The emergence of spillovers from technological advances at the local or national levels may significantly alter the path of a nation's economic development and its dynamic comparative advantage.

Despite these differences with the earlier neoclassical growth model, the new growth theory retains substantial continuity with neoclassicism. Much of the new growth literature is firmly wedded to a general equilibrium framework in which the goods and labor markets clear, thereby automatically generating full employment (Grossman and Helpman 1994, 34). Many of the new growth models also continue to treat the capital accumulation process as the transformation of savings into investment spending. Perhaps most significantly, the new growth theory retains the supply-side emphasis of neoclassical economics, resting on Say's Law that supply creates its own demand.

There are, however, policy implications of the new growth theory that indicate grounds for an increased role for the state in the development process. The stress on the role of human capital in increasing long-run growth potential, while hardly a new idea, could provide a stronger case for government intervention in education and the labor market. More important, Grossman and Helpman suggest a role for industrial policy may exist where technological spillovers from one industry into others are likely to substantially improve a country's dynamic comparative advantage in trade (Grossman and Helpman 1994, 39–40). There may even be circumstances where trade protection to allow domestic industries to "catch up" technologically might increase economic growth rates, though these improvements may not be synonymous with higher economic welfare (Grossman and Helpman 1994, 40–41).

AN INSTITUTIONALIST APPROACH TO DEVELOPMENT

Institutional economics provides an alternative perspective on economic growth and development. It rejects the savings-centered approach of neoclassical economics in favor of a view of development concentrated on the interaction between technology and institutions that gives rise to a path dependent process. Adopting an evolutionary approach, institutionalism is concerned with the effects of circular and cumulative causation, which may result in polarization as much as convergence. As policy prescription, the institutional approach emphasizes the need for institutional adjustment through a reconfiguration of power within and between societies in order to encourage greater social, political, and economic equality.

Both neoclassical growth theory and its offspring, new growth theory, lack a theory of technological change; rather, they have a theory of savings which purports to explain the capital accumulation process. These savings-centered theories hold that fore going current consumption in order to channel a larger share of disposable income into savings will increase the production of investment goods, generating higher GDP growth (Junker 1967). They are, however, incapable of describing the true causes of economic growth. While saving does represent monetary power over productive resources, saving per se does not explain growth. As Clarence Ayres put it bluntly: "No one secretes rails by going without lunch" (Ayres [1944] 1978, 49).

There are two major flaws in the savings-centered approach. First, it implies that consumption goods are always present-oriented while capital goods are future-oriented. However, items often labeled consumption goods are frequently used to sustain things labeled capital. For example, human capital—the skills and knowledge embodied in people—have to be maintained by food and drink, shelter, clothing, and transportation to and from work in order for the flow of benefits to be realized from the use of human capital. As Junker argued, the real distinction is between wasteful and beneficial uses of physical capital (Junker 1967, 42). Second, and most important, the savings-centered approach addresses a symptom rather than a cause of economic progress. The availability of greater savings does not automatically raise the productive capacity of an economy. While saving is the monetary form by which control is exerted over the technological process, it is the technological process itself that expands an economy's ability to deliver higher future output.

Technology and Institutional Change

Institutional economics sees the economic growth and development process as characterized by the interaction of technology and institutions (Ayres [1944] 1978). Economic progress occurs when technological forces, (defined as the combining of skills and tools), create cumulative change that exceeds the limits of institutions that serve to inhibit change. Institutions are habits of thoughts that curb the ability of people to use skills and tools to improve their material existence.

Clarence Ayres identified four principles of economic development from an institutionalist perspective (Ayres [1944] 1978, xxvi–xxxiii). First, the development process is indivisible and irresistible. Second, technological change unfolds in an inverse relationship to the degree of institutional resistance to that change. Third, human capital or the creative capacities of its people determine the pace and extent to which a society can experience economic progress. Fourth, the values underpinning the technological process are universal, instrumental values. These instrumental values supersede ceremonial values expressed through outmoded institutions such as systems of social stratification based on caste, class, and other forms of status and ideology.

Instrumental values are, according to Ayres, a set of mutually inclusive values: freedom, equality, security, abundance, and excellence, with democracy acting as "the procedure by which alone all the other values can be achieved" (Ayres 1961, 282). Thus, greater equality may be achieved by providing greater freedom and security, emphasizing achievement of excellence in the technological process, and enhancing democratic participation in the political and economic processes. In the institutionalist analysis, there is no trade-off between efficiency and equality as in neoclassical economics. Instead, the two are mutually reinforcing.

The dichotomous relationship between technology and institutions results in path dependence—technologies are constrained or channeled by institutions so that development moves in a particular historical, institutionally driven direction. Such path dependence may either retard or propel development, contingent on the degree to which technology can cause institutional change along the lines of instrumental values. Initial historical "accidents" in the application of technology come to be shaped and constrained by institutions. For instance, while the automobile was the outcome of a combination of technical innovations—the internal combustion engine, pneumatic tires, and advances in metallurgy—the evolving auto industry was powerfully directed down a particular path by institutions such as the profit motive, the mass production system, corporate vertical integration, and the antilabor tactics of Henry Ford. Hence, path dependence is not necessarily linked to superior outcomes. Some paths may give rise to inefficiencies, and even those that are efficient may fail to deliver social outcomes according to instrumental valuation.

Circular, Cumulative Causation in an Evolving Economy

An evolving economy is a process involving circular and cumulative causation in which economic convergence or polarization may occur. According to Myrdal, the advantages of growth poles, regions, or nations, where growth proceeds at a faster pace because of a technological or institutional edge, may become cumulative and outstrip backward or slower growing regions or nations (Myrdal 1957). "Spread" effects reinforce growth poles in the form of technological spillovers, the concentration of human capital, and the expansion of infrastructure. Backward regions may experience "backwash" effects as resources are bid away by the more prosperous areas, such as the outmigration of labor, deterioration of infrastructure, and decline of the local community. This polarization between regions within a country or between countries occurs because of an unequal distribution of power over productive resources, which not only becomes an obstacle to attaining greater equality, but also to efficiency and economic growth.

Nicholas Kaldor extended the concept of circular and cumulative causation, attributing it to the existence of increasing returns to scale in the broadest sense (Kaldor 1966, [1970] 1989, 1981). The manufacturing sector, unlike agriculture, is characterized by increasing returns at both the firm and sectoral levels because of technical externalities involving learning by doing, product and process differentiation, and network effects. These technological advantages are cumulative and path dependent or self-reinforcing.

The self-reinforcing effects of cumulative causation are crucially dependent on the growth of effective demand (Kaldor 1981). The growth of demand determines how fast productivity and economic growth will rise. A slowing of demand is likely to lead to economic stagnation which, if it becomes chronic, may result in structural decline. Periodic financial instability may also imperil economic growth during periods of debt deflation as the process of making money impedes that of making goods (Minsky 1986).

Adapting Harrod's foreign trade multiplier analysis, Kaldor ascribed the key source of effective demand as coming from outside the region or nation in which production occurs (Kaldor 1981, 601–5). This led him to advocate an "outward strategy" for LDCs that entailed import substitution but, more significant, export promotion. Kaldor maintained that the success of this outward strategy would depend on "the innovative ability and adaptive capacity [of a nation's] manufacturers" as well as the growth of global demand (Kaldor 1981, 603).

As the outward strategies of LDCs expanded, industrial countries would likely experience a decline in their share of world trade as their export share declined while import penetration rose, much as has occurred in many industrial countries since the 1970s. However, these countries could expect rising demand for their manufactured goods from faster-growing LDCs. Kaldor was not sanguine about the likelihood that the reduced export market share of industrial countries would be fully offset by growth in global demand. His solution was to develop a multilateral system of planned trade between industrial economies so that the balance of payments constraint would not limit their ability to expand domestic demand to maintain full employment (Kaldor 1981, 608).

In international trade, then, circular and cumulative causation is apparent. Countries that capture the benefits of increasing returns to scale through rapid, sustained growth of the manufacturing sector will grow and develop rapidly, while those that do not will be left behind. Domestically, there is likely to be uneven growth and development between regions and local communities, especially in rural areas. Meantime, "leader" industrial countries may encounter structural decline if they are unable to maintain a strong manufacturing sector or a highly productive service sector and export-led growth. Again, within industrial nations, uneven development may take place between growth poles and backward regions.

In the aggregate, all countries cannot successfully adopt an export-led strategy, at least one that would generate current account surpluses for all. At the global level, one country's surplus is another's deficit. Davidson pointed out that the outward strategy is a "beggar thy neighbor" strategy in which one nation's increased employment, economic growth, and trade surplus are achieved at the expense of another's trade deficit, rising unemployment, and slower economic growth (Davidson 1994, 255–62).

The Market Myth and Social Economy

One of the great enabling myths of the past few centuries has been that of the market mentality, which suggests that a self-regulating market system is the optimal organization of the economy and society. Karl Polanyi warned of the perils of the "economistic fallacy" which consists of the error in reading market exchange motives into all social contexts across space and time (Polanyi 1977, 20). Historically, the self-regulating market system was only dominant in nineteenth-century England. Before and since that time, societies have, with varying degrees of success, developed ways to hem in the market system so that the social fabric is not irretrievably damaged by its working. When society fails to take such action to ensure social protection, cultural dislocation may result in the form of the breakdown of family structure, local communities, and national society.

The imperialism of the past two to three centuries involved the penetration of the market system into less developed regions of the world. The result was social disintegration. In the imperial powers, citizens suffered cultural dislocation as the traditional economic system embedded in social relations was swept away by the expanding market system. In the new colonies, communities built on traditions of custom were fractured by the spread of the cash nexus of the marketplace, which was regulated by legal contract rather than traditional rights and duties.

J. S. Furnivall and Julius Boeke investigated the nature of this social disintegration within the context of plural societies such as India, Burma, and the Dutch East Indies (present-day Indonesia) (Furnivall 1939, [1948] 1956; Boeke 1953). Peopled with diverse ethnic and racial groups, plural societies find it difficult to develop a "common will" that would reflect a national consensus. Crucial to the success of social reintegration, Furnivall held, was the need for a strong state to bind together the diverse elements of plural society (Furnivall [1948] 1956, 488–91). However, as he realized, this was a "chicken or egg" dilemma: how could a strong state emerge before a common will had been formed concerning the social, political, and economic direction society should take?

Gunnar Myrdal addressed this inadequacy of the state in the development process with his theory of the *soft state*, which describes a government either unable or unwilling to impose obligations on its citizenry (Myrdal 1968, 1: 66, 2: 895–900). Lacking sufficient autonomy, the soft state becomes a broker state swayed by competing interests, which promote their own narrow self-interests rather than also contributing to the definition and implementation of a public interest. For Myrdal, the poverty trap could be escaped if LDCs adopted "modernization ideals," including such values as rationality, planning, social and economic equalization, improved institutions and attitudes, self-determination, and political democracy (Myrdal 1968). A *hard state,* championing the ideals of modernization, could act as a catalyst for economic and social progress.

While Furnivall studied plural societies in the developing world, some of the problems of plural societies may also be observed in a number of the developed nations. The growing incapacity of social institutions to deal with cultural diversity can be seen in diverse contexts: the civil war in the former Yugoslavia; the separatist movement in Quebec, Canada; the Zapatista uprising in Chiapas, Mexico; the polarization between African-Americans and white Americans; and the demands for greater Maori sovereignty in New Zealand. The problems of plural societies are therefore *not* unique to LDCs but are common ones, though their solutions must be tailored to the unique cultural context.

The Developmental State

In the institutional approach, the state and the market system are complements rather than substitutes (Jones 1981; Dugger 1992). The expansion of the market sector is dependent on the actions of the modern state to recognize and enforce property rights and contracts; provide infrastructure such as basic education, research and development, and roadways; redistribute incomes; and conduct macroeconomic stabilization. The state, in turn, depends on the market sector to deliver a tax base to finance its activities and to provide employment and incomes for citizens.

The state is dichotomous: it carries out both integrative and repressive functions (Stanfield 1991). The former are aimed at integrating the various interests within society to achieve a public interest through collective action. This is the task that Myrdal's soft state is unable to achieve. The latter function, repression, derives from the state's use of its sovereign power to coerce citizens to behave in particular ways. This repressive role may be put to noninstrumental ends such as enforcing social stratification which entrench social, political, and economic inequality. Alternately, it may be used to realize instrumental values by dismantling hierarchies that result in the maldistribution of income and wealth in society. The state's intervention to require universal education, provide a social safety net, regulate the conditions of labor, and promote increased political and economic democracy illustrate the instrumental use of its repressive function. Accordingly, in furthering instrumental values, the state may simultaneously employ integrative and repressive functions. After World War II, an Asian developmental state emerged to superintend rapid economic growth in Japan, Singapore, South Korea, and Malaysia, which had a measure of success in terms of improving equity as well (World Bank 1993). It may serve as a model for LDCs that are less far down the development path (as well as some already in the industrial camp). A number of lessons can be drawn from the Asian experience. A developmental state can deliver rapid economic growth to raise low standards of living, not only by correcting for market failures but by even enhancing efficient market outcomes (Dietz 1992). However, to be successful the state must be "hardened." It must have a vision of the public or national interest and be both prepared and able to move the economy in this direction. The state in many East Asian nations was itself reformed to improve the professional competence of the bureaucracy; adopt criteria for selection, monitoring, and removal of assistance to industry; and conduct controlled "contests" between private sector firms in an industry (World Bank 1993, 79–103).

Successful development may also require administering prices, especially for finance and foreign currency, to attain production and income gains instead of leaving them to the determination of world markets, as implied by the free trade prescription of neoclassical economists. Reiterating the institutionalist message, an export-promotion strategy by itself is insufficient for development success. The successful East Asian economies, as a group, strived for technological autonomy which went beyond merely acquiring the capability of its workforce to use foreign technology effectively in efforts to create, use, and control technologies developed at home (Dietz 1990, 1992). Care was taken to build both backward and forward linkages in the production and exchange processes at the national and international levels. In essence, East Asian economies built themselves an industrial network, with a particular emphasis on strengthening domestic producers. Accelerated development was further advanced by the ability of policymakers to perceive and act upon "strategy switch points" (Dietz 1992, 377). For example, immediately after the oil shock of 1974, the Japanese government and private sector engaged in resource-seeking and then resource-processing investment in many areas outside of Japan in order to secure supplies of resources for Japanese industry (Ozawa 1993). Between the 1960s and 1990s, as its resource shortages and its productive capacities evolved, Singapore progressively moved from import-substitution to manufactured export-promotion and then to knowledge- and service-intensive strategies.

WHAT IS TO BE DONE?

The central problem of the LDCs, as with the already industrialized nations, is the dynamic tension between technological improvement, leading to an enhancement of social provisioning, and the inhibitory forces of outdated institutions. Many LDCs are pluralistic societies, governed by soft states in which vested interests exert power over national policy and establish links with foreign capital to the detriment of the larger share of the population.

A first step in LDC reform is to develop in these societies a public or national interest that addresses the broad interests of the plurality. As the experience of the past four decades shows, this is no easy task for many societies. However, it is possible to "harden" the state, as numerous countries have shown. Existing economic and political power structures may be expected to resist change, but the alternative is persisting social and economic inequality. The combination of old and new institutions may be necessary to bind together the community in a new social fabric while unleashing technological progress. This implies that the economic theory to guide the development of a particular society needs to be applied in the particular cultural context.

Given the centrality of technological change to the development process, a key focal point of reform must be efforts to inculcate the technological way of doing things. LDCs must improve their capacity to adopt and adapt the technological capabilities of their citizens through expanded education and technological transfer. Much technology transfer from the north to the south is tightly controlled by multinational corporations and northern governments. Much of it is also not appropriate for the internal development of the LDCs. Consequently, uncritical technology transfer is not a desirable strategy.

One option is to promote "technological blending," the integration of cutting-edge technologies appropriate to traditional economic activities for lower-income groups in the LDCs (Bhalla and James 1988, 1995). The application of photovoltaic power to small-scale farming, biotechnology to oral rehydration therapy, and environmentally friendly kiln designs for brickmaking are examples of blending that may allow LDCs to leapfrog stages in technology and improve the well-being of the poorest citizens. Beyond technology transfer, LDCs must build their own creative capacity if they are to achieve technological autonomy. This will be difficult to realize unless education, business, and political systems encourage freedom of thought, expression, and association. Individual and civil rights are fundamental elements in an instrumental development process that delivers both higher material and welfare standards of living.

Promoting equality in the LDCs raises the issue of meeting the basic needs of the lower income groups. These needs ought to include both material and nonmaterial requirements which, to name but a few, include self-worth, self-determination, and the sense of belonging. Capitalism may try to treat the human resource as a variable cost, but this is a fiction as far as society is concerned. Society must always cover the overhead costs of human life or risk the very survival of both the individual and the society.

What is needed to ensure social provisioning in the LDCs is "adjustment with a human face," or a basic-needs approach to adjustment (Cornia, Jolly, and Stewart 1987). Such policies would place material floors under the nutrition, health care, and education of the poorest LDC citizens. Structural adjustment programs of the World Bank and LDC government policies need to be reconfigured to place the highest priority on meeting the basic needs of the poor and not on austerity programs directed solely at achieving market efficiency.

Since the mid-1970s, many of the northern nations have encountered slower productivity and GDP growth along with a widening distribution of income and wealth. These developments are set against a backdrop of increasing interdependence in the global economy, which has meant larger trade deficits for a number of industrialized nations, (with the exception of Japan and Germany), until recently. The resulting job loss in trade-sensitive industries has been hardest felt by low-skill, low-wage workers. In the United States, at least, groups at high risk from freer trade—women, minorities, and older and less-skilled workers—are left to carry the burden of adjustment largely on their own. Only some 6 percent of the long term unemployed, among which these groups are disproportionately represented, receive trade adjustment assistance.

Protectionist policies to prevent further job loss in trade-sensitive sectors of the northern nations may be superficially attractive; however, they entail real costs for other sectors of these economies and for the growth of LDCs. Just as export-promotion strategies in aggregate are "beggar thy neighbor" policies, so, too, would be greater import protection against LDC products. A more viable policy package would involve accelerating efforts to improve the education and training of lower-skilled workers; redistributing income from the skilled to the unskilled through the fiscal system; developing an industrial policy to bring about structural upgrading into higher value-added production; redistributing work and leisure on a more equitable basis; and expending significant effort securing a new international system for trade and payments.

The last major effort to build a supranational governance system for the world economy was conducted at the close of World War II. While rightfully the United Nations system can claim some limited successes (for example, the Bretton Woods fixed exchange rate system in effect up until the early 1970s), on balance this international management structure has proved inadequate to the task. The outcome is partly caused by nationalist fears of surrendering some sovereignty to supranational agencies and partly by the staying power of the obsolete market mentality as an enabling myth.

As the pressures of economic and social disintegration mount within and between nations, the need for new, supranational governance arrangements is apparent (McClintock 1995). Many of the international economic problems facing the north and south alike are now beyond the capability of a superpower or small group of large players to manage successfully. Moreover, such approaches in the past have proved to be inherently inequitable because of their exclusionary nature.

A supranational strategy that could deliver benefits to both the north and south and deliver more stable trade would be to link international labor and environmental standards to reductions in trade barriers by the north against imports from the south. Such a multilateral agreement would have the benefit of placing floors underneath the conditions of LDC citizens by international agreement which would be reciprocated by increased market access for the higher wage products of the south. Low-skill workers in the north would gain some measure of protection for their livelihoods, underpinning a material floor for them. Should participating countries infringe the standards, importing nations could levy a social tariff against their goods. Similarly, an importing nation that maintains trade barriers in excess of the agreed levels could be sanctioned to lower the barriers or find its exports subject to a social tariff by trading partners.

The privatized trade and investment management of multinational corporations also needs greater supervision. While they may deliver benefits to host nations in the form of technology transfer, productivity improvements, and higher incomes and employment, they also can lead to costs in terms of the exploitation of labor and the environment, transfer pricing, control over technology, and monopolistic behavior. Supranational monitoring and regulation of the activities of multinationals could mediate the interests of north and south, but it must encompass broad interests and be highly participatory. An international organization for multinational enterprises (OMNE) could be developed that would act to ensure the rights of multinationals to operate in a host country under the same laws as domestic firms (Scaperlanda 1993). It would also enforce the duties of multinationals to adhere to labor and environmental standards and to avoid restrictive practices.

Finally, the international payments system needs to be reformed. The floating exchange rate system and removal of capital controls have increased volatility in trade and financial markets, increasing financial innovations like financial derivatives that have increased the instability of the international financial system (McClintock 1996). The creation of a fixed exchange rate system governed by an international clearing union with the ability to create international liquidity to ensure stable growth in effective global demand, to monitor capital flight, and to recycle current account surpluses is a prerequisite to a more equitable global order (Davidson 1994, 268–72).

The chances of securing greater supranational governance may be even less propitious in the 1990s than in 1945 because of an increasing trend to freer markets and less government. However, the need has never been greater. Greater economic and social polarization in the developing and developed nations is strengthening the forces of disintegration both within and between societies. The question is whether or not the world community is up to the challenge of securing improvements in its citizens' well-being through rising, and more equitable, living standards.

REFERENCES

Abramovitz, Moses. 1986. "Catching Up, Forging Ahead, and Falling Behind." *Journal of Economic History*, 46, no. 2 (June): 385–406.

Ayres, Clarence. 1961. *Toward a Reasonable Society.* Austin: University of Texas Press.

___. [1944] 1978. *The Theory of Economic Progress.* 3rd ed. Kalamazoo, Mich.: New Issues Press.

Bairoch, Paul. 1982. "Discussion." In Just Faaland, ed., *Population and the World Economy in the 21st Century.* New York: St Martin's Press, 162–63.

Bhalla, Ajit S., and Dilmus D. James, ed. 1988. *New Technologies and Development: Experiences in Technology Blending.* Boulder, Colo.: Lynne Rienner.

___. 1995. "Alternative Technologies for Third World Development: Technological Blending Revisited." Paper presented to the Association for Institutional Thought Annual Meeting, April, Oakland, Calif.

Boeke, Julius H. 1953. *Economics and Economic Policies of Dual Societies.* New York: Institute of Pacific Relations.

Cornia, Giovanni Andrea, Richard Jolly, and Frances Stewart, eds. 1987. *Adjustment with a Human Face.* Vol. 1. New York: Oxford University Press.

Davidson, Paul. 1994. *Post Keynesian Macroeconomic Theory.* Aldershot, U.K.: Edward Elgar.

De Long, J. Bradford. 1988. "Productivity Growth, Convergence, and Welfare: Comment," *American Economic Review,* 78, no. 5 (Dec.): 1138–59.

Dietz, James L. 1990. "Technological Autonomy, Linkages, and Development." In James Dietz and Dilmus D. James, eds., *Progress toward Development in Latin America.* Boulder, Colo.: Lynne Rienner, 177–99.

___. 1992. "Overcoming Underdevelopment: What Has Been Learned from the East Asian and Latin American Experiences?" *Journal of Economic Issues,* 26, no. 2 (June): 373–83.

Dugger, William M. 1992. "An Evolutionary Theory of the State and the Market." In William M. Dugger and William T. Waller, Jr., eds., *The Stratified State.* Armonk, N.Y.: M. E. Sharpe.

Fieleke, Norman S. 1994. "Is Global Competition Making the Poor Even Poorer?" *New England Economic Review* (Nov./Dec.): 3–16.

"For Richer, For Poorer." 1994. *Economist,* Nov. 5, 19–21.

Furnivall, J. S. 1939. *Netherlands India: A Study of Plural Economy.* Cambridge: Cambridge University Press.

___. [1948] 1956. *Colonial Policy and Practice.* New York: New York University Press.

Gordon, Wendell. 1994. *The United Nations at the Crossroads of Reform.* Armonk, N.Y.: M.E. Sharpe.

Grossman, Gene, and Elhanan Helpman. 1991. *Innovation and Growth in the Global Economy.* Cambridge: Massachusetts Institute of Technology Press.

___. 1994. "Endogenous Innovation in the Theory of Growth." *Journal of Economic Perspectives,* 8, no. 1 (Winter): 23–44.

Jones, Eric L. 1981. *The European Miracle.* Cambridge: Cambridge University Press.

Junker, Louis. 1967. "Capital Accumulation, Savings–Centered Theory and Economic Development." *Journal of Economic Issues,* 1, no. 3 (June): 25–43.

Kaldor, Nicholas. 1966. *Causes of the Slow Rate of Economic Growth of the United Kingdom.* Cambridge: Cambridge University Press.

___. 1981. "The Role of Increasing Returns, Technical Progress and Cumulative Causation in the Theory of International Trade and Economic Growth." *Economie Appliquee,* 34, no. 4: 593–617.

___. [1970] 1989. "The Case for Regional Policies." Reprinted in F. Targetti and A. P. Thirlwall, eds., *The Essential Kaldor.* New York: Homes and Meier, 311–26.

Kuznets, Simon. 1966. *Modern Economic Growth.* New Haven, Conn.: Yale University Press.

Lucas, Robert E., Jr. 1988. "On the Mechanics of Economic Development." *Journal of Monetary Economics,* 22, no. 1 (July): 3–42.

McClintock, Brent. 1996. "The Financial Derivatives Market and International Financial Instability."*Journal of Economic Issues,* 30, no. 1 (Mar.): 13–33.

___. 1995. "International Trade and the Governance of Global Markets." In Charles Whalen, ed., *Political Economy for the Next Century.* Armonk, N.Y.: M. E. Sharpe, 225–44.

Minsky, Hyman. 1986. *Stabilizing an Unstable Economy.* New Haven, Conn.: Yale University Press.

Myrdal, Gunnar. 1957. *Rich Lands and Poor.* New York: Harper.

___. 1968. *Asian Drama.* Vols. 1, 2. New York: Twentieth Century Fund.

Organization for Economic Cooperation and Development. 1993. *Employment Outlook.* Paris: OECD.

Ozawa, Terutomo. 1993. "Foreign Direct Investment and Structural Transformation: Japan as a Recycler of Market and Industry." *Business and the Contemporary World,* 5, no. 2 (Spring): 129–50.

Polanyi, Karl. 1977. *The Livelihood of Man.* Edited by Harry Pearson. New York: Academic Press.

Rebelo, Sergio. 1991. "Long Run Policy Analysis and Long Run Growth." *Journal of Political Economy,* 99, no. 3 (June): 500–521.

Romer, Paul. 1986. "Increasing Returns and Long-Run Growth." *Journal of Political Economy,* 94, no. 5 (Oct.): 1002–37.

___. 1990. "Endogenous Technological Change." *Journal of Political Economy,* part 2, vol. 98, no. 5 (Oct.): S71–102.

___. 1994. "The Origins of Endogenous Growth." *Journal of Economic Perspectives,* 8, no. 1 (Winter): 3–22.

Scaperlanda, Anthony. 1993. "Multinational Enterprises and the Global Market." *Journal of Economic Issues,* 27, no. 2 (June): 605–16.

Solow, Robert. 1956. "A Contribution to the Theory of Economic Growth." *Quarterly Journal of Economics,* 70 (Feb.): 65–94.

Stanfield, James Ronald. 1991. "The Dichotomized State." *Journal of Economic Issues,* 25, no. 3 (Sept.): 765–80.

Wood, Adrian. 1994. *North-South Trade, Employment and Inequality.* Oxford, U.K.: Clarendon Press.

World Bank. 1993. *The East Asian Miracle.* New York: Oxford University Press.

___. 1994. *World Development Report 1994.* Washington, D.C.: World Bank.

13

Inequality in the 1980s:
An Institutionalist View

Charles M. A. Clark

This chapter offers an institutionalist explanation of the trends in inequality during the last decade. It highlights exactly those operating forces that are behind the income distribution dynamic and which are shielded by neoclassical economic theory.

The chapter first compares the institutional and neoclassical approaches to income distribution. Then, it looks at the dramatic rise in inequality in the United States and its causes. Next, it offers an examination of the trends in income distribution in the 1980s in various other industrial countries. The chapter also shows that it is differing institutional characteristics that explain the levels of inequality in the different countries, rather than the operation of impersonal market forces that adjust relative prices in response to scarcities and surpluses.

EXPLAINING INCOME DISTRIBUTION

The classical economists, who are best exemplified by John Stuart Mill, recognized that historical and social factors played an important role in determining the distribution of income. While Mill held that "natural laws" controlled the sphere of production, distribution was determined by historical and social factors and could be classified as part of the discretionary economy. As part of the overall trend of eliminating history and society from economic theory (Clark 1992), the marginalist revolution argued that both production and distribution were under the domain of natural laws. In a move toward individualistic explanations of all economic phenomena, the marginalists created the theory of marginal productivity to demonstrate that "the distribution of the income of society is controlled by a natural law, and that this law, if it worked without friction, would give every agent of production the amount of wealth which that agent created" (John B. Clark [1899] 1965, v). The political and ideological ramifications of this theory cannot be underestimated, for following the classical approach leads to Marx's theory of exploitation and/or to the popular socialist-labor view of the late nineteenth century of the right of the workers to the whole of their product. Furthermore, as Mill argued, the distribution of income was an area of discretion; that is, it could be changed from what it currently was.

The differences between the classical and neoclassical theories of distribution have carried on up until the present. Erik Olin Wright (1989) labeled these two as the achievement and exploitation theories. Achievement theories view the distribution of income as the sum total of the determination of individual incomes of the group in question.

[A] full account of the individual (non-relational) determinants of individual income is sufficient to explain the overall distribution of income. This suggests that the central empirical task is first, to assemble an inventory of all the individual attributes that influence the income of individuals, and second, to evaluate their relative contributions to explaining variance across individuals in income attainment. (Wright 1989, 918)

Exploitation theories view income distribution as the result of social and economic relations. Income distribution from this perspective is determined by the structure of the relations that allocate income. A person's income is determined by where she fits into the processes that determine incomes, and not by individual achievements based on individual attributes. Exploitation theories concentrate on the distribution and control of those "assets" that put one in the position to appropriate a disproportionate share of social output. These "assets" range from the traditional means of production, in the form of physical and financial capital, to technological knowledge, skills, and organization. Another word for *control of assets* is *power*. Neoclassical theories are the quintessence of achievement type theories, while the institutionalist explanation of income distribution is clearly an exploitation story.

Neoclassical Theory of Income Distribution

At one level, the marginal productivity theory of income distribution was an answer to Marx's theory of exploitation. However, at a deeper level, achievement theories are the natural outcome of the logic of neoclassical economics; the two most important attributes of which (methodological individualism and the emulation of natural science models and metaphors) necessarily exclude what is at the heart of exploitation theories, society, and history and necessitate the type of explanations that are part and parcel of achievement theories.

The neoclassical theory approach to the question of the rise in inequality has been to change the question to one of income determination, of which earnings determination becomes the focal point of all discussions on the topic. Underlying this approach (and, in fact, all neoclassical economics) are the two principles that (1) "all agents in the economy (i.e., individuals, firms, unions, governments) maximize a well-defined objective function; and (2) there exists a market equilibrium which balances the conflicting goals of the various players in the labor market" (Borjas 1988, 21). In the neoclassical story, individual economic agents make choices, based on their preferences and endowments, which, when totaled, determine market outcomes.   Any existing income distribution is merely the outcome of this market process; that is, an individual's income is determined by the price (market outcome) that their particular factor service receives in a competitive market. Any long term income inequality will be the result of differences in productivities or (what is seldom discussed) initial endowments. Short run inequalities might be the result of shortages or surpluses in particular factor markets, but these are alleviated when relative prices, performing the necessary role of sending market signals to individuals, adjust so that such imbalances are eliminated.

For neoclassical economics, the most important choices in terms of income determination involve the accumulation of human capital. Essentially, human capital theory states that individuals acquire education and skill by exchanging current earnings for future earnings, with future earnings being higher than current earnings in order for the exchange to be rational. This creates education/skill differentials in future earnings. Those with more education or skill have invested in their own human capital; they have exchanged their current income (lost wages while at school) for higher future incomes. The underlying rationale of this whole approach is the marginal productivity theory of income distribution, which states that more productive economic agents will earn higher incomes.

The question of rising income inequality is thus addressed as a problem of the determination of income differentials. Assumed from the start is that incomes are market determined prices and that some supply or demand factor is behind the change in relative prices of skills/education or the other characteristics deemed to receive prices. In explaining individual income differentials, the standard procedure is to investigate the relationship between some individual trait or set of traits (gender, education, race, work experience), job characteristics, and earnings. This is usually done by running a regression with income as the dependent variable and the various individual attributes as the independent variables. The coefficients for each trait or job characteristic are interpreted as prices that the market has imputed for these traits and characteristics. Both the causes and the effects of the change in inequality are limited by the adherence to methodological individualism—to examining phenomena that can be depicted only in terms of individuals. Even when group or collective effects are investigated, such as the effect of unions, the mode of investigation is at the individual level, with participation in the particular group being one more individual trait. Changes in income distribution are thus analyzed via changes in the supply and demand for the various attributes. The rise in the education differential, a frequent topic in this literature, is seen as a reflection of either an increase in the demand for educated workers (usually attributed to the rising use of computers in the workplace) and or changes in the supply of educated workers.

Recent work on earnings inequality has given institutional factors more of a role in explaining why different countries have different levels of earnings inequality (Blau and Khan 1995). Here, a dichotomy is presented between market and institutional factors. Market factors included the determination of skills prices through the interaction of supply and demand, whereas institutional factors include "extent of collective bargaining coverage, the scope of collective bargaining where it occurs, union pay policies, and government policy toward the labor market" (Blau and Khan 1995, 5–6). Institutional factors are depicted as deviations from the competitive market norm, as market imperfections. Implicit in this analysis is the idea that these "imperfections" produce suboptimal outcomes, as they are non-competitive in nature. Even though there is a large and growing literature within the neoclassical tradition dealing with institutions, the final term in their analysis is always the maximizing individual, with institutions only being beneficial if it can be shown that markets cannot operate in a particular setting, namely, market imperfection or failure.

This markets versus institutions distinction should be seen as a false dichotomy, for it is a comparison of a myth and reality. The hypothetical free market exists only in the minds of economists and on the pages of economics textbooks. In reality all markets are instituted processes, which only exist—can only exist—by being institutionalized. *Markets are institutions*, and the process by which they are instituted is the process by which the standards, practices, expectations, and sanctions of specific exchange processes are established and legitimated.

In reality, individual markets are instituted with their own individual set of rules, customs, and procedures. Markets are institutionalized arenas of exchange. They are institutions that institute, regulate and legitimate exchange activity, enabling the market "system" to exist (Hodgson 1988). Markets are human creations and not natural phenomena (Dugger 1989), and thus the outcome of markets should be seen as a social product, an expression of the underlying social order. It is from this perspective that the institutional theory of income distribution begins.

Institutionalist Theory of Income Distribution

There are four pillars of institutionalism (Mayhew 1987): evolution, culture, cultural relativity, and instrumental valuation. The institutionalist theory of income distribution thus is an extension of these concepts into the area of how society distributes the social product in its solution to the primary economic question: how to provide for society's material reproduction. The net effect of Veblen's stress on the importance of the evolutionary perspective in economic analysis is that such analysis should be historically based; that to understand economic activity we must understand the institutional arrangements by which such activity is made possible. Moreover, any such analysis of these institutions must view them as the by-product of institutional arrangements that existed in the past and the interests and activities of individuals who are adjusting old, and forming new, institutions (Veblen [1899] 1909, 188). This evolutionary perspective means that the economy and economic activity are cultural phenomena and can only be understood as such. To use Veblen's most famous example, consumption is not merely an individual act (the meeting of physical needs or the satisfying of subjective wants and desires) but a social activity, whose significance as a device for social communication is as important—in fact, for an affluent society, more important—as its role in fulfilling basic needs. Veblen's great insight into conspicuous consumption was not that people keep up with the Joneses, but that the act of consumption was an essential part of the overall legitimation and recreation of the social order. The importance of culture in questions of income distribution cannot be exaggerated, as it leads directly to the idea of cultural relativity: all economic phenomena can only be understood in the context in which it takes place and, over time and with institutional changes and adjustments, the meaning of the activity will change.

The last of the four pillars, instrumental valuation, also has its roots in Veblen, in what has become known as the Veblenian dichotomy. Veblen was not interested in giving different answers to the question raised by neoclassical economic theory, but in asking different questions. Specifically, he was interested in understanding the process of cumulative change, the process of institutional evolution. Given the idea of cultural relativity, and its abandonment of universal categories and teleological outcomes, Veblen had to account for the process in terms of the process, that is the evolution of institutions as a function of the interaction between and within institutions. For Veblen, this is the result of the interaction between two types of institutions: industrial and pecuniary. "Institutions ... may be roughly distinguished into two classes or categories, ... they are institutions of acquisition or of production; ... they are pecuniary or industrial institutions; or in still other terms, they are institutions serving either invidious or the non-invidious economic interests" ([1899] 1909, 208). The distinction Veblen is making here is fundamental. It distinguishes between forces that promote the well-being of the community and those that promote the status and power of those with power. These two types of institutions, or aspects of a single institution, are most often in conflict. Most social institutions are inherently conservative and supportive of the status quo. Nevertheless, the dynamic of life never stops, and one important institution that Veblen often stressed, the community's collective knowledge—technology— continually disturbs the status quo. Social evolution is the interaction of these two types of institutions, with no predetermined path of development.

However, the Veblenian dichotomy is not merely a tool for understanding cumulative change. Just as important, it is a tool for instrumental valuation. The industrial, noninvidious institutions, or aspects of institutions, promote the well-being of the community (an admittedly difficult concept to define). The acquisitive, pecuniary, invidious institutions, or aspects thereof, promote and perpetuate status and power, frequently retarding the interests of the community. This distinction was generalized by latter institutionalists as the instrumental/ceremonial dichotomy (see Waller 1982).

Thus an institutionalist theory of income distribution starts off with—in fact, highlights—the historical path by which what neoclassical economists call initial endowments are allocated (an issue neoclassicals avoid like the plague). It also emphasizes that incomes are cultural products and part of the overall social order, playing a social, political, and ethical role as well as an economic one. Moreover, the more affluent a society, and an individual, the less "economic" concerns enter into the determination of incomes. Incomes, like most of the economy, are mostly discretionary factors and could be otherwise distributed.

Bill Dugger (1987) discusses three modes of income distribution: industry, market, and hierarchy. These are not mutually exclusive categories, for the same activity can have elements of more than one mode, and over time, through the process of institutional change, can move from one mode to another. The industrial mode is akin to the instrumental in the Veblenian dichotomy. It is a distribution that promotes the well-being of society. That is, it is a distribution regime that plays an integral part in solving an economic problem in an efficient manner. What exactly is an industrial distribution will depend on the society in question. In a supply-constrained economy with a low standard of living, it would be a distribution that best allocates the social product to promote the increased production capabilities of a society. In an affluent society, in which "our industrial capacity to produce affluence outstrips our institutional ability to absorb affluence" (Dugger 1987, 729), an industrial distribution might emphasize consumption. A hierarchial mode of distribution is akin to the ceremonial, that is, it determines incomes so as to support existing income distinctions between classes and perpetuate the status quo of an existing social order.

The market mode is a mixture of both industrial and hierarchical modes. In neoclassical theory, where prices, including incomes, serve the role of signaling individual economic agents to adjust their behavior in line with relative surpluses or shortages, all in a perfectly competitive setting, the market mode would generate the same results as the industry mode (assuming consumer sovereignty and perfect knowledge). However, again staying in the world of neoclassical analysis, once market imperfections enter the scene, the market distribution begins to reflect the relative economic power of various economic agents, and thus we end up with hierarchy. However, this analysis has been very uninstitutional in that the social context has been left out. Real markets are instituted process and not merely the interaction of impersonal forces. A real market distribution would have the element of hierarchy in that it reflects given endowments and the assignment of property and other rights. This is particularly important in that the assignment of costs is fundamental to the determination of the distribution of the social product. Production includes the process by which goods, services, and pollution are generated, yet costs are often shifted to those who receive none of the benefits of production. Moreover, hierarchy is built into the conceptions of fair and honorable incomes based on one's social and economic status. Thus, hierarchy is part of society's values.

In the real world, we end up with a mixture of industrial and hierarchical modes. Given the structure of the economy, "industrial prices" or "instrumental prices" would be ones that reflect the needs of production (technology and the structure of demand), and industrial incomes would be those that promoted both the future production of goods and services and the absorption of past production. Some prices and incomes might adjust to reflect shortages and surplus, but that would be the exception rather than the rule. Incomes, like prices, are administered, reflecting relative power, and thus hierarchy. A change in relative power could adjust them closer to "instrumental" incomes.

The institutional analysis of income distribution emphasizes the inherent conflict that is at the heart of the income distribution dynamic. It is an exploitation theory, not only in its emphasis on structure (social, political, and economic) as determining distribution, but also in its emphasis on the exploitative nature of how incomes are determined in a "market" economy. As Dugger explains in his chapter in this volume, class inequality is exploitative, and differential incomes are due to the acquisition of differential advantages and the exercise of differential powers. Furthermore, he argues that such differentials are supported by enabling myths that become stronger as the differentials widen. The whole class, race, gender, and nation complex of differentials and myths is cumulative; it is not counterbalancing and does not tend toward an equilibrium. In this institutionalist context, the changes in income distribution that took place during the 1980s can be seen as a change in the relative power of the groups struggling over the economic pie. It is a story of institutional change and the dominance of hierarchy.

Any discussion of inequality must necessarily be one of values. As Gunnar Myrdal explained, what we look at as social scientists is a reflection of our values (Myrdal 1958, 1). This is particularly so in income distribution, where almost all of what is written is either a defense of the status quo (or the means by which it has been produced) or a call for change. However, at a deeper level, the existence of inequality is an expression of a community's values and the working out of these values through behavior. For example, racial discrimination against blacks in America, while no longer state sanctioned (at least by statute), is carried out in the millions of small acts and decisions made by Americans in their daily lives. When shoppers show a preference for white-owned over black-owned shops, the incomes of the white owners will be higher than those of black owners. Similarly, if employers feel that white employees will generate greater business than black employees, they will hire more whites than blacks. Both these tendencies will affect the distribution of income, and in a very neoclassically methodological, individualistic manner, that is, through the preferences of individuals in the marketplace. However, racism is not genetic, nor is it spontaneous. It is learned; it is institutionalized. Thus, we cannot examine it out of the context of the society in question. Similarly, the values that produce higher or lower levels of inequality are learned and are expressions of the overall values of society. However, contrary to neoclassical economics, these values do not arise from a spontaneous order of autonomous preferences balancing in equilibrium, but rather reflect the history of the community and the interests of those with power. The inability to place such activity in its historical and social context is why neoclassicals like Milton Friedman have such a hard time understanding racism. Friedman has argued that discrimination is economically irrational, since there are profits to be earned by capitalist hiring black or female employees at rates under white males, thus bidding up the black and female rates and bidding down the white male rate. According to these enabling myths, the market should not only produce optimal results, it should eliminate racism and sexism.

Once we get away from the market myth, however, we can see that the prices we observe serve many functions and can be (and are), the result of many different types of activities. They are not the result of a mere summation of autonomous individual preferences and relative scarcities. Most prices are, in fact, administered, that is, they are the result of a firm's pricing policy and not the sole result of impersonal market forces. Supply-and-demand considerations are often important in the determination of a firm's pricing policy, but this is a far cry from the world of market mythology. Of particular importance is the role of power, that is, the ability to influence or control prices. To some extent this is the phenomena of "market" power, in that market structure can, and often does, influence pricing power. However, pricing power is institutionalized, always being the result of custom, tradition, legislation, adjudication, and politics. The role of power and the existence of administered prices gives us a new perspective with which to view income distribution. If one group can raise the price for the service or good they sell (that is, increase their income), and others cannot, then the distribution of income will be altered. Any change in the institutions that support and regulate markets that alters these power relations will have an income distribution effect. An examination of the changing distribution of income in the United States will show that this is exactly what has been happening.

THE RISE IN INEQUALITY IN THE UNITED STATES

After making a dramatic move towards equality in the early post-World War II era (Goldin and Margo 1992), the distribution of income remained relatively stable for most of the postwar era. The 1960s saw a gradual decrease in inequality, while the 1970s experienced a similarly gradual increase. (This coincides with the beginning of the decline in union strength, the use of monetary policy to fight inflation, and the upward trend in unemployment rates —the result of the reliance on monetary policy to fight inflation.) The Gini coefficient for pre-tax family income was 0.365 in 1960, falling to a low of

0.348 in 1967–1968, and then gradually rising again to 0.365 in 1980. This is contrasted with the movement in the Gini coefficient since 1980, where it steadily rose from 0.365 to the 1993 level of 0.420. This dramatic rise in inequality in the 1980s is widely recognized. It has involved a fundamental shift in the flow of real income upward toward the higher strata in the United States. (see Table 13.1).

Table 13.1
Changes in Median Income and Income Distribution

Year	Median Income (1991 $)	Bottom 40%	Middle 40%	Top 20%	Top 5%	Gini
1970	32,540	17.6	41.4	40.9	15.6	0.354
1975	33,248	17.2	41.7	41.1	15.5	0.358
1979	36,051	16.8	41.6	41.7	15.8	0.365
1981	33,843	16.3	41.8	41.9	15.3	0.370
1983	33,741	15.8	41.4	42.8	15.9	0.382
1985	35,107	15.5	41.1	43.5	16.7	0.389
1987	37,131	15.3	40.8	43.8	17.2	0.393
1989	37,579	15.2	40.2	44.6	17.9	0.401
1993	36,258	14.3	39.6	46.2	19.1	0.420

Source: U. S. Bureau of the Census, *Current Population Reports*, Series P-60 and for 1993 (Mishel and Bernstein 1994).

From 1980 to 1989, all income quintiles except the top experienced a fall in their share of aggregate income. The top quintile share rose from 41.7 to 44.6. This increase is largely the result of the increase in the share of aggregate income going to the top 5 percent, which rose from 15.3 percent in 1980 to 17.9 percent in 1989, accounting for 87 percent of the top quintile share increase. This trend is continued in the 1989–1993 period, with the top 5% share rising to 19.1 percent, which accounted for 75 percent of the top quintile's increase to 46.2 percent in 1993. The gains in income share were highly concentrated in the upper strata.

The so-called longest boom in peacetime history was an upper-class party, with 40 percent of the population actually worse off at the end of the decade than they were at the start. For each year of the 1980s except 1989, the lowest quintile had a real income of $471 to $1,279 below their 1979 level. The cumulative loss in income for this group ($7,667), was greater than their mean income in any year since 1979 (calculated by subtracting each year's actual mean income for the lowest quintile, in 1992 dollars, from the 1979 mean income). Since the median family income from 1979 to 1989 only rose by 4.2 percent, the dramatic 16.7 percent rise in income of the top quintile (with the even more dramatic rise of 23.3 percent of the top 5 percent), clearly came from a reslicing of the economic pie and not from its expansion. The real income flow shifted the most toward those who needed it the least. Table 13.2 shows how each quintile's income changed during 1959–1993.

Table 13.2

Change in Mean Family Income by Quintiles in Constant Dollars

PERIOD	Q1*	Q2	Q3	Q4	Q5	Top 5%
ACTUAL CHANGE						
1959-69	2,914	5,006	6,805	9,279	15,289	23,497
1969-79	-78	-45	1,333	2,774	5,500	6,932
1979-89	-285	-89	687	2,525	10,319	21,883
1989-93	-1,195	-2,125	-2,648	-2,253	-230	5,037
PERIOD	Q1	Q2	Q3	Q4	Q5	Top 5%
PERCENTAGE CHANGE						
1959-69	58.7	40.9	38.2	39.1	37.3	37.1
1969-79	-1.0	-0.3	5.4	8.4	9.8	8.0
1979-89	-3.7	-0.5	2.6	7.1	16.7	23.3
1989-93	-10.9	-8.3	-6.7	-3.9	-0.2	2.9

Source: U.S. Census Bureau, *Money Income of Households, Families and Persons in the United States, 1991*, No. 180, and for 1989–1993 data, Mishel and Bernstein (1994) and author's calculations.

*Q1 is the first quintile, and so forth.

The 1989–1993 data show how each income quintile was affected by the 1990–1992 recession. The lowest quintile had its income fall the most. However, the top 5 percent wealthiest Americans actually had their mean family income rise 2.9 percent, while the median family income fell by 3.5 percent. Furthermore, the income shares of the lowest 80 percent fell, while the top quintile's share rose to 46.2 percent. From 1983 to 1989, when the economy was expanding and median income rose from $33,741 to $37,579, the Gini coefficient rose 4.9 percent, from 0.382 to 0.401. However, from 1989 to 1993, when the economy was stagnant or shrinking and median family income fell from $37,579 to $36,258, the Gini coefficient rose again, from 0.401 to 0.420, a further 4.7 percent. This provides further evidence (if any was needed) that the policies of the 1980s and early 1990s are making the rich richer and the poor poorer. Observers, other than neoclassical economists, should not be surprised, however. After all, it was the rich or the politicians they elected who implemented those very policies.

Neoclassical explanations either concentrate on changes in earnings inequality or demographic changes. Frank Levy and Richard J. Murnane's (1992) survey of the literature on earnings inequality demonstrates the inherent bias of neoclassical analysis. Their primary concern is evaluating how changes in productivities, or in supply and demand factors, can explain the rise in earnings inequality. Of their 48-page article, only six short paragraphs are devoted to "other" factors, which they limit to changes in "wage-setting" institutions and macroeconomic factors. The wage-setting institutions referred to are the decline in union membership and the decline in the real value of the minimum wage, which is only mentioned in passing. However, even when these "other" factors are mentioned, their analysis of them is in terms of individual characteristics and not as part of the institutional environment. "Changes in wage setting institutions" we are told, have brought "wages closer to marginal products" (Levy and Murnane 1992, 1369). The implication is that a decline in unions has resulted in less distortion in market forces. The three paragraphs devoted to the influence of the macroeconomic environment treat it as another factor that has influenced and reinforced supply and demand shifts.   Levy and Murnane's conclusion is:

The increase in inequality, and particularly trends in earnings between groups defined by education and age, reflect both supply and demand shifts. Critical aspects of supply shifts are the 1970s entry into the labor market of the large, relatively well educated baby boom cohorts, and the deceleration in the 1980s of both the overall rate of labor force growth, and the rate at which the education attainments of the labor force were increasing. Supply shifts alone cannot explain the trends in earned income inequality, however; a steady increase in the demand for skilled workers relative to unskilled workers is also necessary. Part of this demand shift consisted of changes in the structure of final demand, with the trade deficit working directly to reduce the number of jobs in manufacturing, the traditional high wage employer of less educated men. (1992, 1372)

The Levy and Murnane article concentrates on explanations of the increasing inequality in earnings, yet the increase in earning inequality is only part of the story of rising inequality, leaving out the relative income shares going to capital and labor. From 1980 to 1986 the Gini coefficient for all earnings increased 2.5 percent (Karoly 1988, cited in Levy and Murnane 1992, 1343), whereas the Gini coefficient for family income rose 7.4 percent for the same period. If we compare the change in the Gini coefficient for earnings with that for family income we see that the earnings story, by the authors' own standards, explains about a third of the change in income equality. Furthermore, as Table 13.3 demonstrates, the rise in wage inequality, while significant from 1973 to 1989, actually decreased from 1989 to 1991, then increased again to just below the 1989 level. However, the increase in inequality continued, with the Gini coefficient rising another 4.7 percent.

Table 13.3
Wage Inequality, 1973–1993

Year	80th-to-20th Percentile Ratio
1973	2.35
1979	2.45
1989	2.75
1991	2.66
1993	2.74

Source: Author's calculations from Mishel and Bernstein 1994, 121.

Table 13.3 shows that wage inequality from 1979 to 1989 rose 12.3 percent, while family income inequality, using the same 80th-to-20th percentile ratio measure, rose 21.2 percent, from 8.0 to 9.7. (The 80/20 distance ratio is calculated by taking the mean income of the top quintile and dividing it by the bottom quintile, which for 1979 is: 61,725 divided by 7,714 = 8.0, and for 1989: 72,044 divided by 7,431 = 9.7.) Furthermore, most of the rise in inequality is a redistribution of income from the bottom 80 percent to the top 5 percent. This could hardly be attributable to changing wage inequality. More important has been the change in factor income—the shift from labor income to capital income.

Table 13.4 demonstrates the move away from labor income and toward capital income in the 1979–1989 period.

Table 13.4
Shares of Market-Based Personal Income by Type, 1979–89

Income Type	1979	1989	Change
Total Capital Income	15.3%	19.7%	28.8%
Rent	0.5%	-0.3%	-60.0%
Dividends	2.7%	3.2%	18.5%
Interest	12.1%	16.9%	39.4%
Total Labor Income	74.9%	71.6%	-4.4%
Wages and Salaries	68.1%	65.2%	-4.3%
Fringe Benefits	6.8%	6.4%	-4.5%
Proprietor's Income	9.9%	8.8%	-11.1%
Total	100.0%	100.0%	
Realized Capital Gains	1.5	3.7	146.7%

Source: Mishel and Bernstein 1994.
Note: Totals may not add up to 100 due to rounding; realized capital gains are shown as a percentage of personal income.

The share of wages and salaries in total personal income fell from 70 percent in 1970 to 68.1 percent in 1979 and 65.2 percent in 1989, while the share of personal interest income rose from 8 percent in 1970 to 12.1 percent in 1979, and finally to 16.9 percent in 1989. The rise in real interest rates and the dramatic increase in indebtedness in the 1980s is at the root of this increase in interest income. Basil Moore has demonstrated that "since 1980 the 2.3 per cent fall in wage's share in personal income was more than fully reflected by the rise in average mark-ups by firms in the fix-price sector in response to the sharp rise in interest rates and the cost of debt finance" (Moore 1989, 33–34). The effect on personal income distribution, Moore concludes, has been that given the high level of concentration of wealth in America, and the fact that the wealthy are large net creditors, "the rise in interest income can explain 4.8 per cent of the observed increase of 5.6 per cent in the income share received by the top 10 per cent of families" (1989, 38). In 1989, 72.5 percent of financial net wealth was in the hands of the top 5 percent richest Americans—exactly the group that benefits most from the recent rise in inequality—while the bottom 80 percent holds 5.7 percent. (For an overview, see Wolf 1993.) Furthermore, realized capital gains doubled as a percentage of personal income.

Table 13.5
Distribution of Labor and Capital Incomes, 1977–1989

Income Group	Shares of Capital Income			Shares of Labor Income		
	1977	1980	1989	1977	1980	1989
All	100%	100%	100%	100%	100%	100%
Bottom	1.8%	1.5%	0.9%	2.8%	2.6%	2.6%
Second	5.1%	4.2%	3.5%	10.0%	9.8%	8.9%
Third	7.9%	6.9%	7.1%	16.8%	16.6%	15.3%
Fourth	12.3%	12.3%	11.6%	24.8%	25.1%	23.7%
Top Fifth	72.6%	74.7%	77.5%	46.0%	46.5%	50.3%
Top 1%	33.1%	34.9%	39.7%	5.8%	5.9%	9.2%

Source: Mishel and Bernstein (1994).

The shift to capital income clearly benefits the top quintile, and especially the top 1 percent, whose share in total family income rose from 8.7 percent in 1977 to 13 percent in 1989. The separation of labor and capital income is a difficult task, and we see from Table 13.5 that the top 1 percent experienced a rise in both capital and labor income. However, I do not think that their rise in labor income can be attributed to the usual arguments that are used to explain wage inequality. Certainly if there is any group that has power over setting their wages, it is this group, which is made up mostly of professionals, corporate managers, and entertainers. Executive pay levels from 1979 to 1989 rose 99 percent, from an average of $308,200 to $612,800 (Mishel and Bernstein 1994, 186). The after-tax increase was even larger (1994, 186). Real median income rose by only 4.2 percent in the same period.

The change in relative power between capital and labor is mostly the result of the weakened position of labor in America. While the causes of this fact are many and are well beyond the scope of this chapter, the rise in conservative politics has played an important role. The decline in union representation and strength has been part of an overall assertion of power by management, which has been supported by government policy. The percentage of workers represented by unions has fallen steadily during the period of increased inequality, from 30 percent in 1970 to 12.7 percent in 1992. As Mitchell noted:

Since the advent of the Reagan Administration, unions have not found encouragement in the process of labor market regulation. While there have been no changes in basic labor legislation, administration appointments and changes at agencies such as the National Labor Relations Board (NLRB) are perceived by unions as hostile to their interests. Although legal scholars can debate the wisdom of this or that NLRB or court decision, there is little doubt that the changes in the regulatory climate have complicated union efforts to win substantial pay advances, preserve jobs, and engage in new organizing. Regulatory changes that hamper job preservation and organization, in particular, open the door to more nonunion competition and resultant management resistance to union demands. (1985, 588)

Richard Freeman reinforces Mitchell's conclusions, stating that "the decline in union density is due in large part to employer opposition to union organizing in National Labor Relations Board representation election campaigns. The effectiveness of this opposition (motivated by the loss of profits due to unionism) gives employers a great deal of influence over the decision of workers to join unions" (1992, 147). Freeman's work has shown that unions redistribute income towards wages and away from profits in the companies in which they exist. The general decline in unions, especially given their spread effects, thus must be seen as altering the balance of power between labor and capital and thus, between income from capital and income from labor. The decline in union representation was also promoted by the decline in manufacturing jobs. This, too, was greatly encouraged by government policy.

As significant as the decline in union representation has been the decline in strength of existing unions. This decline in union strength can be seen by the fall in the average number of work stoppages per year, which for the 1970s was 289, contrasted with the 1982–1992 average of 56 work stoppages per year. Even more telling has been the trend in wage concessions and real wage declines in union settlements. In the 1970s the average proportion of workers who had wages frozen or cut was 2.2 percent, with an average of 24.1 percent receiving wage settlements below the consumer price index (CPI), thus leaving 26.8 percent with a fall in their real income. From 1981 to 1985, the proportion of workers who received a freeze or cut in wages climbed to 27 percent, with the total proportion of workers to experience either a freeze, a cut, or an increase below the CPI reaching 56.6 percent. Daniel Mitchell (1985) has demonstrated that in the early 1980s, unions received wage increases substantially lower than economic conditions would justify. The reduced strength in unions is a significant factor, dramatically changing the structure of the U.S. labor force, yet it is not something that would be captured in a model that looks at union membership simply as a characteristic whose relative price has changed, causing a change in income distribution. Furthermore, countries with high union representation rates and strong unions have, for the most part, not experienced a dramatic rise in inequality in the 1980s.

A neoclassical analysis of the influence of unions views union representation as another individual characteristic for which the market has determined a relative price. Unions also are seen as market imperfections, influencing wages only through their ability to impact on the labor supply available in a particular market, and thus causing a distorted price. The decline in union representation is seen as allowing markets to act more efficiently, by lowering individual wages closer to individual marginal products.

Unions are the primary avenue for low-skilled workers to earn higher wages, and unions compress the structure of wages, thus lowering the within plant dispersion of wage levels. Thus, even within the logic of neoclassical economics, they can be seen as a possible factor in income distribution. Davis and Haltiwanger (1991) have investigated this possibility, but conclude that unions have had little influence on wage dispersion in manufacturing. They claim that their investigations show that the influence of industry level union density is "trivial," about "one penny an hour" (1991, 169). Their approach is practically designed to not capture the role that declining union strength has had on increasing inequality. First, by its own admission, this approach does not have an adequate data set to test unionization as a factor in determining income differentials, that is, a data set in which union membership could be viewed as another characteristic with a market price. Second, it ignores the systematic effects of unionization on labor-management relations and the relative power each has in determining wage rates.

Minimum wage policy is another factor that has contributed to the increase in inequality and the weakening of labor. Since 1970, the value of the minimum wage as a percentage of average manufacturing wages has fallen, from 48 percent to 43 percent in 1980 and to 32 percent in 1989. In constant 1992 dollars, the minimum wage fell from $5.50 in 1979 to $3.78 in 1989. (Two increases in the minimum wage raised it to $4.25 in 1992). Recently, Michael Horrigan and Ronald Mincy have argued that the minimum wage is not an important factor in income distribution and that since minimum-wage workers are almost equally distributed between income quintiles, an increase in the minimum wage would not improve the distribution of income (Horrigan and Mincy 1993). However, according to William Spriggs and Bruce Klein, this analysis is seriously misleading. First, only hourly wage workers are counted as minimum-wage workers. Excluded are workers on salaries that, if calculated by the hour, would in fact equal minimum-wage rates. (They suggest that this group could outnumber hourly workers.) Furthermore, unlike part-time workers, who often live with their parents, full-time minimum-wage workers are much more highly concentrated in the lower two quintiles. Second, the full impact of minimum-wage rates goes well beyond those who receive such rates, influencing a contour of wages. Spriggs and Klein estimated that in 1989, 58.98 percent of all high-school educated workers had their wages tied to the minimum wage (up from 46.96 percent in 1979). Given that high school graduates accounted for 40.5 percent of the 1989 share of employment (Mishel and Bernstein 1992, 8) it is easy to see how significant the minimum wage is to the structure of wages.

INEQUALITY IN OTHER INDUSTRIAL COUNTRIES IN THE 1980s

In examining the levels of inequality in other industrial countries and the changes in those levels in the 1980s, we can see further evidence of the primacy of institutional factors. Measures of income inequality are notoriously problematic, particularly when making international comparisons, where differences in income definitions can greatly effect the measure of inequality. Therefore, we will use a variety of inequality measures and studies. Our interest is in overall trends and the general picture, not in exact measures and rankings. Table 13.6 presents the distribution of family income for ten industrial countries at the beginning of the 1980s. Family income is defined as market income plus public and private transfers minus direct (income and payroll) taxes.

Table 13.6
Family Income Distribution, 1979–1983

Decile	Austrl	Can	Ger	Ire	Neth	Nor	Swed	Switz	UK	US
1	1.9	1.8	2.6	1.7	2.1	2.2	2.9	1.5	2.3	1.4
2	3.5	3.6	4.4	3.5	4.8	4.1	5.1	3.8	3.5	3.3
3	5.0	5.2	5.9	5.1	6.0	5.7	6.1	5.2	4.8	4.9
4	6.6	6.8	7.1	6.6	7.2	7.2	7.1	6.5	6.6	6.4
5	8.2	8.3	8.2	7.9	8.4	8.7	8.2	7.6	8.3	8.0
6	9.8	9.6	9.5	9.3	9.6	10.3	9.2	8.8	9.9	9.2
7	11.4	11.6	11.1	11.0	11.0	11.8	11.0	10.1	11.5	11.6
8	13.5	13.5	13.1	13.0	12.7	13.5	13.5	12.0	13.5	13.9
9	15.4	16.2	15.4	16.2	15.3	15.5	16.1	14.7	16.2	16.8
10	23.6	23.3	22.7	25.7	23.0	21.2	20.8	29.8	23.2	24.0
Gini	.344	.338	.307	.360	.308	.306	.288	.378	.338	.359
10/1	12.3	13.0	8.7	15.1	11.2	9.6	7.2	20.6	10.1	16.9

Source: Bishop, Formby, and Smith (1991), and for Ireland, Callan and Nolon (1993).

From Table 13.6 we can rank countries by levels of inequality in two ways, by Gini and by the ratio of income from the richest decile to the poorest decile (last row of the table). Table 13.7 does so.

Table 13.7
Ranking of Countries by Levels of Inequality

Country	Gini	Rank	10/1	Rank
Sweden	.2875	1	7.24	1
Norway	.3057	2	9.64	3
Germany	.3070	3	8.73	2
Netherlands	.3076	4	11.16	5
Canada	.3383	5	12.99	7
UK	.3377	6	10.14	4
Australia	.3439	7	12.28	6
USA	.3592	8	16.88	9
Ireland	.3600	9	15.11	8
Switzerland	.3783	10	20.57	10

Source: Bishop, Formby, and Smith (1991).

The purpose of the Bishop, Formby, and Smith (1991) paper, from which Tables 13.6 and 13.7 are derived (with the exception of the data on Ireland) is to provide a comparison of income inequality using tests for Lorenz dominance using different measures of income. Our interest is not so much in ranking countries, but in giving a general idea of the variety in income distribution experiences and a sense of how changing the measure of distribution can influence such rankings. While Germany, Norway, Netherlands, Australia, US, and Ireland experience marginal changes, the UK goes from sixth to fourth and

Canada goes from fifth to seventh. Table 13.8 shows the relationship between factor, and gross and net income for a slightly different selection of countries.

Table 13.8
Distribution and Redistribution of Income: Income shares (%) of quintiles of Persons Ranked by Family Gross Income

	Quintile	Can	US	UK	WG	Swed	Nor	Ire
FACTOR	1	5.4	4.2	4.0	2.3	6.5	4.4	2.2
INCOME	2	14.9	12.8	15.0	13.8	18.5	17.0	8.7
	3	19.2	19.2	19.9	17.1	18.8	19.6	16.6
	4	24.5	25.1	24.9	22.0	23.0	24.2	25.2
	5	36.0	38.8	36.3	44.7	33.2	34.9	47.7
	5/1	6.67	9.12	9.08	19.43	5.11	7.93	21.68
GROSS	1	9.5	7.5	10.9	10.7	13.7	12.0	9.2
INCOME	2	15.6	14.3	15.6	14.7	20.5	17.8	11.6
	3	18.7	18.8	18.7	16.2	18.6	18.4	16.5
	4	23.0	23.6	22.0	20.1	20.1	21.6	22.9
	5	33.2	35.9	31.9	38.2	27.1	30.3	40.2
	5/1	3.49	4.79	2.93	3.57	1.98	2.53	4.37
NET	1	10.8	9.0	12.4	13.1	16.4	14.7	11.2
INCOME	2	16.4	15.9	15.9	15.3	21.3	18.6	13.1
	3	18.8	19.5	18.6	16.0	18.3	18.6	16.9
	4	22.6	23.6	22.4	19.3	19.9	21.0	22.3
	5	31.4	32.0	30.6	36.2	24.2	27.2	36.8
	5/1	2.91	3.56	2.47	2.76	1.48	1.85	3.29

ADDENDUM TO TABLE 13.8:
Net Income Inequality as a Percent of Factor Income Inequality

Can	US	UK	WG	Swed	Nor	Ire
43.5%	39.0%	27.2%	14.2	29.0%	23.3%	15.2%

Source: Callan and Nolon (1992), 188

Table 13.8 and its addendum gives us a good idea of how levels of inequality are achieved. One can have a high level of inequality in factor income, as in Germany and, through transfers and taxes, achieve a moderate level of inequality in net income; or one can follow the Swedish model of having a low level of inequality in factor income and, mostly through transfers, achieve a high level of equality. In fact, in Sweden the second quintile's post transfer income is higher than that of the third and fourth quintiles. Germany and Ireland had the highest level of redistribution, while Canada and the United States had the lowest. The United States starts out with a moderately high level of inequality in factor income (ranked five out of seven) and ends up with the highest level of inequality in net income.

Table 13.9 provides some measures of inequality from the mid 1980s, while Table 13.10 notes the changes in inequality for the same group of countries. In Table 13.9 we see the family income (after taxes and transfers) distribution for nine industrial countries. In the percentage of median income of the 10th and the 90th deciles, the United States is clearly separated from the rest of the group. This is also reflected in its distance ratio being 40 percent larger than the next largest (Australia). It is obvious from this Table that U.S. inequality comes both from the rich being very rich and from the poor being very poor.

Table 13.9
Family Income Distribution: Percentage of the Median, Mid-1980s*

Country and Year	10th Percentile	90th Percentile	Distance Ratio (90/10)
Australia, 1985	45.0	191.5	4.26
Canada, 1987	45.8	184.5	4.03
France, 1984	55.4	192.8	3.48
W. Germany, 1984	56.9	170.8	3.00
Italy, 1986	48.9	197.9	4.05
Netherlands, 1987	61.5	175.0	2.85
Sweden, 1987	55.6	151.5	2.72
UK, 1986	51.1	194.1	3.80
US, 1986	34.7	206.1	5.94

Source: Mishel and Bernstein (1994).
* Adjusted for family size. The entries in columns 1 and 2 are the percent of family income at the decile of the median.

The strong correlation between speaking English and inequality is shown by Table 13.9. Only Italy's 4.05 distance ratio breaks a perfect relationship. The levels of inequality are at least partly cultural, since all the English speaking countries have a similar cultural tradition (Ireland's level of inequality is second only to that of the United States, as measured in Callan and Nolan 1993, and Saunders, O'Connor, and Smeeding 1994). Furthermore, the U.S. increase in inequality cannot be dismissed simply as part of an international trend, for Table 13.10 shows that the changes in inequality are by no means uniform.

Table 13.10
Income Distribution: Changes in Percentage of the Median over the 1980s

Country and Years	Change in Distance from Median			Distance Ratio
	10th	*90th*	*95th*	*90/10*
Australia (81-85)	-1.0	5.2	10.9	0.2
Canada (81-87)	0.9	1.8	6.5	0.0
France (79-84)	1.8	6.3	1.2	0.0
Netherlands (83-87)	-3.3	-1.1	-1.7	0.1
Sweden (81-87)	-5.9	0.6	3.4	0.3
UK (79-86)	0.2	14.4	23.2	0.3
US (79-86)	-3.4	18.5	25.4	1.0

Source: Mishel and Bernstein (1994).

Family income distribution is determined by family composition, factor income distribution, earnings distribution, and taxes and government transfers. Family composition includes male and female participation rates.   Male participation rates are fairly similar across countries. Female rates vary widely, but are converging. Although female labor participation is often cited as a factor in some particular countries' income distributions, there seems to be no clear relationship between female participation and income distribution (Saunders, O'Connor, and Smeeding 1994).

Factor income distribution is the share of national income going to labor income and capital income. The dividing line between the two is often fuzzy, especially with regard to self-employment. In the corporate sector of the economy, with the advent of the separation of ownership and control in the early twentieth century, a significant portion of management's income, especially top management, is hard to conceive as labor income.

The most discussed aspect of changes in factor income has been the increase in wage inequality. In Table 13.11 we see the change in wage inequality from the early 1970s to the late 1980s for 14 industrial countries. While we can clearly see a trend toward greater wage inequality, most countries experienced very modest increases. The exceptions are Denmark, which had no change, and France and Norway, which experienced decreasing wage inequality. The United Kingdom and the United States had the largest increases in wage inequality, followed by Belgium and Canada.

Table 13.11
Wage Inequality Trends: 1970s and 1980s

Country	1973-75 D9/D1*	1979-81 D9/D1	1985-87 D9/D1	1989-91 D9/D1	Change from 1979-81 to 1989-91
Australia	2.0	2.0	2.2	2.2	-0.2
Austria	n.a.	3.4	3.5	3.5	-0.1
Belgium	n.a.	2.0	2.0	2.4	-0.4
Canada	3.7	4.0	4.5	4.4	-0.4
Denmark	n.a.	2.2	2.2	2.2	0.0
France	3.3	3.1	3.0	3.0	0.1
Germany	n.a.	2.2	2.6	2.4	-0.2
Italy	n.a.	2.0	2.0	2.1	-0.1
Japan	n.a	2.6	2.7	2.8	-0.2
Netherlands	2.0	2.2	2.2	2.3	-0.1
Norway	n.a	2.1	2.2	2.0	0.1
Sweden	2.1	2.0	2.0	2.1	-0.1
U.K.	2.5	2.4	2.9	3.2	-0.8
U.S..	5.0	4.8	5.5	5.6	-0.8

Source: Organization for Economic Cooperation and Development (1993).
*D9 and D1 refer to the upper limits of the ninth and first deciles, respectively.

Tables 13.11 and 13.12 show that the institutions that make up the labor market clearly affect wage inequality. Countries with high union density and collective bargaining coverage tend to have less wage inequality and have experienced less of a change over the 1980s than those with low values.

Countries with either union density or coverage ratio of 70 percent or higher (Australia, Austria, Belgium, Denmark, France, Germany, Netherlands, Norway, and Sweden) had an average D9/D1 earnings differential of 2.44, compared with countries with low union density and coverage ratios (Canada, Japan, United Kingdom, and United States), which had an average of 4.0. Out of the 13 countries considered here, 3 buck the general trend. Both Austria and France have high wage differentials (3.5 and 3.0, respectively), while Japan has a relatively low wage differential (2.8). Austria's declining union density, from 62.2 percent in 1970, to 56.2 percent in 1980 and finally to 46 percent in 1990, indicates a decline in the power of those institutions that support workers in Austria. Similarly, France's union density fell more than half since 1970.

Table 13.12
Union Density, Collective Bargaining Coverage, Labor
Standards, and Social Protection

Country	Union Density 1990	Coverage Ratio* 1990	Synthetic Index ** 1990	Social Protection*** 1990
Australia	40	80	n.a.	n.a.
Austria	46	98	5	24.5%
Belgium	51	90	4	25.2
Canada	36	38	2	18.8
Denmark	71	n.a.	2	27.8
France	10	92	6	26.5
Germany	32	90	6	23.5
Italy	39	n.a.	7	24.5
Japan	25	23	n.a.	n.a.
Netherlands	26	71	5	28.8
Norway	56	75	5	28.7
Sweden	83	83	7	33.1
U.K.	39	47	0	22.3
U.S.	16	18	0	14.6

Source: Organization for Economic Cooperation and Development OECD (1994).
*Collective Bargaining Coverage Ratio (OECD 1994). Data are for 1990, except for France (1985), Germany (1992), and Japan (1991).
**Index of labor standards complied by OECD. It is a summary index of "the extent to which certain labor standards are determined by government regulations." It includes five factors: Working time, fixed-term contracts, employment protection, minimum wages, and employees' representation rights. For each category a value of "2" means regulations are strict, a value of "0" means they are non-existent, and a value of "1" represents the intermediate case (OECD 1994).
***Total public expenditures on social protection as a percentage of GDP.

The synthetic index, which is designed to measure the extent of government regulation in the labor market, is a telling statistic. All countries with a synthetic index of 5 or more had a change in wage inequality of less than 10 percent in the 1980s, while those with a synthetic index of less than 5, with the notable exception of Denmark, experienced wage inequality increases of more than 10 percent. However, Denmark's low synthetic index is misleading. Denmark receives a "0" for minimum wage in its synthetic index because it is not a matter of government regulation. Nevertheless, minimum wages are set in Denmark by collective bargaining agreements and cover 80 to 85 percent of workers. A similar situation exists for most worktime regulations. With over 70 percent of the labor force unionized, Danish workers generally have very good protection. Total public expenditures on social protection also are divided in a similar manner, with high union density and collective bargaining countries all spending more than 23 percent, (an average of 26.9 percent), while the low union density and collective bargaining countries were all below 23 percent (an average of 18.6 percent).

Union density has been shown (OECD 1993) to have a high and negative correlation with wage inequality, especially with the spread between the bottom decile and the median. Freeman and others have shown that unions generate lower levels of inequality by compressing wages and redistributing some of the monopoly profits of firms down toward the workers. Keith Cowling and Ian Molho (1982) have shown, looking at data for the United Kingdom, that unions tend to raise the wage share, counteracting the tendency for concentration to lower it. With the decline in unions in many industrial countries, we should expect inequality, both wage and income, to increase—and this is exactly what we find.

In the late 1970s and early 1980s, fighting inflation became the number one policy objective for most industrial countries. This was coupled with the rise to power of many conservative governments, with the Ronald Reagan government in the United States and the Margaret Thatcher government in the United Kingdom being the most prominent. The rhetoric of politicians and academics became increasing hostile to the "welfare state," and governments began to attempt, sometime successfully and sometimes not, to scale down or dismantle the welfare state programs built up over the past 40 years. The attack on the welfare state is producing a dramatic change in the institutional structure of industrial countries, the consequences of which will take generations to feel and fully know. Its impact on the level of inequality, however, has been rather quick and can be seen already. This attack on the welfare state has been most successfully waged in the United States, and the rise in inequality there has been amply demonstrated in this chapter. The extent to which the welfare state has been dismantled in other industrial countries has varied considerably, as have the levels and changes in inequality.

In conventional explanations, much of the increase in earnings inequality in the United States is attributed to an increase in the relative value of skills and education. As the story goes, the need for individuals with computer skills has increased, so market forces send out the appropriate signal of higher differential prices for computer skills. In terms of neoclassical theory, the productivity of workers with computer skills relative to those without has increased; thus, their relative incomes should also increase. However, measuring such causes are not as easy as measuring the effects. The standard proxy for measuring skill is education, so this conventional theory's main evidence is the increase in the education differential, even though the education differential may be a reflection of something other than, or in addition to, the differential market value of skills.

Table 13.13 shows the change in education differentials for males from the late 1970s-early 1980s to the mid- to late 1980s. As with our other international comparisons, we see a great diversity in changing "skills" differentials, with the United States and United Kingdom having significant increases, Germany and the Netherlands having equal or greater decreases, and Canada, Japan, and Sweden pretty much staying the same.

The so-called skills differential, the average of which did not change for these seven countries, is thus a weak explanation of rising inequality. Furthermore, a rise in the education premium is consistent with the hierarchy explanation of rising inequality. Afterall, the groups at the top of the corporate hierarchies, which determine wage structures in the first place have, on average, much more schooling than other groups of workers. Education is used as a rationing device for most entry level positions into the technostructure. It is a class/hierarchy variable, not a skill/market variable. Thus, a rise in the education premium is not a response to market signals, but the result of the increasing power of corporate managers and bureaucrats to determine pay structures that favor them. The ratio of CEO to manufacturing worker pay shows great international diversity, from the low of 6.5 in Germany, to 7.6 in Italy, 8.9 in France, 9.5 in Canada, 12.4 in the United Kingdom, and 17.5 in the United States. Such differences cannot be explained by recourse to marginal productivity theory and must instead be cultural and institutional (i.e., due to relative power and public policy).

Table 13.13
International Education Differentials for Males over the 1980s
Ratios of Mean or Median College-Equivalent Wage to High-School-Equivalent Wage*

Country	1979 or Early 80s	Mid- to Late 1980s	Average 5-year Change
Canada	1.40	1.42	0.02
W. Germany	2.00	1.94	-0.06
Japan	1.26	1.26	0.00
Netherlands	1.50	1.22	-0.35
Sweden	1.16	1.19	0.03
UK	1.53	1.65	0.07
US	1.37	1.51	0.09
Average	1.46	1.46	0.00

Source: Mishel and Bernstein (1994), 347.

*Except for the Netherlands and Germany, all figures control for changes in age composition of educational groups.

CONCLUSION

The level of inequality in a modern industrial country is made up of four factors: the distribution of factor or market-based incomes, the distribution of transfer incomes, and the percentage of factor and transfer income in total income, and the level of progressivity of the tax system. The distribution of factor income is determined by the level of earnings inequality, the shares going to capital and labor, and the distribution of the ownership of capital. The distribution of transfer incomes is a matter of public policy, as is the percentage of transfer income in the total income (shown for eight countries in Table 13.14). Furthermore, the tax system is a matter of public policy.

Table 13.14
Percentage of Disposable Income from Specified Sources
in Families with Earnings, Mid-1980s

Country	Factor Income	AB	Child	MN	UN	Other	Total
Australia	86	0	4	2	4	4	100
Canada	83	0	4	6	5	2	100
France	78	1	18	0	0	3	100
Germany	89	0	5	1	3	2	100
Netherlands	86	0	9	2	1	2	100
Sweden	63	10	15	8	3	1	100
UK	76	1	12	6	2	3	100
US	91	0	2	3	1	3	100

Source: Rainwater (1993), 9.

Note: Child = child allowance and child support; AB = sickness and maternity; MN = income tested, and UN = unemployment.

This leaves the distributional consequences of factor incomes as the only aspect that is not explicitly a matter of public policy. However, even here the role of the state is important. In the United States and the United Kingdom, monetarist monetary policy has a major impact in the distribution of income by raising the income going to capital (interest income) and by creating mass unemployment and thus lowering the earnings income of those in the lower income categories. Moreover, high unemployment weakens labor in general in its bargaining with management, further eroding the income of workers. Additionally, as we have seen, public policy has an important effect on the structure of the labor market, that is, in setting the "rules of the game." Supportive public policy, an indication of which is the synthetic index used in Table 13.12, will promote greater wage equality, while hostile public policies (particularly antiunion policies as seen in the United States and the United Kingdom), will weaken labor and thus promote greater wage inequality.

This chapter concludes that the level of inequality and the recent changes in the level of inequality are in the sphere of the economy that institutionalists call "discretionary." They are a response to changes in the power relations in particular societies and to the public and corporate policies brought about by these changes. Given the diversity of the international experience in inequality, we must agree with John Stuart Mill that the distribution of income is determined by institutional factors, especially power relations, and "might be still more different, if mankind so chooses " (Mill [1848] 1987, 200).

REFERENCES

Bishop, John A., John P. Formby, and W. James Smith. 1991. "International Comparisons of Income Inequality: Tests for Lorenz Dominance across Nine Countries." *Economica*, 58: 461–77.

Blau, Francine D., and Lawrence M. Kahn. 1995. "International Differences in Male Wage Inequality: Institutions versus Market Forces." Paper presented at the American Economic Association meetings, January 1995.

Borjas, George J. 1988. "Earnings Determination: A Survey of the Neoclassical Approach." In Garth Mangum and Peter Philips, eds., *Three Worlds of Labor Economics*. Armonk, N.Y., and London: M. E. Sharpe.

Callan, Tim, and Brian Nolon. 1992. "Income Distribution and Redistribution: Ireland in Comparative Perspective." In J. H. Goldthorpe and C. T. Whelan, eds., *The Development of Industrial Society in Ireland.* Oxford, U.K.: Oxford University Press.

___. 1993. "Income Inequality and Poverty in Ireland in the 1970s and 1980s." Economic and Social Research Institute Working Paper 43.

Clark, Charles M. A. 1992. *Economic Theory and Natural Philosophy.* Aldershot, U.K.: Edward Elgar.

Clark, John B. [1899] 1965. *The Distribution of Wealth.* New York: Augustus M. Kelley.

Cowling, Keith, and Ian Molho. 1982. "Wage Share, Concentration and Unionism." *The Manchester School*, 50, no. 2: 99–115.

Davis, Steve J., and John Haltiwanger. 1991. "Wage Dispersion between and within U.S. Manufacturing Plants, 1963–86." *Brookings Papers on Economic Activity* (special issue): 115–180.

Dugger, William M. 1987. "Three Modes of Income Distribution: Market, Hierarchy, and Industry." *Journal of Economic Issues*, 21, no. 2: 723–731.

___. 1989. "Instituted Process and Enabling Myth: The Two Faces of the Market." *Journal of Economic Issues*, 23 (June): 607–16.

European Federation for Economic Research. 1989. *Trends and Distribution of Incomes: An Overview.* Luxembourg: EFER.

___. 1992. "Minimum Pay in 18 Countries." *European Industrial Relations Review*, 225 (Oct.): 14–21.

Freeman, Richard. 1992. "Is Declining Unionization of the U.S. Good, Bad, or Irrelevant?" In Lawrence Mishel and Paula B. Voos, eds., *Unions and Economic Competitiveness.* Armonk, N.Y., and London: M.E. Sharpe.

Gimble, Daniel E. 1991. "Institutionalist Labor Market Theory and the Veblenian Dichotomy." *Journal of Economic Issues,* 25, no. 3 (Sept.): 625–48.

Goldin, Claudia, and Robert A. Margo. 1992. "The Great Compression: The Wage Structure in the United States at Mid-Century." *Quarterly Journal of Economics*, 107, no. 1: 1–34.

Hodgson, Geoffrey M. 1988. *Economics and Institutions: A Manifesto for a Modern Institutional Economics.* Cambridge: Polity Press.

Horrigan, Michael W., and Ronald B. Mincy. 1993. "The Minimum Wage and Earnings and Income Inequality." In Sheldon Danziger and Peter Gottschalk, eds., *Uneven Tides Rising Inequality in America.* New York: Russell Sage Foundation, 173–203.

Karoly, Lynn A. 1988. "A Study of the Distribution of Individual Earnings in the United States from 1967 to 1986." Ph.D. dissertation, Yale Department of Economics, New Haven, Conn.

Katz, Lawrence F. and Kevin M. Murphy. 1992. "Changes in Relative Wages, 1963–1987: Supply and Demand Factors." *Quarterly Journal of Economics*, 107 (Feb.): 35–78.

Levy, Frank, and Richard J. Murnane. 1992. "U.S. Earnings Levels and Earnings Inequality: A Review of Recent Trends and Proposed Explanations." *Journal of Economic Literature*, 30 (Sept.): 1333–81.

Mayhew, Anne. 1987. "The Beginnings of Institutionalism." *Journal of Economic Issues*, 21, no. 3 (Sept.): 971–98.

Mill, John Stuart. [1848] 1987. *Principles of Political Economy*. Edited, with an introduction, by William Ashley. Fairfield, N.J.: Augustus M. Kelley.

Mishel, Lawrence, and Jarel Bernstein. 1992. "Declining Wages for High School and College Graduates: Pay and Benefits Trends by Education, Gender, Occupation, and State, 1971–1991." Economic Policy Institute, Briefing Paper 31.

___. 1994. *The State of Working America 1994–95*. Armonk, N.Y.: M. E. Sharpe.

Mitchell, Daniel. 1985. "Shifting Norms in Wage Determination." *Brookings Papers on Economic Activity*, no. 2: 575–99.

Moore, Basil J. 1989. "The Effects of Monetary Policy on Income Distribution." In Paul Davidson and Jan A. Kregel, eds., *Macroeconomic Problems and Policies of Income Distribution: Functional, Personal, International*. Aldershot, UK: Edward Elgar, 18–41.

Myrdal, Gunnar. 1958. *Value in Social Theory*. Edited by Paul Streeten. London: Routledge and Kegan Paul.

Organization for Economic Cooperation and Development (OECD). 1993. *Employment Outlook 1993*, Paris: OECD.

___. 1994. *Employment Outlook 1994*. Paris: OECD.

Peach, James T. 1987. "Distribution and Economic Progress." *Journal of Economic Issues*, 21 (Dec.): 1495–1530.

Rainwater, Lee. 1993. "The Social Wage in the Income Package of Working Parents." Luxembourg Income Study Working Paper No. 89.

Saunders, Peter, Inge O'Connor, and Timothy M. Smeeding. 1994. "The Distribution of Welfare: Inequality, Earnings Capacity, and Household Production in a Comparative Perspective." Luxembourg Income Study Working Paper No. 122.

Smeeding, Timothy M., Michael O'Higgins, and Lee Rainwater. 1990. *Poverty, Inequality and Income Distribution in Comparative Perspective*. Washington, D.C.: Urban Institute Press.

Spriggs, William E., and Bruce W. Klein. 1994. *Raising the Floor: The Effects of the Minimum Wage on Low-Wage Workers*. Washington, D.C.: Economic Policy Institute.

United States Census Bureau, 1992. *Money Income of Households, Families and Persons in the United States, 1991*. No. 180. Washington, D.C.: U.S. Government Printing Office.

United States Department of Labor. 1994. *Report on the American Workforce*. Washington, D.C.: U.S. Government Printing Office.

Veblen, Thorstein. [1899] 1909. *The Theory of the Leisure Class*. New York and London: Macmillan.

Waller, William T. 1982. "The Evolution of the Veblenian Dichotomy: Veblen, Hamilton, Ayres and Foster." *Journal of Economic Issues*, 16, no. 3 (Sept.): 757–71.

Wolf, Edward N. 1993. *The Rich Get Increasingly Richer: Latest Data on Household Wealth during the 1980s*. Economic Policy Institute Briefing Paper 36.

Wright, Erik Olin. 1989. "Inequality." In John Eatwell, Murray Milgate, and Peter Newman, eds., *The New Palgrave: A Dictionary of Economics*. London: Macmillan, 851–919.

Part IV

CASE STUDIES

14

The War on Drugs: A Legitimate Battle or Another Mode of Inequality?

Jim Horner

The American public perceives the "drug problem" to be one of the most important issues facing the country. Only poverty and the economy are seen as more important (United States 1991b). The concern about drugs makes sense on the surface. Gang wars, violence, corruption in law enforcement, and other drug-related problems would seem to justify a War on Drugs and the current boom in the prison industry. However, a closer look at these social concerns reveals a different situation. The War on Drugs is really an attack on constitutional rights, the poor, minorities, women, and selected countries in the Third World. It reinforces inequality, and as it does so, has become an exercise in social pathology rather than an attempt at social amelioration. This war is best understood in terms of predatory behaviors and invidious distinctions made among select groups, both domestically and abroad.

Conventional economics has provided a framework for understanding supply and demand in the drug market. Milton Friedman and others (Friedman 1972, 1990; Ostrowski 1990; Boaz 1990) have even explored some of the unintended effects of drug prohibition, such as an increase in drug-related crimes, more violence, and a shift toward the consumption of less expensive but more dangerous substitutes. They have also provided policy analysis that strongly suggests that the War on Drugs should be abolished.

While some conventional economists have built and bravely supported their own case for legalizing drugs, they have not provided the necessary framework for understanding the invidious and predatory nature of the War on Drugs. Their neoclassical framework of analysis is incapable of supporting the needed inquiry—strong hearts, weak heads? Radical institutionalist analysis, especially that of Veblen, provides the framework needed to explore the predatory nature of the War on Drugs as it relates to race, class, gender, and nation. The extended analysis provides for more humane policy proposals in dealing with drug-related problems.

THE VEBLENIAN DICHOTOMY

Radical institutionalism draws heavily from Thorstein Veblen's dichotomy. As J. Ron Stanfield notes, "The foundation of Veblenian economics is the celebrated dichotomy between the ceremonial and technological aspects of human society" (1989, 84). However, Stanfield believes that the Veblenian dichotomy is often misunderstood. The ceremonial function is not just ritual behavior that retards progress; rather, it is more often an expression or a reinforcement of invidious uses of power. Stanfield also cautions that the technological function is not descriptive of the best techniques and tools of production. The technological function has to do with the "habit of the mind" in improving the human process. Thus, the most important dichotomy is between the "invidious" economic interest and "noninvidious" economic interest (Stanfield 1989, 84).

Invidious distinctions are defined as the "process of valuation of persons in respect of worth or value" (Veblen 1904, 34). These valuations are made on the basis of wealth, race, class, gender, and national origin. Invidious evaluation raises one person by lowering another. Noninvidious evaluations do not diminish one person's integrity in order to recognize the dignity of another person (Tool 1979, 295).

Veblen analyzed society in terms of institutions or "habits of thought." Institutions change with changing circumstances of society, and the development of these institutions is "the development of society." Institutions of the past shape current institutions and current institutions shape future institutions through a "selective and coercive process" (Veblen 1931, 190).

Veblen charged that, in communities of a diverse ethnic background, one ethnic group "or type of body or temperament" would dominate. Further, "a process of selective adaptation of habits and thoughts" would favor the dominant group. The dominant group takes the institutions from the past and reshapes them into their own likeness. However, the current institutions (what Veblen refers to as "the present scheme of life") do not entirely fit current circumstances. Institutions resist change and encourage conformity with the overall scheme of life of the dominant class. In Veblen's own words:

Men's habits of thought tend to persist indefinitely, except as circumstances force a change. These institutions which have so been handed down, these habits of thought, points of view, mental attitudes and aptitudes, or what not, are therefore themselves a conservative factor. This is the factor of social inertia, psychological inertia, conservatism. (Veblen 1931, 191)

Social and psychological inertia characterize America's drug policy debate. There is ample evidence to support the hypothesis that the War on Drugs has been lost. However, for policy makers to oppose the War on Drugs would be similar to opposing U.S. involvement in Vietnam, Central America, or the Persian Gulf. There is the risk of appearing "unpatriotic."

Current drug policy promotes political gain for both conservatives and liberals. The conservative can continue exploiting the "crime issue" (a new statement of old bigotry) and call for more expenditures for the growing prison industry. Representative Gerald Solomon (R.-NY) advocates increasing the intensity of the War on Drugs. He suggests expanding drug testing in the private sector and denying state assistance and summer employment to drug users. He introduced legislation (House Resolution 1453) that would deny tax-exempt status to any organization that advocates the legalization of drugs and further legislation (H.R. 135) that would deny federal funding to any group that would do any research into the question of legalization. The liberal, who generally fears appearing "soft" on crime, can call for harsh penalties and expanded funding to fight the War (Andreas and Youngers 1989; Trebach and Inciardi 1993). Both Senator Joseph Biden (D.-DE) and Charles Rangel (D.-NY) advocate stepping up the War on Drugs. The bi-partisan support for a continued predatory drug policy does great harm to disenfranchised groups. The policy is implemented by making invidious distinctions among people based on class, race, gender, and nation.

UNEQUAL JUSTICE: CLASS AND RACE DISTINCTIONS

Jeffrey Reiman recognizes that the arrangement of social institutions defines and determines a significant share of the crime in contemporary society. Although he acknowledges the Marxian concept of the "repressive function" of the criminal justice system, his analysis is more concerned with the system's "ideological function." Reiman concentrates on the failure of the system to reduce crime rather than its success in repressing the poor on behalf of the rich. A more complete understanding of crime in America requires an investigation of the social process that defines what a crime is, who the criminal is to be, and how the criminal justice system discriminates among people and behavior (Reiman 1990, 8).

The criminal justice system becomes "successful" as it "fails" to really address the widespread nature and occurrence of crime. By allowing crime to continue, the "system" can continue to punish minorities and the poor for their crimes. The punishment does not end crime, but it does stigmatize the poor and minorities who are punished. Furthermore the system escapes any blame for the plight of the least advantaged. As long as the crime and punishment continue, the underdogs can be seen as the perpetrators of serious crime and, as such, can be seen as the enemies of a normal and reasonable society. Consequently, the poor are thought to be more prone to crime because they are poor of their own choosing, and thus participate in criminal activity on their own volition. The system is thus excused from any complicity in their plight.

Certain activities are crimes by their nature if they disrupt the recreation of community or take away from the life process. The paradox is that the criminal justice system does not include all such harm to others as being part of criminal activity, or at least does not treat the same crimes equally. There is one system of justice for the poor and minorities, while another exists for the most economically and politically powerful.

For example, one may directly assault another by physical harm or through the threat of the use of a weapon. This is the "criminal activity" that registers in the minds of most people. Reiman contends that more physical harm and loss of income and property are a direct result of "white-collar" crime but "white-collar criminals" are treated in a very different way (Reiman 1990, 89–91). The crimes of the poor draw harsh sentences and punishment while the crimes of the more affluent (the white-collar strata of seemingly respectable, professional and managerial groups) usually result in very mild punishment, if any at all.

Armed robbers addicted to crack cocaine risk the health and lives of others to hold up grocery stores. They make a conscious decision to carry out such an act for profit. Corporate managers addicted to powder cocaine make conscious decisions that risk the health and lives of employees by not installing safety equipment or enforcing certain safety rules. Profit is the motivation for such decisions. While such armed robbers are often imprisoned or executed as criminals, such corporate managers are often rewarded as pillars of the community (Reiman 1990, 38–47).

Clearly, race plays a major role in the War on Drugs. The overt racism that once characterized the United States has given way to more subtle and sophisticated forms of expression. George Bush won the presidential election in 1988 by running against a code word, a racist image—"Willie Horton." (That name was used to conjure up in the fearful minds of many white voters the stereotypical images of dreadfully violent black criminals.) Other code words include "quotas," "neighborhood schools," and taking back control of "our cities." All are subtle tools of racism, as is the War on Drugs. Black felons are viewed differently from white felons and are treated differently by the justice system. The mental image of "black crime" is not one of "tax evasion or embezzling from brokerage firms," but one of violent crime and drugs (Hacker 1992, 181–82).

Police are more likely to question and arrest blacks (and other minorities) than whites. Table 14.1 shows the ratio of black arrests to all arrests for various crimes. It also shows the disproportion of black arrests. The disproportion measure is the black arrest ratio adjusted for the ratio of black population to the total population, which is less than 12 percent. With the exception of driving while intoxicated, a disproportionate amount of blacks are arrested for each crime. The disproportion rate of black versus white arrests for drug violations is greater than three to one.

Andrew Hacker maintains that when whites hear that "the police are coming," it usually implies that "help is on its way." For blacks, however, it more often means questioning, search and seizure, and arrest. For example, the state of

Florida has adopted a program that stops cars whose drivers fit a "profile" of a drug dealer (Blachman and Sharpe 1989–1990, 141). This profile primarily fits young blacks in expensive cars. As a result, a disproportionate number of young blacks are stopped and their cars searched. An increased number of arrests have resulted from these actions. However, any type of search and seizure policy will increase arrests. The "profile" of a drug user in Florida is a "ceremonial" profile of minorities that stems from invidious distinctions.

Table 14.1
Arrests of Blacks, 1990

Crimes	Black Share of All Arrests	Disproportion of Black Arrests
Robbery	61.2%	5.1
Murder and Manslaughter	54.7%	4.5
Gambling	47.5%	3.9
Rape	43.2%	3.6
Receiving Stolen Property	41.2%	3.4
Vagrancy	40.8%	3.4
Drug Violation	40.7%	3.4
Weapons Possession	39.8%	3.3
Prostitution	38.9%	3.2
Motor Vehicle Theft	38.4%	3.2
Aggravated Assault	38.4%	3.2
Forgery and Counterfeiting	34.0%	2.8
Disorderly Conduct	32.4%	2.7
Embezzlement	32.1%	2.7
Domestic Violence	30.3%	2.5
Burglary	30.1%	2.5
Vandalism	22.6%	1.9
Curfew and Loitering	17.7%	1.5
Driving While Intoxicated	8.7%	0.9

Source: Hacker, *Two Nations* (1992).

Once arrested, blacks face further discrimination. Blacks (especially the young) are disproportionately poor and have less chance of making bail. Being incarcerated impedes their ability to build a better defense. Public defenders, who are appointed by the court to represent indigent defendants, are not able to provide as good a defense for the accused as would a private attorney. Public defenders often persuade their clients to plea-bargain in order to obtain a lesser sentence. Thus, blacks (along with other underdogs) have a greater chance of being convicted and imprisoned (Reiman 1990, 95). Table 14.2 shows the prison population over a 60-year period. The proportion of black prisoners increased over this time period, while the proportion of white prisoners decreased.

The criminal justice system succeeds by stigmatizing the underdogs and punishing people, some of whom have committed crimes. It also succeeds by failing to control crime so that the public's fear continues to justify the stigmatization and punishment of underdog groups. The latter is its real success, because doing so promotes inequality. The War on Drugs is a facilitating factor in this process, and it works a special hardship on women.

Table 14.2
Prison Population In the United States, 1930–1990

Years	Whites	Blacks	Other
1930	76.7%	22.4%	0.9%
1940	73.0%	n.a.	n.a.
1950	69.1%	29.7%	1.2%
1960	61.0%	37.0%	2.0%
1970	60.5%	35.8%	3.7%
1980	47.0%	44.0%	9.0%
1990	45.0%	43.0%	12.0%

Sources: Hacker, Two Nations, (1992); United States (1986); United States (1993b).

WOMEN AT RISK: THE WAR ON DRUGS AND GENDER

Women are also particular targets in this War as they face unique problems in terms of health, family, and community. The "get tough" drug policies result in women being imprisoned at higher rates than ever before (United States 1991c). As Table 14.3 indicates, the number of female inmates in state prisons grew an astonishing 75 percent during the period 1986–1991. Drug offenses account for more than half of the increase (United States 1991a).

Table 14.3
Increase in Number of Women in State Prisons

	1986	1991	Percent Change
Female	22,777	39,917	75.2%
Male	464,603	728,246	52.9%

Source: United States (1991c).

The imprisonment of women is tearing families and communities apart and the result is discontinuity in the "re-creation of community," which Marc Tool defines as "reconstituting the social fabric of that social order to provide for continuity by utilizing effectively the stock of human wit and wisdom" (1979, 295). Communities are going concerns and are composed of language, custom, and culture. A noninvidious re-creation of community requires the adoption of instrumental values based on current knowledge and a rejection of values and behavior that maintain the status and abuse of economic/political power (Tool 1979, 295).

Invidious distinctions are often made according to gender in the matter of substance abuse. This differential treatment is what Dugger calls, in this volume, the enabling myth of "otherness." Thinking of men as being superior requires "otherness," so that the "other" (women) can be inferior. The "superior" man should be in the world, and the "inferior" woman should be at home.

The mythology of "otherness" as it relates to substance abuse is not new. Mark Lender and James Kirby Martin describe the female alcoholic in Victorian America as being thrown into a "social catastrophe." The role of a woman was to be the home's defender, but the alcoholic woman "imperiled" the home. At the turn of the century, Dr. Albert Day stated, "A debauched woman is always, everywhere a more terrible object to behold than a man" (Day quoted in Lender and Martin 1987, 117–18). The double standard led to hidden alcoholic behavior among women which still exists today.

Women bear a disproportionate amount of shame and guilt for their substance abuse and related behavior. Whereas men are likely to be accepted for sexual exploits and for "holding their liquor," women are more likely to be condemned for the same activities. As a result, women are often discouraged from seeking treatment due to their fear of losing their children, employment, and freedom. The fear is especially acute in terms of fetal endangerment (Weiss 1991, 9).

The proliferation of fetal endangerment cases has only added to the problems of poor women in gaining access to proper medical care. Fetuses may be endangered by a whole range of parental activities. The ingestion of alcohol, cocaine, nicotine, heroin, and other substances by the fetus's mother or father can cause it harm. However, only the mother risks prosecution for any of these activities, and even then, only the ingestion of illegal drugs can land her in court. Many poor women are hesitant to go for medical examination for fear of the detection of illegal drugs in their blood and urine tests. In some cases, addicts are afraid to give birth in hospitals for fear of detection and arrest.

Although female users/addicts in general are being ravaged by the drug crisis, black female addicts/users receive especially harsh treatment. Although there is very little difference in the proportion of black and white pregnant women who use drugs, physicians report black women in greater proportions than white women (Lusane 1991, 55). There may be a lack of medical facilities for pregnant addicts/users, but a growing prison industry welcomes them.

For many women, incarceration is an extension of the stigmatization and victimization that they face in society. Female prisoners are subject to nude body searches which humiliate them as guards (male and female) explore their private areas. Such actions bring back the trauma of rape and other physical violations (Albor 1995, 235–37).

Females in American society have been charged with the function of nurturing and raising children, so their imprisonment works an extra hardship for the family unit. Male prisoners have a better chance than do females of leaving children with the other parent while serving time. Even when females do leave their children with other family members, this causes concern that their children may be subjected to the same abuse they faced in their youth.

The American War on Drugs not only promotes inequality according to gender (and other factors) but also promotes inequality beyond domestic borders. Understanding the international impact of drug policy requires understanding the institutional nature of "nation."

NATION: AN EXTRATERRITORIAL MODE OF INEQUALITY

Veblen described the concept of nation as a predatory organism that creates a "community interest in getting something for nothing by force and fraud." The predatory and dynastic state not only implements force and fraud against other nations but also creates a "penalized subservience of this underlying population at home." (Veblen 1923, 442).

Continued support for foreign domination and militarization is enhanced by the "infatuation with patriotism" and the habitual creation of enemies. To appear unpatriotic is to be charged with "presumptive criminality." The Cold War offers a striking example of the abuses of the predatory state. Opposition to nuclear proliferation or wars against communism was met with charges of being unpatriotic.

The rhetoric of national predation changed after the breakup of the Soviet Union and the dissolution of the communist satellite country relationships. Without the contrived threat to the United States from the Russians and Chinese, new enemies had to be created to justify continued high levels of military expenditures. Terms such as "communist menace" and "evil empire" have been replaced by "state-sponsored terrorism," the "Islamic threat," and "drug-dealing dictators."

The War on Drugs has provided an additional justification for continued militarization as evidenced by the invasion of Panama in 1989. The George Bush administration claimed that Panamanian General Manuel Noriega was selling and facilitating the flow of drugs into the United States. This justified the invasion in the mind of the administration as well as in the mind of the public; nonetheless, the street price of drugs in the United States fell within a few weeks after the invasion. The lower price suggests that the invasion did not affect the supply of drugs. It did, however, affect the lives (and deaths) of many innocent Panamanians.

An important consequence of the War on Drugs is the militarization of law enforcement. For almost a century, the Posse Comitatus Act of 1876 made a clear distinction between civilian law enforcement and the military. However, the distinction between the two began to erode in the 1970s when the military was allowed to offer temporary "indirect help" in the enforcement of drug laws. Amendments to the Posse Comitatus Act allowed the military to gather intelligence, lend equipment, and deploy personnel to civilian law enforcement. During the 1980s, the navy became directly involved in drug interdiction (although it kept coast guard personnel around at all times to give the appearance of civilian authority), and Congress allowed the national guard to assist in antidrug operations. Morris J. Blachman and Kenneth E. Sharpe describe these actions as dangerous because they may have opened the door for the military to make "non-drug-related" arrests (Blachman and Sharpe 1989, 148–53).

However, even critics of the military involvement in the War on Drugs miss the invidious nature of drug prohibition. Bruce Michael Bagley criticized the Ronald Reagan administration for banking on military action and interdiction while dedicating far too little time, energy, and resources to the development of a long-term policy to deal with the Columbian cocaine trade. He asserts that the focus should have been on institution building and multilateral cooperation. (Bagley 1989–1990, 63). William H. Overbolt (1989-90) made a similar argument about U.S. military involvement in Burma's drug trade. He thinks America's War on Drugs in Southeast Asia could be won by supporting a "decent and moderate regime" (1989-90, 117). Overbolt and Bagley are on target as they describe the futility of military involvement in the War on Drugs. What they overlook is that a more drug-moderate regime would probably be as oppressive in trying to control trafficking. Attempts at institution building and multilateral cooperation will result in the same predatory behavior on the part of the state that now exists, as the failure of drug prohibition to check drug sales and consumption is built into the policy itself. The American prohibition against drugs is a driving force behind the drug problems in South America, Central America, and Asia. The best policy to address the international drug problem is to legalize drugs in the United States. To best address the drug problems in America requires, not only legalization, but also social reform and a harm reduction program.

CONCLUSION: HARM REDUCTION AND NON-INVIDIOUS POLICY

The War on Drugs has already been   lost to vested interests. It increases, rather than decreases, the scope and complexity of the illegal drug market. Those who are not consumers or sellers of drugs have been harmed as the result of drug-related crimes. The users/addicts have been harmed beyond what would normally be the case without drug prohibition.

Who are winners in the War on Drugs? They may be the prosecution (drug-law enforcement), the prosecuted (drug dealers), and politicians (both conservative and liberal) who oppose legalization. Under legalization, the $12 billion spent on drug law enforcement (United States 1993a, 61) may be allocated to fight other crimes or to treatment and rehabilitation efforts. Prices would fall, as would the profits of the dealers. Conservative politicians would have one less tool of discrimination against economically disenfranchised groups and liberal politicians would have one less opportunity to get tough on crime. After all, to get tough on drug crimes is to make invidious distinctions on the basis of class, race, gender, and nation and to exercise predatory behavior.

The United States needs a harm reduction program that will reduce the damage done to all groups involved. The legalization of drugs would bring about changes similar to those seen during the repeal of prohibition (Boaz 1990). The health of the user/addict would be less endangered due to the ability to buy drugs from reputable sources. There would be less associated crime, as drugs would be more available at lower prices and in legally institutionalized markets. Lower-income groups would be less likely to face an unfair justice system. Economic policy (to reduce unemployment, and raise minimum wages and income supports) and the justice system could both concentrate on reducing crime, including white-collar, political, race, and gender crime as well as property crime. We might even surprise ourselves by addressing war crimes. All these should be done instead of concentrating on punishing and stigmatizing the underdogs, some of whom do commit crimes. Legalization could be accompanied with regulations on the grading of drugs, proper warning labels, legal age limits, and restrictions on advertising. These types of regulations are similar to those on alcohol and tobacco.

Legalization alone will not suffice. Reforms are required in the legal and economic system. A first step in legal reform would require a rethinking of the prison system. Currently, the United States has over 1 million people incarcerated in jails, and state and federal prisons. Table 14.4 reflects almost a threefold increase in the rate of prisoners per 100,000 population over a 30-year period. As of 1993, drug offenders accounted for 61 percent of the prison population in federal prisons, 21 percent in state prisons, and almost 25 percent in local jails (United States 1991a). Imprisonment is one of the most ineffective forms of public policy, *if* its purpose is the reduction of crime. As Reiman notes, "Prison produces more crime than it cures" (Reiman 1990, 25).

Table 14.4
Federal and State Prisoners

Year	Number of Prisoners	Prisoners per 100,000 Population
1960	212,953	118.6
1970	196,429	96.7
1980	315,974	139.2
1985	480,568	216.5
1986	522,084	230.4
1987	560,812	229.0
1988	603,732	244.0
1989	680,907	274.3
1990	739,980	295.0
1991	789,347	309.6

Source: United States (1993b).

Effective public policy must encourage the recreation of community and noninvidious distinctions among people. Addressing the problems of unemployment and poverty is a more moral and ethical policy than incarcerating the poor. Funding universal access to prenatal care contributes more to society than prosecuting fetal endangerment cases. Young blacks, pregnant women, and the poor would gain more by access to jobs, education, medical care, and income supports than by facing arbitrary justice and incarceration. Drug treatment facilities are more useful to society than prisons.

Ending the War on Drugs cannot solve the drug problem or eliminate crime. Nor can it eradicate all drug-induced damage to self, family, and community. However, it is certain that continuing the War on Drugs only makes these problems much more severe. Many addicts/users could live a relatively normal life under legalization. Such people should be held accountable for the damage inflicted on others while under the influence, but not for their choice to consume.

Legalization is not the same as encouraging or sanctioning drug abuse. Fighting the War on Drugs, however, is the same as waging a war on the poor, minorities, women, and on selected developing nations. Such a war should stop.

REFERENCES

Albor, Teresa. 1995. "The Women Get Chains." *Nation*, Feb. 20, 234–37.

Andreas, Peter, and Coletta Youngers. 1989. "Busting the Andean Cocaine Industry: America's Counterproductive War on Drugs." *World Policy Journal*, 6 (Summer): 529–62.

Bagley, Bruce Michael. 1989–1990. "Dateline Drug Wars: Columbia: The Wrong Strategy." *Foreign Policy*, 77 (Winter): 154–71.

Blachman, Morris, and Kenneth E. Sharpe. 1989–1990. "The War on Drugs: American Democracy Under Assault." *World Policy Journal*, 7 (Winter): 135–63.

Boaz, David, ed. 1990. *The Crisis in Drug Prohibition*. Washington, D.C.: Cato Institute.

Friedman, Milton. 1972. "Prohibition and Drugs." *Newsweek*, May 1, 104.

___. 1990. "An Open Letter to Bill Bennett." In David Boaz, ed., *The Crisis in Drug Prohibition*. Washington D.C.: Cato Institute, 114–16.

Hacker, Andrew. 1992. *Two Nations*. New York: Ballantine Books.

Hyde, Henry. 1995. *Forfeiting Our Property Rights*. Washington, D.C.: Cato Institute.

Lender, Mark Edward, and James Kirby Martin. 1987. *Drinking in America*. New York: Free Press.

Lusane, Clarence. 1991. *Pipe Dream Blues*. Boston: South End Press.

Nell, Edward J. 1994. "The Dynamics of the Drug Market." *Challenge*, Mar.–April, 13–30.

Ostrowski, James. 1990. "Thinking about Drug Legalization." In David Boaz, ed., *The Crisis in Drug Prohibition*. Washington, D.C.: Cato Institute, 45–76.

Overbolt, William H. 1989–90. "Dateline Drug Wars: Burma: The Wrong Enemy." *Foreign Policy*, 77 (Winter): 171–91.

Reiman, Jeffrey. 1990. *The Rich Get Richer and the Poor Get Prison*. New York: Macmillan Publishing.

Stanfield, J. Ron. 1989. "Recent U.S. Marxist Economics In Veblenian Perspective." In William M. Dugger, ed., *Radical Institutionalism: Contemporary Voices*. Westport Conn..: Greenwood Press, 83–104.

Tool, Marc R. 1979. *The Discretionary Economy*. Santa Monica, Calif.: Goodyear Publishing.

Trebach, Arnold S., and James A. Inciardi. 1993. *Legalize It? Debating American Drug Policy*. Washington, D.C.: American University Press.

United States. Department of Justice. 1986. *Historical Corrections Statistics in the United States, 1850–1984*. Washington, D.C.: Bureau of Justice Statistics.

___. 1991a. *Drugs and Crime Facts.* Washington, D.C.: Bureau of Justice Statistics.

___. 1991b. *Drugs, Crime, and the Justice System.* Washington, D.C.: Bureau of Justice Statistics.

___. 1991c. *Women in Prison.* Washington, D.C.: Bureau of Justice Statistics.

___. 1993a. *Sourcebook of Criminal Justice Statistics.* Washington D.C.: Bureau of Justice Statistics.

___. 1993b. . Washington, D. C.: Government Printing Office.

Veblen, Thorstein. 1904. *The Theory of Business Enterprise.* New York: Charles Scribner and Sons.

___. 1923. *Absentee Ownership.* New York: Viking.

___. 1931. *The Theory of the Leisure Class.* New York: Modern Library.

___. 1945. *Absentee Ownership.* New York: Viking Press.

Weiss, Carol J. 1991. "Women and Chemical Dependency: Stigma, Shame, Guilt." *Drug Policy Letter,* Fall, 9–11.

15

Regional Income Inequality Revisited: Lessons from the 100 Lowest-Income Counties in the United States

James Peach

As it relates to the United States, the phrase "regional income inequality" is a polite way of saying that some areas of the nation are desperately poor. The case of Shannon County, South Dakota, is a good illustration. In 1990, according to data from the most recent census, Shannon County, South Dakota had the dubious distinction of having the lowest per capita income of the nation's 3,147 counties or county equivalents (United States 1993). Shannon County's per capita income was $3,417, or 23.7 percent of the national average of $14,420. The average household in Shannon County contained 4.4 persons (nearly twice the national average) and 45.7 percent (nearly three times the national average) of these households had a total income of less than $10,000. Low income relative to the rest of the nation is not a new phenomenon for Shannon County, which has been among the 100 lowest-income counties in each of the last four censuses (1960, 1970, 1980, and 1990).

In 1990 there were 9,902 residents of Shannon County, 94.1 percent of whom were Native Americans. Native Americans in Shannon County had a per capita income of $3,029, or 33.4 percent of the per capita income of whites ($9,074) in the county. Among persons 18 years old and older in Shannon County, 41.8 percent had not finished high school in 1990. The unemployment rate in 1990 was 30.5 percent, roughly six times the national average of 6.2 percent. Of those who were employed, 58.4 percent were federal, state, or local government employees.

Shannon County is not unique. Regional income inequality is a persistent feature of the American economy. The Shannon County data correctly suggest that regional income inequality can be as brutal, nasty and ugly as other forms of inequality.

Like other forms of inequality, regional income inequality is a reflection of genuine deprivation for the people who live in the poorest areas in the nation.

Regional income inequality is important also because it is closely related to other forms of inequality. Racial inequality and regional inequality, for example, are mutually reinforcing aspects of the overall problem of income distribution.

The obstacles to reducing extreme regional variations in income in the U.S. are not insurmountable. John Kenneth Galbraith ([1964] 1967) offered an incomplete, but sensible, policy for reducing regional inequality. Galbraith argued that:

There is no place in the world where a well-educated population is really poor. If so, let us here in the United States select, beginning next year, the hundred lowest income counties ... and designate them as special education districts. These would be equipped (or re-equipped) with a truly excellent and comprehensive school plant, including primary and secondary schools, transportation and the best in recreational facilities. ([1964] 1967, 129)

Galbraith also described the other support that would be necessary to make such a program work. His main point, of course, was that with adequate education, the people of the 100 lowest-income counties could not remain poor for long.

Galbraith's proposal can be criticized from many perspectives, but his concern with the 100 lowest-income counties in the nation provides a unique analytical focal point for examining regional inequality in the U.S.

The main portion of this chapter is a statistical description of the nation's 100 lowest-income counties. In a very meaningful sense, the data do "speak for themselves." The statistical description is based mainly on data from the 1990 Census of Population and Housing. Where appropriate, the 1990 data are compared to data from earlier censuses. Comparisons are also made between characteristics of the 100 lowest-income counties with those of the 100 highest counties and the nation as a whole. The statistical description begins after two brief digressions. First, some brief comments about the truly vast literature on regional income inequality are both ceremonially and instrumentally warranted. Second, equally brief comments about the data and its limitations are necessary. A concluding section contains intentionally invidious remarks about the future of the 100 lowest-income counties in the context of the current political climate.

THE LITERATURE ON REGIONAL INCOME INEQUALITY

The approach taken in this chapter differs considerably from the methods commonly used in the literature on regional income inequality. Reviews of that literature are available from several sources (e.g., Amos 1989; Fan and Casetti 1994) and will not be repeated here. Some brief comments about the literature are necessary to place the current study in an appropriate context.

Essentially, two main questions are addressed in the literature. First, many authors (e.g., Al-Samarrie and Miller 1967; Thurow 1969; Bishop, Formby, and Thistle 1992) have investigated the "determinants" of regional inequality.

Sometimes the emphasis is on a single variable such as federal government expenditures. More typically, studies are cross-sectional analyses using multiple regression. Among the variables that have been investigated are natural resource endowments, the industry mix, state and local economic development programs, the age distribution of the population, the national trend toward greater income inequality, the internationalization of the economy, state and federal expenditure and tax policies, and rapid technological change. These variables are important determinants of patterns of regional inequality. This chapter is not, however, a study of the determinants of regional inequality.

The second main question addressed in the literature concerns the time-path of patterns of regional inequality. These studies (e.g., Amos 1989; Barro and Sala-I-Martin 1995, 1994; Fan and Casetti 1994) often address the question of convergence (or divergence) of regional incomes in the context of the development process. The beginning of the convergence debate is usually attributed to Simon Kuznets (1955), who suggested an inverted-U relationship between regional inequality and development. Kuznets argued that in the initial stages of development, regional inequality was likely to be minimal since all regions were likely to be equally poor. As the development process proceeded, some regions were likely to develop more rapidly than others. Eventually, however, factor mobility suggests a decline in regional income inequality.

Many neoclassical economists (e.g., Barro and Sala-I-Martin 1995) continue to assert that regional income convergence is a reasonable expectation in a nation without legal barriers to labor or capital mobility. According to basic neoclassical theory, in such a nation, the factors of production should flow from the low to the high-income region until incomes in the two regions reach equilibrium (equality). However, there has been a noticeable trend towards greater regional inequality in the United States since the mid-1970s (Amos 1989). Neoclassical theory offers no explanation of why regional incomes might diverge in a modern economy, like the United States.

The literature has produced some genuinely useful insights into both the determinants of regional inequality and the convergence/divergence issue. The value of these contributions should not be lightly dismissed. However, no attempt is made in this chapter to resolve either of the main issues addressed in the literature. Rather, the question is posed as to what can be learned by examining the characteristics of the 100 lowest-income counties.

THE DATA AND ITS LIMITATIONS

Most of the data for this study are from the 1990 Census of Population and Housing (United States 1993). The per capita income figures from the census differ considerably from the estimates of per capita income reported by the U.S. Bureau of Economic Analysis (BEA) on an annual basis. Only 65 of the counties listed among the 100 lowest income counties according to the 1990 census appear on a comparable list using the BEA estimates (United States 1995).

The population used to derive per capita income is the number of persons as of the census enumeration date (April 1 of years ending in zero), while the income figure used in the numerator of per capita income represents income for the year prior to the census. Following the customary practice, population will be referred to in terms of the census year (e.g., 1990) while income data from the same census will be referenced as of the year prior to the census (e.g., 1989). Also important is the fact that the population data are truly 100 percent census counts, while the income data are from a sample consisting, on average, of somewhat less than 20 percent of all households.

The use of data from earlier censuses (1960, 1970, and 1980) for comparisons poses two problems. First, the Census Bureau has periodically made changes to the definition of its concept of money income. For the most part, these changes are minor and present no major obstacle. Second, the number of counties in the United States does not remain constant from decade to decade. For example, Cibola County, New Mexico, which appears on the 1990 list of the 100 lowest-income counties, did not exist when the census was taken in 1980.

THE 100 COUNTIES: POPULATION AND INCOME

As shown in Map I (Figure 15.1), the 100 lowest-income counties in 1990 are highly concentrated in five major regional groupings. These are: (1) Appalachia (26 counties in Kentucky, West Virginia, and Tennessee); (2) the Deep South (31 counties in Mississippi, Louisiana, Alabama, and Georgia); (3) the U.S.–Mexico Border area (14 counties in Texas); (4) the Four Corners area (9 counties in Arizona, New Mexico, Colorado, and Utah); and (5) the Northern Plains region (10 counties in North Dakota, South Dakota, and Montana). A complete list of the 100 lowest (and highest) income counties in 1990 is available from the author.

Table 15.1 contains selected characteristics of the 100 lowest-income counties from the four most recent censuses. The counties were selected on the basis of per capita income as reported in the 1990 census. For purposes of comparison, the same data are reported for the 100 highest-income counties and for all counties.

According to the four censuses, the 100 lowest-income counties contain on average slightly less than 1 percent of the U.S. population, while about 15 percent of the nation's people live in the 100 highest-income counties. In 1990, only 17 of the low-income counties had a population exceeding 25,000 persons and only 3 of the low-income counties had more than 100,000 residents. In contrast, 65 of the high-income counties had more than 100,000 residents in 1990. Stated differently, while the high-income counties were 91.6 percent urban in 1990, the low income counties were only 44.9 percent urban.

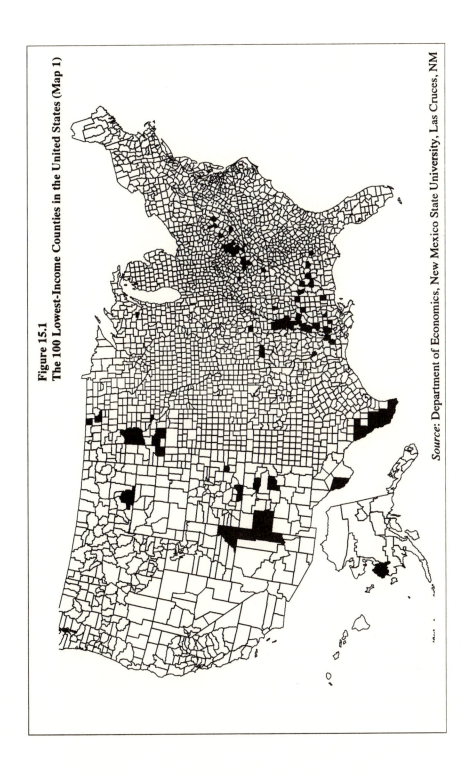

Figure 15.1
The 100 Lowest-Income Counties in the United States (Map 1)

Source: Department of Economics, New Mexico State University, Las Cruces, NM

Table 15.1
Selected Characteristics of U.S. Counties: 1960, 1970, 1980, and 1990

	Lowest 100	Highest 100	Nation
1990			
Population	2,129,613	39,775,463	248,709,873
Percent*	0.86	16.0	100.0
Urban Population	956,391	36,421,466	187,051,543
Percent**	44.9	91.6	75.1
Per Capita Income (1989)	6,633	20,376	14,420
Percent***	46.0	143.8	100.0
1980			
Population	1,973,493	35,075,879	226,545,805
Percent*	0.87	15.5	100.0
Per Capita Income (1979)	4,011	9,356	7,298
Percent***	55.0	128.2	100.0
1970			
Population	1,659,144	31,711,389	203,302,031
Percent*	0.82	15.6	100.0
Per Capita Income (1969)	1,451	4,039	3,119
Percent***	46.5	129.5	100.0
1960			
Population	1,773,428	24,749,488	179,323,175
Percent*	1.0	13.8	100.0
Per Capita Income (1959)	783	2434	1850
Percent***	42.3	131.6	100.0

Source: Author computations from U.S. Bureau of the Census Data. The 100 lowest-income counties and 100 highest-income counties are based on 1990 rankings in all cases.
*Percent of U.S. population.
**Percent of population in the area listed.
***Percent of U.S. per capita income.

The data in Table 15.1 show that the 100 lowest-income counties have made little progress in terms of relative income during the four census periods. In 1989, the 100 lowest-income counties had a per capita income of $6,633, or 46.0 percent of the national average of $14,420. Only 7 of the 100 lowest-income counties in 1989 had a per capita income of 50 percent of the national average, and none of the 7 exceeded 51 percent of the national figure. The 100 lowest-income counties in 1989 had a 1959 per capita income of $738, or 42.3 percent of the national average of $1,850 (United States 1967). Seventy-five of the 100 lowest-income counties in 1989 had a lower per capita income as a percent of the national average than they did in 1959.

The data for 1969 produce similar results. The 100 lowest-income counties in 1989 had a 1969 per capita income of 46.5 percent of the national average. The low-income counties had a per capita income in excess of 50 percent of the national average in only one census reporting period (1979), and a decade later, that apparent progress had disappeared.

For several reasons, considerable change in the list of the nation's 100 lowest-income counties over time could be expected. First, the change in per capita income required to produce a change in rankings at the low end of the distribution of county incomes is small. In 1959, for example, only $98 separated the 100th lowest-income county from the 200th lowest-income county. Second, the census bureau has periodically altered its definition of money income as well as its data-processing and data-collection procedures. Third, there have been considerable changes in the structure of the nation's economy.

There is, however, remarkable stability during the four census periods among both the 100 lowest- and 100 highest-income counties. Table 15.2 contains the relevant rankings. In order to avoid the question of which census year should serve as the base year for defining the list of 100 lowest (highest) income counties, the rankings are shown in Table 15.2 using data from each census year as the basis for the list. A second reason for using each census year as the basis for the list is that the total number of counties has changed between census years. Of the 100 lowest-income counties in 1979, 64 were among 1989's 100 lowest-income counties and an additional 22 counties from 1979's list ranked no higher than the bottom 200 counties in 1989. Indeed, 93 of 1979's 100 lowest-income counties ranked no higher than the bottom 10 percent (311) of counties in 1989. Of 1959's 100 lowest-income counties, 45 were among 1989's lowest 100. Moreover, 76 of 1959's 100 lowest-income counties ranked no higher than the bottom 10 percent of counties in 1989—30 years later.

Table 15.2
1990 County Rankings Compared to 1960, 1970, and 1980

100 Lowest Income Counties	1 to 100	101 to 200	201 to 311	Missing
1960 Counties in 1990	45	18	13	0
1970 Counties in 1990	60	16	12	0
1980 Counties in 1990	64	22	6	0
100 Lowest Income Counties				
1990 Counties in 1960	45	14	12	3
1990 Counties in 1970	60	20	13	1
1990 Counties in 1980	64	18	8	1
100 Highest Income Counties				
1960 Counties in 1990	43	23	16	0
1970 Counties in 1990	62	24	10	0
1980 Counties in 1990	65	21	6	0
100 Highest Income Counties				
1990 Counties in 1960	43	14	6	10
1990 Counties in 1970	62	17	3	0
1990 Counties in 1980	65	20	8	0

Source: Author computations from U.S. Bureau of the Census data.

Like the 100 lowest-income counties, the nation's 100 highest-income counties also exhibit stability over time. In 1989, these counties had a per capita income of $20,736, or 143.8 percent of the national figure. These same counties in 1959 had a per capita income of $2,434, or 131.6 percent of the national figure. From a different perspective, 82 of 1959's 100 highest-income counties ranked among the top 10 percent of counties in 1989.

Race and Ethnicity

The racial and ethnic composition of the population in the 100 lowest-income counties differs substantially from the distributions found in the 100 highest-income counties and the nation. As can be seen in Table 15.3, the white, non-Hispanic population of the 100 lowest-income counties was 37.1 percent of the total population which is less than half of the percent of white, non-Hispanics found in either the 100 highest-income counties or the nation. Compared to a resident of the 100 highest-income counties, a person living in the 100 lowest-income counties was almost twice as likely to be black, nearly 20 times as likely to be Native American and slightly more than 5 times as likely to be Hispanic.

Table 15.3
Race and Ethnicity in 1990: Number and Percentage of Persons

Race or Ethnicity	Lowest Counties Number*	Percent	Highest Counties Number*	Percent	Nation Number*	Percent
White	790	37.1	30,954	77.8	188,425	75.8
Black	312	14.7	3,479	8.8	29,285	11.8
U.S. Indian	165	7.8	149	0.4	1,867	0.8
Asian	4	0.2	1,986	5.0	6,994	2.8
Other	2	0.1	40	0.1	239	0.1
Hispanic	857	40.2	3,168	8.0	21,900	8.8
Totals	2,129	100.0	39,775	100.0	248,710	100.0

Source: Author computations from United States (1993).
Note: Persons of Hispanic origin may be of any race. The racial categories (white, black, American Indian, and other) do not include persons of Hispanic origin. Columns may not sum to totals due to rounding.
*Number is in thousands.

The averages for the 100 counties conceal the regional concentration of minorities. The 31 counties in the Deep South are 56.3 percent black. The 14 counties in the U.S.–Mexico Border area are 86.2 percent Hispanic. The population of the 9 counties of the Four Corners region is predominantly Native American (58.5 percent) and Hispanic (18.5 percent). In the Northern Plains region, 67.1 percent are Native American. Only Appalachia has a predominantly white, non-Hispanic population (97.5 percent).

The relationship between regional income inequality and racial and ethnic income inequality becomes more apparent when per capita incomes are examined on a regional basis by race and ethnicity. In the Deep South counties, blacks have a per capita income of $3,971, only 38.0 percent of the per capita income of whites ($10,462). Given the original 1990 rankings of all 3,147 U.S. counties, a county with the per capita income of whites in the Deep South counties would rank 1,403.

In the Northern Plains region, Native Americans have a per capita income of $3,834, or 38.5 percent of the corresponding figure for whites ($9,947). If the Northern Plains counties all had the per capita incomes of whites in those counties, none would currently rank lower than 1,067.

In the U.S.–Mexico Border and the Four Corners regions, the story is similar but more complicated because of the nature of the census data. Both regions have a large percentage of Hispanics. The census provides per capita income data for Hispanics and for all whites but does not provide a separate income figure for the white, non-Hispanic population. It is possible, however, to calculate a very close approximation of the per capita incomes of the white, non-Hispanic population. The details of the estimation are available from the author on request.

For the 14 counties of the U.S.–Mexico Border region, the per capita income of the white, non-hispanic population is estimated to be $15,733. Hispanics in the region had a per capita income of $5,152, or 32.7 percent of the white, non-Hispanic population. In short, the counties in the Border region would rank in the upper half of all counties if they had the per capita incomes of the white, non-Hispanic population within the region.

The data cited are consistent with the conclusions of numerous other authors (Perloff et al. 1960; Al-Sammarie and Miller 1967; Thurow 1969; Frisbie and Niedert 1977) who have observed a relationship between racial and regional inequality. With the notable exception of the Appalachian counties, the relationship between race, ethnicity, and regional inequality is too strong to ignore. Furthermore, if Appalachian whites are considered a distinct ethnic group of underdogs, (the pejorative word for them in some quarters is "hillbilly") then no exception to the relationship is found. Racial and ethnic enclaves are not found exclusively in unfortunate regions like the former Yugoslavia.

Educational Attainment

Table 15.4 contains data on the educational attainment of persons 18 years old and older in 1990. The data on educational attainment provide substantial support for John Kenneth Galbraith's proposal to attack regional inequality by providing educational opportunity for the people of the 100 lowest-income counties. Nearly half (49.3 percent) of the population 18 years old and older in the 100 lowest-income counties had not completed high school. In the 100 highest-income counties, only 17.4 percent had not completed high school. The comparable figure for the nation was 18.3 percent.

At the high end of the educational attainment scale, the differences are also dramatic. In the 100 lowest income counties, 8.4 percent of those 18 years old and older had achieved a Bachelor's degree or higher. The comparable figures were 29.1 percent for the 100 highest-income counties and 13.8 percent for the nation as a whole.

Table 15.4
Educational Attainment in 1990: Percentage of Persons 18 Years Old and Older

Attainment	Lowest Counties	Highest Counties	Nation
Less than 9th Grade	29.1	6.2	7.0
9th–12th Grade, No Diploma	20.2	11.2	11.3
High School Graduate	25.2	25.8	22.4
Some College, No Degree	13.7	21.3	15.5
Associate Degree	3.3	6.5	4.5
Bachelor's Degree	5.6	18.6	9.1
Grad. or Professional Degree	2.8	10.5	4.7

Source: Author computations from United States (1993).

Labor Force Characteristics

Table 15.5 contains selected labor force characteristics for persons 16 years old and older as of 1990. The unemployment rate in the 100 lowest-income counties (14.2 percent) is more than three times as high as it is in the 100 highest-income counties (4.6 percent) and more than twice as high as the national average (6.2 percent). None of the 100 lowest-income counties had an unemployment rate below the national average. In contrast, only 9 of the 100 highest-income counties had an unemployment rate higher than the national average.

Table 15.5
Selected Labor Force Characteristics in 1990: Number and Percentage of Persons 16 Years Old and Older

Characteristic	Lowest Counties	Highest Counties	Nation
In Labor Force	771,461	22,104,287	125,182,378
Percent of Persons 16 +	52.0	70.1	65.3
Employed	622,102	21,076,176	117,390,130
Unemployed	109,359	1,028,111	7,792,248
Unemployment Rate	14.2	4.6	6.2
Not In Labor Force	713,258	9,443,621	66,646,893
Percent of Persons 16 +	48.0	29.9	34.7
16 Years Old and Older	1,484,719	31,547,908	191,829,271
Percent of Total Population	69.7	79.3	77.1

Source: Author computations from United States (1993).

The labor force participation rate (LFPR) of the 100 lowest-income counties (52.0 percent) is substantially lower than in either the 100 highest-income counties (70.1 percent) or the nation (65.3 percent). Without pushing cause and effect too far, low LFPRs are at least consistent with high unemployment rates.

The higher the unemployment rate, the more likely it is that some potential workers will become discouraged and drop out of the labor force.

Some Tentative Conclusions

What can we learn from this statistical description of the 100 lowest-income counties? First, and perhaps most important, they have been low-income counties for a long time. At a minimum, for the vast majority of these counties there is no evidence indicating meaningful improvement in per capita incomes relative to the national average during the four census periods examined. This fact does not confirm or falsify any of the various theories of regional income convergence. The 100 lowest-income counties, which are the focus of this study, constitute only 3.2 percent of the total number of counties in the United States. The convergence hypothesis was neither the focus of the study nor the target of statistical tests. However, it is apparent that for the people who live in the 100 lowest income counties, regional income convergence is a process that, at best, will take a very long time.

Second, the racial and ethnic composition of the population of the 100 lowest-income counties is difficult to ignore. Whether examined as a single group or analyzed on the basis of regional groupings, there is a distinct pattern of racial and ethnic concentration in the 100 lowest-income counties. This fact alone does not suggest that racism is the major cause of low per capita incomes in these counties. After all, the Appalachian counties in the study group are 97.5 percent white and non-Hispanic. Nevertheless, when racial and ethnic income differentials are examined on a regional basis, there appears to be more than an inconsequential relationship between racially and ethnically based income inequality and regional income inequality.

Third, while Galbraith's proposal to concentrate on providing a decent education for the people of the 100 lowest-income counties may be limited and incomplete, the data on educational attainment strongly reinforce his contention. Fourth, the 100 lowest-income counties are characterized by high unemployment rates and low labor force participation rates. These labor market facts are overwhelming—so is the need for job creation.

Fifth, the 100 lowest-income counties, while they share many characteristics, do not constitute a homogeneous group. Most of the counties are small and rural, but a few are highly urbanized. The vast majority of the counties have populations with a high concentration of minorities. More than a quarter of the counties are nearly all white and non-Hispanic. The problem of low per capita incomes in the U.S.–Mexico Border area is not the same as in Appalachia.

Finally, the problem of omitted variables deserves mention. As noted in the brief literature review, many variables have been shown to be statistically significant determinants of patterns of regional income inequality. Also noted was the fact that this chapter is not a study of such determinants. The conclusions reached from the statistical description of the 100 lowest-income counties are not weakened by the omitted variables problem.

A POSTSCRIPT

In a large wealthy nation, such as the United States, there is no reason to tolerate the high degree of regional inequality, which has been a persistent feature of the economy. There are no technological obstacles to reducing regional inequality, and natural resources are not a relevant issue.

The obstacles to improving the economic well-being of the people of the 100 lowest-income counties are institutional. Especially, these obstacles are political. Market forces, even in the absence of legal barriers to labor and capital mobility, have not produced great progress in the 100 lowest-income counties. Apparently, the invisible hand is not large enough to hold these counties. Genuine progress in the low-income counties requires collective action, which means federal government action in the form of systematic regional policies and sufficient resources to make those policies meaningful.

However, if past trends are a reasonable guide to the future, it is highly likely that most of the 100 lowest-income counties in 1990 will remain low-income counties for the next several decades. A less-than-optimistic prognosis for the low-income counties is reinforced by the current political climate in the United States. Budget cutting and reducing the size of government are the dominant guidelines for determining public policy in both major political parties. A serious effort to implement effective regional policies is almost unimaginable in such a political atmosphere.

Although it is probably not terribly important in a political sense, the concept of regional income convergence, which some neoclassical economists still maintain is the natural tendency in market economies, can easily be construed as providing academic legitimacy to the absence of explicit regional policies. If regional income convergence is the norm, the neoclassical solution of "letting the market work" (read this as "do nothing") would be an appropriate policy response. However, trends over the last two decades indicate that divergence as well as convergence can occur in a modern economy.

The possibility of establishing effective regional policies is also diminished by the fact that deliberately regional policies were once attempted in the United States. Regional policies were a key feature of the Lyndon Johnson Administration's War on Poverty. The regional commissions, established during the height of the War on Poverty, were dismantled by the early 1980s. With the closing of the commissions, explicit regional policies on the part of the federal government were also abandoned. Whether the regional commissions accomplished any notable successes no longer really matters. This previous effort to implement regional policies provides powerful political reasons why such policies should not be tried again.

Moreover, the people of the 100 lowest-income counties are politically powerless in the national context. They constitute less that 1 percent of the nation's population; they are more likely to be members of a minority group than the population as a whole; and they are geographically dispersed. Quite obviously, they do not have high incomes. They are not a political interest group with the ability to effectively demand a systematic regional policy.

Nevertheless, political and economic trends do change. The Soviet Union has been dissolved (at least partially because of regionalism). Newt Gingrich is only temporarily the speaker of the U.S. House of Representatives. In a different political climate, designing policies to attack regional income inequality would not be a difficult task. No new research is needed, as the data described above are readily available for any regional grouping of counties, and the essential elements of an effective regional policy are reasonably obvious.

REFERENCES

Al-Samarrie, Ahmed, and Herman P. Miller. 1967. "State Differentials in Income Concentration." *American Economic Review,* 57 (Mar.): 59–72.

Amos, Orley M., Jr. 1983. "The Relationship Between Regional Income Inequality, Personal Income Inequality and Development." *Regional Science Perspectives*, 13, no. 1: 3–14.

___. 1989. "An Inquiry into the Causes of Increasing Regional Income Inequality in the United States." *Review of Regional Studies,* 19. no. 2: 1–12.

Barro, Robert J, and Xavier Sala-I-Martin. 1995. "Empirical Analysis of Regional Data Sets." In Robert J. Barro and Xavier Sala-I-Martin, eds., *Economic Growth.* New York: McGraw-Hill, 382–413.

Bishop, J. A., J. P. Formby, and P. D. Thistle. 1992. "Explaining Interstate Variation in Income Inequality." *Review of Economics and Statistics,* 74: 553–57.

Fan, C. C. and E. Casetti. 1994. "The Spatial and Temporal Dynamics of US Regional Income Inequality." *Annals of Regional Science*, 28, no. 2: 177–96.

Frisbie, W. Parker, and L. Neidert. 1977. "Inequality and the Relative Size of Minority Populations: A Comparative Analysis." *American Journal of Sociology*, 82 (Mar.): 1007–30.

Galbraith, John Kenneth. [1964] 1967. "Let Us Begin: An Invitation to Action on Poverty." *Harpers Magazine,* Mar. Reprinted in Lester C. Thurow, ed., *American Fiscal Policy: Experiment for Prosperity.* Englewood Cliffs, N.J.: Prentice Hall, 123–30.

Kuznets, Simon. 1955. "Economic Growth and Income Inequality." *American Economic Review,* 45, no. 1: 1–28.

Maxwell, Nan L. 1990. *Income Inequality in the United States, 1947–1985.* Westport, Conn.: Greenwood Press.

Perloff, Harvey S., Edgar S. Dunn, Jr, Eric E. Lampard, and Richard F. Muth. 1960. *Regions, Resources and Economic Growth.* Baltimore, Md.: Johns Hopkins University Press.

Thurow, Lester C. 1969. *Poverty and Discrimination.* Washington, D. C: Brookings Institution.

United States. Bureau of the Census. 1967. *County and City Data Book: 1967.* Washington, D. C.: U.S. Bureau of the Census.

___. 1983. *1980 Census of Population and Housing, Summary Tape File 3C* [Machine-Readable Data File]. Washington, D.C.: U.S. Bureau of the Census.

___. 1992. *USA Counties: A Statistical Abstract Supplement* [CD-ROM]. Washington, D.C.: U.S. Bureau of the Census.

___. 1993. *1990 Census of Population and Housing, Summary Tape File 3C* [CD-ROM]. Washington, D.C.: U.S. Bureau of the Census.

___. Bureau of Economic Analysis. 1995. Regional Economic Information System [CD-ROM]. Washington, D.C.: Bureau of Economic Analysis.

16

Racial Inequality and Radical Institutionalism: A Research Agenda

Steven Shulman

The contributions that institutionalists have made to the study of racial discrimination are few and far between. John Harvey (1991, fn. 3) lists three articles on black economic development which have appeared in the *Journal of Economic Issues* (JEI) since its inception in 1967. All told, fewer than a dozen articles on the topic of race have appeared in the JEI, the main journal of institutionalism. Nor have institutionalists been much inclined to publish in journals such as the *Review of Black Political Economy*. Institutionalists are proud of their critical attitudes toward American society, but they have had little to say concerning its most profound and hypocritical contradiction.

This lack of attention is surprising. The only institutionalist ever to have won the Nobel prize, Gunnar Myrdal, built his reputation in part upon *An American Dilemma* (1972; first published in 1944), which, a half century after its original publication, remains one of the most comprehensive and influential studies of U.S. race relations ever undertaken. However, in his wide ranging and sympathetic book on Myrdal and his impact upon "racial liberalism," Walter Jackson (1990) finds little to say about the responses of institutionalists. This quiescence is all the more surprising given that the institutionalist method (as I will argue) is well suited to the analysis of a phenomenon such as racism, which conjoins culture, community, power, and markets. One would have thought that institutionalists would have picked up this ball and run with it. The reasons why they have not will not detain us here, but the fact that they have not has had some consequences for the modern analysis of race.

In the absence of a strong institutionalist voice, the main economic analyses of race have come from neoclassicals and orthodox Marxists. The two are in direct opposition insofar as neoclassicals conclude that capitalism erodes discrimination while Marxists conclude that capitalism reproduces discrimination. Both, however, are based on a purely dollars-and-cents type of reasoning, which is necessarily limited in its historical and contemporary relevance. Neoclassicals argue that discrimination is unstable because it raises search and hiring costs and thereby lowers profits. Marxists (at least of the orthodox variety) argue that discrimination is stable because it reduces labor solidarity and bargaining power, and thereby raises profits. However, neither has had much to say about the conditions in which their *a priori* reasoning would hold in the real world. Therein lies the failure of economism and the opportunity for institutionalism.

U.S. race relations are based on historical patterns of violent subjugation (slavery, terrorism, white riots, and Jim Crow), and a social and physical separation that until recently, was close to complete. Ghettoization and segregation were deliberately created by realtors, bankers, and public officials, as well as by the mass aversion to integration among whites, and have resulted in the almost total isolation of a large segment of the African-American community (Massey and Denton 1993). The contemporary consequences of these historical patterns, in conjunction with continuing discrimination, have left blacks disproportionately vulnerable to poverty, unemployment, and their attendant social ills. At the same time, the personal and political struggles of large numbers of African-Americans, combined with economic growth and progressive public policies, have made it possible for many blacks to enter the middle class. These advances are tenuous since middle-class blacks are more likely than their white counterparts to work for the government and since their gains relative to whites have slowed or stopped since the mid-1970s (Bound and Freeman 1989); nonetheless, overt bigotry has dramatically declined and some government and corporate employment policies now favor the previously disadvantaged.

These complex trends cannot be explained by simple recourse to the logic of the marketplace. While pecuniary incentives do matter (particularly with respect to the way in which discrimination can vary over the business cycle), the way in which they work themselves out depends upon the context in which they operate. It is here that institutionalists could have made a great deal of difference to the analysis of race. The anthropological approach to economic behavior, the view of markets as "embedded" in culture and community, the emphasis on history and institutions (both in the sense of organizations and social relationships), and the explicit reference to instrumental values in the critique of domination are all elements of institutionalism that seem perfectly positioned to offset (or perhaps complement) the neoclassical focus on markets and the Marxian focus on class conflict as methodologies for racial analysis (for a synthesis, see Albelda, Drago and Shulman 1995, ch. 8).

The purpose of this chapter is to suggest some ways in which institutionalists can start making these contributions. I will discuss three interdependent areas that seem to be particularly promising: cultural norms and ethical judgments, positive feedback effects, and evolutionary holism. Throughout I will refer to the pioneering work of Myrdal, but my focus is more on the future than the past.

I will attempt to flesh out some elements of an institutionalist analysis of race with an eye toward potential research directions. While these will certainly not be the only productive avenues for future work, my hope is that they will spark new ideas and research agendas within an old and distinguished tradition.

CULTURAL NORMS AND ETHICAL JUDGEMENTS

Race is a social category. The groups we call "black" and "white"—the focus of this paper—are differentiated by a biologically arbitrary, but socially real, criterion wherein *any* African ancestry defines one as black. In the United States, to be white is to be completely free of African ancestry. This definition is by no means universal. For example, any discernible Caucasian ancestry is suffcent to define one as white in Brazil. Not only do the patterns of racial etiquette and conflict vary from society to society, but the very definitions of racial groups vary as well. Race exists as a cultural and historical artifact; consequently, it cannot be understood in purely economic terms.

As one would expect from the more rigid U.S. definition, racial conflict has been much greater in the United States than in countries such as Brazil, and the dehumanization of nonwhites has been more extreme. The United States has only been able to reconcile its racism with its pride in having a government "of the people, by the people and for the people" by using stringent cultural norms of white superiority and black inferiority. White supremacy resolved the ethical contradiction between racism and democracy by denying that blacks had the capacity for self-governance. For this reason Pierre van den Berghe (1978, 77), a leading scholar of comparative race relations, describes the pre–civil rights United States as a "*Herrenvolk* democracy."

The civil rights movement proved that the ethical contradiction could not be denied forever. The contradiction between American democratic ideals and racial realities so acutely described by Myrdal was resolved in favor of the ideals. This represented a dramatic shift in popular white ideologies: no longer could claims of black inferiority be used to justify racial inequality. In this sense the traditional culture of white supremacy was reduced to a fringe element. For a time it seemed as though inequality could no longer be rationalized by "blaming the victim." The hostile reaction that greeted the Moynihan Report (which called attention to black family instability) a quarter of a century ago made it clear that discrimination was the only acceptable explanation for racial inequality in the eyes of the intelligentsia.

This is no longer the case. Today it is fashionable to resolve the ethical contradiction between racism and democracy by claiming that racism is a thing of the past. Democracy, however, is thought to be threatened by the breakdown of the family. The socialization needed to create responsible citizens is supposedly collapsing under the weight of fatherless families, which lack authority and stability. The moral territory has been staked out by conservatives under the banner of family values, a banner that is waved with particular vigor in the faces of African Americans.

In this manner the debates about inequality conjoin economics, ethics, and culture. Inequality reinforces the culture of individualism, and in turn is rationalized by it. What has always been seen to be true for inequality in general is now applied to racial inequality in particular. Is economic opportunity for blacks now limited, in a painful irony of history, only by their own values and behaviors? The answer to this question hinges upon a socioeconomic analysis which should be grist for the institutionalist mill. If democractic ideals have conquered racial subordination, then continuing racial inequality must be due to the peculiarities of black culture. However, if democratic ideals have been compromised by racial subordination, then continuing racial inequality must be due to the peculiarities of white culture. Clearly, it is possible for democratic ideals to be real but imperfectly realized so that both cultures play a role in creating and sustaining inequality. The relation between culture and inequality is at the heart of the modern debates about race. The inability of either neoclassical or Marxian economists to come to grips with this relation suggests that research in the institutionalist tradition could be especially rewarding.

Conservatives such as Thomas Sowell (1983) emphasize that a group's economic success and failures are more determined by internal cultural factors than by treatment by the larger society. If a group's culture does not emphasize savings, entrepreneurship, hard work, education, and stable families, it will do poorly compared to a group whose culture does emphasize such behaviors. Since Marxists have tended to ignore the issue of the cultural distinctiveness of African Americans and its impact on economic well-being, or have simply labeled the issue as racist, the field for cultural analysis has been left open for the conservatives.

Institutionalists could contribute a progressive alternative to the conservative critique of black culture. Consider, for example, the issue of female-headed households. This is one of the most-talked about issues of our time and is cited repeatedly by those who insist that blacks are responsible for their own social and economic problems. Indeed, the fraction of all births to unmarried women was relatively stable from 1940 to 1960 but rose rapidly after 1960. Both the level and the rate of change were much greater for black women than for white women. By the mid-1980s, six black births in ten, compared to one white birth in eight, were to unmarried women (Jaynes and Williams 1989, 518). Female-headed households are a causal factor in the social problems that dispropotionately afflict the black community, such as crime, drug abuse, gangs and school dropouts (for a review, see Whitehead 1993).

The rise in the fraction of all births that are out-of-wedlock is not due to increasing fertility among unmarried women, but rather to declining fertility among married women combined with later, less frequent, and shorter marriages. In 1960, the white–black difference in the percent of 15-to-44-year-old women living with husbands was 17 points; by 1985 it had risen to 27 points. Only 28 percent of this cohort of black women were living with husbands in 1985, compared to 52 percent in 1960 (Jaynes and Williams 1989,

522). The problem of out-of-wedlock births and female-headed households is thus fundamentally a problem of the institution of marriage.

Why has marriage declined so dramatically among African Americans? It is hard to believe that discrimination is worse today than it was prior to the Civil Rights Act (but see Hill 1990). Consequently, conservatives argue that the decline in marriage and the rise in the out-of-wedlock birthrate must be due to other factors, such as an increase in welfare dependency and a collapse of traditional family values in the African-American community.

There is an alternative view. Wilson (1987, 83) argues that the rise in female-headed households is in part due to a steep drop in the availability of marriageable men. Williams (1990, 174) shows that the ratio of 25-to-44-year-old (i.e., prime marriage age) male/female ratio is 100.5 for whites but only 86.5 for blacks. He cites another study that concludes that "there may be no more than one black man for every five single black women in the United States" (1990, 176) once homosexuals, men who are already married or who are uninterested in marriage, and men who for other reasons are unacceptable (e.g., unemployed or in prison) are factored out. This is an interesting and plausible explanation for the decline in marriage among African Americans which needs to be fleshed out both quantitatively and qualitatively. Can trends in the availability of men be estimated, and do they correspond to the trends in female headship? Has marriage declined for different reasons among blacks and whites, and if so what is the significance of the difference? Is it reasonable to expect black women to avoid childbearing if their economic opportunities are insufficient to allow them to support their children? What is the impact of the welfare system on female headship and male unemployment? How do segregation and discrimination affect family structure, and how does family structure affect economic behaviors and outcomes?

White culture raises a different set of questions. Historically, Europeans who emigrated to the United States assimilated by replacing their ethnic roots with a racial identity as whites which overlapped with their national identity as Americans. As Lawrence Fuchs parenthetically notes at the outset of his massive study of race and ethnicity, "The freedom of Americans to worship, speak, assemble and petition their government, and their protection under equal laws (for whites only) bound them in a national community even though their political interests were often diverse" (1990, 3). Nonwhites were, by definition, excluded from this national community, and the civic culture it generated. However, in the post–civil rights era, the civic culture has been deracialized. Even—or especially—conservatives claim to favor racial equality and the principle of a colorblind society. They do so by denying institutional racism and reducing discrimination to the status of an individual grievance. The structural dynamics of inequality, such as housing segregation and localized schemes of public school finance (Kozol 1991), are ignored. Racial ideology has been rearticulated in the discourse of individual rights, and as such attacks group remedies (e.g., affirmative action) with a principled fervor while relying upon code words (e.g., welfare and crime) to get across that it is still "us" versus "them" (Omi and Winant 1986, 113–14; Edsall and Edsall 1991, chs 9–11).

White culture today thus stands in sharp contrast to the past in that it denies its own racial content. Few whites would even accept that there is such as thing as "white" culture. Instead they would call it "American" culture, or simply "individualism" in the sense of meritocracy. From this standpoint, it would be interesting to ask how they can justify racially systematic differences in the allocation of "public" resources such as schooling, firefighting, and police protection, or the use of "public" monies to rebuild the urban centers in a way which consistently bypasses the nonwhite poor. The experience of the 1980s shows that economic growth, even when combined with black political power, is no guarantee of reduced inequality or increased opportunities for those who are isolated in the inner cities (Orfield and Ashkinaze 1991). The role of race in the conservative backlash and the role of conservative economic policies (which have been followed even under Democratic administrations since the late 1970s) in distributing the fruits of growth would make a fascinating study, especially if informed by the instrumental values which institutionalists hold so dear.

Questions concerning both black and white culture could be placed in a provocative interpretive framework by institutionalists. The overthrow of traditional white supremacy and the sudden decline in marriage are perhaps the two most fundmental social and cultural changes of the century. They both took place at about the same time. Is there a connection between them? Gender dynamics intersect with race relations to differentiate black and white patterns of family formation. We are desperately in need of a fusion of cultural and economic analyses to understand the causes and effects of these patterns. Neoclassical economists cannot provide it since they take culture as a given and analyze family dynamics with a misplaced analogy to the market. Marxist economists cannot provide it since they see culture as a pallid reflection of the more fundamental forces of class struggle. The institutionalist thesis that culture is a powerful force in its own right, one which changes in response to social and economic conditions but which also affects those conditions, could provide a worthwhile contribution if it were applied to the topic of racial inequality and family structure.

This is true in a positive as well as a negative sense. We need to understand what has gone wrong with American families (and especially African American families), but we also need to understand what has gone right. When Myrdal wrote An American Dilemma, he felt it necessary to write only 5 pages (out of over 1,000) on the topic of the black family. He said that the black family had characteristics that made it "disorganized," but also noted that blacks "have certain other cultural traits which tend to reduce the disorganizing effect of those characteristics" (Myrdal 1972, 934). The reliance on extended families, the emotional bonds between women, the high value placed on children, the lack of stigma attached to illegitimacy (described by Myrdal as a "healthy social custom") and the refusal to condemn people for divorce or other personal problems are traits which deserve appreciation and study. The distinctive characteristics of African-American culture can account for the survival of an entire people in the face of overwhelming hostility and danger. The topic of racial inequality pushes us toward the question of why blacks have done so poorly, but the flip side of the question is how they have done so well in the face of such overwhelming adverse odds. Culture is a key part of the answer to both the positive and negative questions. It is a natural research area for institutionalists, and one can only wonder why more of them have not seized upon it.

POSITIVE FEEDBACK EFFECTS

One of the clearest contrasts between institutionalism and neoclassicism concern feedback effects, which refer to the way in which economic activities are offset (negative feedback) or reinforced (positive feedback) by their own consequences. Neoclassicism emphasizes negative feedback effects, since these make problems self-correcting. When excess supply results in lower prices and thus increased sales, a negative feedback effect has automatically solved a problem. Negative feedback effects are the basis of the laissez-faire belief that markets are self-regulating. In contrast, nonneoclassical methodologies such as Marxism, institutionalism, and post Keynesianism emphasize positive feedback effects, which make problems self-reinforcing.

Because racial inequality is multifaceted and context dependent, positive feedback effects are especially pertinent. The four main sources of positive feedback effects are perception, socialization, choice, and institutional interactions (Shulman, Drago and Albelda 1995). Perception refers to white stereotypes of blacks, socialization refers to community and family influences on the development of children, choice refers to ways in which individual decision-making responds to external constraints, and institutional interactions refer to the mutual reinforcement of racial inequality in housing, education, work, finance and government policy. Each of these provides a means by which inequality can become a self-reproducing process. All deserve attention, but for the sake of brevity I will confine my comments to perception.

Racial oppression in the modern period may have originated with capitalism, and in particular with the impetus for capital accumulation created by the slave trade and slave labor (Williams 1966), but racism is never purely economic. The psychological, cultural, and social baggage carried by slavery became forces in their own right and have infected the mentality and behavior of both whites and blacks to the present day. The political systems that first legitimated property in human beings and then mandated their separation, as well as the institutions (both public and private) that presupposed and reproduced white supremacy, continue to be creatures of their past. The task facing any analyst of modern race relations is to disentangle these forces so that particular aspects of race relations can be exposed and understood.

One approach is to examine the interactions between economic inequality and the popular ideologies which have rationalized black subordination. Myrdal argued that poverty created behaviors and life conditions among African Americans which reinforced racist stereotypes among whites, thereby perpetuating discrimination and black poverty:

This depreciation of the Negro's potentialities is given a semblance of proof by the low standards of efficiency, reliability, ambition, and morals actually displayed by the average Negro. This is what the white man "sees," and he opportunistically exaggerates what he sees. He "knows" that the Negro is not "capable" of handling a machine, running a business or learning a profession. As we know that these deficiencies are not inborn in him...we must conclude that they are caused, directly or indirectly, by the very poverty we are trying to explain...Poverty itself breeds the conditions which perpetuate poverty. (1972, 208)

It would be a mistake to interpret this statement as an early version of the culture of poverty. Myrdal was emphatic that "little if anything could be scientifically explained in terms of the peculiarities of the Negroes themselves"—it was a "white man's problem" (1972, lxxiii).

The white man's problem today is perhaps expressed in a somewhat more subtle fashion, but there is little doubt that racial inequality continues to reinforce racist stereotypes, which in turn reinforce racial inequality. A clear example is education. The parents of black students tend, on average, to have lower incomes and to be less well educated than the parents of white students. Parental income and education is associated with success of children in school, and teachers know it. Poor teacher perceptions of black student capacities results in low expectations which in turn reduce student performance, thereby creating (at least in part) racial inequality in educational outcomes (Chunn 1991). Inequality in educational outcomes is a factor in creating inequality in labor market outcomes, and so the circle goes round for the next generation.

The interaction between education, employment, and racial inequality is (or should be) a natural field of study for institutionalists. The intersection of the public and private domains, of socialization and individuation, of authority and meritocracy, and of culture and economics can all be found at this crossroads. To pick one telling if narrow example, consider the models of so-called "statistical discrimination."

Statistical discrimination occurs when individuals are treated in terms of the average characteristics of their groups. A commonly used example concerns gender differences in turnover. Women are said to be less stable employees because their primary commitment is to their family. Even if a female applicant has no intention of having a family, an employer will minimize his or her risks by treating her as an average female in comparison to an average male. It is simply too expensive and time consuming to verify the stated intentions of each applicant. Gender functions as an inexpensive screening device, and employers who use it will on average wind up with more stable employees even if they thereby discriminate against particular women some of the time. Statistical discrimination thus combines the irrational (i.e., non–productivity-based) treatment of individuals with the rational (i.e., productivity-based) treatment of groups. It is simultaneously a story of discrimination and human capital differences, in contrast to most stories which pit one explanation against the other. For this reason it is particularly interesting.

The key to the neoclassical interpretation of statistical discrimination is that perceptions of group differences must be accurate. If they are not, then employers should learn about their mistakes and correct them. An employer who persists in believing myths will wind up with less productive workers (or will pay more to find equally productive workers), and so will be driven out by the competition.

The problem is that employers do not seem to go through this type of learning process. Although the turnover example is widely used, it happens to be false: the turnover rates of women and men are similar when job characteristics are similar (Blau and Kahn 1981; Alexander 1991). Furthermore, men are more likely to be criminals, to be alcoholics or drug addicts, to be violent, to get into car accidents, and to be absent on any particular day. However, these risk factors do not seem to result in employer preferences for women; why, then, should the risk factor of turnover result in employer preferences for men?

It seems to be the case that statistical discrimination is based upon stereotypes, not reality. It is this recognition that allows for an institutionalist interpretation of statistical discrimination. The rigidity of stereotypes is quite different than the fluid knowledge presumed by neoclassical economists. If an employer never or only rarely sees a woman in a position of authority, with what evidence can the stereotype be overturned? Stereotypes become self-fulfilling prophecies because they generate the evidence that confirms them: women are not hired into positions of authority because of sexist stereotypes, and because they are not hired, these stereotypes persist. In this manner (among others) positive feedback reinforces occupational sex segregation.

Similar arguments can be made about statistical discrimination by race. Employers perceive black applicants (and black males in particular) as being less productive or more risky than ostensibly comparable white applicants. Instead of investigating the characteristics of each individual applicant, they treat all as members of a group whose average productivity is lower (or whose average risk is higher) than comparable whites. Consequently they discriminate against individuals in the process of treating groups in terms of their perceived characteristics. Neoclassical statistical discrimination treats these perceptions as accurate; institutional statistical discrimination would treat them as stereotypes. The question is: why would blacks be perceived to be less productive than comparable whites?

The answers here are speculative since statistical discrimination models have been applied to gender more than race. Say that whites and blacks are comparable in the sense of having equal amounts of education. There are three possible reasons why blacks would still be less productive or more risky hires: differences in educational quality, differences in culture, and differences in intelligence. I will discuss each in turn.

Blacks and whites who have completed an equal number of years of schooling may nonetheless be differentiated by employers if they have a perception that black education is qualitatively inferior. Black education may be inferior if blacks attend segregated schools with fewer resources, or if blacks get lower grades or test scores in integrated schools (indicating that the receipt of a degree is a riskier proxy for educational attainment). For example, Card and Krueger (1992) showed that 20 percent of the decline in the black–white earnings gap between 1960 and 1980 is due to improvements in the quality of black schools. Some of the remaining gap may therefore be due to persistent differences in the quality of black and white schools.

Blacks score lower than whites on achievement tests even when years of schooling are held constant. For example, there are large black–white differences in literacy within each educational level (Jaynes and Williams 1989, 352). While test bias may play a role, motivation and academic background are also implicated (Johnson 1991). This means that employers may have an incentive to treat black and white applicants differently even if they have completed equal years of schooling. A particular black applicant may be superior to the average white applicant, but if the employer uses skin color as a cheap screening device, preference will be given to the white applicant. The perception of group differences will thus generate racial inequality as a result of statistical discrimination.

However, statistical discrimination due to differences in the qualities of black and white education cannot be taken as a given. The black–white gap in test scores has been declining over the past quarter-century (Jaynes and Williams 1989, 348–54), and funding gaps between black and white schools have been reduced (at least in some states). Furthermore, differences in the resources and characteristics of schools do not seem to bear a strong relationship to differences in student achievement (Hanushek 1987). This suggests that the belief that black education is qualitatively inferior should be weakening over time, or else is a proxy for something other than schooling differences. This takes us to the second possible reason for statistical discrimination by race: culture.

It is commonly argued that cultural differences can explain economic differences. For example, Thomas Sowell (1983, 91–2) explains the success of Jews in the United States in terms of a tradition of entrepreneurship and education. Similarly, the difficulties experienced by blacks are explained in terms of their lack of such traditions (1983, 132). While Sowell's work on race and ethnicity is well-known, it tends to be descriptive and laden with simplistic generalizations. However, Borjas comes to the same conclusion on the basis of a much more technical analysis: "the intergenerational progress of workers belonging to ethnic groups that have relatively low levels of human capital is retarded by the low average quality of the group ... [and] the role played by ethnic capital in intergenerational mobility partly explains the slow rates of economic progress experienced by blacks" (1992, 124). Individual mobility, in other words, is a function of the characteristics of ethnic group to which the individual belongs. Racial inequality persists because blacks are held back by the "low human capital"—primarily group attitudes toward work, family and education—of their group as a whole.

If economic success depends on ethnic background, then two workers who are equal in all respects except ethnic background may differ with respect to productivity. An employer may then expect that black and white applicants with equal educations may have different average productivities. Again, this lays the basis for statistical discrimination. Is it reasonable? Darity (1989) argues that the different economic experiences of different ethnic groups has more to do with their class background in their country of origin and their experience with discrimination in the United States than with an ill-defined "culture." Certainly, one would expect that mobility patterns would converge over time as cultural homogenization overwhelms ethnic differentiation.

It is sometimes argued that upper income blacks have adopted the cultural norms of the wider society while lower income blacks are caught up in a destructive culture of welfare dependency. Sometimes welfare dependency is explained in terms of a rational response to incentives (Murray 1984); and sometimes it is explained in terms of an irrational breakdown of mainstream values (Kelso 1984). The notion that the culture of poor blacks (identified with crime, drugs, violence, female-headed households, lack of self-respect, and antieducation, antiwork attitudes) is to blame for black poverty is a widely held belief among the nonpoor, black as well as white. If culture is to blame for black poverty, then one would expect that all these problems would be changed in tandem and be concentrated among well-defined groups of people (e.g., ghetto residents). In fact, different problems are often found among different people and different problems have been trending in different directions (Jencks 1991), suggesting that particular problems are caused by particular circumstances rather than an allegedly common culture. Nonetheless, if employers believe that cultural differences matter, so that blacks are less productive or more risky hires than comparably educated whites, then black applicants may be treated on the basis of their group membership rather than their individual characteristics.

The third possible reason for statistical discrimination is differences in intelligence. Herrnstein and Murray (1994) argue that intelligence plays a stronger role in determining economic success and failure than socioeconomic background. One does not have to accept their additional arguments concerning the genetic determination of intelligence to recognize that intelligence (wherever it comes from), in the sense of analytical abilities, varies between individuals, and that more intelligence improves the odds for success in an increasingly knowledge-based economy. Logically, this is no different than saying that musical abilities vary between individuals, and that more musical ability improves the odds for instrumental success. Individual differences in intelligence may be wholly due to environmental factors (though this is unlikely), but once they are in place they will create predictable differences in labor market outcomes.

The argument becomes more problematic when applied to groups, particularly racial groups. The notion of group differences in intelligence is repugnant to many of us because of its association with eugenics, Naziism, and white supremacy; nonetheless, it is a fact of life that blacks score lower than whites on intelligence tests even within educational and socioeconomic categories. This finding is not an artifact of Herrnstein and Murray's ideological predispositions, nor is it due to test bias. It is possible (though dubious) to deny that the tests measure something we call "intelligence," but it is not possible to deny that these tests capture something associated with educational and economic success.

If employers believe that blacks on average are less intelligent than whites even though they have equivalent educational credentials, then they would have another motive for statistical discrimination. Of course, they could solve this problem by giving their applicants intelligence tests (a workable one can be given in under 15 minutes). This would allow them to separate out high IQ blacks and avoid lumping them in with their group. However, this has been illegal since the *Griggs* decision. (The *Griggs* decision in 1971 held that an employer had to show that a job requirement was in fact related to job performance if it disproportionately disadvantaged blacks.) The paradoxical result of a decision designed to reduce discrimination is that it may increase statistical discrimination against highly intelligent blacks.

The foregoing is a statement about neoclassical statistical discrimination since it presumes that blacks and whites actually do differ in their average intelligence. To be clear, I call this "neoclassical" statistical discrimination because it presumes that employer perceptions of average group differences are accurate, not because most neoclassicals believe that blacks are less intelligent than whites (the preceeding two explanations for neoclassical statistical discrimination are much more common). An institutionalist interpretation of this argument would be directed toward showing that the perception of group differences in intelligence is persistent and widespread but wrong. Group differences in average intelligence could be shown to be a racist stereotype if IQ tests are biased or inaccurate measures of intelligence, or if intelligence is too multi-faceted to be captured by a single numerical index. The history of intelligence testing certainly does not promote confidence in the objectivity of the testing process (Gould 1981). Alternatively, institutionalists could focus on the environmental conditions which influence cognitive development as the basis for public policies to promote equal opportunity and offset the inequality generating effects of the marketplace.

Statistical discrimination models are one means by which the perception of group differences can create positive feedback: the perception of inequality generates actual inequality which in turn reinforces the perception. The institutionalist interpretation differs from the neoclassical approach by stressing rigid stereotypes over fluid knowledge. The institutionalist paradigm, with its stress on the cultural norms that rationalize and reproduce inequality, would appear to be well positioned to develop these models and apply them to the analysis of the mechanisms of contemporary discrimination.

Positive feedback in general, and statistical discrimination models in particular, are clearly related to the issue of cultural norms discussed in the preceeding section. The cultural norms created by the historical contexts of capitalism and white supremacy are a fusion of meritocracy and the stereotypes of black inferiority: blacks are less likely to succeed (according to white cultural norms) because they are less deserving of success, whether due to inferior education, cultural inadequacies or lower intelligence. In turn, positive feedback is one example of the process of evolutionary holism, to which I now turn.

EVOLUTIONARY HOLISM

Evolutionary holism is an explanation for change. Capitalism is viewed as a dynamic system whose momentum cannot be reduced to any single factor, such as "individual choice" or "class struggle." Instead, social and political conflict, technology, popular ideologies and cultural norms, organizational structures, public policies and market incentives interact in a way which determines how power is exercised and how its effects are distributed.

John Harvey (1991, 118–19) prefers the phrase "institutional dynamics" to emphasize that evolutionary holism must include environmentally conditioned goal seeking behavior portrayed in terms of negative and positive feedback loops. While I find the phrase "evolutionary holism" to be more expressive, I agree that it can suggest an analytical approach which can be overly relativistic and vague. The way in which *evolutionary holism* is used in this paper is consistent with Harvey's admonitions. "Evolutionary" refers to a process of change based on adaptation to changing circumstances. "Holistic" refers to the impact of the whole on each of the parts. Capitalism is built up from its constituent institutions and social relationships, but it also imposes its own "nature and logic" (Heilbroner 1985) on each of them. It does so in a way that adapts to changes in the conditions that govern the process of capital accumulation.

Capital accumulation is the fundamental goal-seeking behavior around which other economic processes are organized and to which they must respond. However, capital accumulation only takes place in particular contexts, and the ways in which it occurs responds to changes in these contexts. The "institutional environment within which the capitalist accumulation process is organized" is called a "social structure of accumulation" (SSA). It is a "collective set of institutions" which primarily include the organization of firms and markets, the structure of the monetary system, the available types of technologies, intraclass organizations and interclass conflicts, international relations, and feasible state policies (Gordon, Edwards, and Reich 1982, 9). These are the concrete manifestations of the capital/labor, capital/capital, labor/labor, and citizen/state relationships, which combine to give historical periods their specific character. The SSA is one expression of evolutionary holism: dynamic, context dependent, multi-factoral and goal oriented. As such, it provides a workable framework for analyzing long-term trends in race relations and their interaction with the capitalist system.

According to Gordon, Edwards and Reich, an SSA typically goes through three phases, which they label exploration, consolidation, and decay. As the conditions that fostered capital accumulation are undermined by internal contradictions or made obsolete by external events, one social structure of accumulation will be transformed into another. These transformations are connected by the "long-swings" which characterize the capitalist growth process. As capitalism has undergone these long-swings, its SSAs have changed and overlapped from an initial period of proletarianization (1820s to 1890s) to a period of labor homogenization (1870s to World War II) and then to a period of labor segmentation (1920s to the present). The names of these SSAs reflect the concern with the labor process that is at the heart of the SSA framework.

A social structure of accumulation should also have characteristic effects on race relations. A dramatic example would be the conflict between the SSAs of proletarianization and slavery, which was one factor in setting off the Civil War. Gordon, Edwards, and Reich do not call slavery an SSA; in fact, they say virtually nothing about slavery at all aside from commenting that blacks "remained outside the capitalist sector, by and large, until the end of European immigration" (1982, 152). This may be true by definition if wage-labor is identified with capitalism, but it hardly seems true in substance given the widespread use of slave production and the slave trade to foster capital accumulation (Williams 1966). On the basis of this consideration, it seems reasonable (if contentious) to characterize slavery as another SSA. Its clash was not with capitalism in general, but with the requirements of a particular, emerging SSA. The transition from the period of proletarianization to the period of homogenization overlapped with the Civil War. The relationship of slavery and the Civil War to the decay of one SSA and the exploration of another remains to be written. It is fertile ground for institutionalists interested in economic history.

Because race relations always interact with capitalism in particular phases of its historical development, the use of the SSA typology to analyze the transitions from slavery (in relation to proletarianization) to sharecropping (in relation to homogenization) to wage-labor (in relation to segmentation) holds promise as a fruitful avenue of inquiry. Race relations are part of the social environment of capital accumulation, i.e., they are part of the SSA, and they transform it just as it transforms them. The long-swings of capitalist development should bear a systematic relationship to long-term transformations in the structure of race relations. But this avenue remains unexplored by authors working within the SSA framework. Perhaps this is because the SSA analysis comes out of the Marxian tradition with its primary focus on class. Gordon, Edwards, and Reich (1982, 32) refer to the "relatively independent logic and dynamics" of race and gender relations in an apologetic aside before they proceed to ignore them. Heilbroner (1985), using the same framework, makes even less reference to race (i.e., zero) in a book devoted to summarizing the underlying structure and historical trends of U.S. capitalism. It is remarkable that the most glaring ethical and social contradiction of our society can be ignored in books with this ambition. It is an obvious opening for researchers interesting in analyzing race from an institutionalist perspective.

Another example of an unexplored but potentially productive research area is the so-called capital-labor accord. The accord refers to the cooperative relationship between corporate management and organized labor in the postwar period. It was based on the legalization of collective bargaining, and it resulted in job security and grievance procedures for workers, no-strike provisions, and an end to radical unionism for management, and an agreement by both to share the fruits of productivity gains (Edwards and Podgursky 1986, 19–28). The accord was the social contract which established labor peace and turned America into a middle-class society after World War II.

The accord was the cornerstone of labor market segmentation, which was a central feature of the postwar SSA. The labor market was split between those included in the accord and those excluded from the accord. Workers in the "primary subordinate segment" (primarily transportation, mining, and heavy industry) were covered by the accord. Those not covered by the accord were either in a segment above it or a segment below it. Workers in the "primary independent segment" were in the technical, administrative, managerial, and professional positions which expanded rapidly after the war. These workers were able to achieve mobility outside of unions due to their educational credentials and knowledge-based skills. The other group of workers outside the accord were in the "secondary segment" consisting of low-wage jobs in services, wholesale and retail trade, and light manufacturing. These workers were left out of the economic prosperity which characterized the quarter-century following World War II. Barriers to intersegment mobility—including discrimination—meant that labor market structure was fundamentally noncompetitive in the postwar period.

Edwards and Podgursky acknowledge that "the accord primarily organized white male workers" and that women and minorities were largely excluded (1986, 21). But neither they nor other writers working with the SSA framework have analyzed the causes or consequences of this exclusion. Women had filled most industrial jobs during the war; afterwards, they were fired *en masse* and restricted to the home or to low-wage, secondary-sector jobs. Black men who had fought with distinction came home from the war to discover that they were still second-class citizens. Segregation and discrimination (*de jure* in the south and *de facto* in the north) were defended with vigor. Apparently, white supremacy was acceptable as long as it was practiced by Americans. Rigid racial and gender hierarchies were reconstructed in a moment when the fight against Naziism could have led into a fight against all forms of racism. The establishment of the labor accord was a step forward in terms of the labor movement but a step backwards in terms of the movements for race and gender equity.

Why did an institutional shift based on class struggle—and one that is usually perceived to be progressive in these terms—turn out to be the basis of a new form of economic oppression for women and minorities? This is a problem, not only for Marxism (which suggests that progress in terms of class should also mean progress in terms of race and sex), but also for neoclassicism (since the fight against Naziism should have reduced the preferences for discrimination). Herbert Hill (1989) believes that the union movement has always tried to restrict job competition on the basis of race, and perhaps simple self-interest can explain why progress in terms of class was combined with retrogression in terms of race and gender. However, the culture of white supremacy may have something to do with it as well. The ideology of class solidarity trumpeted by the CIO was never as powerful as the racial solidarity which white ethnics craved. The fight against Naziism was both a fight against racism and a fight with racism, particularly with respect to the segregation of the services, the war against the Japanese, and the refusal to take any measures to save the Jews. In addition, the anticommunist crusades of the 1950s were used to undermine the fragile commitment of the white dominated labor movement to racial equality. These cultural and political factors interacted with changes in industrial organization, labor relations, and the role of the state to create labor market segmentation in the postwar period. Their analysis would provide an important addition to the work on labor market structure for which institutionalism is justly famed.

This period is also important in terms of institutional developments. The emergence of Roosevelt's welfare state accomodated the Jim Crow laws and other forms of racial oppression. After World War II, ghettoization deepened and spread as a result of deliberate public policies and business practices as well as white flight (Massey and Denton 1993, 42–57; Hirsch 1983). The great migration of blacks to the north is a critical part of the story of the postwar labor market (especially given the crucial role of rapid urbanization). The SSA literature speaks in terms of the national labor market when the concrete historical questions concern the interaction of the industrialized north, where segmentation emerged and became dominant, with the decline of southern agriculture and the consequent migration, urbanization and ghettoization of millions of African-Americans. Nor has it ever attempted to characterize the SSA which predominated in the postwar south (in tandem with its failure to apply the SSA framework to slavery or Jim Crow). Even within the north the SSA literature—which by all rights should be concerned with the emergence of barriers to mobility—has ignored the connection between the distribution of housing and the distribution of jobs (i.e., between ghettoization and unemployment). The emergence of the 2-to-1 ratio between black and white unemployment rates, which we now take for granted, did not emerge until the early 1950s. This phenomemon has yet to be placed within the SSA framework. It would be a worthwhile accomplishment for an institutionalist to do so.

The SSA literature treats workers as actors. Labor market segmentation is explained in terms of the conflict between management and labor, not the simple domination of the former over the latter, but the same consideration is not given to race. To the extent that race is discussed, blacks are treated as victims. The impact which their resistance movements have had on labor relations and labor market structure has so far been ignored. This omission is especially egregious with respect to the civil rights movement, which was the main impetus for the growth of government in the postwar period. Usually the claim is that big government originated in the New Deal and World War II. This is true but incomplete. The modern role for government—and the one that has created the conservative backlash—has to do with the expansion of its regulatory interventions, which originated in the civil rights movement. The struggle of African Americans for political freedom increased the willingness of the state to intervene in labor contracts and to further restrict the employment-at-will doctrine. Furthermore, that struggle dramatically increased the role of the federal government in the provision of public education, and the expansion of public education is central to the development of the modern labor market. While the SSA literature emphasizes the political determinants of labor market structure, it seems stuck in the New Deal period. An enterprising institutionalist could bring this story up to date by focusing on the response of the state to racial struggles, and the impact of that response on the modern political economy.

A similar set of questions could be asked about the prognosis that the postwar SSA is in a period of decay, in part due to the breakdown of the labor accord (Edwards and Podgursky 1986, 28–53). This breakdown has occurred during a period of racial progress, at least in the senses of public policy, educational attainment, and occupational mobility. Again we see an inverse relation between progress in terms of class and progress in terms of race. The civil rights movement took off as the union movement started to decline, and as the social and political changes created by the civil rights movement became institutionalized, the decline in unionization accelerated. Can the civil rights movement be implicated in the decline of the labor movement, and conversely, has the decline of the labor movement offset some of the gains of the civil rights movement? One could tentatively hypothesize that unions raise black and white wages by equal amounts. If true, would this mean that the decline in unionism is irrelevant to the trends in racial inequality? How has the union movement altered its traditional racial practices in its efforts to attract new members and reverse its long-term decline? What does the increasing diversity of the U.S. labor force imply for the future of the labor movement? Questions such as these are natural ones for institutionalists to ask given the long and distinguished tradition established by institutionalists in the field of labor relations.

CONCLUSIONS

Institutionalism has not lived up to the promise created by Gunnar Myrdal's *An American Dilemma*. While its modern contributions to the study of racial inequality have been sparse, its method is potentially fruitful. The insistence of radical institutionalists that economic outcomes can only be understood when market mechanisms are placed in the context of history, culture and power is particularly appropriate for the topic of racial inequality. This chapter has attempted to show how some of the basic concepts of institutionalism—cultural norms and ethical judgements, positive feedback effects, and evolutionary holism—can be applied to the analysis of racial inequality and discrimination. A research agenda was suggested that develops a variety of questions concerning culture and family structure, statistical discrimination and racial stereotypes, and social structures of accumulation and the interaction of class and race relations. Others could easily be added, such as class divisions within the black community (e.g., why have improvements in opportunities for the black middle class coincided with a decline in opportunities for the black poor?), the relationship of race to gender (e.g., what is the significance of the equalization between black and white women's wages?), the impact of economic growth on racial inequality (e.g., why did racial inequality go up when unemployment went down over the 1980s?), or the impact of political policies and institutions on racial inequality (e.g., has affirmative action hurt whites? Have property tax based systems of public school finance hurt blacks?).

In addition to its attention to cultural norms, positive feedback effects, and evolutionary holism, institutionalism is uniquely suited to racial analysis due to its emphasis on the problem of power. This issue is ignored by neoclassicals but it has received some attention by Marxists, and for this reason I have not devoted much space to it in this chapter. But the exercise of power which subordinates blacks is complex due to the interaction of class relations and race relations. Racism may benefit both capitalists and white workers in particular ways, and it may hurt both of them in particular ways. The distributional consequences of discrimination may vary between historical periods and economic contexts. Furthermore, power is embedded in the hierarchical structure of organizations, and as such is a component in the social relations of both class and race. The instrumental values which institutionalists advocate provide a normative basis for a critique of the exercise of power, including white supremacy. Institutionalists could add a unique voice to the debates over these questions if they began to give the topic of racial inequality the sustained attention it deserves.

REFERENCES

Albelda, Randy, Robert Drago, and Steven Shulman. 1995. *Level Playing Fields? Discrimination and Wage Inequality.* New York: McGraw-Hill.
Alexander, Kari. 1991. "Turnover and Its Relation to Discrimination and Sexual Inequality." Unpublished masters thesis, Fort Collins, Colorado State University.
Baron, James. 1991. "Organizational Evidence of Ascription in Labor Markets." In Richard Cornwall and Phanindra Wunnava, eds., *New Approaches to Economic and Social Analyses of Discrimination.* New York: Praeger, 113–44.
Becker, Gary. 1971. *The Economics of Discrimination.* Chicago: University of Chicago Press.

Blau, Francine, and Lawrence Kahn. 1981. "Race and Sex Differences in Quit Rates by Young Workers." *Industrial and Labor Relations Review,* 34 (July).

Bonancich, Edna. 1976. "Advanced Capitalism and Black/White Race Relations in the United States: A Split Labor Market Interpretation." *American Sociological Review,* (Feb.).

Borjas, George. 1992. "Ethnic Capital and Intergenerational Mobility." *Quarterly Journal of Economics,* 107, no. 1, (Feb.): 365–89.

Bound, John, and Richard Freeman. 1989. "Black Economic Progress: Erosion of the Post-1965 Gains in the 1980s?" In Steven Shulman and William A. Darity, Jr., eds., *The Question of Discrimination: Racial Inequality in the U.S. Labor Market.* Middletown, Conn.: Wesleyan University Press, 32–49.

Card, David, and Alan Krueger. 1992. "School Quality and Black-White Relative Earnings: A Direct Asessment." *Quarterly Journal of Economics,* 107, no. 1 (Feb.).

Chunn, Eva Wells. 1991. "Sorting Black Students for Success and Failure: The Inequality of Ability Grouping and Tracking." In Willy Smith and Eva Chunn, eds., *Black Education: A Quest for Equity and Excellence.* New Brunswick, N.J: Transaction Publishers.

Darity, William Jr. 1989. "What's Left of the Economic Theory of Discrimination?" In Steven Shulman and William Darity, eds., *The Question of Discrimination.* Middleton, Conn.: Wesleyan University Press, 335–76.

Edsall, Thomas, and Mary Edsall. 1991. *Chain Reaction: The Impact of Race, Rights and Taxes on American Politics.* New York: W. W. Norton.

Edwards, Richard, and Michael Podgursky. 1986. "The Unraveling Accord: American Unions in Crisis." In Richard Edwards, Paolo Garonna, and Franz Todtling, eds., *Unions in Crisis and Beyond: Perspectives from Six Countries.* Dover, Mass.: Auburn House, 14–60.

Fuchs, Lawrence. 1990. *The American Kaleidoscope: Race, Ethnicity and the Civic Culture.* Hanover N.H: University Press of New England.

Gordon, David, Richard Edwards, and Michael Reich. 1982. *Segmented Work, Divided Workers:The Histtorical Transformation of Labor in the United States.* New York: Cambridge University Press.

Gould, Stephen. 1981. *The Mismeasure of Man.* New York: W. W. Norton.

Hanushek, Eric. 1987. "The Economics of Schooling: Production and Efficiency in the Public Schools." *Journal of Economic Literature,* 24 (Sept.).

Harvey, John. 1991. "Institutions and the Economic Welfare of Black Americans in the 1980s." *Journal of Economic Issues,* 25, no. 1 (Mar.): 115–35.

Heilbroner, Robert. 1985. *The Nature and Logic of Capitalism.* New York: W. W. Norton.

Herrnstein, Richard, and Charles Murray. 1994. *The Bell Curve: Intelligence and Class Structure in American Life.* New York: The Free Press.

Hill, Herbert. 1989. "Black Labor and Affirmative Action: An Historical Perspective." In Steven Shulman and William Darity, Jr., eds., *The Question of Discrimination.* Middleton, Conn.: Wesleyan University Press, 190–267.

Hill, Robert. 1990. "Economic Forces, Structural Discrimination and Black Family Instability." In Cheatham and Stewart, eds., *Black Families: Interdisciplinary Perspectives.* New Brunswick, N.J.: Transaction Publishers.

Hirsch, Arnold. 1983. *Making the Second Ghetto: Race and Housing in Chicago 1940–1960.* New York: Cambridge University Press.

Jackson, Walter. 1990. *Gunnar Myrdal and America's Conscience: Social Engineering and Racial Liberalism, 1938–1987.* Chapel Hill: University of North Carolina Press.

Jaynes, Gerald, and Robin Williams, eds. 1989. *A Common Destiny: Blacks and American Society.* Washington, D.C: National Academy Press.

Jencks, Christopher. 1991. "Is the American Underclass Growing?" In Christopher Jencks and Paul Peterson, eds., *The Urban Underclass.* Washington, D.C.: Brookings Institution, 28–102.

Jennings, Ann. 1993. "Public or Private? Institutional Economics and Feminism." In Marianne Ferber and Julie Nelson, eds., *Beyond Economic Man: Feminist Theory and Economics.* Chicago: University of Chicago Press, 111–30.

Johnson, Sylvia. 1991. "Test Fairness and Bias: Measuring Academic Achievement Among Black Youth." In Willy Smith and Eva Chunn, eds., *Black Education: A Quest for Equity and Excellence.* New Brunswick, N.J.: Transaction Publishers.

Kelso, William. 1984. *Poverty and the Underclass: Changing Perceptions of the Poor in America.* New York: New York University Press.

Kiefer, David, and Peter Philips. 1988. "Doubts Regarding the Human Capital Theory of Racial Inequality." *Industrial Relations,* 27, no. 2 (Spring): 251–62.

Kozol, Jonathan. 1991. *Savage Inequalities: Children in America's Schools.* New York: Crown Publishers.

Massey, Douglas, and Nancy Denton. 1993. *American Apartheid: Segregation and the Making of the Underclass.* Cambridge: Harvard University Press.

McCrate, Elaine. 1991. "Discrimination, Returns to Education, and Teenage Childbearing." In Richard Cornwall and Phanindra Wunnava, eds., *New Approaches to Economic and Social Analyses of Discrimination.* New York: Praeger, 281–94.

Murray, Charles. 1984. *Losing Ground: American Social Policy 1950–1980.* New York: Basic Books.

Myrdal, Gunnar. 1972. *An American Dilemma: The Negro Problem and Modern Democracy.* Vols. 1, 2. New York: Pantheon Books.

Omi, Michael, and Howard Winant. 1986. *Racial Formation in the United States: From the 1960s to the 1980s.* New York: Routledge and Kegan Paul.

Orfield, Gary, and Carole Ashkinaze. 1991. *The Closing Door: Conservative Policy and Black Opportunity.* Chicago: University of Chicago Press.

Reich, Michael. 1981. *Racial Inequality: A Political Economic Analysis.* Princeton, N.J.: Princeton University Press.

Shulman, Steven. 1987. "Discrimination, Human Capital and Black–White Unemployment: Evidence from Cities." *Journal of Human Resources,* 22, no. 3 (Summer): 361–76.

___. 1989a. "Controversies in the Marxian Analysis of Racial Discrimination." *Review of Radical Political Economics,* no. 4 (Winter): 73–80.

___. 1989b. "Racism and the Making of the American Working Class." *Politics, Culture and Society,* no. 3 (Spring): 361–66.

___. 1992. "Metaphors of Discrimination: A Comparison of Gunnar Myrdal and Gary Becker." *Review of Social Economy,* 50, no. 4 (Winter):432–52.

Shulman, Steven, Robert Drago, and Randy Albelda. 1995. "The Political Economy Model of Discrimination." Fort Collins, Colo.: Mimeo.

Sowell, Thomas. 1983. *The Economics and Politics of Race.* New York: Quill.

van den Berghe, Pierre. 1978. *Race and Racism: A Comparative Perspective.* New York: John Wiley and Sons.

Whitehead, Barbara Dafoe. 1993. "Dan Quayle Was Right." *Atlantic Monthly,* Apr.

Williams, Eric. 1966. *Capitalism and Slavery.* New York: Capricorn Books.

Williams, Michael. 1990. "Polygamy and the Declining Male to Female Ratio in Black Communities: A Social Inquiry." In Cheatham and Stewart, eds., *Black Families: Interdisciplinary Perspectives.* New Brunswick, N.J.: Transaction Publishers.

Wilson, William. 1980. *The Declining Significance of Race.* Chicago: University of Chicago Press.

___. 1987. *The Truly Disadvantaged: The Inner City, The Underclass, and Public Policy.* Chicago: University of Chicago Press.

Index

Ginsburg, Helen, 117, 121
Gintis, Herbert, 72, 76
Global Economy, 73
Globalization, 164
Goldberg, Marilyn, 49
Goldin, Claudia, 204
Goodsell, Charles T., 162
Gordon, David M., 69, 263–65
Gordon, Linda, 144–47, 149
Gould, Stephen Jay, 34, 262
Governance, supranational, 181, 193
Government, 43, 72; achievements,
   157; decentralized, 159; fiscal
   outcomes, 153–56; ideology, 148;
   role, 88, 94, 120, 153–57
Governments: number in the United
   States, 153, 161–62, state and local,
   159
Great Depression, 41, 72; output lost,
   118; poverty, 146
Greed, 103
Green, Philip, 104
Grossman, Gene, 184, 185
Growth, 112, 172, 256
Guest Worker, 72, 73

Habituation, 33
Hacker, Andrew, 228
Haltiwanger, John, 210–11
Hamilton, David, 143, 145
Hanushek, Eric, 260
Hardin, Garrett, 171
Harmonization, 160
Harvey, David, 171
Harvey, John, 251, 263
Haveman, Robert, 141
Head Start program, 123
Health Care, 119–20, 122, 133
Heilbroner, Robert L., 128, 263–65
Helpman, Elhanan, 184, 185
Herrnstein, Richard, 261
Hickerson, Steven R., 124
Hill, Herbert, 255, 266
Hillbilly, 245
Hillman, Mayer, 172

Hirsch, Arnold, 266
Hispanics, 244–45
Hitler, Adolf, 46
Hochschild, A. R., 129
Hodgson, Geoffrey M., 58, 114, 200
Holism, 39–40, 263–67
Horrigan, Michael, 211
Horton, Willie, 228
Households, female-headed, 254–55
Housework, 50
Housing, 27, 148
Humphrey-Hawkins Bill, 121
Hutchison, Robert, 172
Huxley, Julian, 111

Ideas, 41
Imbalance, social, 128, 130
Imperialism, 189
Imprisonment, 230
Income, 6–8; class, 23, 27–28;
   distribution, 74–80, 92, 173–74,
   204–211, 214; factor, 208–209;
   family, 206; inequality, 116–17;
   policies, 121, 206, 218–19
Incrementalism, 164
Individualism, 88–90, 95; John Dewey,
   176; Mahatma Gandhi, 177–78;
   methodological, 199
Individuality, 178
Industrialization, 47–48
Industry, 4, 10
Inequality, xi, 14, 25, 61, 173–74;
   antidotes, 22; costs, 104, 116–20;
   institutionalized, 142; international,
   173–74, 182, 211–18; modes, 13,
   21, 23; regional-racial-ethnic, 237–
   49; United States, 204–211. See also
   Class; Gender; Nation; Race
Inferiority, 29, 45; black, 253; crime,
   230–31; development, 46; profit, 49
Inflation, 71, 121, 217
Infrastructure, 121–22
Insatiability, 177
Instinct, 12–13
Institutional Economics, 128;

About the Editor and Contributors

DOUG BROWN is Associate Professor of Economics at Northern Arizona University. His current research interests include the economics of global sustainability and social economics. He has written *Towards a Radical Democracy* and coedited, with Janice Peterson, *The Economic Status of Women Under Capitalism*. His articles have appeared in the *Journal of Economic Issues*, *Review of Social Economy*, and *Latin American Perspectives*.

CHARLES M. A. CLARK is Associate Professor of Economics at St. John's University, Jamaica, New York, and was recently Visiting Professor of Economics at University College Cork, Ireland. His publications include *Institutional Economics and the Theory of Social Value* (editor), *History and Historians of Political Economy* (editor), and *Economic Theory and Natural Philosophy*. His current research interests are income distribution and basic income policies.

JAMES DEVINE studied economics at Yale University (B.A.) and the University of California at Berkeley (Ph.D.). He is a Professor of Economics at Loyola Marymount University in Los Angeles, California. His interests and publications range from political economy, Marx, macroeconomics, labor economics, and money and banking to U.S. economic history.

WILLIAM M. DUGGER is Professor of Economics at the University of Tulsa, Oklahoma. Along with other works in institutional and social economics, he has authored *An Alternative to Economic Retrenchment, Corporate Hegemony* and *Underground Economics*. He has edited *Radical Institutionalism* and coedited, with William Waller, *The Stratified State*.

JOHN E. ELLIOTT has been Professor of Economics at the University of Southern California, Los Angeles, since 1966. His Ph.D. in economics is from Harvard University. He has published widely, including articles in the *Quarterly Journal of Economics, Economic Inquiry, History of Political Economy, Journal of Economic Issues,* and *Review of Social Economy.* His interests include political economy, the history of thought, and comparative systems.

JIM HORNER is Professor of Economics at Cameron University in Lawton, Oklahoma, and is often a Visiting Professor at American University in Paris. His Ph.D. is in Political Economy from the University of Texas at Dallas. He has published widely on institutional economics, and his current interests include drug policy, social justice, the history of thought, and Henry George.

BRENT McCLINTOCK is Assistant Professor of Economics at Carthage College, Kenosha, Wisconsin. He has worked in both academia and the government sector in the areas of international political economy and macroeconomics. He has published widely in institutional economics, and his interests include trade adjustment policies of the welfare state and international finance.

EDYTHE S. MILLER is an unaffiliated economist. Her previous affiliations include the Colorado Public Utilities Commission and the Metropolitan State College in Denver, Colorado. She has chaired the Association for Evolutionary Economics and the Transportation and Public Utilities Group of the American Economics Association, as well as served on the Board of Editors of the *Journal of Economic Issues.* She has published widely on institutional economics and is interested in economic philosophy and public utility economics.

JAMES PEACH is Professor of Economics at New Mexico State University, Las Cruces. He received his Ph.D. from the University of Texas at Austin in 1978. He edited the *Journal of Borderlands Studies* for the past decade. He has published widely on institutional economics and his interests include income inequality, population economics, and economic development.

JANICE PETERSON is Associate Professor of Economics at the State University of New York, Fredonia. She is the coeditor of *The Economic Status of Women under Capitalism,* with Doug Brown. Her articles have appeared in the *Journal of Economic Issues, Social Science Journal,* and *Review of Social Economy.* Her interests include feminism and institutional economics.

ZAHID SHARIFF is in political science at Evergreen State College in Olympia, Washington. His teaching and research interests have focused on the changing functions and impacts of government in contemporary society. He has published widely in such journals as the *Social Science Quarterly, Administration and Society,* and *Social Policy.*

HOWARD J. SHERMAN is Professor and former Chair of the Department of Economics, University of California, Riverside. He has published 75 articles and 15 books. One of his textbooks, coauthored with David Kolk, is *Business Cycles and Forecasting* (1995). His most recent book is *Reinventing Marxism* (1995).

STEVEN SHULMAN is Professor of Economics at Colorado State University, Fort Collins. His articles on racial inequality have appeared in the *Journal of Human Resources, Review of Black Political Economy, Journal of Economic Issues*, and other journals. He is the coeditor of *The Question of Discrimination* and is currently working on the issues of equal opportunity and economic justice.

JACQUELINE BLOOM STANFIELD is Associate Professor and Chair of the Department of Sociology at the University of Northern Colorado, Greeley. She is the author of *Married with Careers* and has published widely on family and gender relations.

JAMES RONALD STANFIELD is Professor of Economics at Colorado State University, Fort Collins. He is Past President of the Association for Social Economics and 1995 President of the Association for Institutional Thought. He is the author of *The Economic Surplus and Neo-Marxism; Economic Thought and Social Change; The Economic Thought of Karl Polanyi; Economics, Power, and Culture*; and *John Kenneth Galbraith.*

RICK TILMAN is Chairman of the Department of Public Administration at the University of Nevada, Las Vegas. He works in the areas of political economy, modern social theory, and American intellectual history. He is the author of *C. Wright Mills* and *Thorstein Veblen and His Critics*, and is writing a trilogy on Veblen. Currently, he is the Director of the International Thorstein Veblen Association.

MARC R. TOOL is Professor Emeritus of Economics at California State University, Sacramento, and editor emeritus of the *Journal of Economic Issues*. He is the author of four books on institutional and evolutionary economics, a contributor to collected volumes, and the editor or coeditor of nine other works. He received the Veblen-Commons Award of the Association for Evolutionary Economics in 1988.